D1280176

President Dad Vol. 2

Created by Rhim Ju-Yeon

Translation - Jennifer Hahm
English Adaptation - Ryan Shankel
Retouch and Lettering - Eva Han
Production Artist - Eric Pineda
Graphic Designer - Jose Macasocol, Jr.
Cover Design - Gary Shum

Editor - Jodi Bryson
Digital Imaging Manager - Chris Buford
Pre-Press Manager - Antonio DePietro
Production Managers - Jennifer Miller and Mutsumi Miyazaki
Art Director - Matt Alford
Managing Editor - Jill Freshney
VP of Production - Ron Klamert
Editor-in-Chief - Mike Kiley
President and C.O.O. - John Parker
Publisher and C.E.O. - Stuart Levy

A  **TOKYOPOP**® Manga

TOKYOPOP Inc.
5900 Wilshire Blvd. Suite 2000
Los Angeles, CA 90036

E-mail: info@TOKYOPOP.com
Come visit us online at www.TOKYOPOP.com

ISBN: 1-59532-235-3

First TOKYOPOP printing: March 2005

10 9 8 7 6 5 4 3 2 1

Printed in the USA

President Dad™

by
Rhim Ju-Yeon

Volume 2

HAMBURG // LONDON // LOS ANGELES // TOKYO

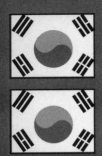

President Dad

Ami Won is just your average high school girl— she's into pop-singing idols and hanging out with her friends. But two extraordinary events have changed her life forever. One is that just recently she lost her mother, who was little Ami's guardian, her friend, the person she most trusted in the whole world. The other is her father, who... well, read on...

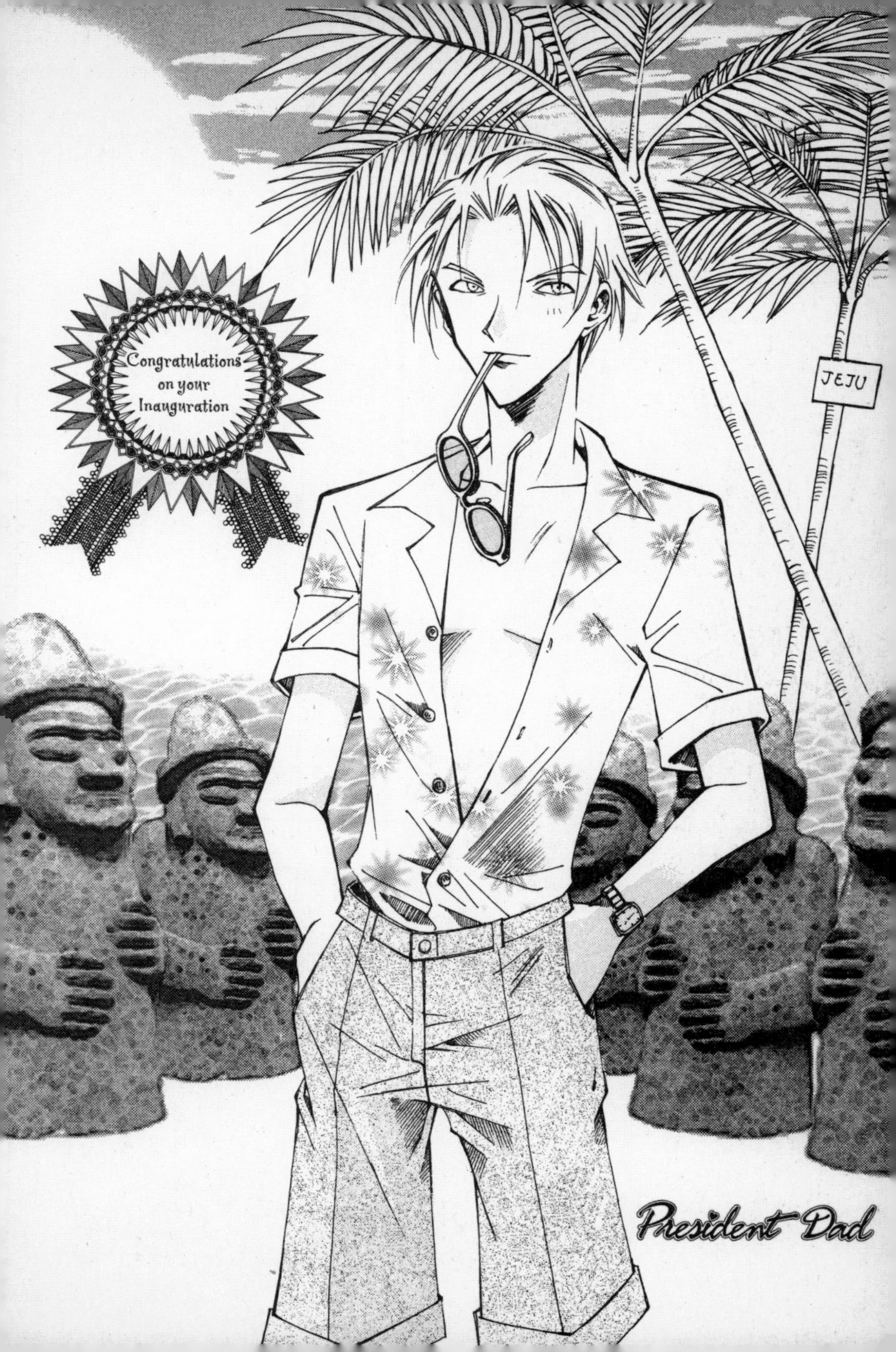

Congratulations on your Inauguration
JEJU
President Dad

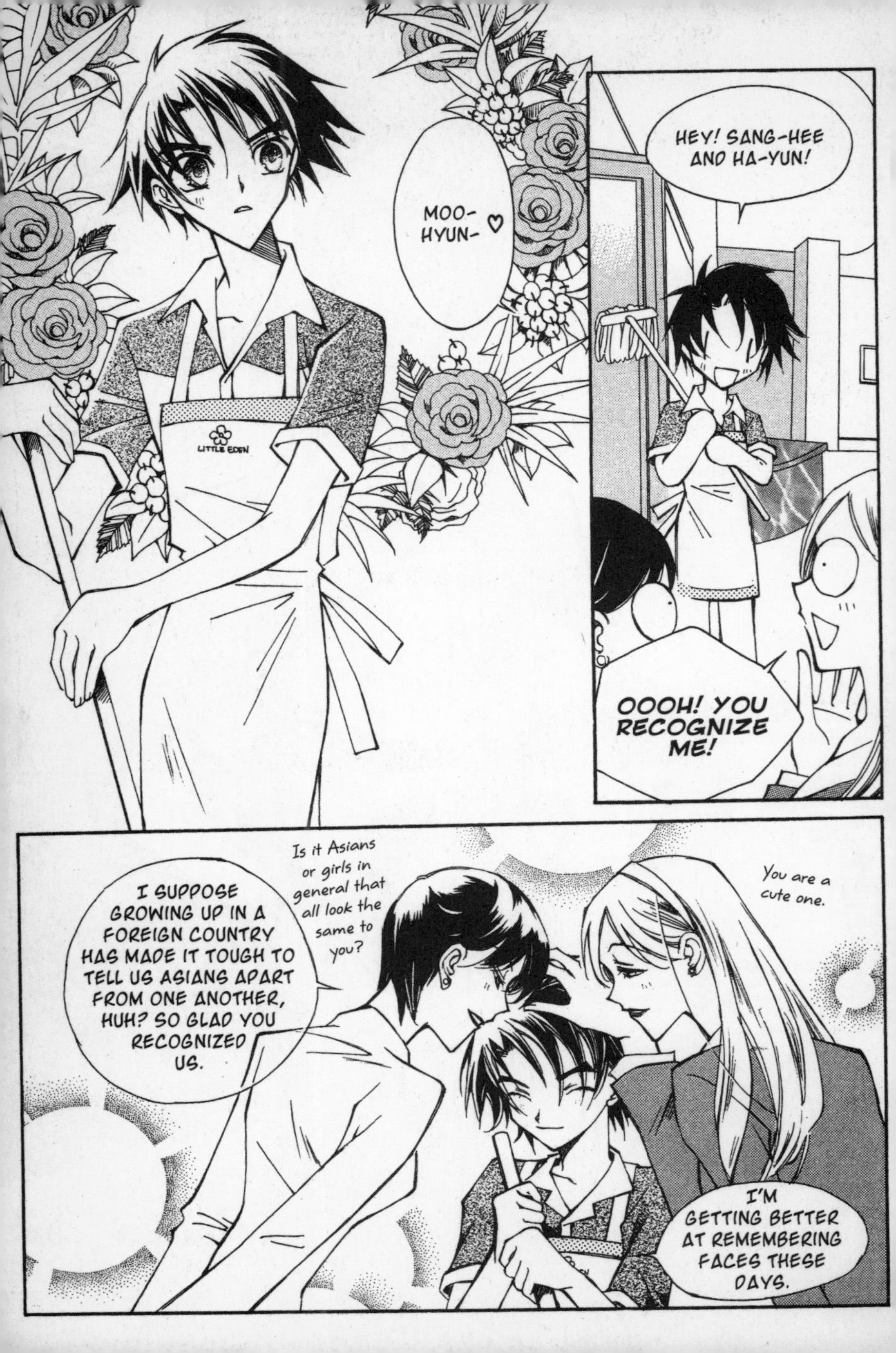
MOO-HYUN-♡
LITTLE EDEN
HEY! SANG-HEE AND HA-YUN!
OOOH! YOU RECOGNIZE ME!
I SUPPOSE GROWING UP IN A FOREIGN COUNTRY HAS MADE IT TOUGH TO TELL US ASIANS APART FROM ONE ANOTHER, HUH? SO GLAD YOU RECOGNIZED US.
Is it Asians or girls in general that all look the same to you?
You are a cute one.
I'M GETTING BETTER AT REMEMBERING FACES THESE DAYS.

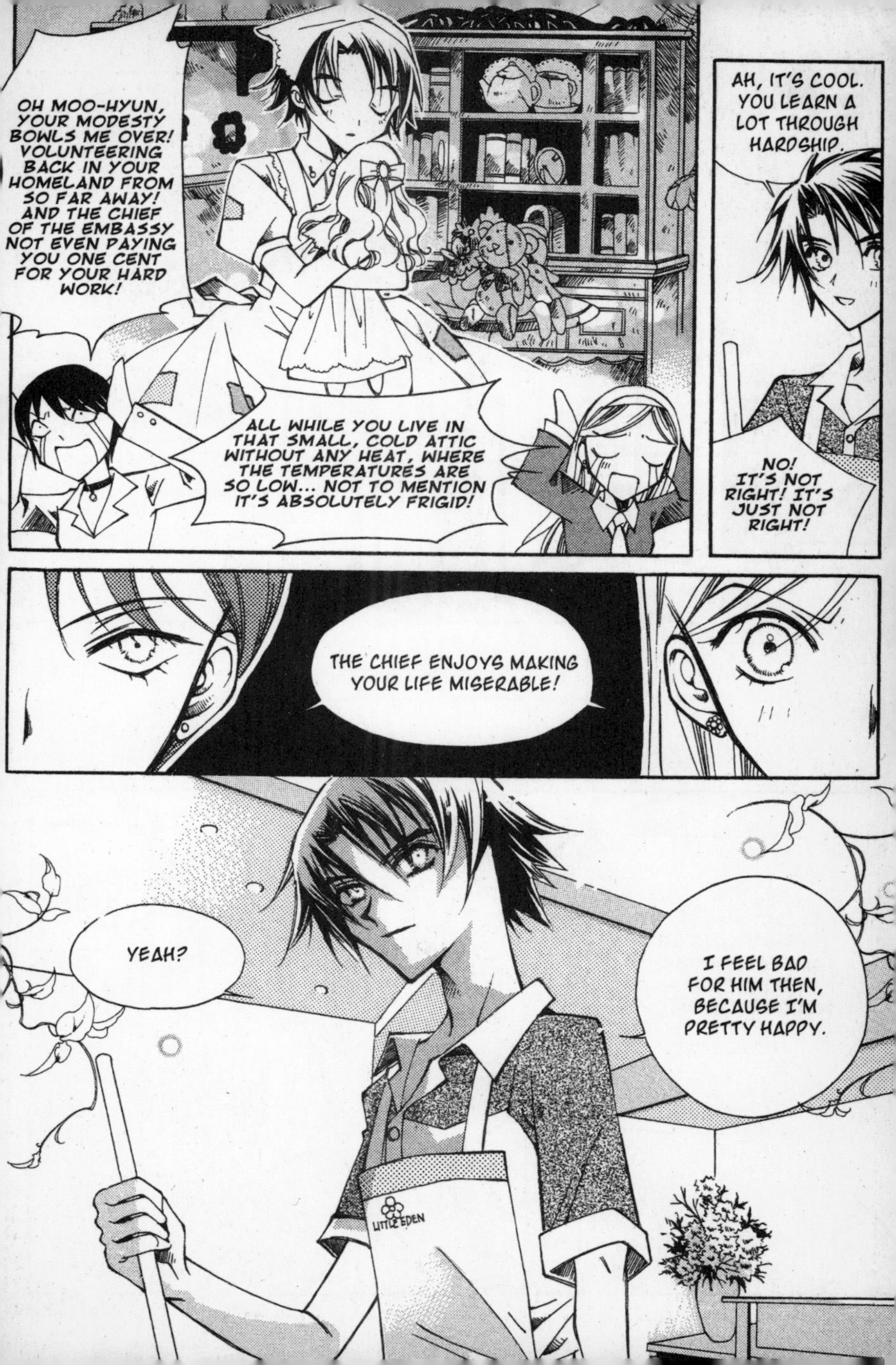
OH MOO-HYUN, YOUR MODESTY BOWLS ME OVER! VOLUNTEERING BACK IN YOUR HOMELAND FROM SO FAR AWAY! AND THE CHIEF OF THE EMBASSY NOT EVEN PAYING YOU ONE CENT FOR YOUR HARD WORK!
ALL WHILE YOU LIVE IN THAT SMALL, COLD ATTIC WITHOUT ANY HEAT, WHERE THE TEMPERATURES ARE SO LOW... NOT TO MENTION IT'S ABSOLUTELY FRIGID!
AH, IT'S COOL. YOU LEARN A LOT THROUGH HARDSHIP.
NO! IT'S NOT RIGHT! IT'S JUST NOT RIGHT!
THE CHIEF ENJOYS MAKING YOUR LIFE MISERABLE!
YEAH?
I FEEL BAD FOR HIM THEN, BECAUSE I'M PRETTY HAPPY.
LITTLE EDEN

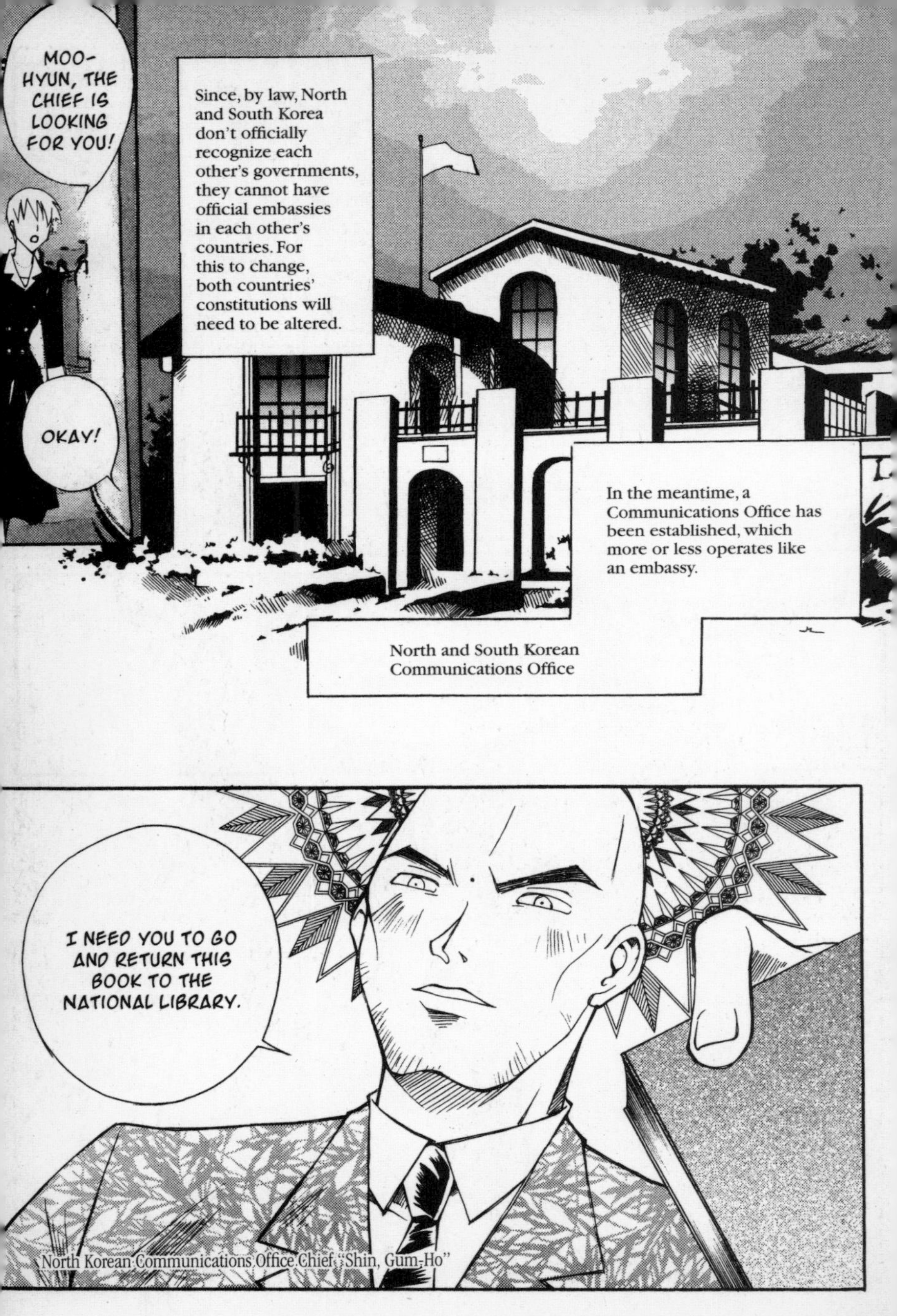
MOO-HYUN, THE CHIEF IS LOOKING FOR YOU!
OKAY!
Since, by law, North and South Korea don't officially recognize each other's governments, they cannot have official embassies in each other's countries. For this to change, both countries' constitutions will need to be altered.
In the meantime, a Communications Office has been established, which more or less operates like an embassy.
North and South Korean Communications Office
I NEED YOU TO GO AND RETURN THIS BOOK TO THE NATIONAL LIBRARY.
North Korean Communications Office Chief "Shin, Gum-Ho"

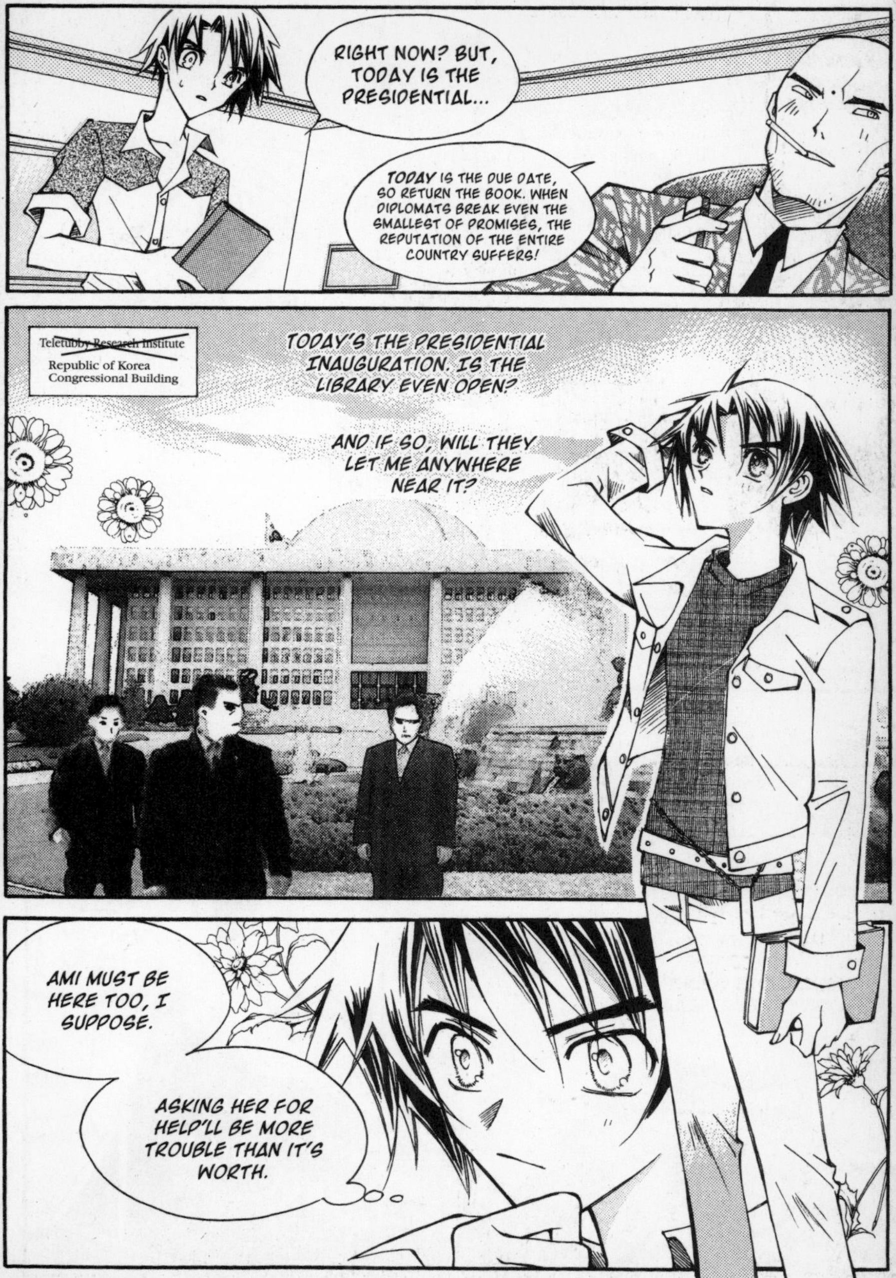
RIGHT NOW? BUT, TODAY IS THE PRESIDENTIAL...
TODAY IS THE DUE DATE, SO RETURN THE BOOK. WHEN DIPLOMATS BREAK EVEN THE SMALLEST OF PROMISES, THE REPUTATION OF THE ENTIRE COUNTRY SUFFERS!
Teletubby Research Institute
Republic of Korea Congressional Building
TODAY'S THE PRESIDENTIAL INAUGURATION. IS THE LIBRARY EVEN OPEN?
AND IF SO, WILL THEY LET ME ANYWHERE NEAR IT?
AMI MUST BE HERE TOO, I SUPPOSE.
ASKING HER FOR HELP'LL BE MORE TROUBLE THAN IT'S WORTH.

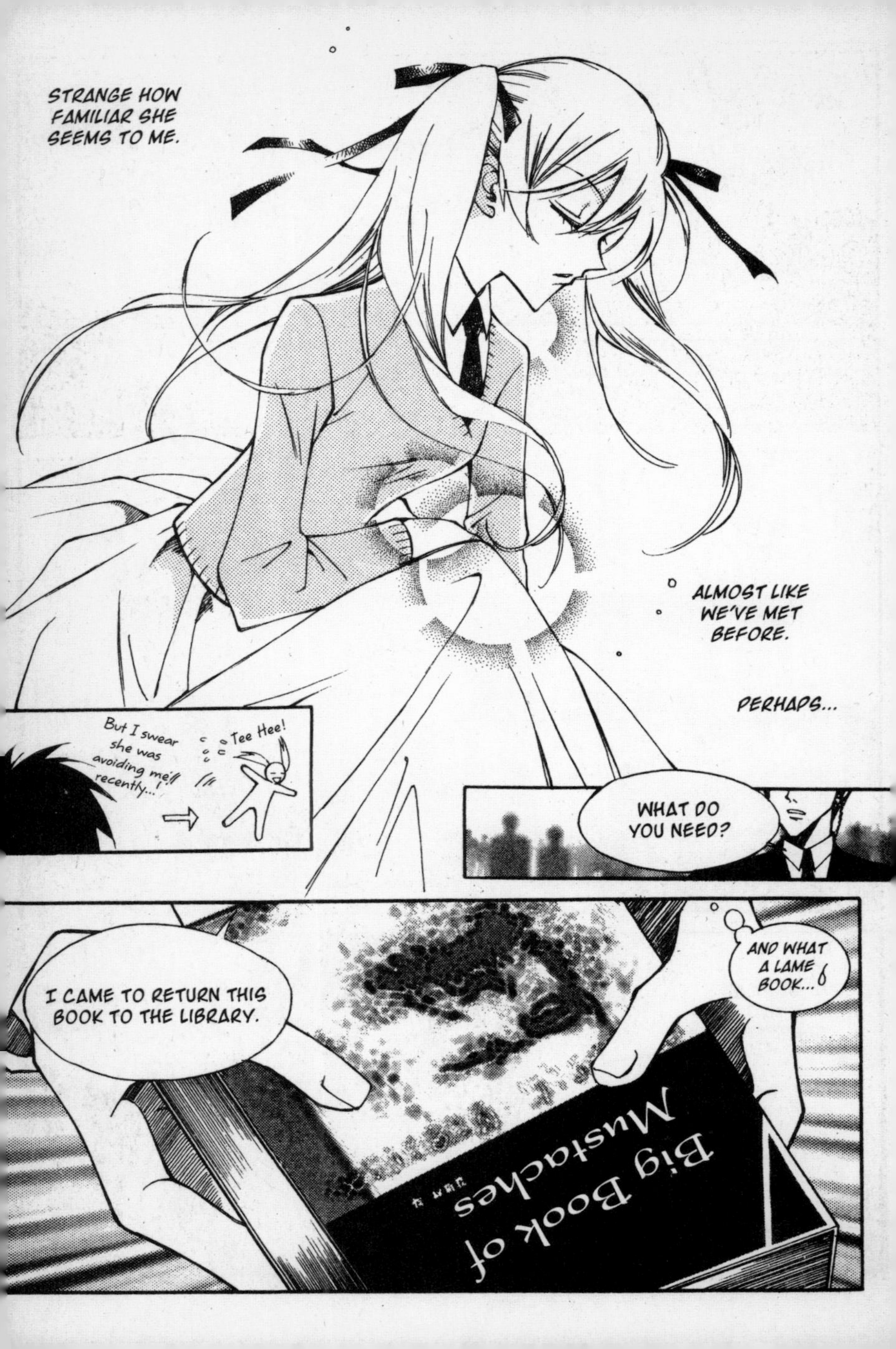
STRANGE HOW FAMILIAR SHE SEEMS TO ME.
ALMOST LIKE WE'VE MET BEFORE.
PERHAPS...
But I swear she was avoiding me!! recently...!
Tee Hee!
WHAT DO YOU NEED?
I CAME TO RETURN THIS BOOK TO THE LIBRARY.
AND WHAT A LAME BOOK...
Big Book of Mustaches

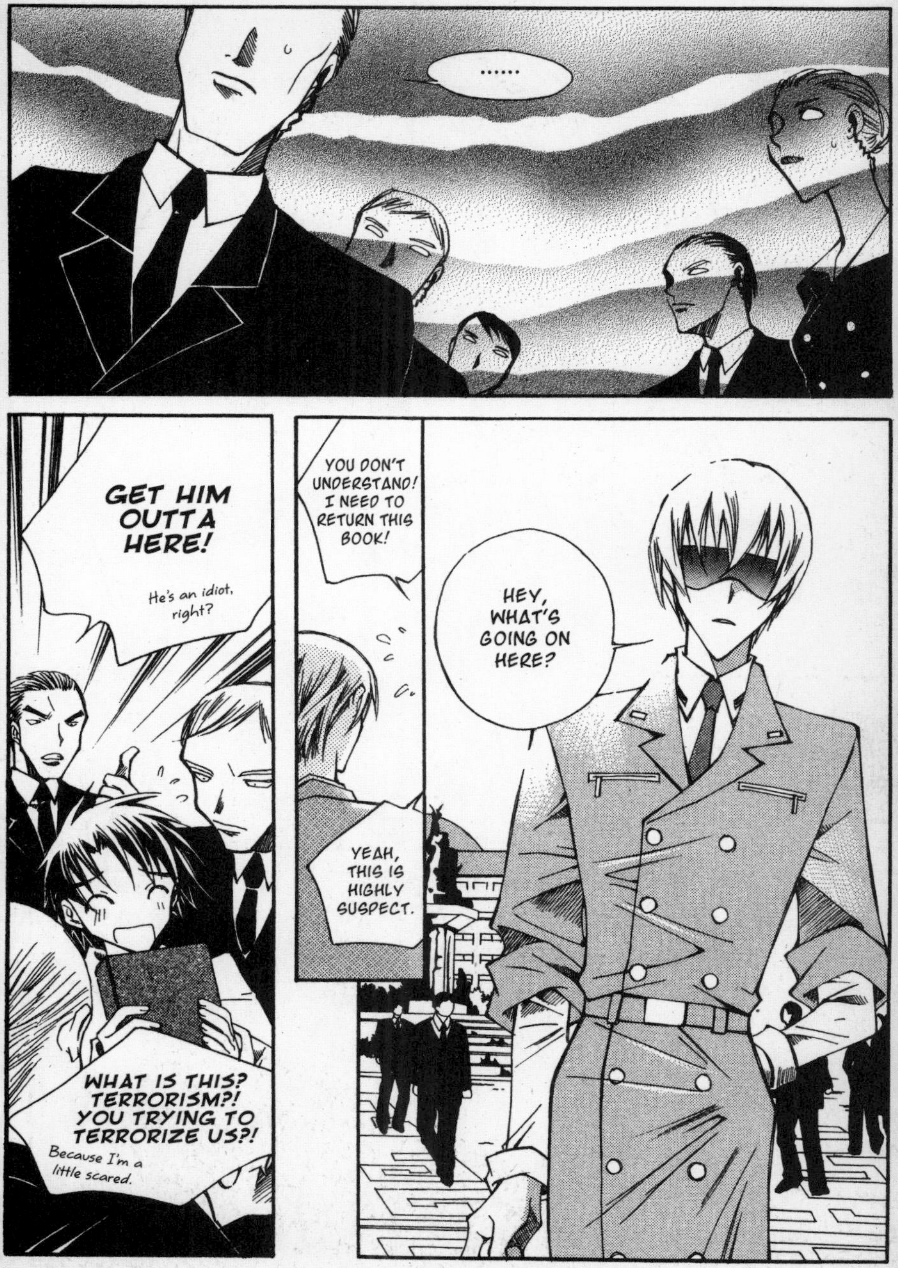
......
GET HIM OUTTA HERE!
He's an idiot, right?
WHAT IS THIS? TERRORISM?! YOU TRYING TO TERRORIZE US?!
Because I'm a little scared.
YOU DON'T UNDERSTAND! I NEED TO RETURN THIS BOOK!
HEY, WHAT'S GOING ON HERE?
YEAH, THIS IS HIGHLY SUSPECT.

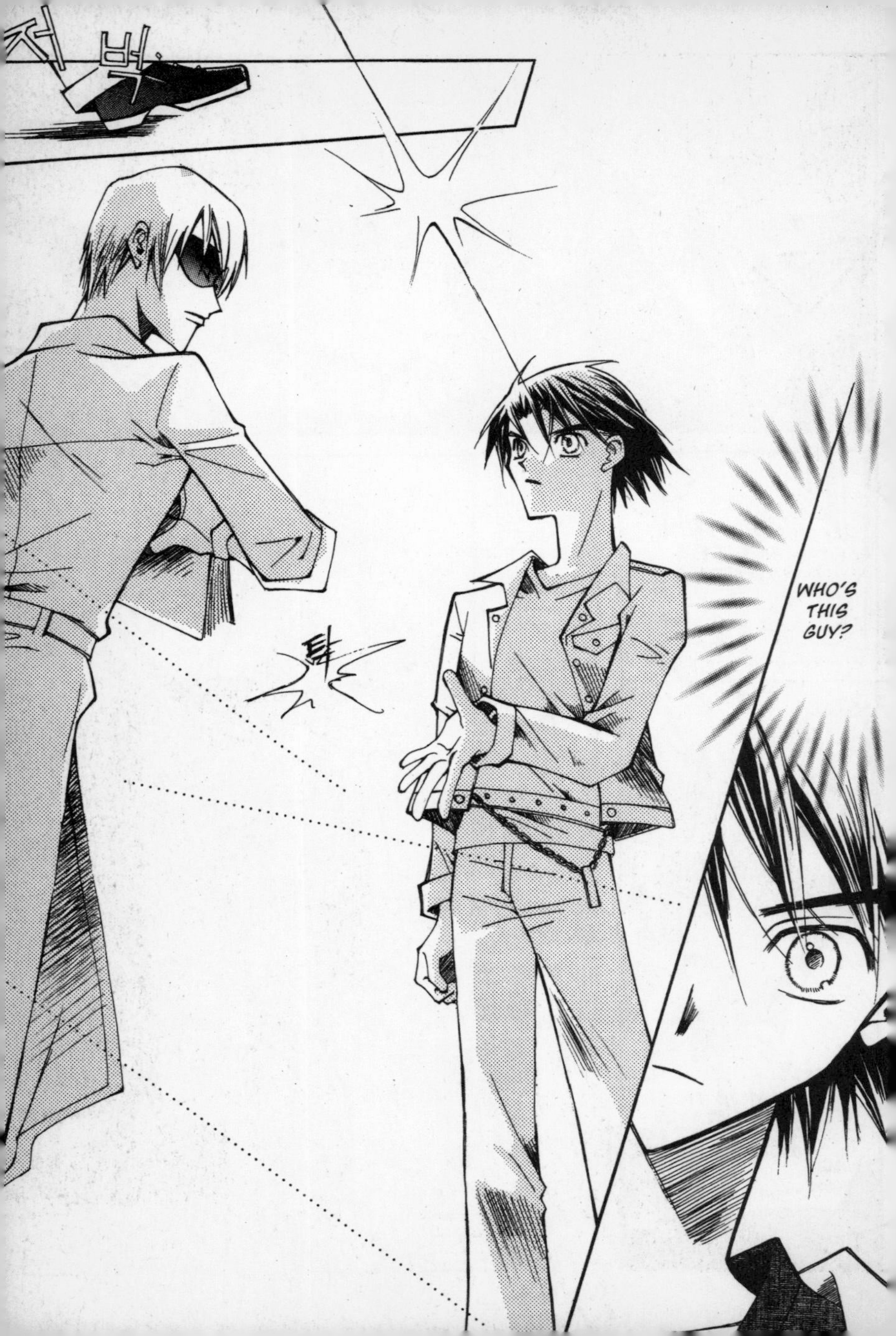
탁
WHO'S THIS GUY?

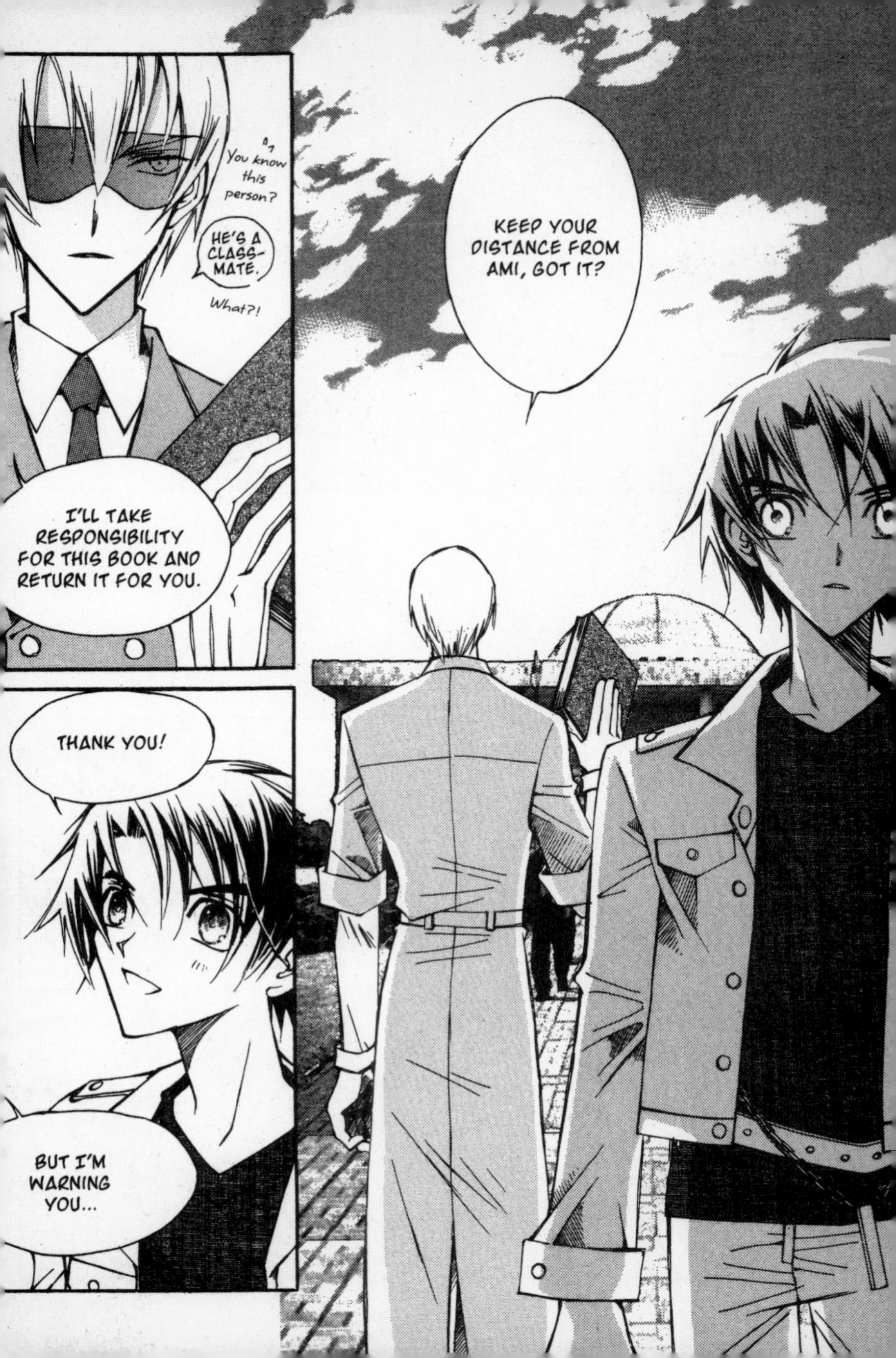
You know this person?
HE'S A CLASSMATE.
What?!
I'LL TAKE RESPONSIBILITY FOR THIS BOOK AND RETURN IT FOR YOU.
THANK YOU!
BUT I'M WARNING YOU...
KEEP YOUR DISTANCE FROM AMI, GOT IT?

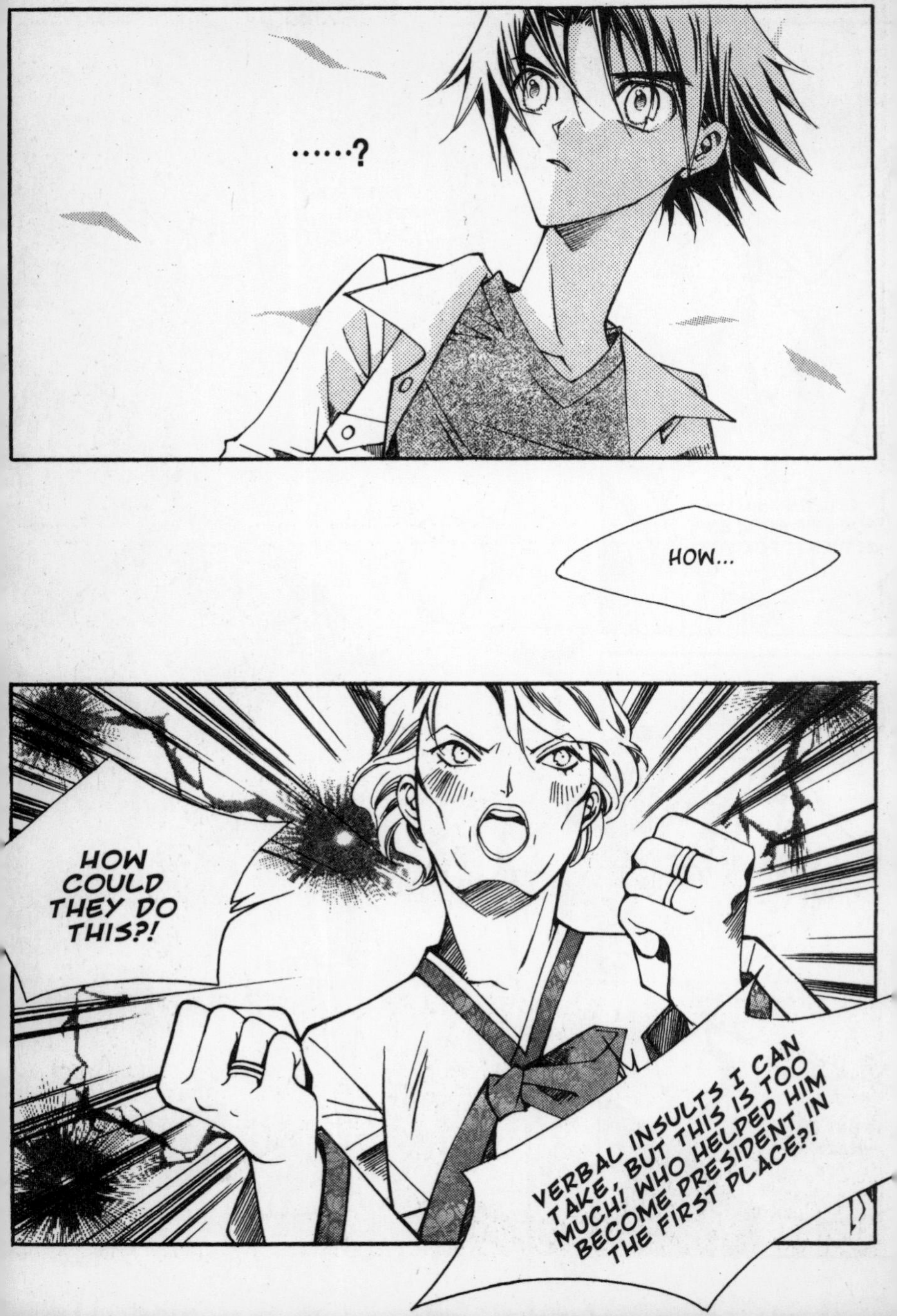
......?
HOW...
HOW COULD THEY DO THIS?!
VERBAL INSULTS I CAN TAKE, BUT THIS IS TOO MUCH! WHO HELPED HIM BECOME PRESIDENT IN THE FIRST PLACE?!

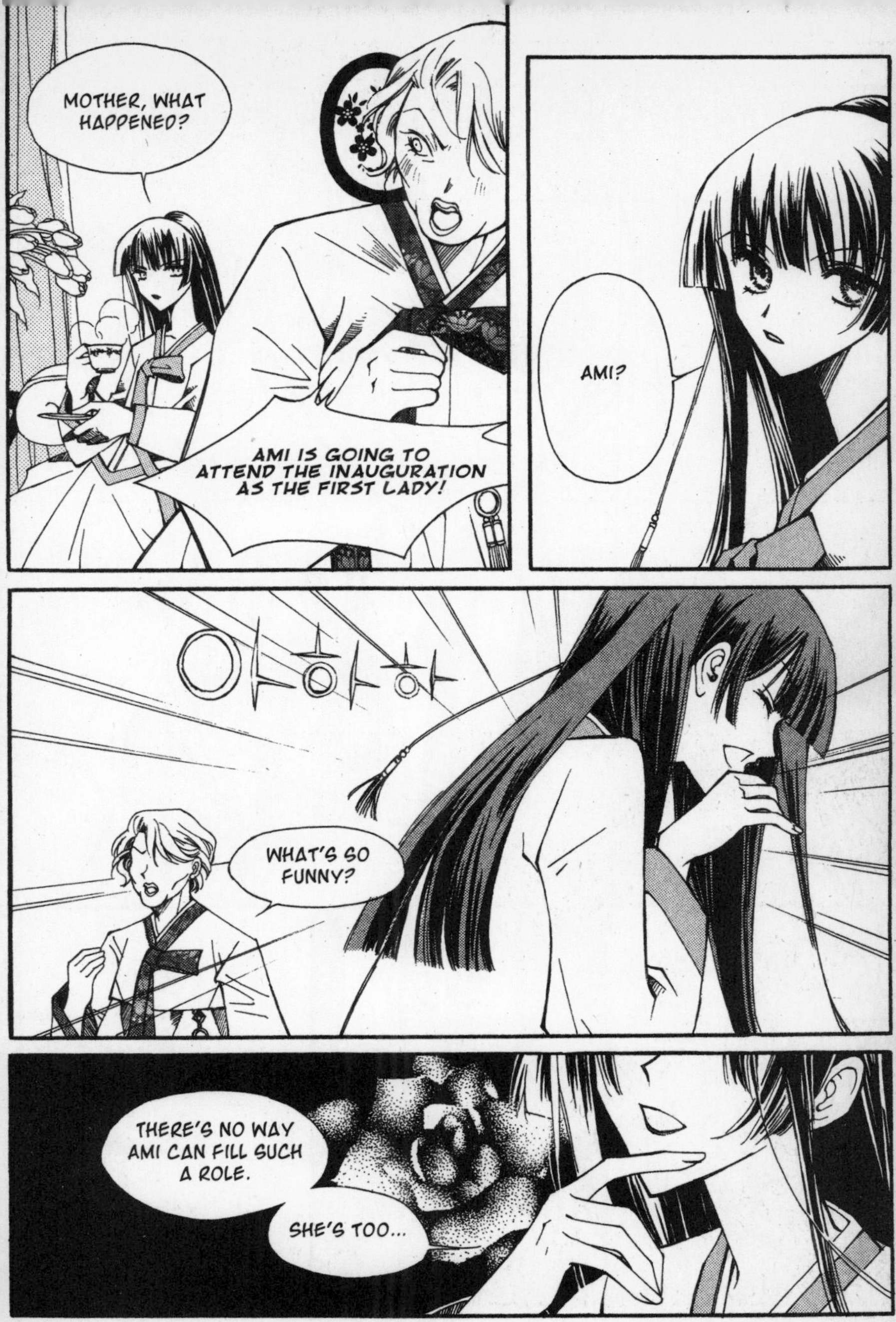
MOTHER, WHAT HAPPENED?
AMI IS GOING TO ATTEND THE INAUGURATION AS THE FIRST LADY!
AMI?
WHAT'S SO FUNNY?
THERE'S NO WAY AMI CAN FILL SUCH A ROLE.
SHE'S TOO...

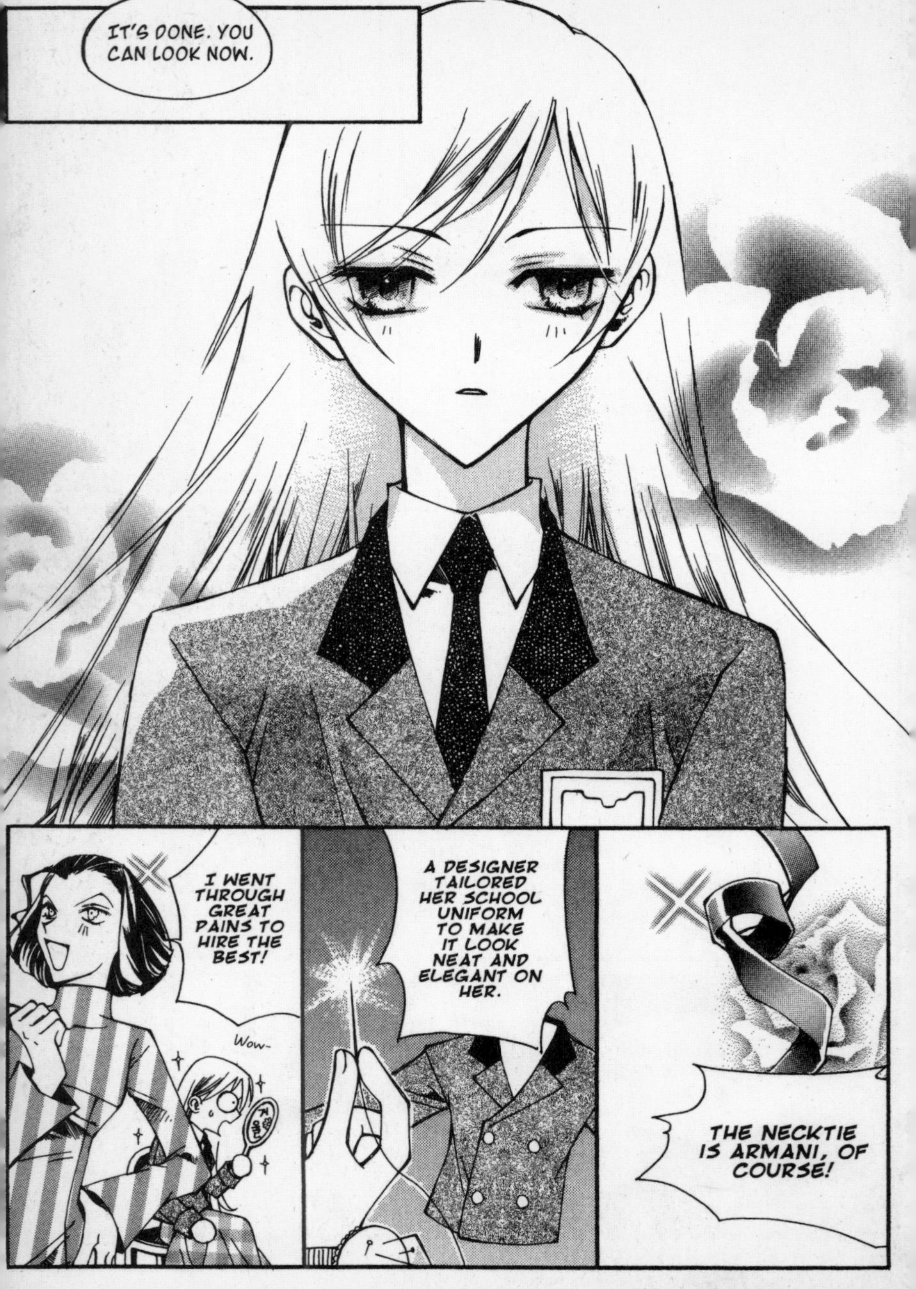
IT'S DONE. YOU CAN LOOK NOW.
I WENT THROUGH GREAT PAINS TO HIRE THE BEST!
Wow-
A DESIGNER TAILORED HER SCHOOL UNIFORM TO MAKE IT LOOK NEAT AND ELEGANT ON HER.
THE NECKTIE IS ARMANI, OF COURSE!

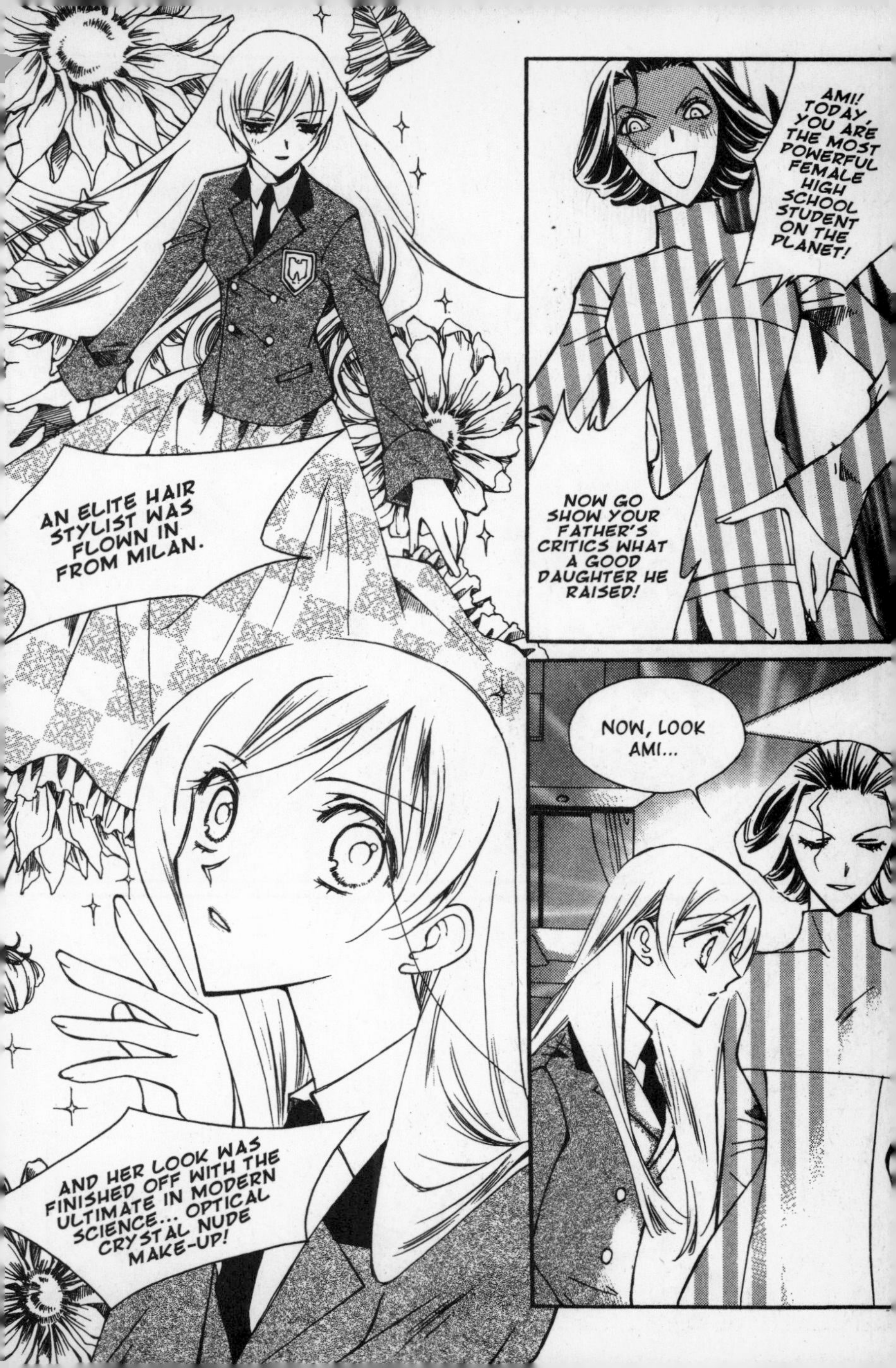
AN ELITE HAIR STYLIST WAS FLOWN IN FROM MILAN.
AND HER LOOK WAS FINISHED OFF WITH THE ULTIMATE IN MODERN SCIENCE... OPTICAL CRYSTAL NUDE MAKE-UP!
AMI! TODAY, YOU ARE THE MOST POWERFUL FEMALE HIGH SCHOOL STUDENT ON THE PLANET!
NOW GO SHOW YOUR FATHER'S CRITICS WHAT A GOOD DAUGHTER HE RAISED!
NOW, LOOK AMI...

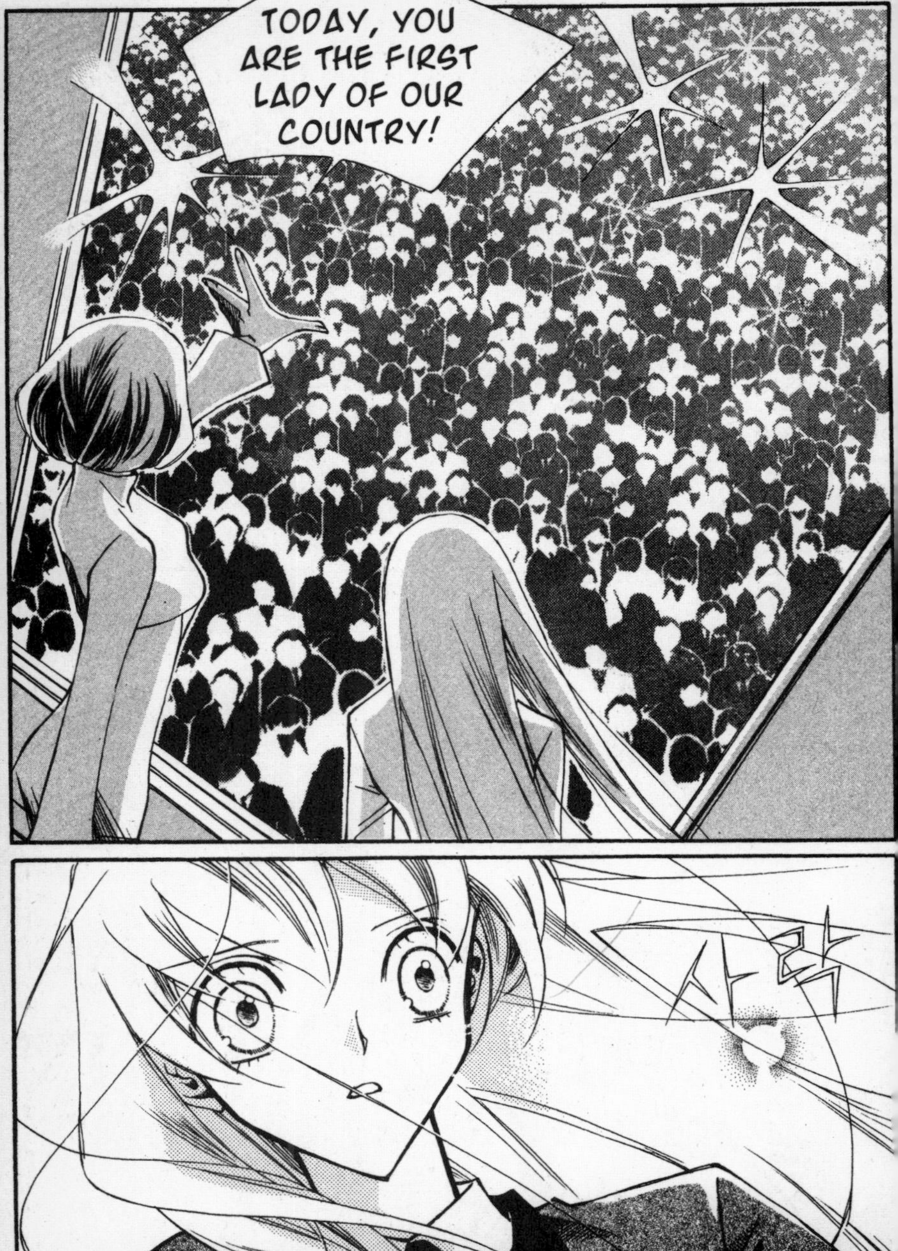
TODAY, YOU ARE THE FIRST LADY OF OUR COUNTRY!
사락

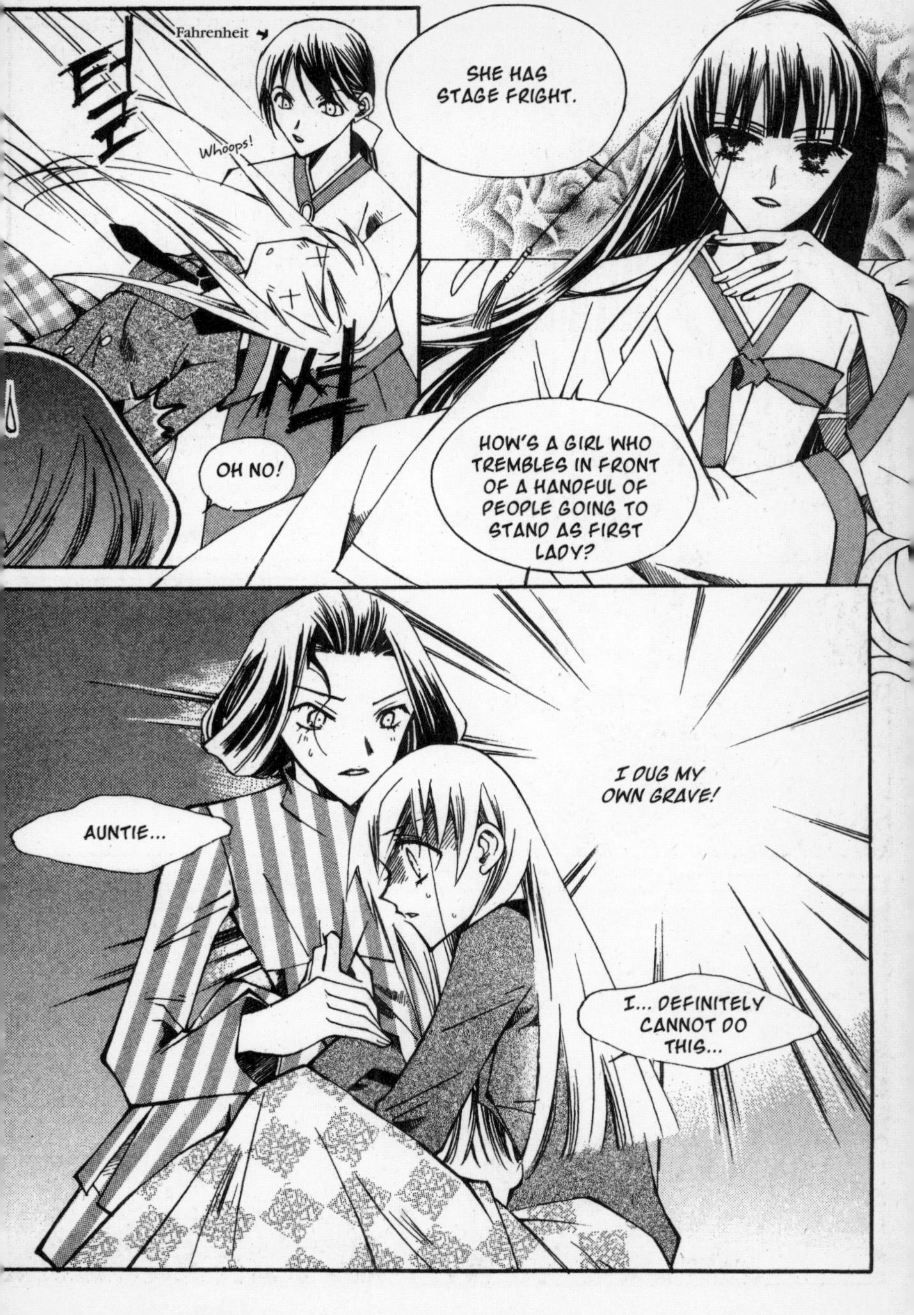
Fahrenheit
Whoops!
OH NO!
SHE HAS STAGE FRIGHT.
HOW'S A GIRL WHO TREMBLES IN FRONT OF A HANDFUL OF PEOPLE GOING TO STAND AS FIRST LADY?
AUNTIE...
I DUG MY OWN GRAVE!
I... DEFINITELY CANNOT DO THIS...

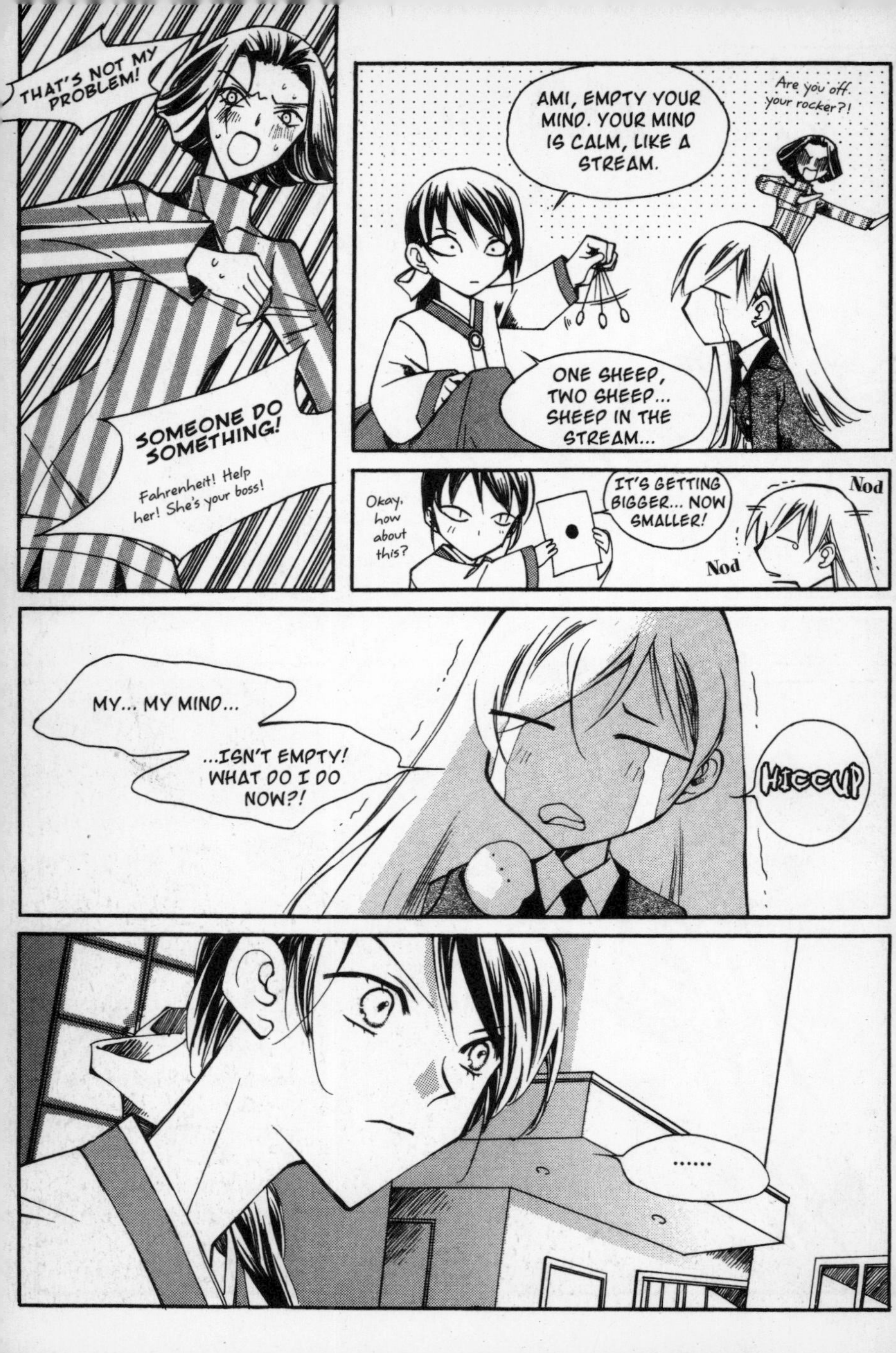
THAT'S NOT MY PROBLEM!
SOMEONE DO SOMETHING!
Fahrenheit! Help her! She's your boss!
AMI, EMPTY YOUR MIND. YOUR MIND IS CALM, LIKE A STREAM.
Are you off your rocker?!
ONE SHEEP, TWO SHEEP... SHEEP IN THE STREAM...
Okay, how about this?
IT'S GETTING BIGGER... NOW SMALLER!
Nod
Nod
MY... MY MIND...
...ISN'T EMPTY! WHAT DO I DO NOW?!
HICCUP
......

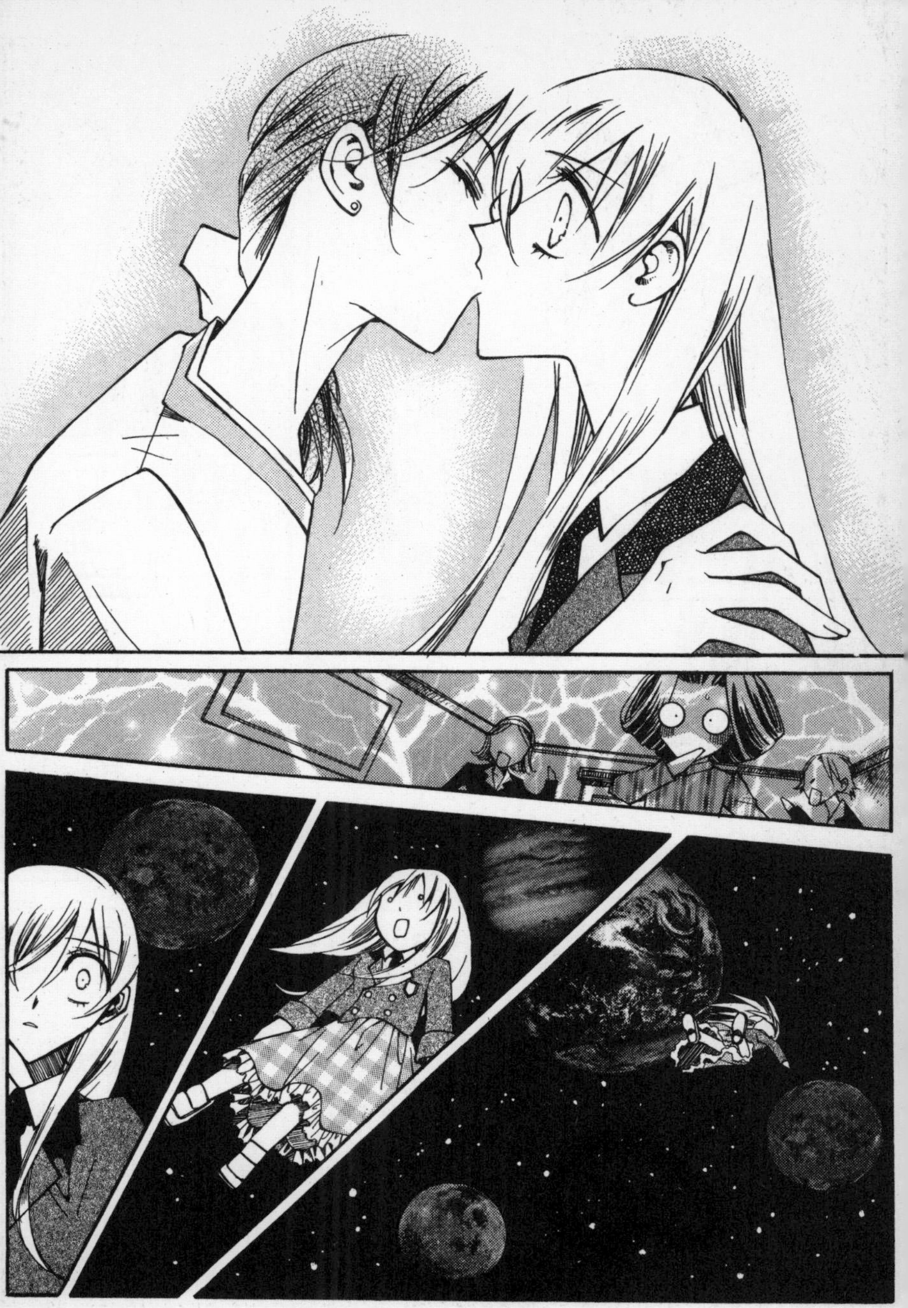

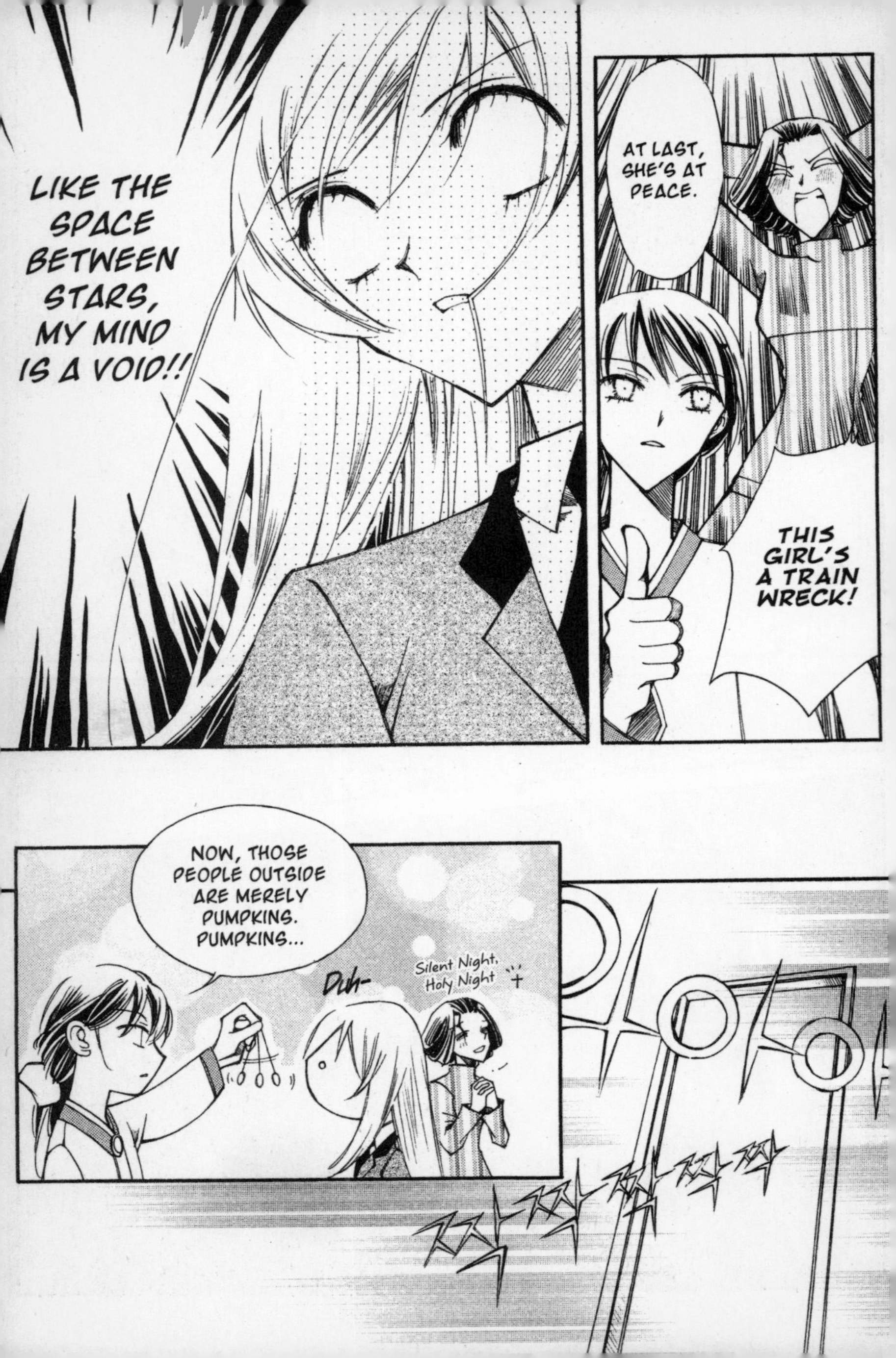
LIKE THE SPACE BETWEEN STARS, MY MIND IS A VOID!!
AT LAST, SHE'S AT PEACE.
THIS GIRL'S A TRAIN WRECK!
NOW, THOSE PEOPLE OUTSIDE ARE MERELY PUMPKINS. PUMPKINS...
Duh-
Silent Night, Holy Night

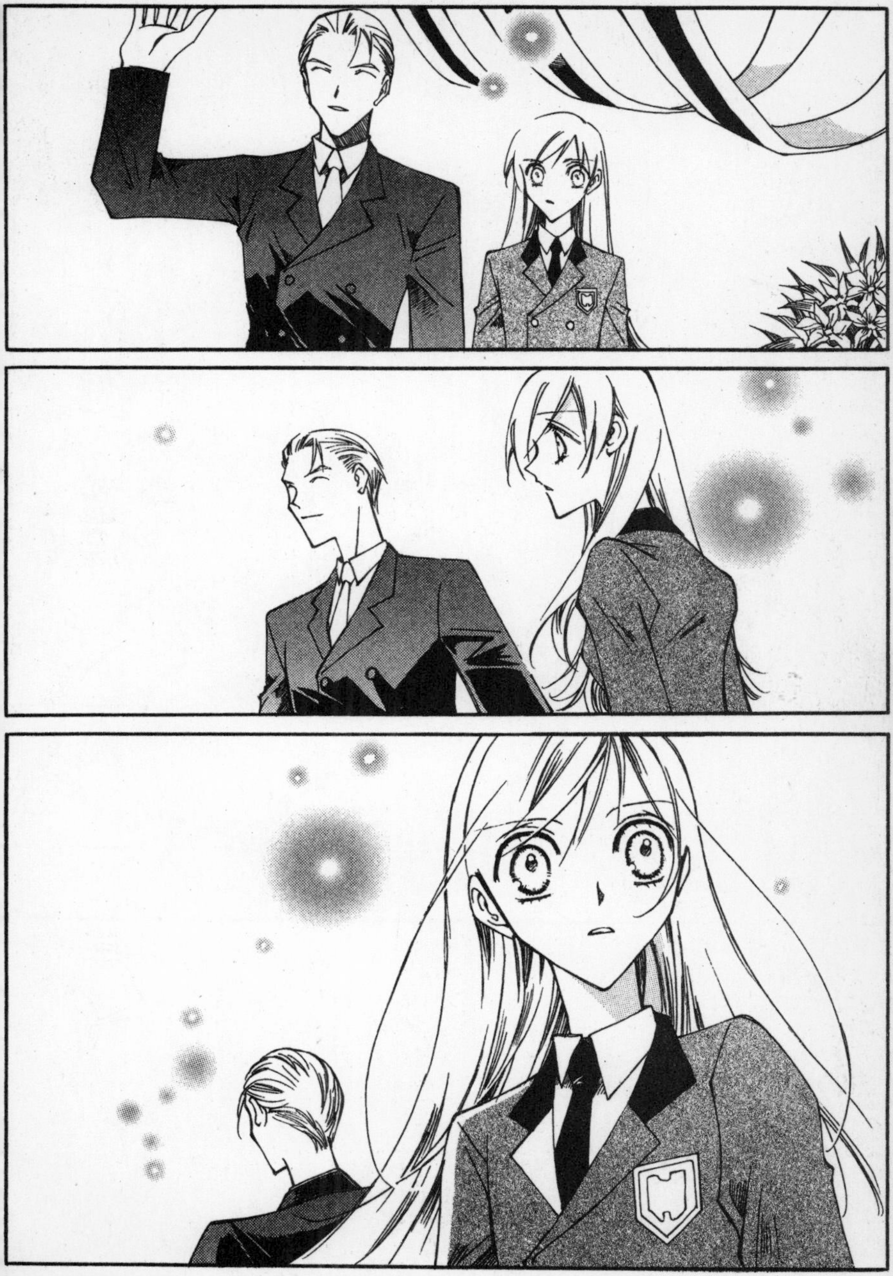

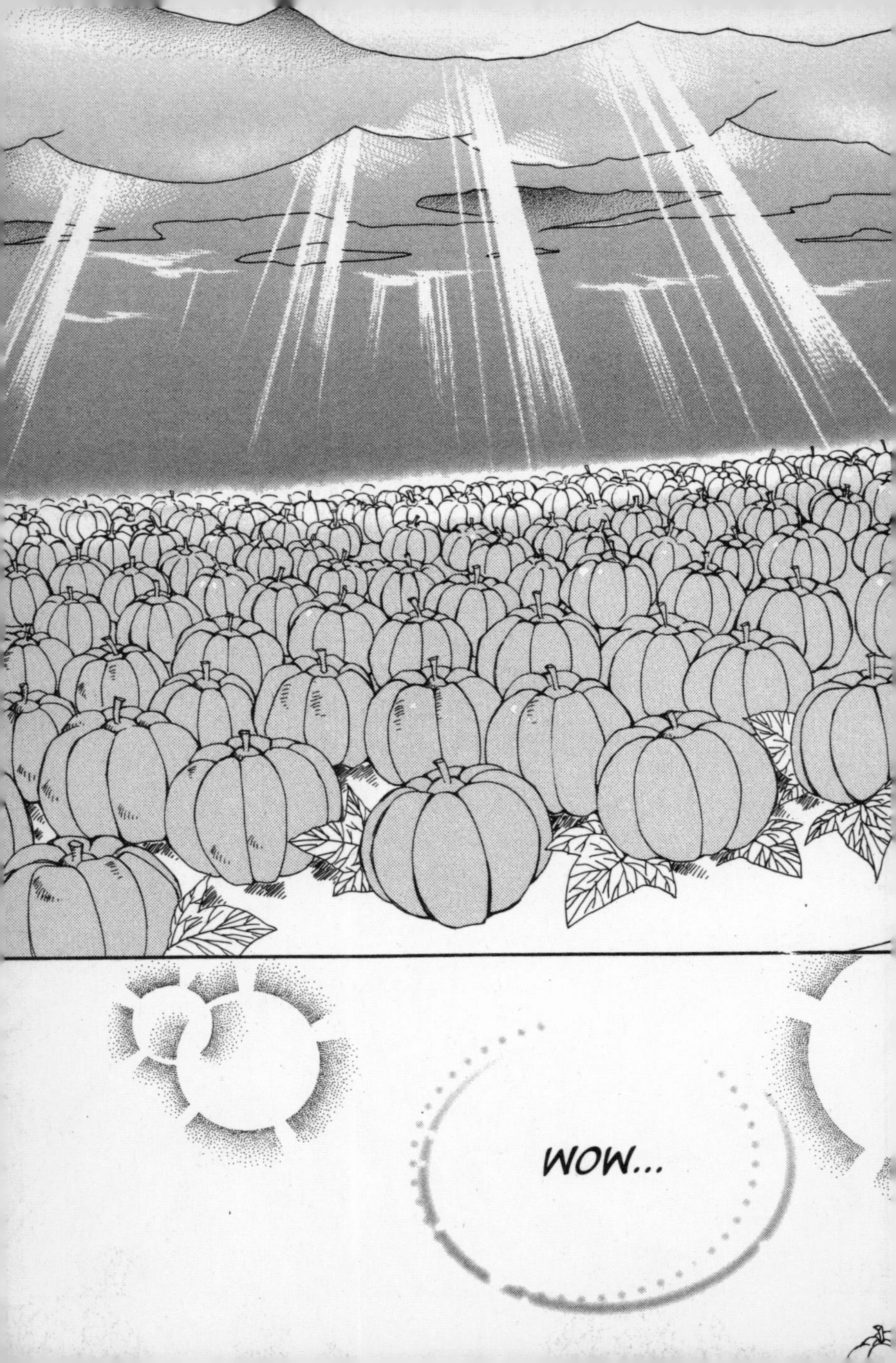
WOW...

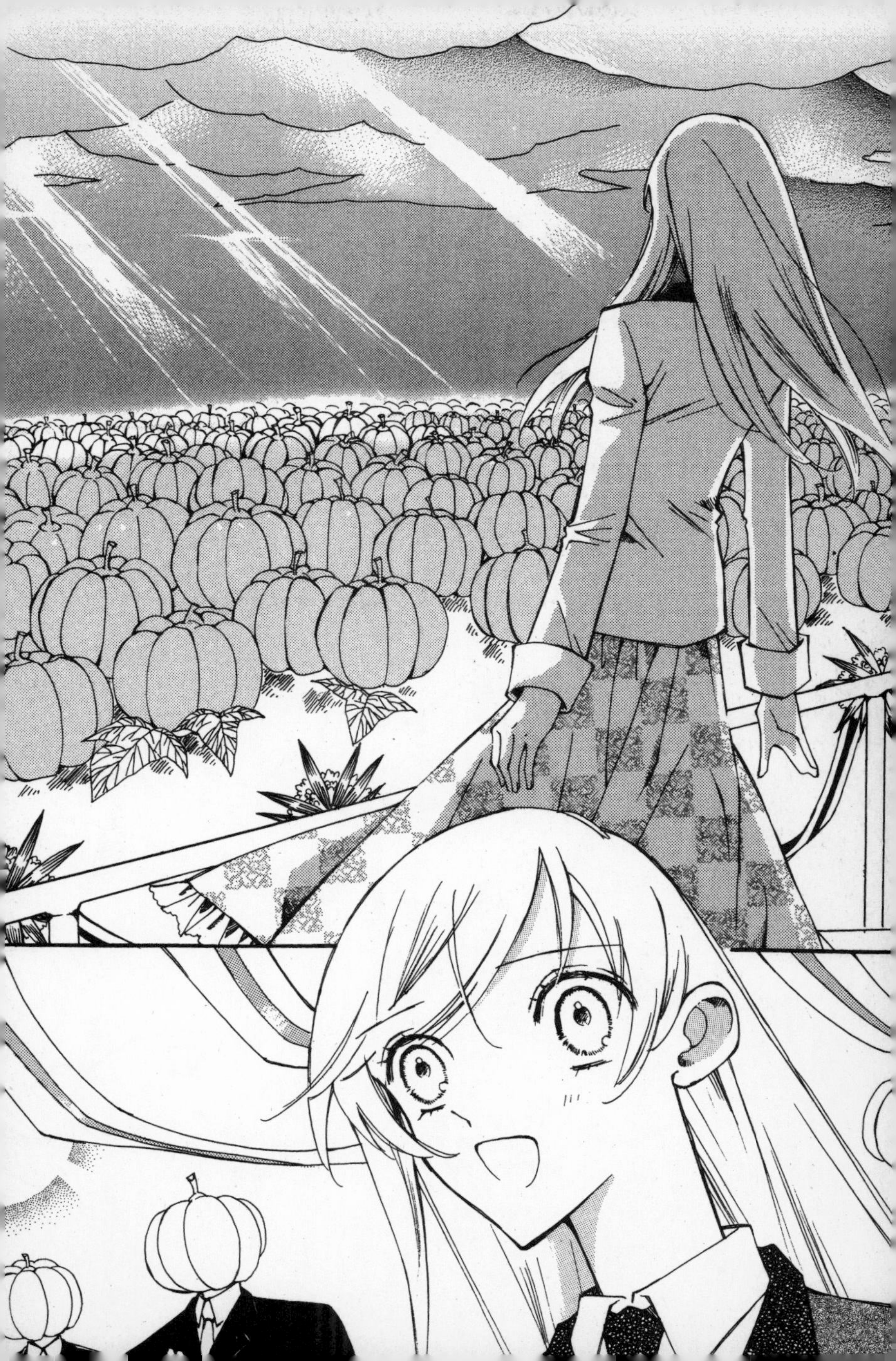

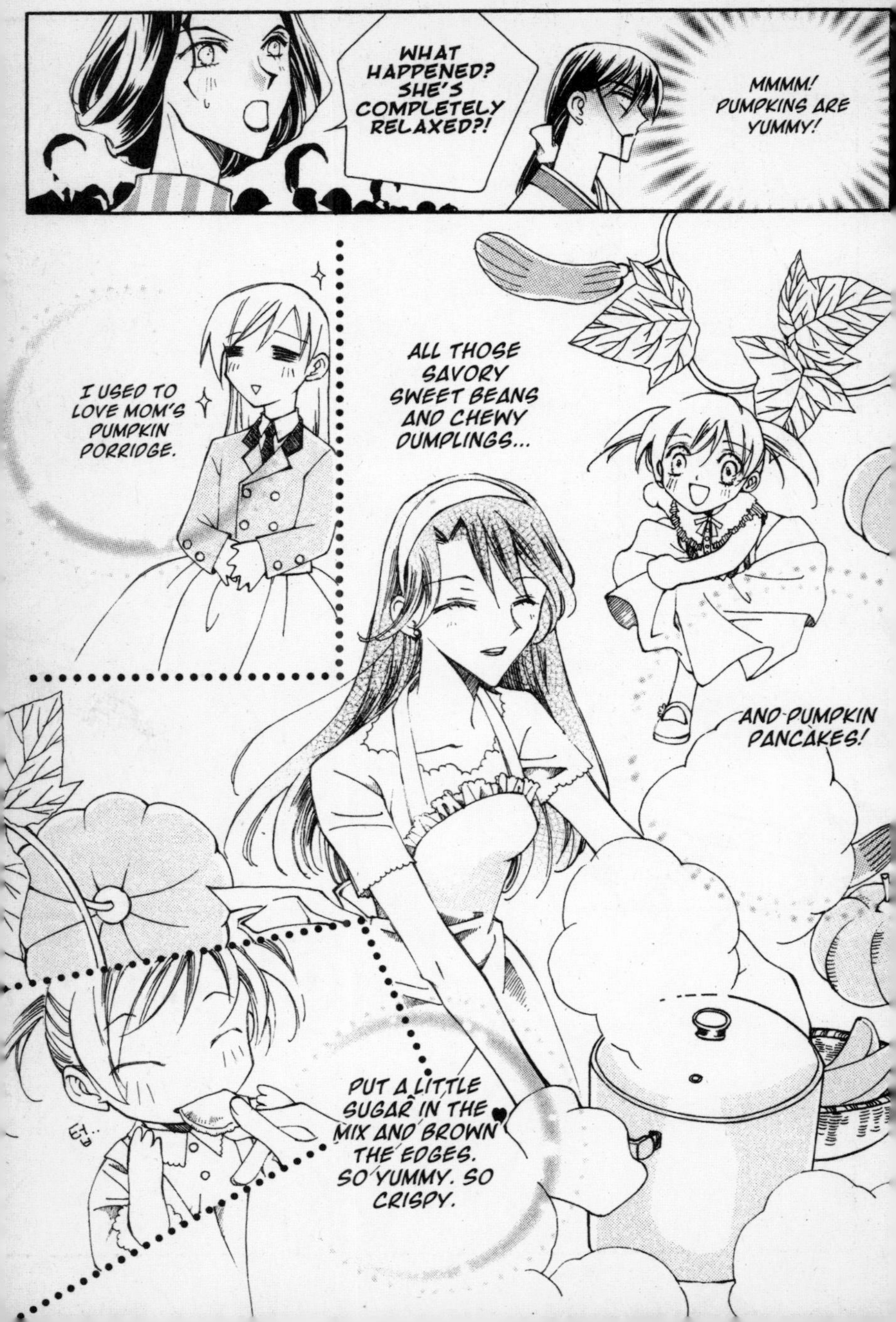
WHAT HAPPENED? SHE'S COMPLETELY RELAXED?!
MMMM! PUMPKINS ARE YUMMY!
I USED TO LOVE MOM'S PUMPKIN PORRIDGE.
ALL THOSE SAVORY SWEET BEANS AND CHEWY DUMPLINGS...
AND-PUMPKIN PANCAKES!
PUT A LITTLE SUGAR IN THE MIX AND BROWN THE EDGES. SO YUMMY. SO CRISPY.

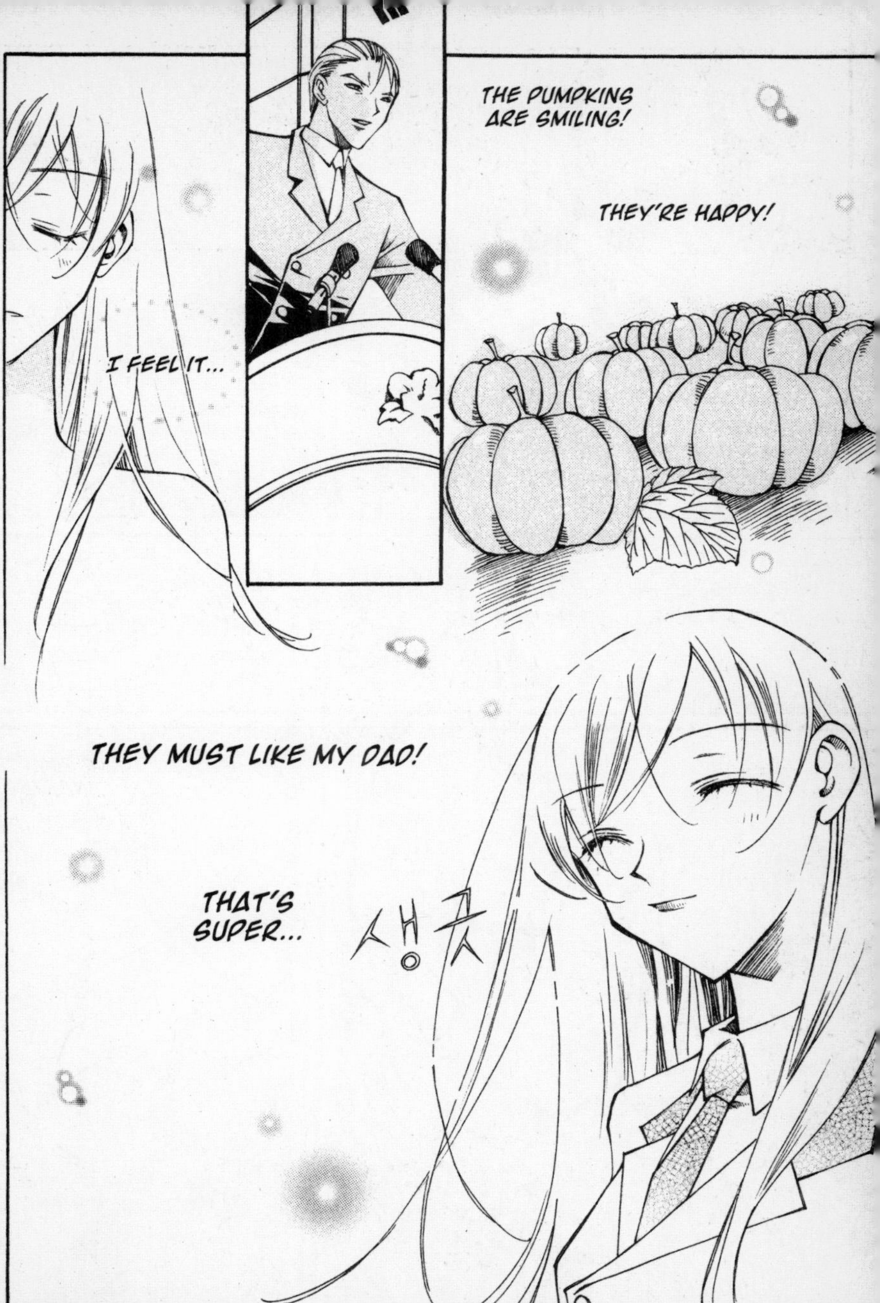
I FEEL IT...
THE PUMPKINS ARE SMILING!
THEY'RE HAPPY!
THEY MUST LIKE MY DAD!
THAT'S SUPER...
생긋

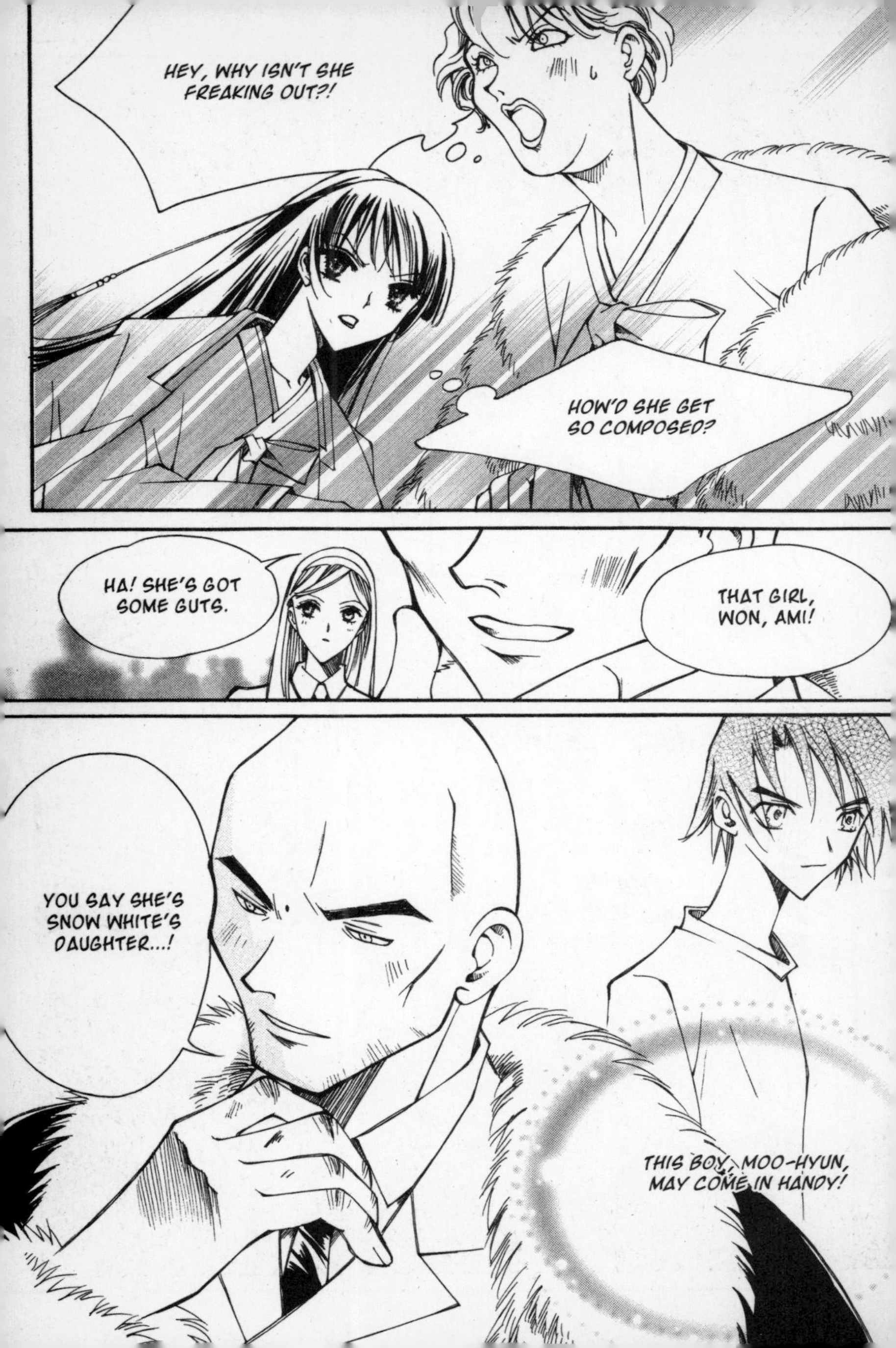
HEY, WHY ISN'T SHE FREAKING OUT?!
HOW'D SHE GET SO COMPOSED?
HA! SHE'S GOT SOME GUTS.
THAT GIRL, WON, AMI!
YOU SAY SHE'S SNOW WHITE'S DAUGHTER...!
THIS BOY, MOO-HYUN, MAY COME IN HANDY!

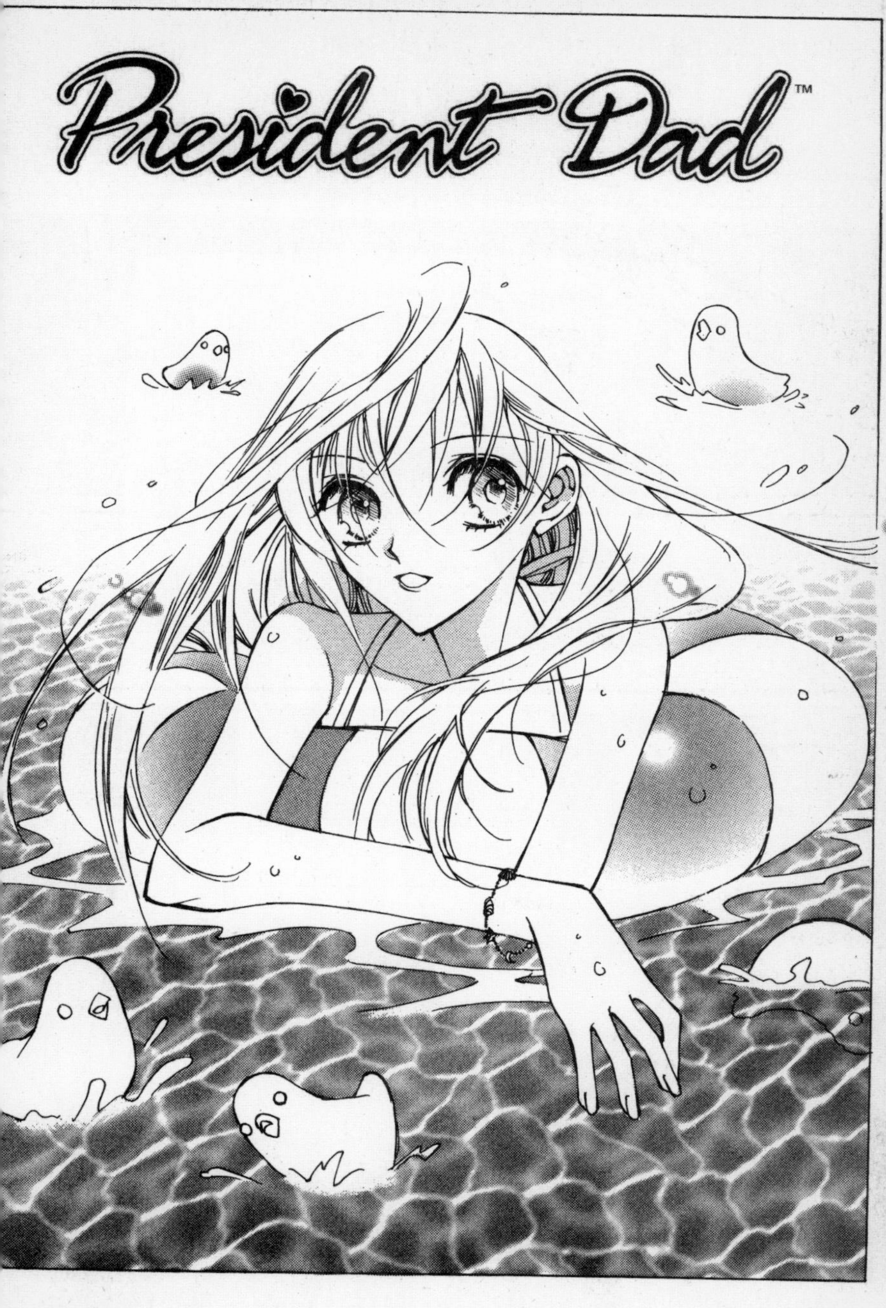
President Dad™

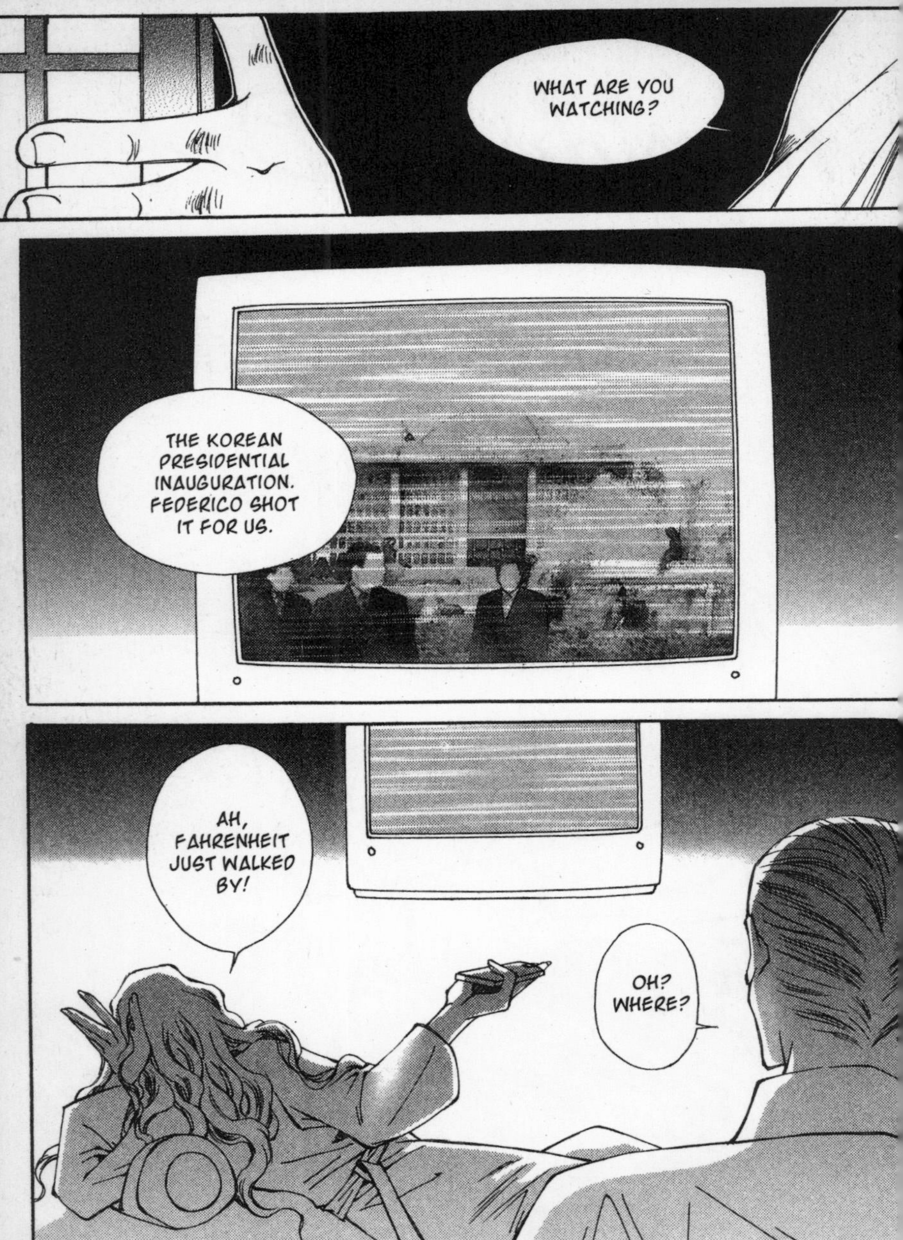
WHAT ARE YOU WATCHING?
THE KOREAN PRESIDENTIAL INAUGURATION. FEDERICO SHOT IT FOR US.
AH, FAHRENHEIT JUST WALKED BY!
OH? WHERE?

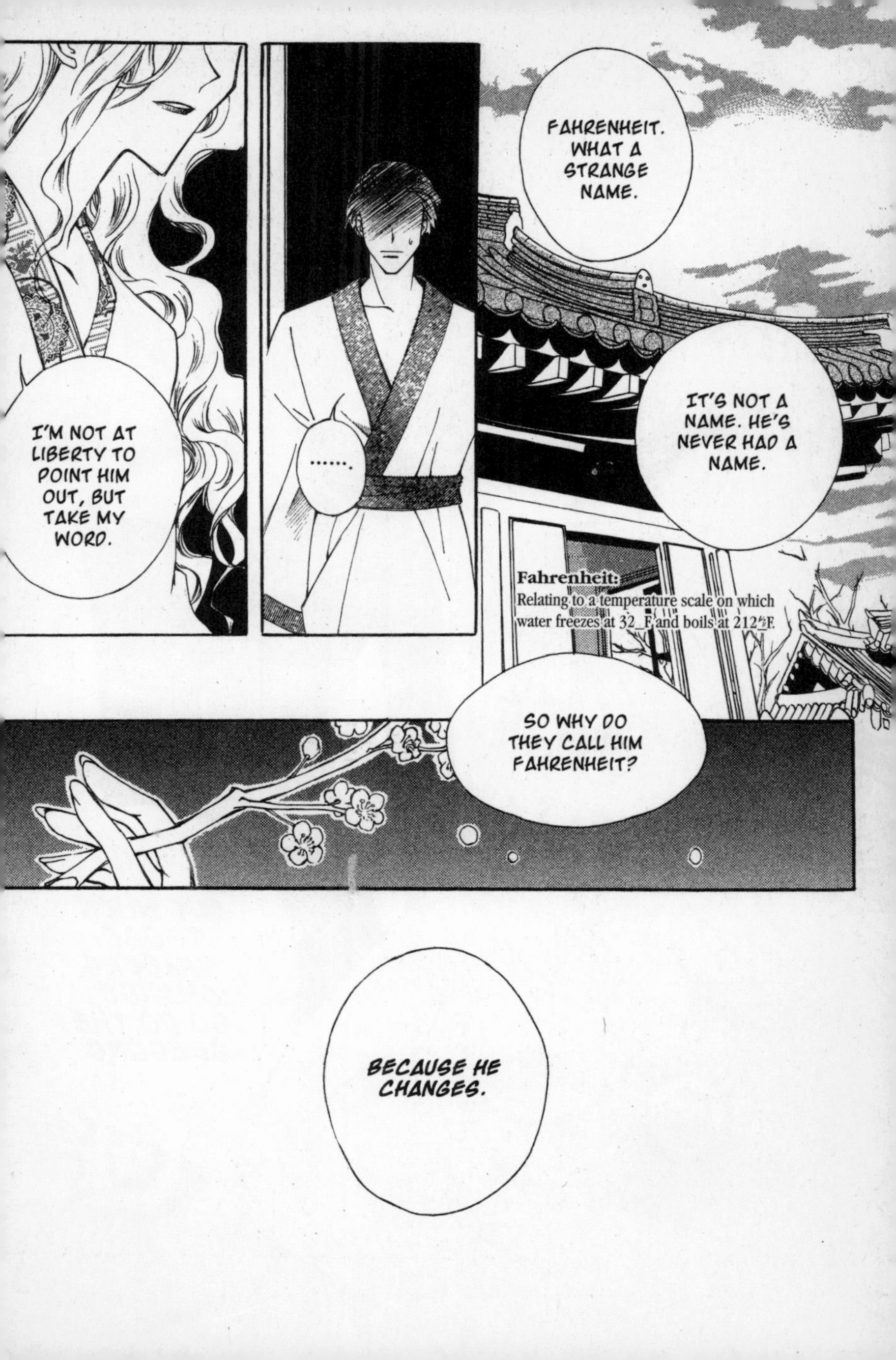
I'M NOT AT LIBERTY TO POINT HIM OUT, BUT TAKE MY WORD.
....
FAHRENHEIT. WHAT A STRANGE NAME.
IT'S NOT A NAME. HE'S NEVER HAD A NAME.
Fahrenheit:
Relating to a temperature scale on which water freezes at 32_F and boils at 212½F.
SO WHY DO THEY CALL HIM FAHRENHEIT?
BECAUSE HE CHANGES.

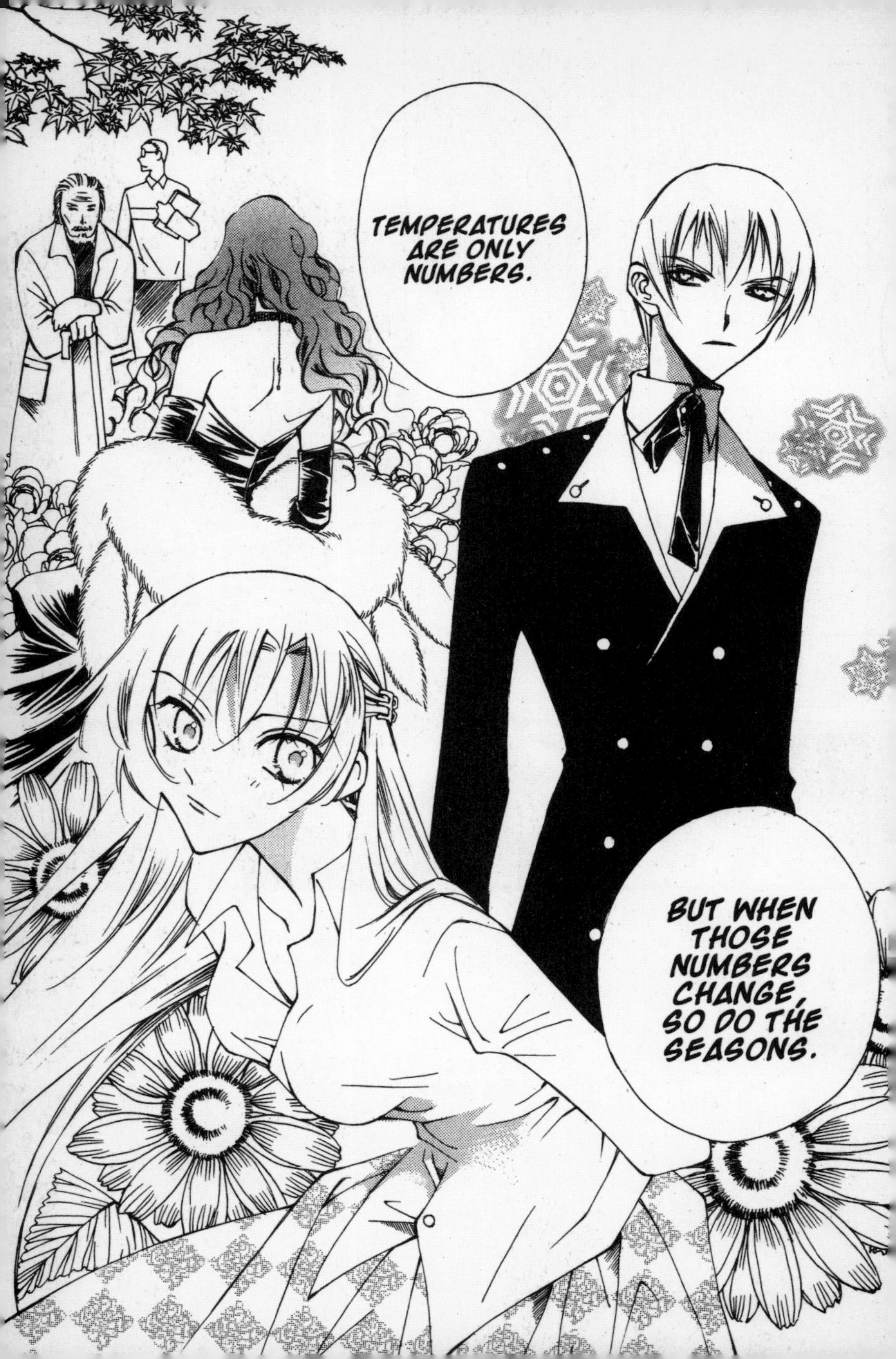
TEMPERATURES ARE ONLY NUMBERS.
BUT WHEN THOSE NUMBERS CHANGE, SO DO THE SEASONS.

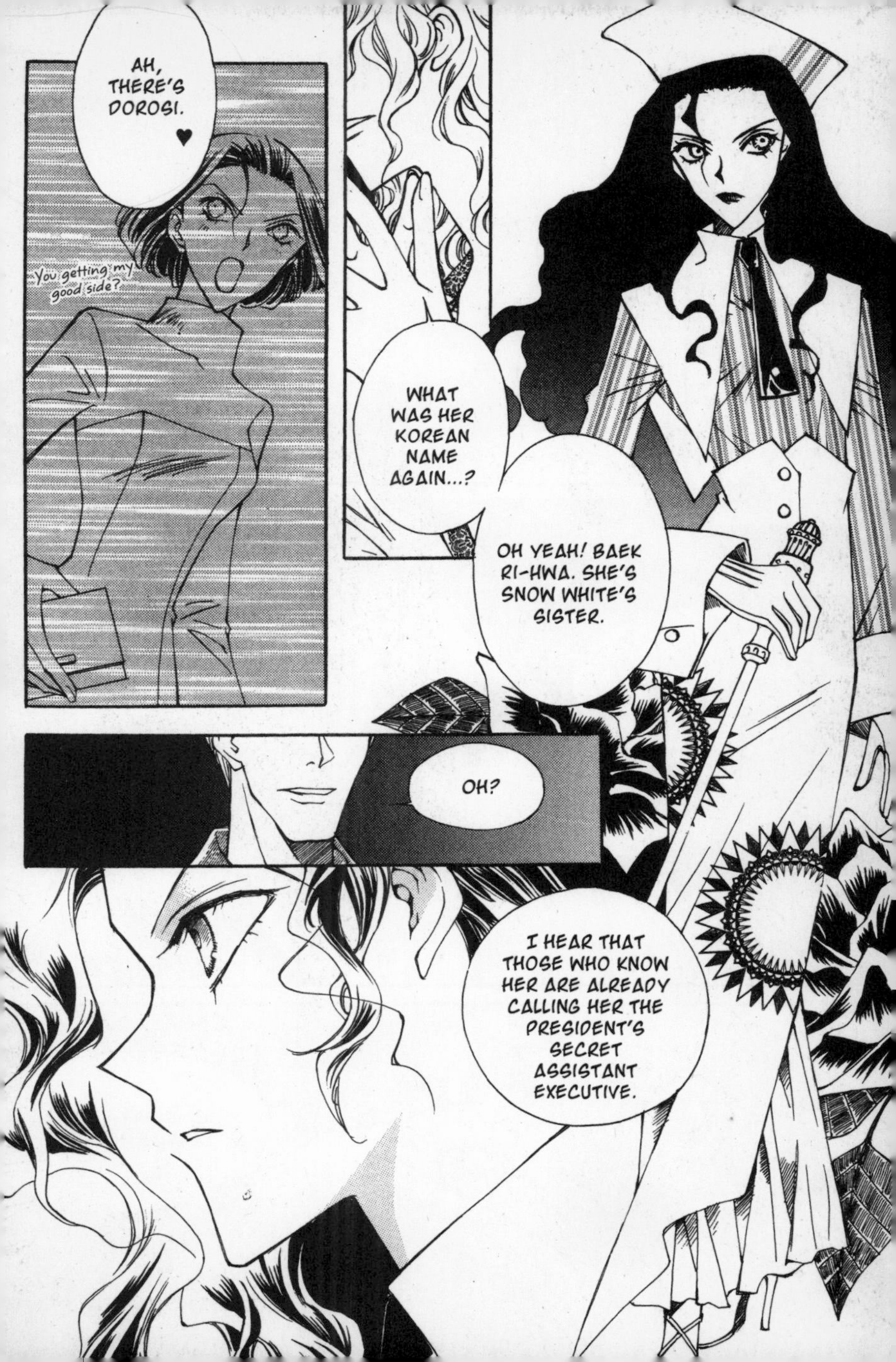
AH, THERE'S DOROSI. ♥
You getting my good side?
WHAT WAS HER KOREAN NAME AGAIN...?
OH YEAH! BAEK RI-HWA. SHE'S SNOW WHITE'S SISTER.
OH?
I HEAR THAT THOSE WHO KNOW HER ARE ALREADY CALLING HER THE PRESIDENT'S SECRET ASSISTANT EXECUTIVE.

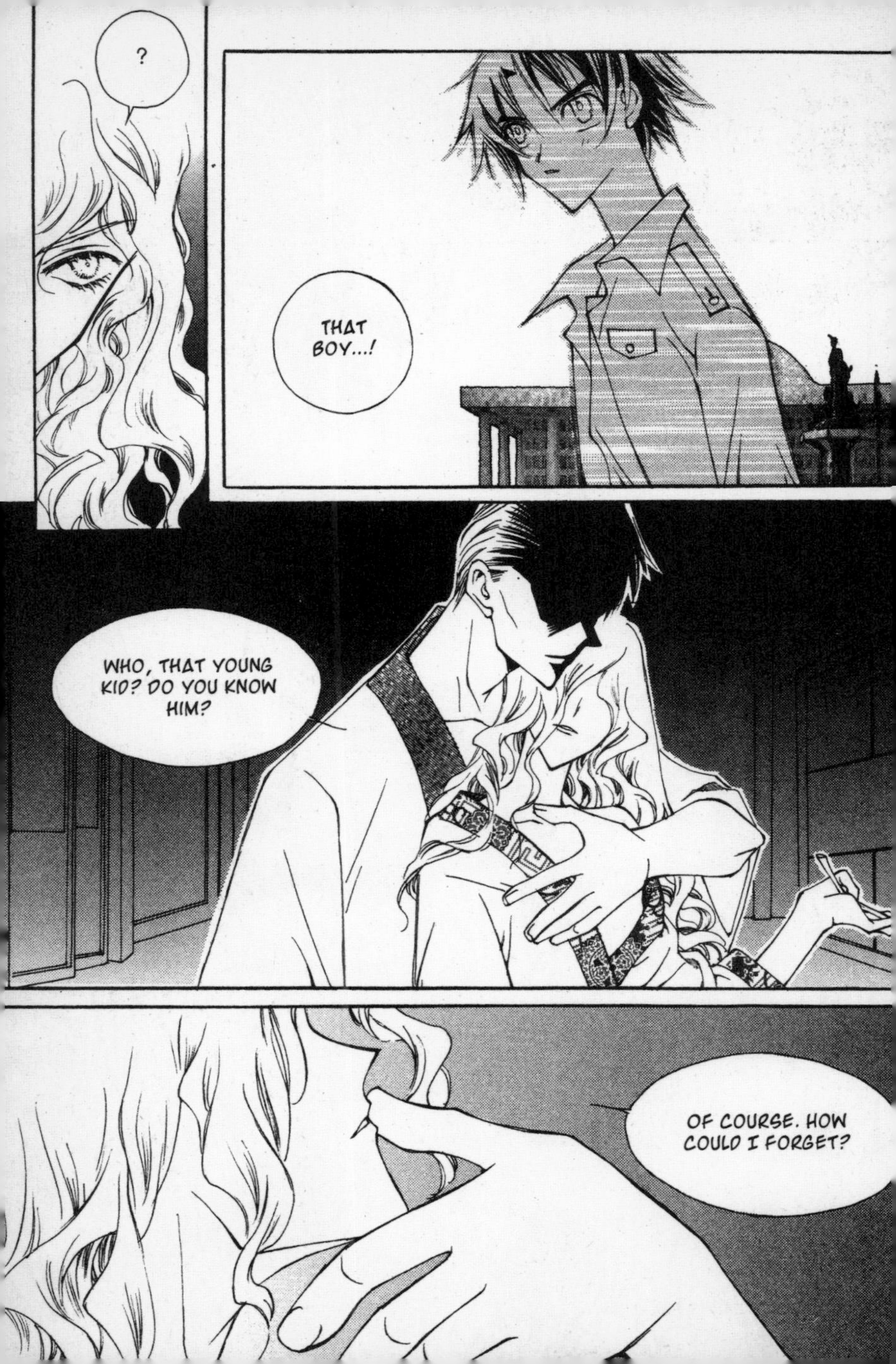
?
THAT BOY...!
WHO, THAT YOUNG KID? DO YOU KNOW HIM?
OF COURSE. HOW COULD I FORGET?

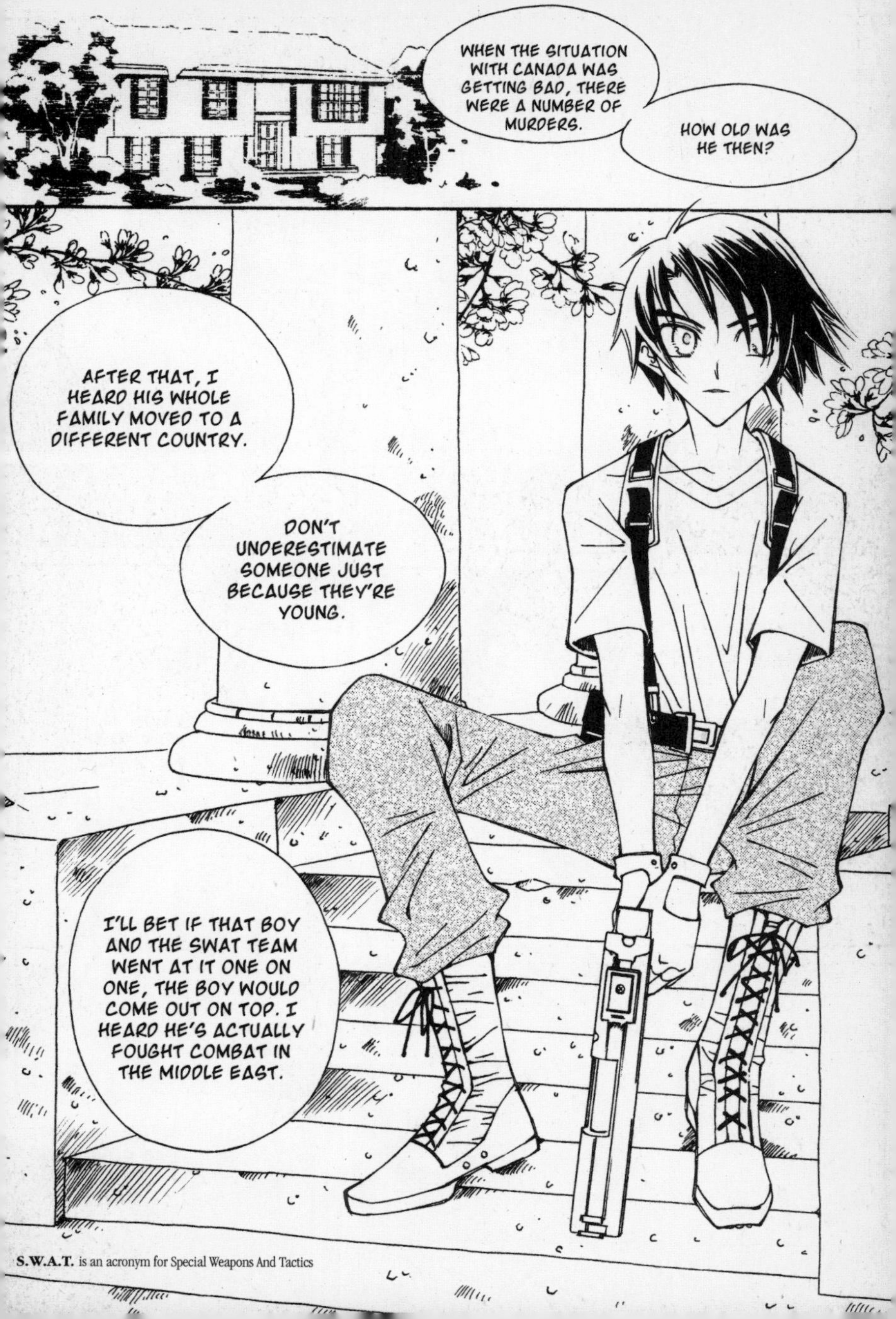
WHEN THE SITUATION WITH CANADA WAS GETTING BAD, THERE WERE A NUMBER OF MURDERS.
HOW OLD WAS HE THEN?
AFTER THAT, I HEARD HIS WHOLE FAMILY MOVED TO A DIFFERENT COUNTRY.
DON'T UNDERESTIMATE SOMEONE JUST BECAUSE THEY'RE YOUNG.
I'LL BET IF THAT BOY AND THE SWAT TEAM WENT AT IT ONE ON ONE, THE BOY WOULD COME OUT ON TOP. I HEARD HE'S ACTUALLY FOUGHT COMBAT IN THE MIDDLE EAST.

S.W.A.T. is an acronym for Special Weapons And Tactics

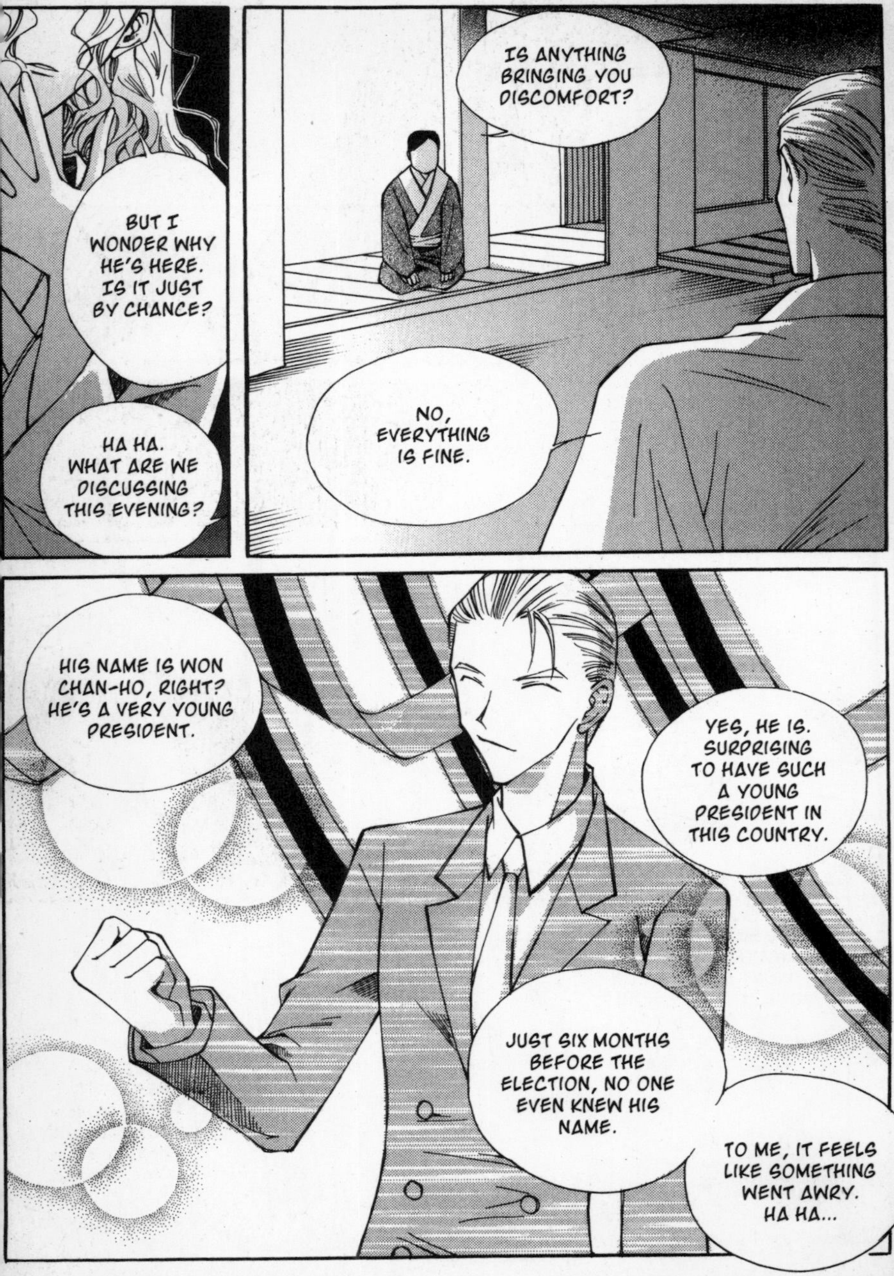
BUT I WONDER WHY HE'S HERE. IS IT JUST BY CHANCE?
HA HA. WHAT ARE WE DISCUSSING THIS EVENING?
IS ANYTHING BRINGING YOU DISCOMFORT?
NO, EVERYTHING IS FINE.
HIS NAME IS WON CHAN-HO, RIGHT? HE'S A VERY YOUNG PRESIDENT.
YES, HE IS. SURPRISING TO HAVE SUCH A YOUNG PRESIDENT IN THIS COUNTRY.
JUST SIX MONTHS BEFORE THE ELECTION, NO ONE EVEN KNEW HIS NAME.
TO ME, IT FEELS LIKE SOMETHING WENT AWRY. HA HA...

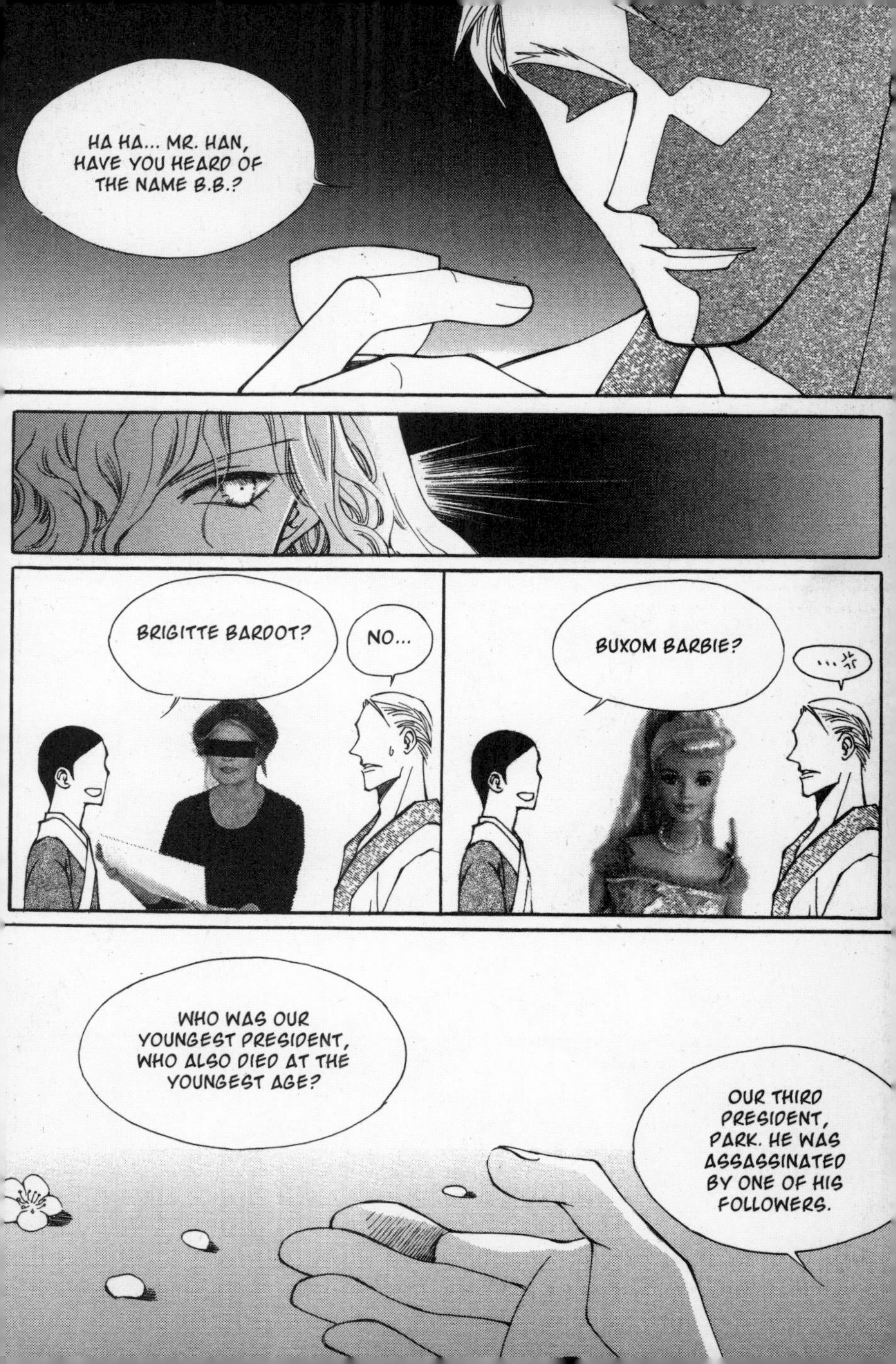
HA HA... MR. HAN, HAVE YOU HEARD OF THE NAME B.B.?
BRIGITTE BARDOT?
NO...
BUXOM BARBIE?
...
WHO WAS OUR YOUNGEST PRESIDENT, WHO ALSO DIED AT THE YOUNGEST AGE?
OUR THIRD PRESIDENT, PARK. HE WAS ASSASSINATED BY ONE OF HIS FOLLOWERS.

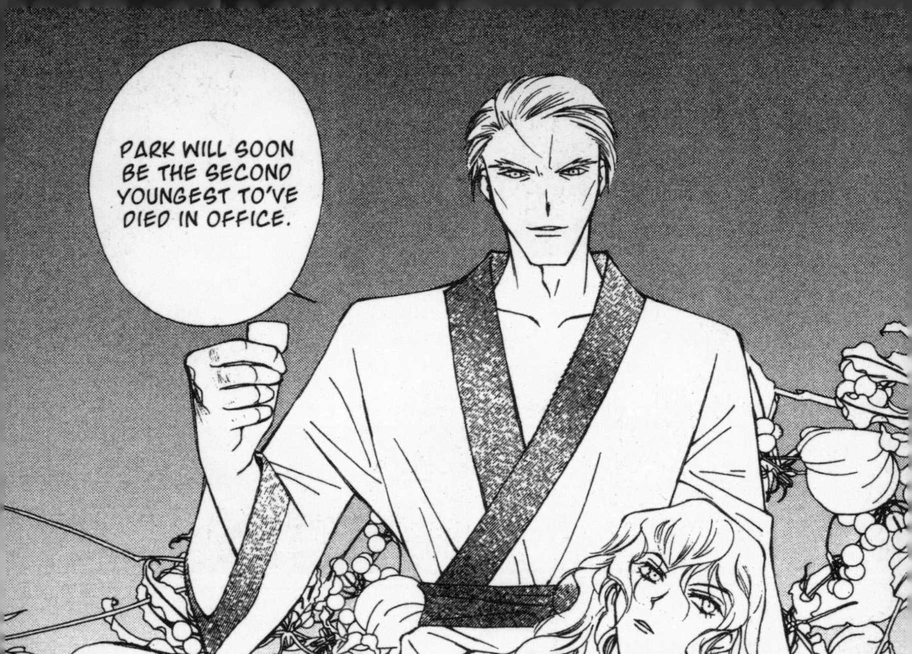
PARK WILL SOON BE THE SECOND YOUNGEST TO'VE DIED IN OFFICE.
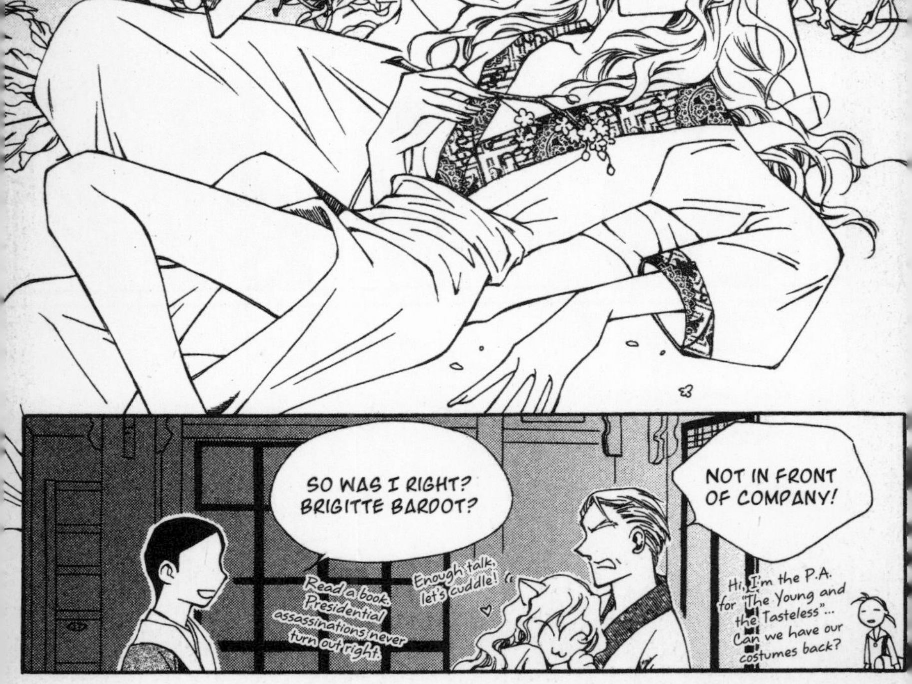
SO WAS I RIGHT? BRIGITTE BARDOT?
Read a book. Presidential assassinations never turn out right.
Enough talk, let's cuddle!
NOT IN FRONT OF COMPANY!
Hi, I'm the P.A. for "The Young and the Tasteless"... Can we have our costumes back?

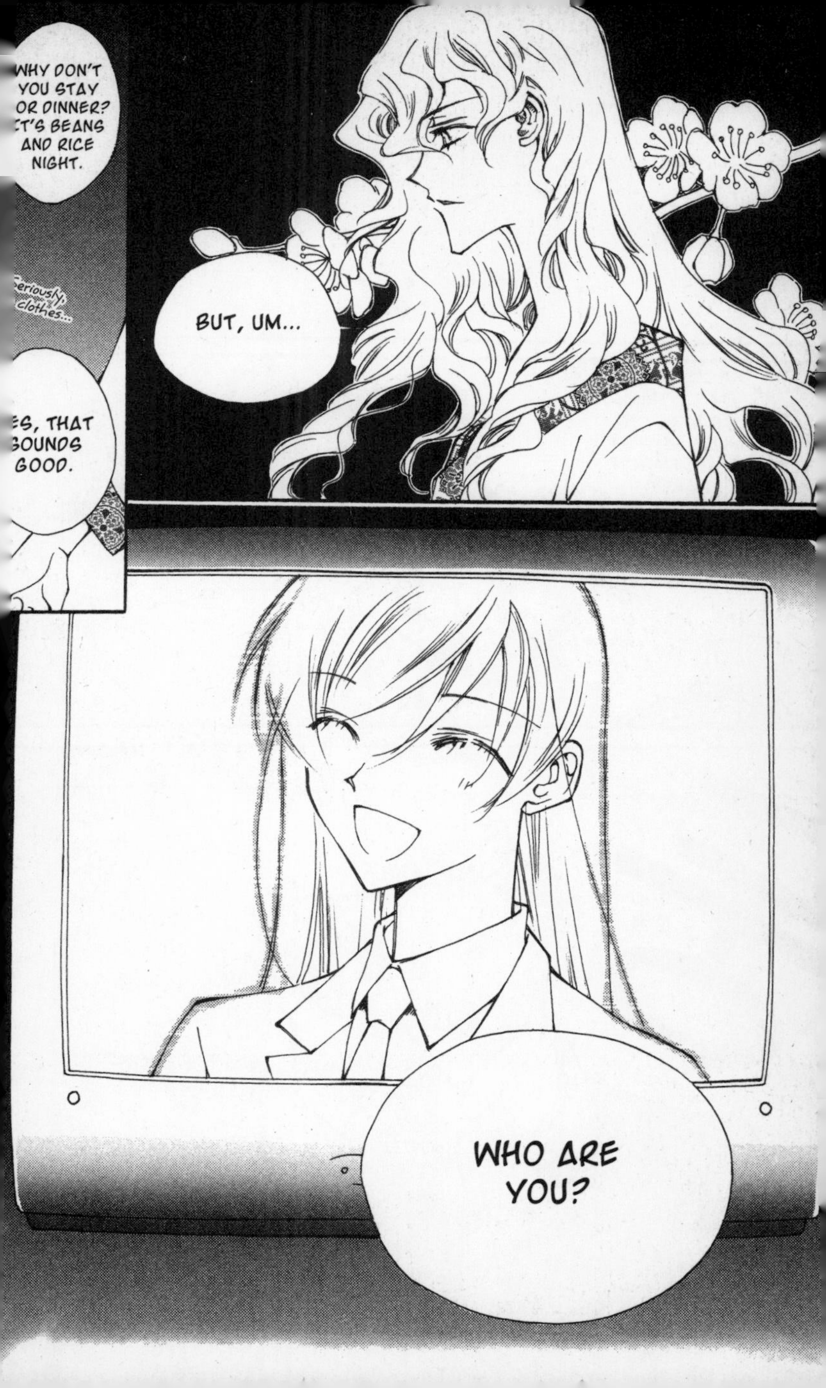
WHY DON'T YOU STAY OR DINNER? T'S BEANS AND RICE NIGHT.
Seriously, clothes...
ES, THAT SOUNDS GOOD.
BUT, UM...
WHO ARE YOU?

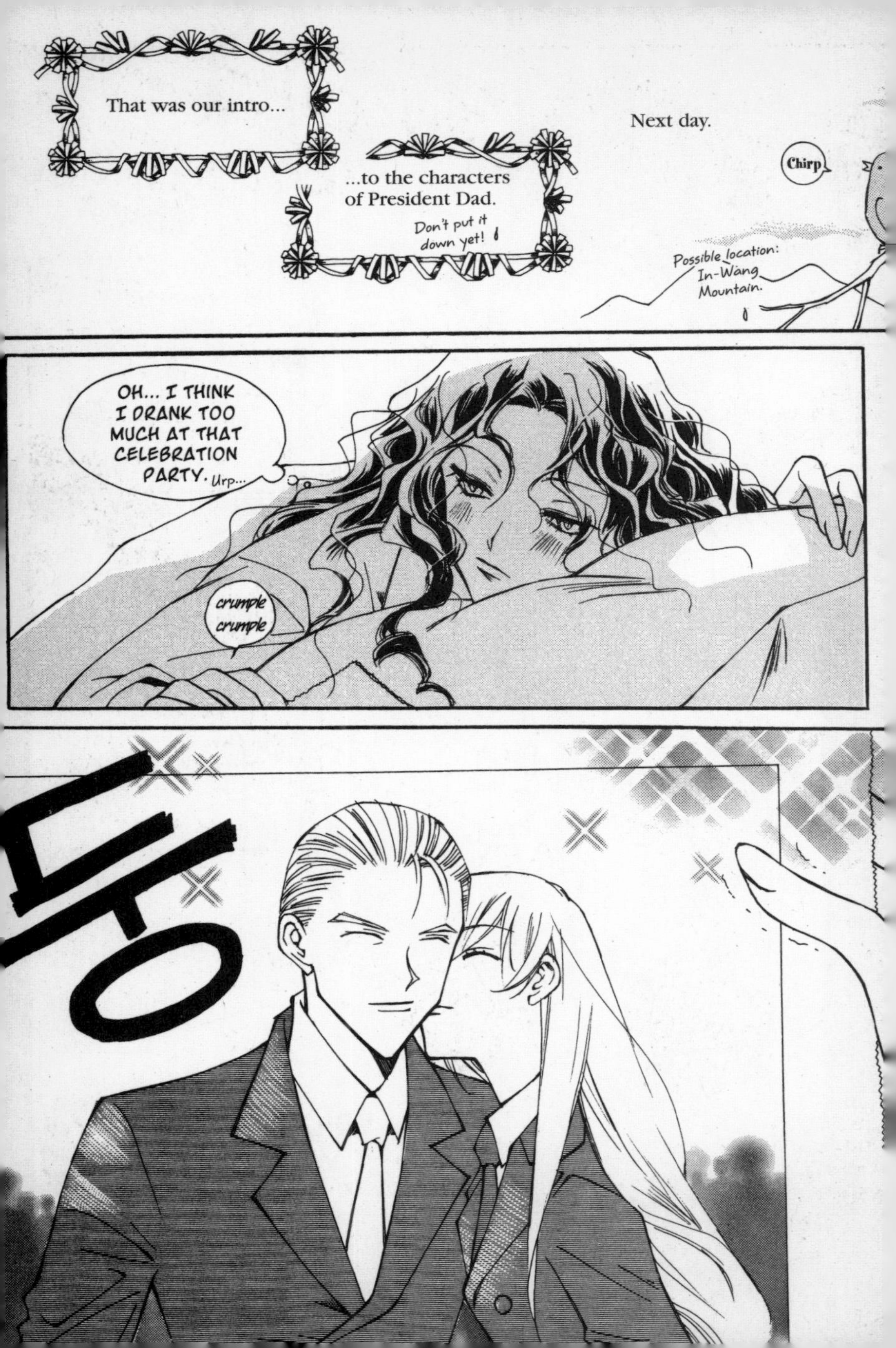

That was our intro...
...to the characters of President Dad.
Don't put it down yet!
Next day.
Chirp
Possible location: In-Wang Mountain.
OH... I THINK I DRANK TOO MUCH AT THAT CELEBRATION PARTY. Urp...
crumple crumple

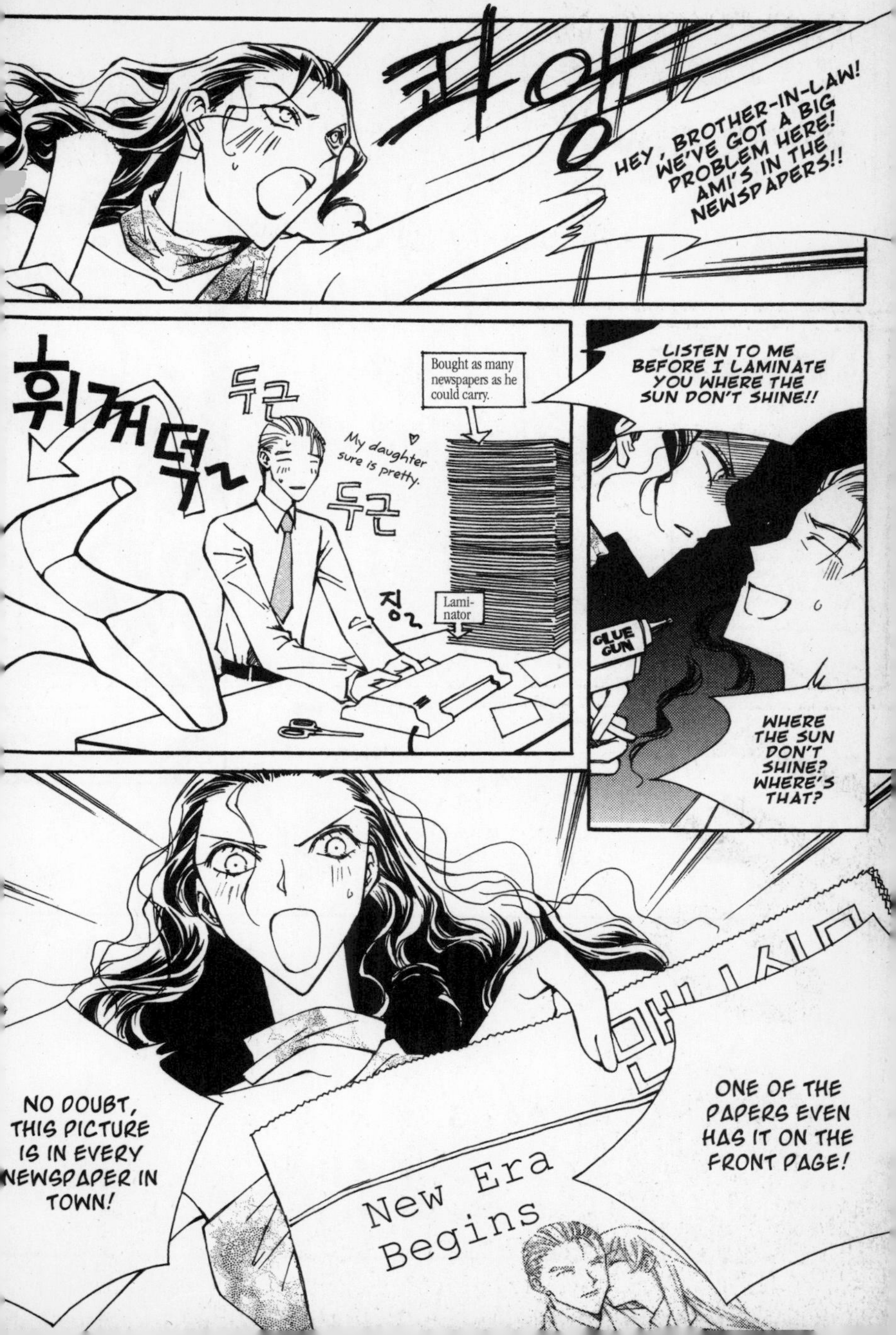

쾌앵
HEY, BROTHER-IN-LAW! WE'VE GOT A BIG PROBLEM HERE! AMI'S IN THE NEWSPAPERS!!
휘께덕~
두근
Bought as many newspapers as he could carry.
My daughter sure is pretty. ♡
두근
징~
Lami-nator
LISTEN TO ME BEFORE I LAMINATE YOU WHERE THE SUN DON'T SHINE!!
GLUE GUN
WHERE THE SUN DON'T SHINE? WHERE'S THAT?
NO DOUBT, THIS PICTURE IS IN EVERY NEWSPAPER IN TOWN!
ONE OF THE PAPERS EVEN HAS IT ON THE FRONT PAGE!
New Era Begins

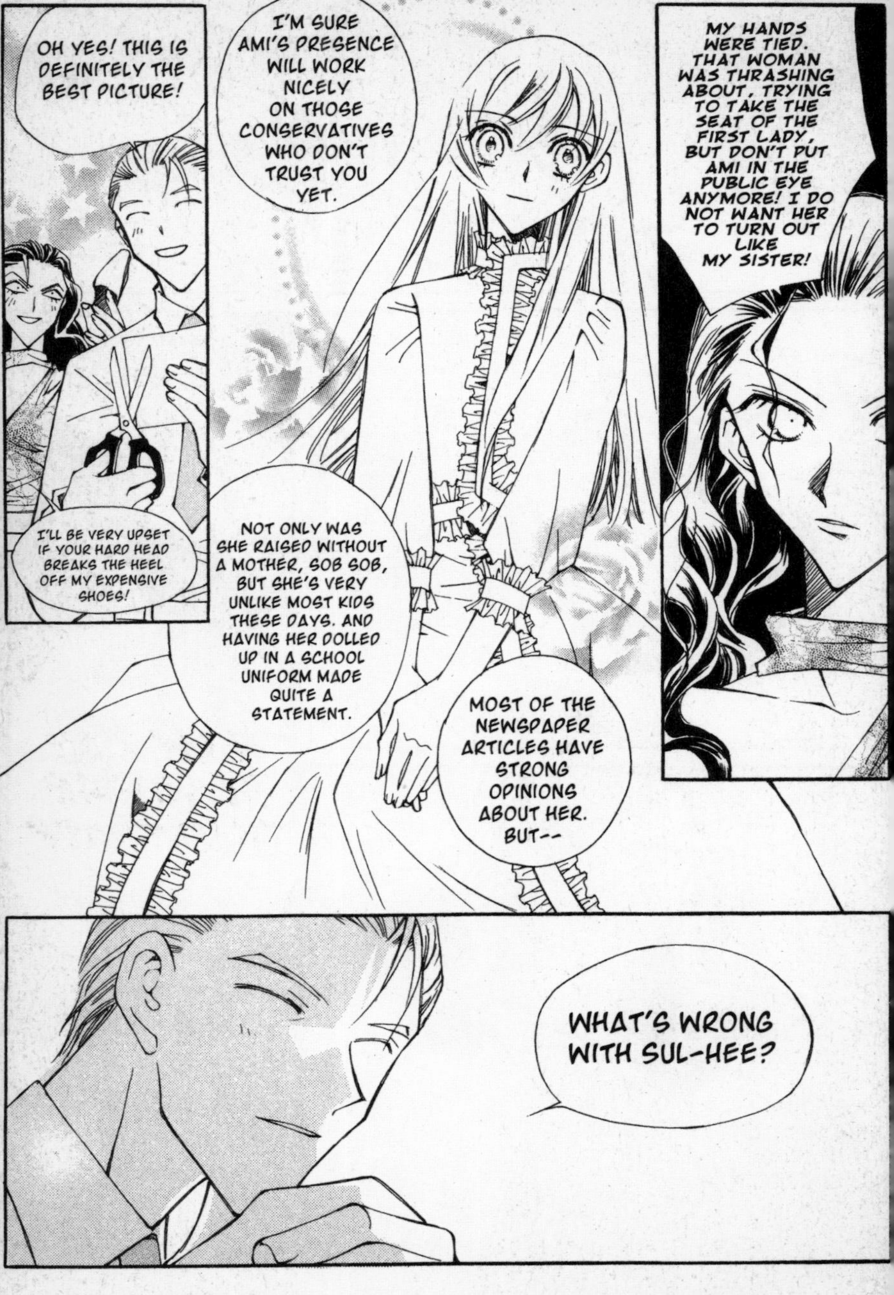
OH YES! THIS IS DEFINITELY THE BEST PICTURE!
I'LL BE VERY UPSET IF YOUR HARD HEAD BREAKS THE HEEL OFF MY EXPENSIVE SHOES!
I'M SURE AMI'S PRESENCE WILL WORK NICELY ON THOSE CONSERVATIVES WHO DON'T TRUST YOU YET.
NOT ONLY WAS SHE RAISED WITHOUT A MOTHER, SOB SOB, BUT SHE'S VERY UNLIKE MOST KIDS THESE DAYS. AND HAVING HER DOLLED UP IN A SCHOOL UNIFORM MADE QUITE A STATEMENT.
MOST OF THE NEWSPAPER ARTICLES HAVE STRONG OPINIONS ABOUT HER. BUT--
MY HANDS WERE TIED. THAT WOMAN WAS THRASHING ABOUT, TRYING TO TAKE THE SEAT OF THE FIRST LADY, BUT DON'T PUT AMI IN THE PUBLIC EYE ANYMORE! I DO NOT WANT HER TO TURN OUT LIKE MY SISTER!
WHAT'S WRONG WITH SUL-HEE?

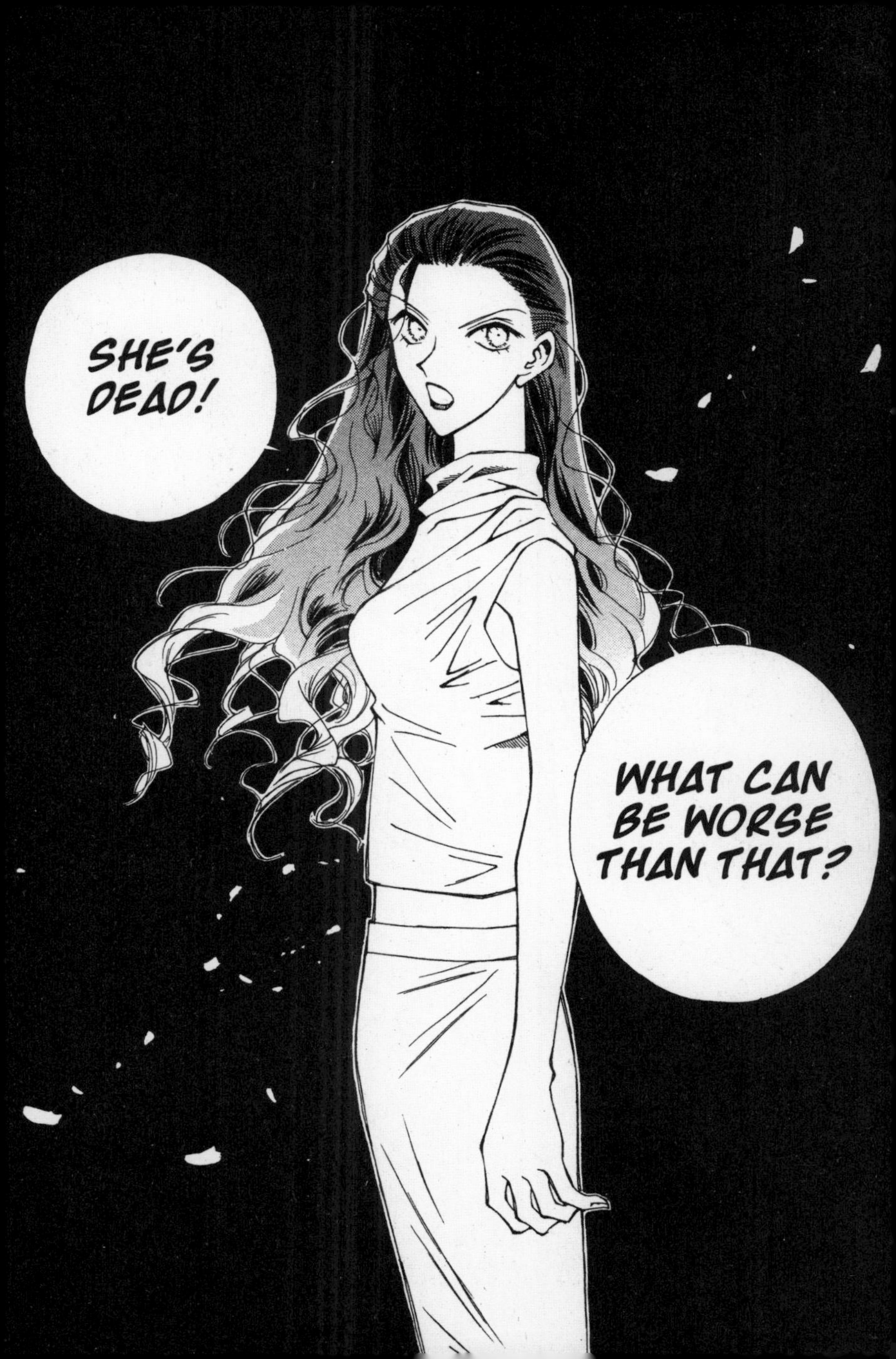
SHE'S DEAD!
WHAT CAN BE WORSE THAN THAT?

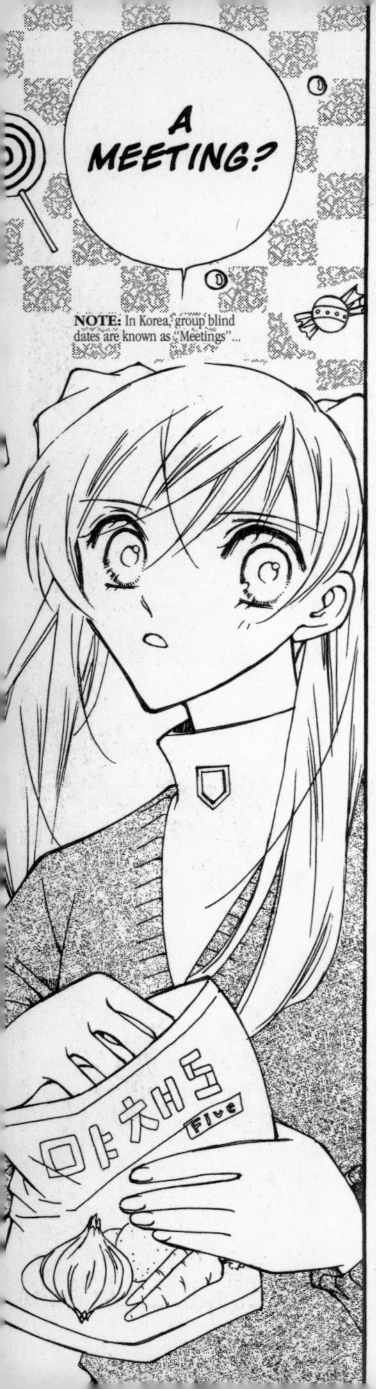
A MEETING?
NOTE: In Korea, group blind dates are known as "Meetings"...
Five

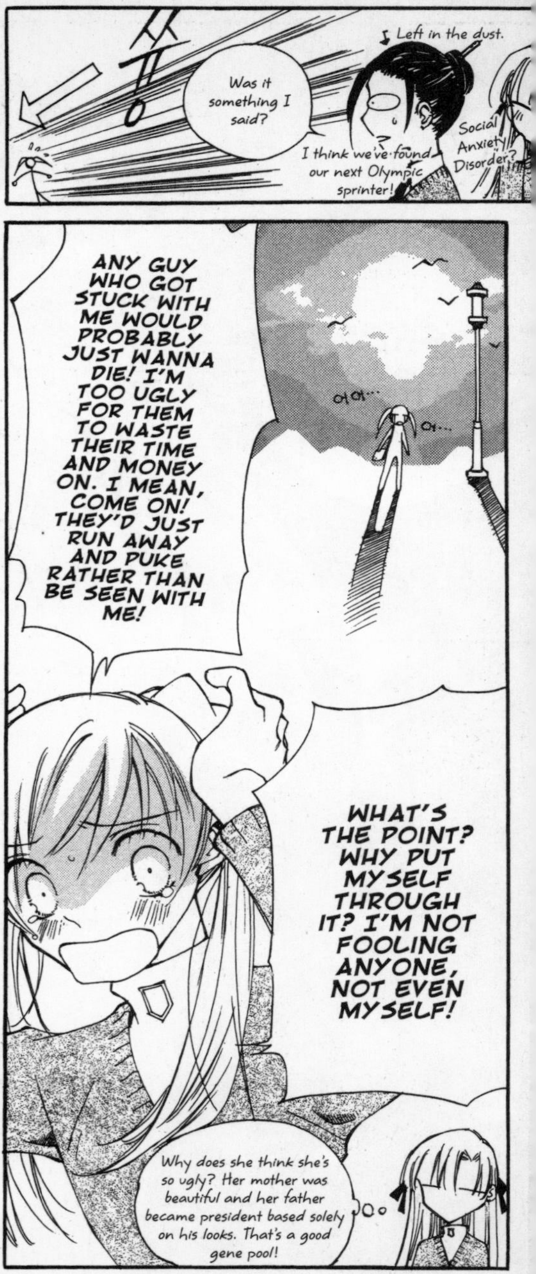
Was it something I said?
Left in the dust.
I think we've found our next Olympic sprinter!
Social Anxiety Disorder?
ANY GUY WHO GOT STUCK WITH ME WOULD PROBABLY JUST WANNA DIE! I'M TOO UGLY FOR THEM TO WASTE THEIR TIME AND MONEY ON. I MEAN, COME ON! THEY'D JUST RUN AWAY AND PUKE RATHER THAN BE SEEN WITH ME!
WHAT'S THE POINT? WHY PUT MYSELF THROUGH IT? I'M NOT FOOLING ANYONE, NOT EVEN MYSELF!
Why does she think she's so ugly? Her mother was beautiful and her father became president based solely on his looks. That's a good gene pool!

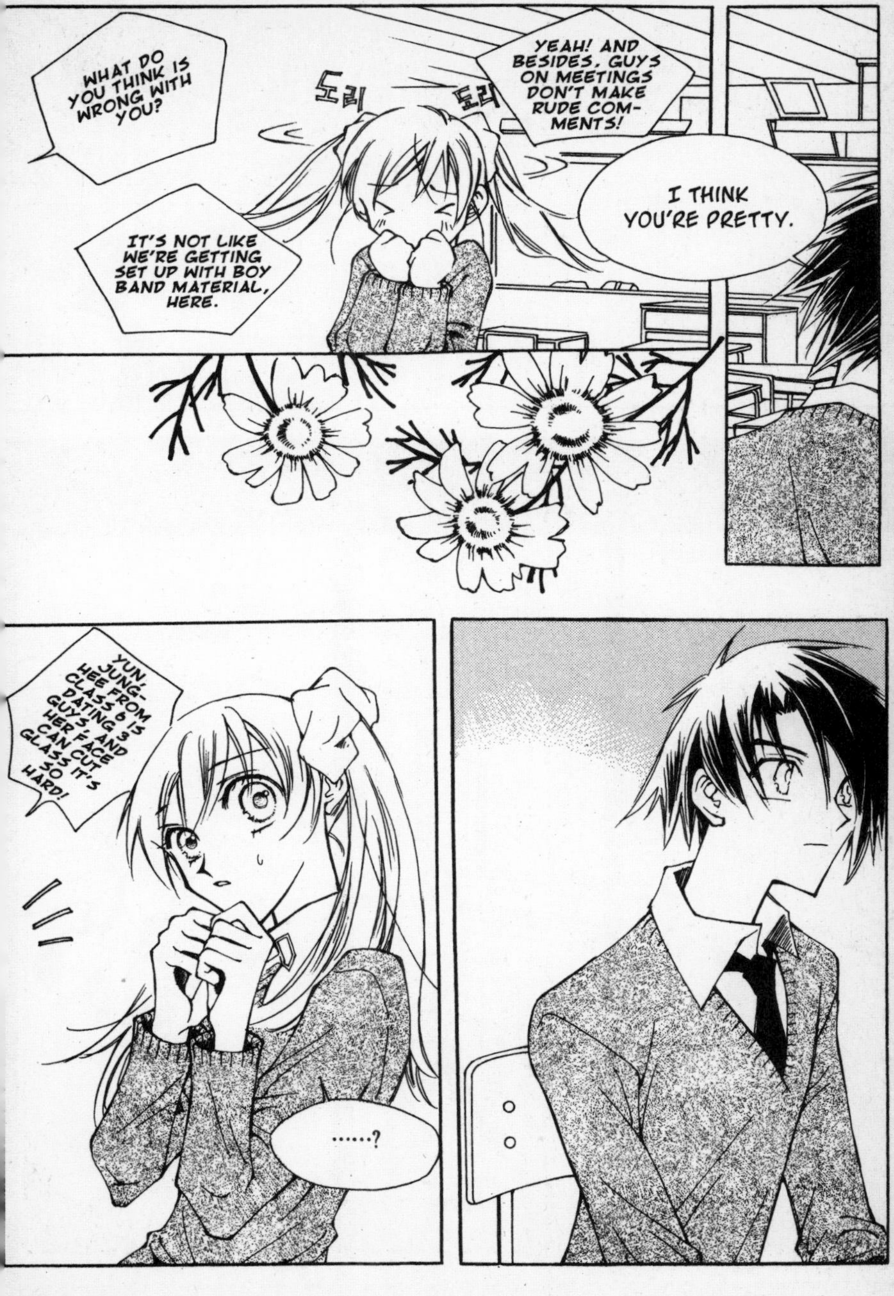
WHAT DO YOU THINK IS WRONG WITH YOU?
도리 도리
YEAH! AND BESIDES, GUYS ON MEETINGS DON'T MAKE RUDE COMMENTS!
IT'S NOT LIKE WE'RE GETTING SET UP WITH BOY BAND MATERIAL, HERE.
I THINK YOU'RE PRETTY.
YUN, JUNG-HEE FROM CLASS 6 IS DATING 3 GUYS, AND HER FACE CAN CUT GLASS SO IT'S HARD!
......?

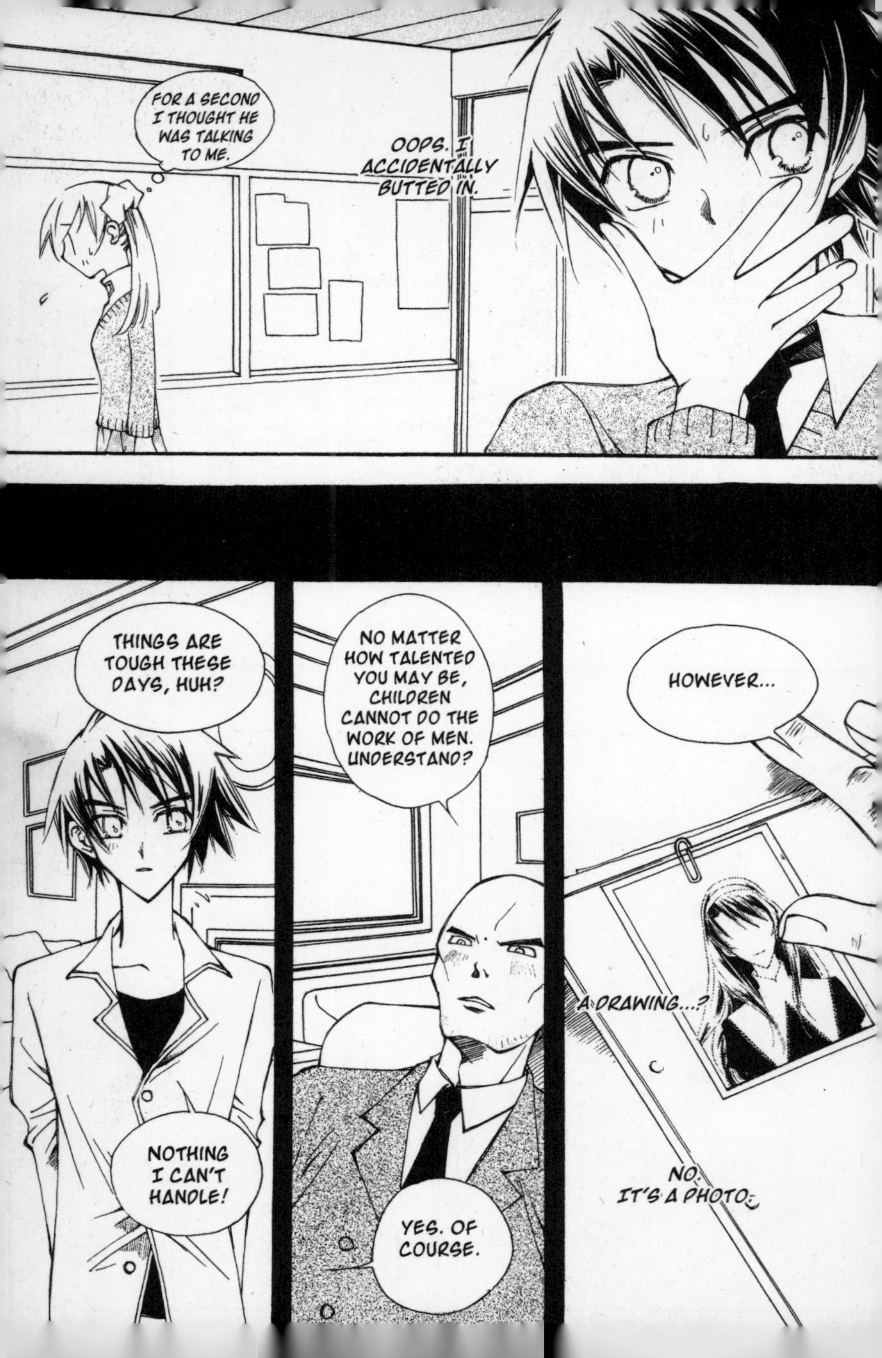
FOR A SECOND I THOUGHT HE WAS TALKING TO ME.
OOPS. I ACCIDENTALLY BUTTED IN.
THINGS ARE TOUGH THESE DAYS, HUH?
NOTHING I CAN'T HANDLE!
NO MATTER HOW TALENTED YOU MAY BE, CHILDREN CANNOT DO THE WORK OF MEN. UNDERSTAND?
YES. OF COURSE.
HOWEVER...
A DRAWING...?
NO. IT'S A PHOTO.

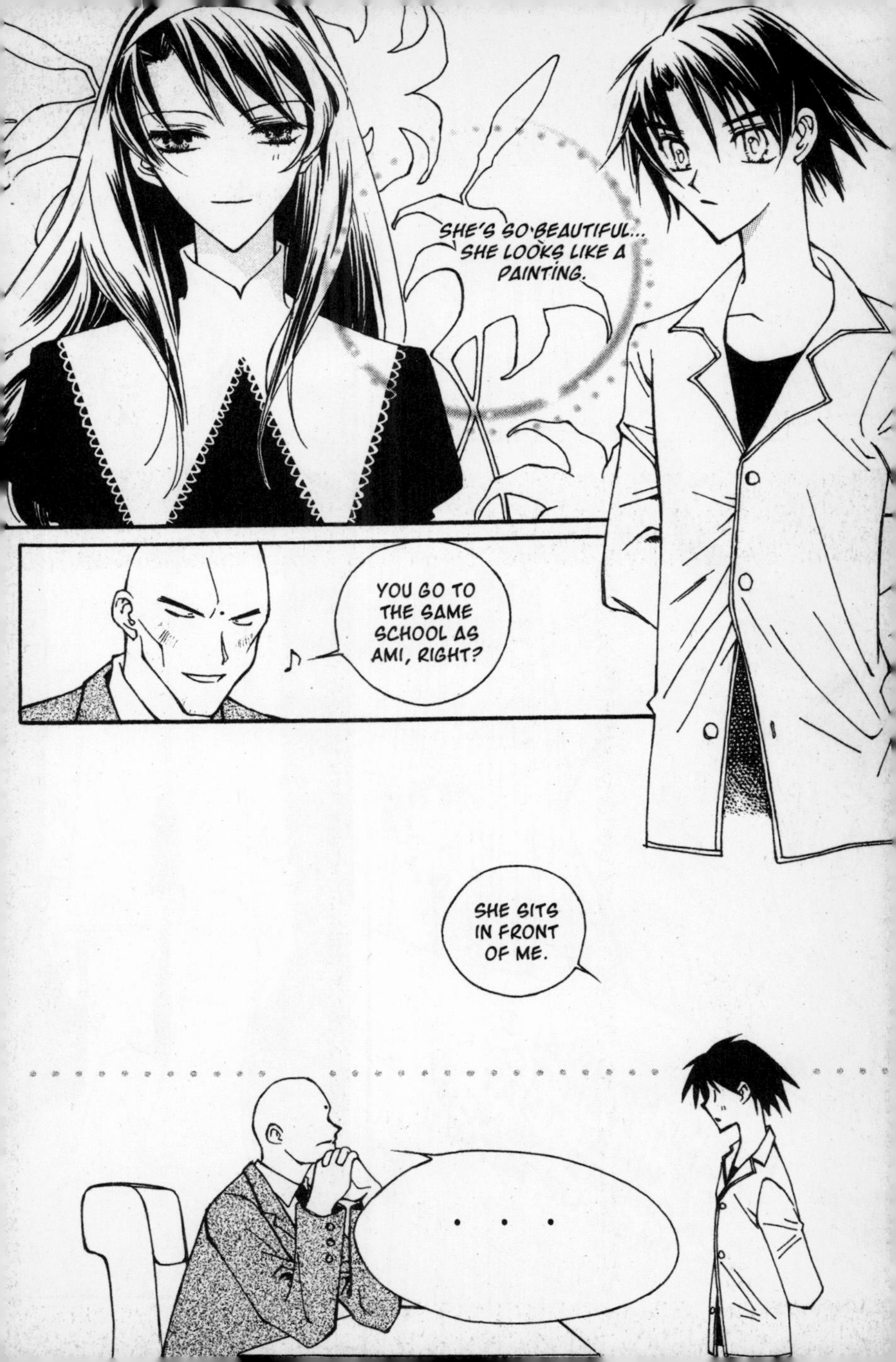
SHE'S SO BEAUTIFUL... SHE LOOKS LIKE A PAINTING.
YOU GO TO THE SAME SCHOOL AS AMI, RIGHT?
SHE SITS IN FRONT OF ME.
. . .

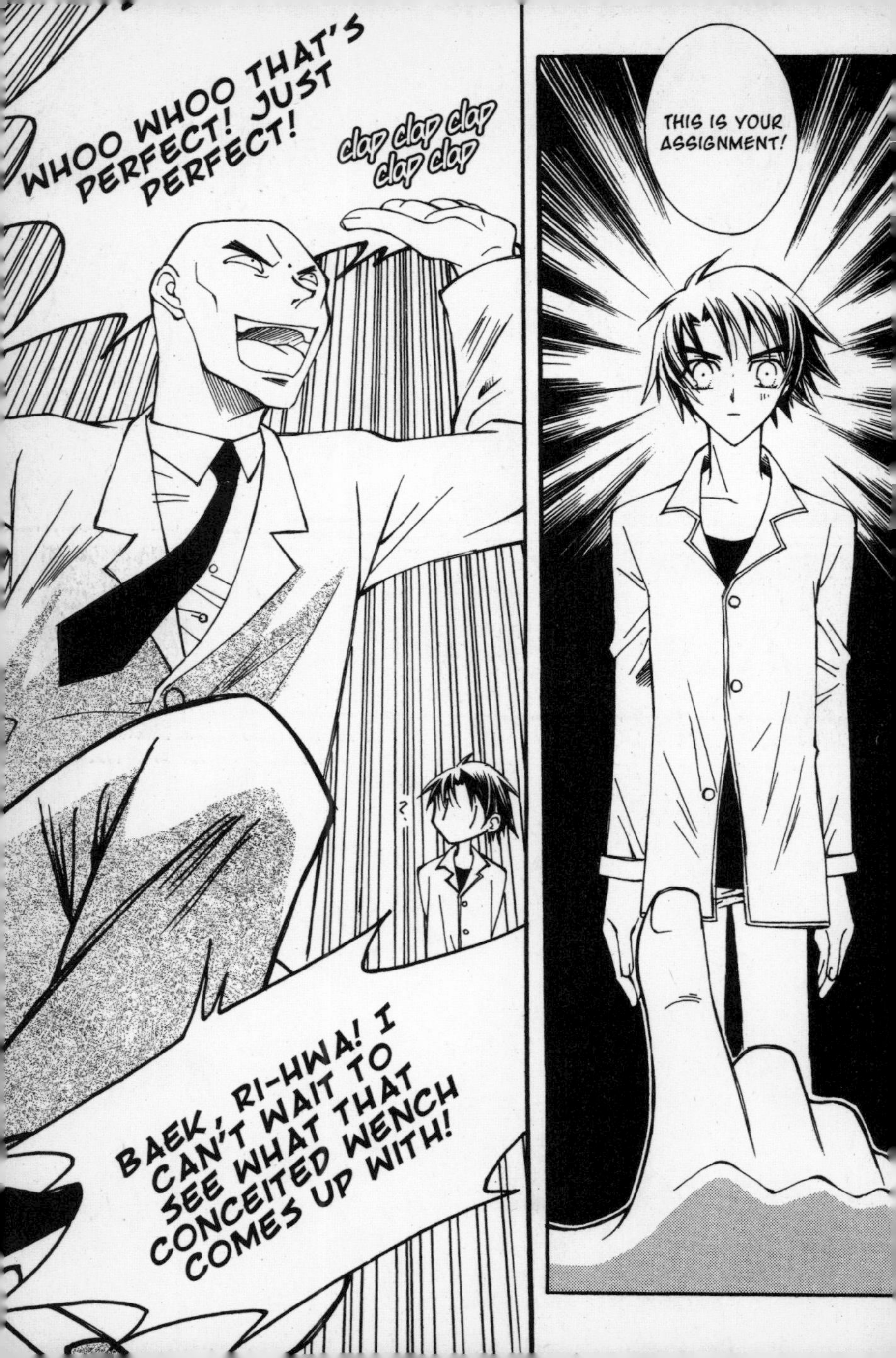
WHOO WHOO THAT'S PERFECT! JUST PERFECT!
clap clap clap clap clap
?
BAEK, RI-HWA! I CAN'T WAIT TO SEE WHAT THAT CONCEITED WENCH COMES UP WITH!
THIS IS YOUR ASSIGNMENT!

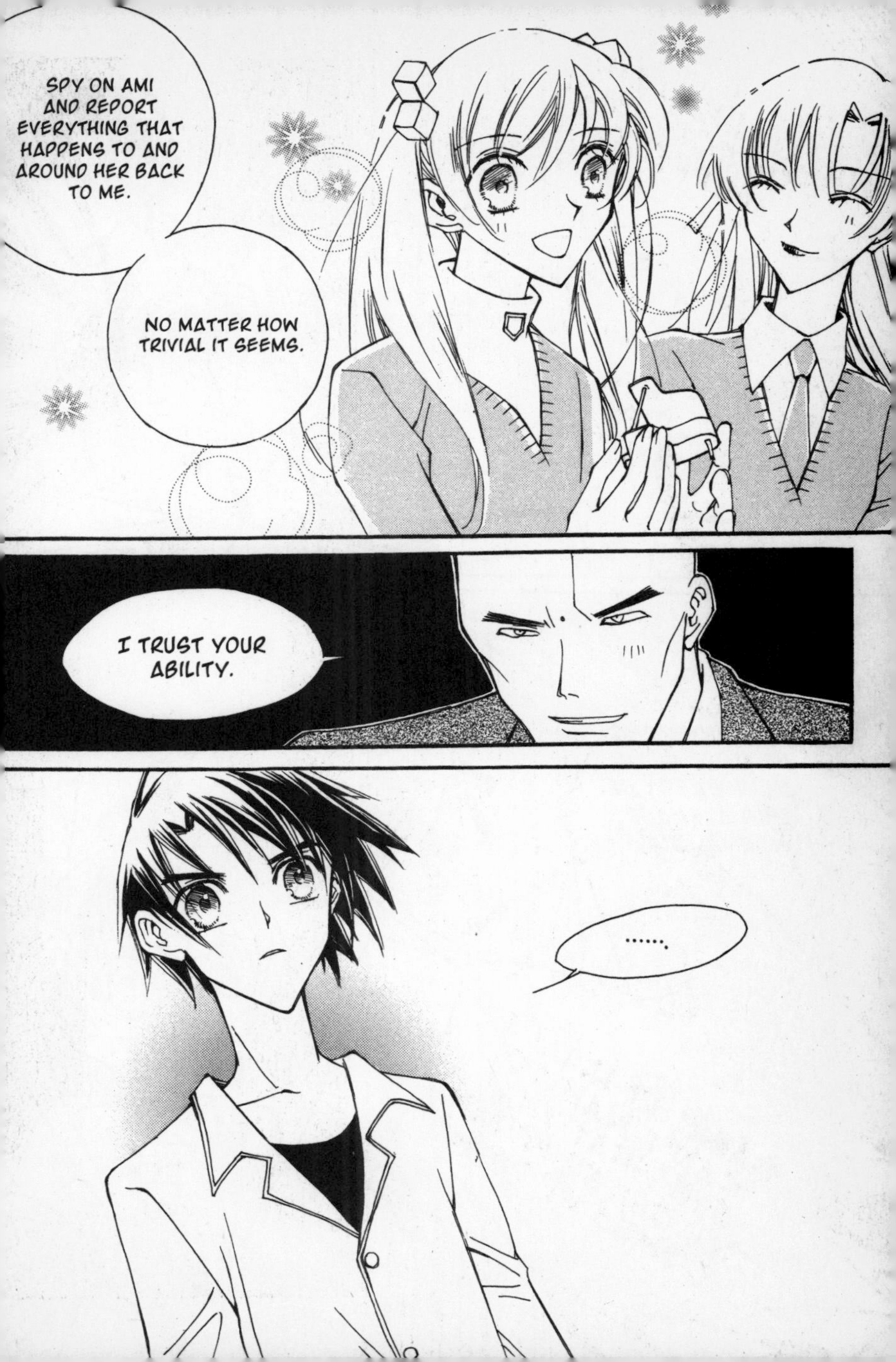
SPY ON AMI AND REPORT EVERYTHING THAT HAPPENS TO AND AROUND HER BACK TO ME.
NO MATTER HOW TRIVIAL IT SEEMS.
I TRUST YOUR ABILITY.
......

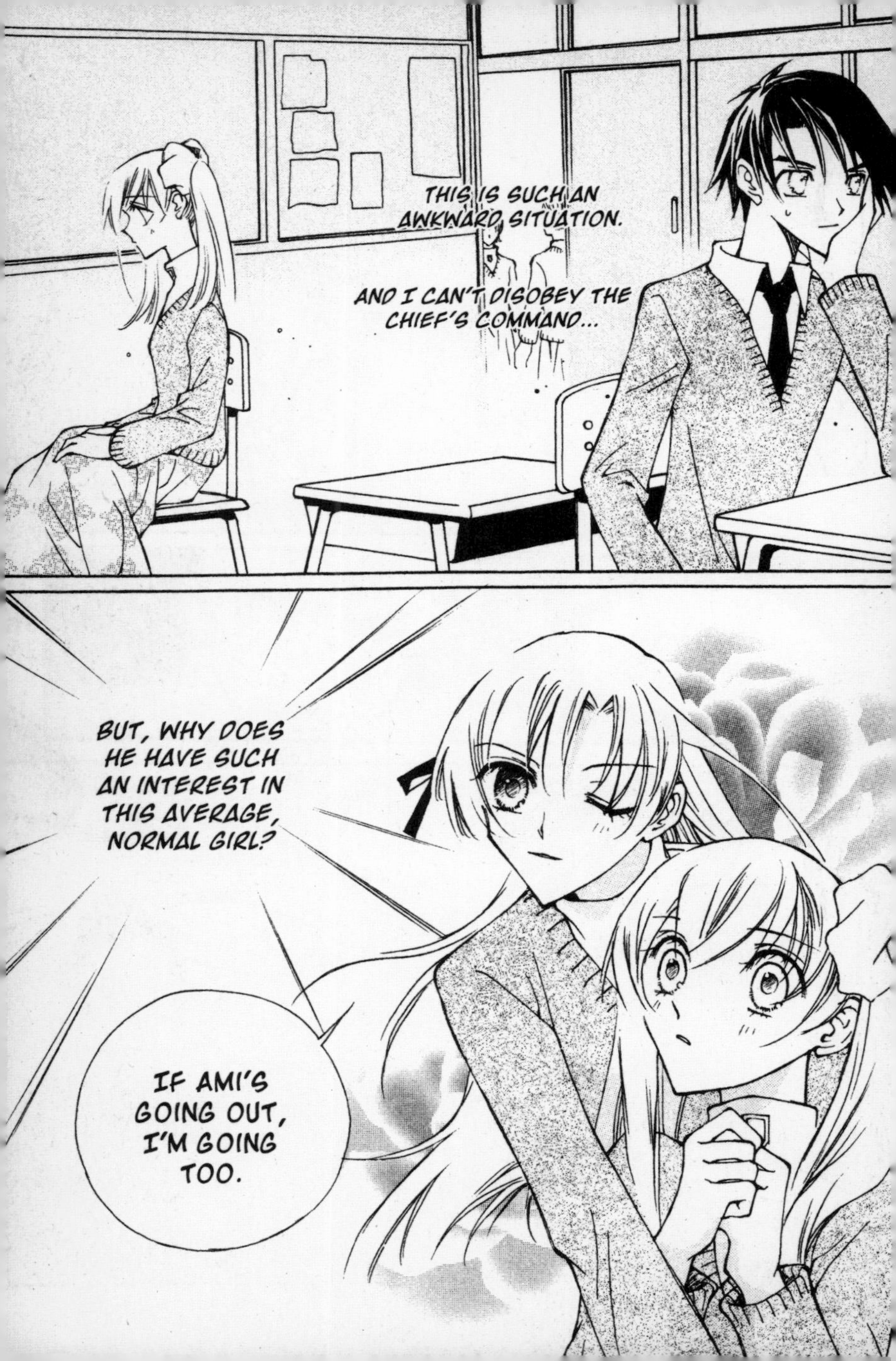
THIS IS SUCH AN AWKWARD SITUATION.
AND I CAN'T DISOBEY THE CHIEF'S COMMAND...
BUT, WHY DOES HE HAVE SUCH AN INTEREST IN THIS AVERAGE, NORMAL GIRL?
IF AMI'S GOING OUT, I'M GOING TOO.

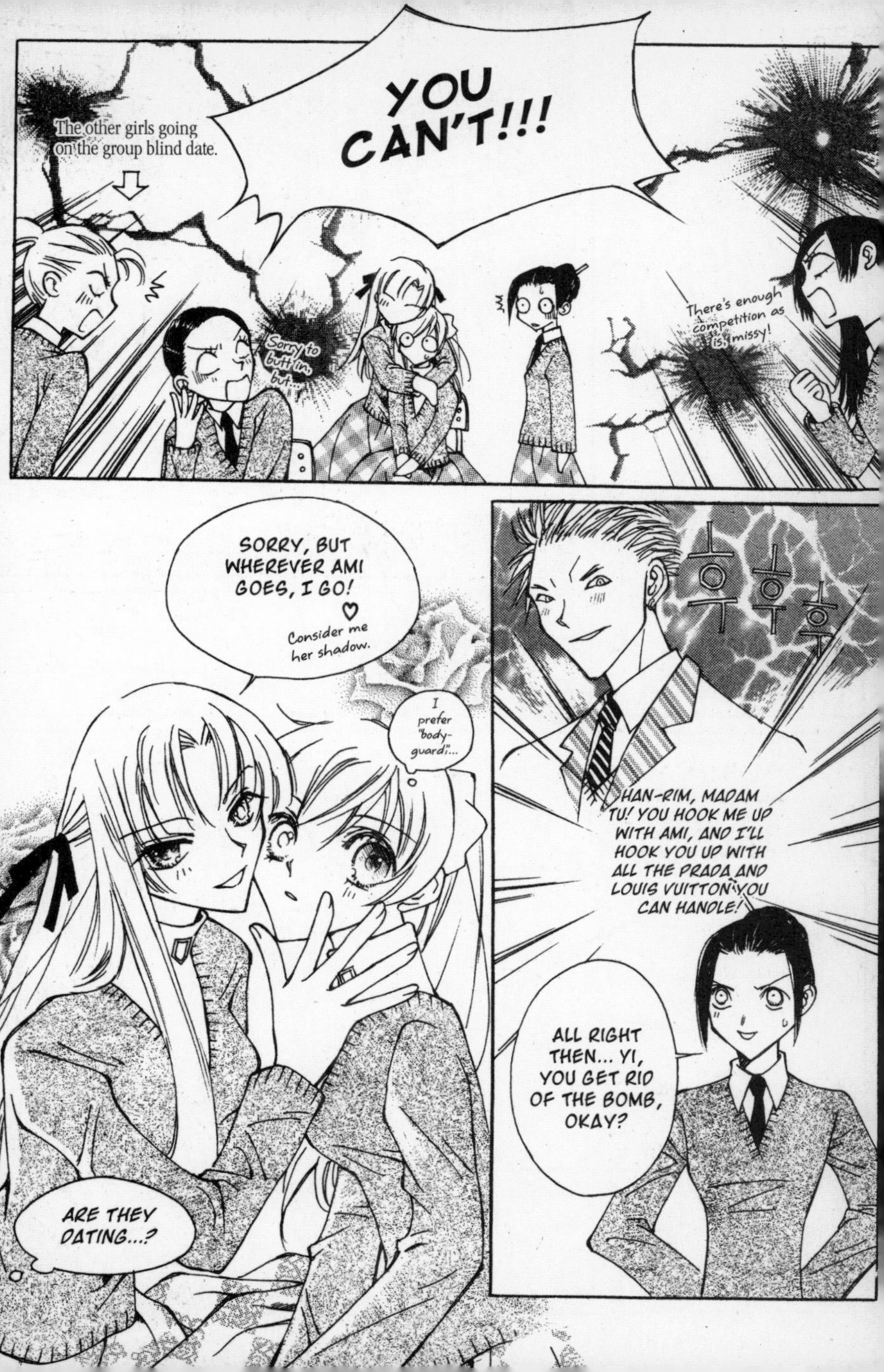
The other girls going on the group blind date.
YOU CAN'T!!!
Sorry to butt in, but...
There's enough competition as is, missy!
SORRY, BUT WHEREVER AMI GOES, I GO! ♡
Consider me her shadow.
I prefer "bodyguard"...
ARE THEY DATING...?
후후후
HAN-RIM, MADAM TU! YOU HOOK ME UP WITH AMI, AND I'LL HOOK YOU UP WITH ALL THE PRADA AND LOUIS VUITTON YOU CAN HANDLE!
ALL RIGHT THEN... YI, YOU GET RID OF THE BOMB, OKAY?

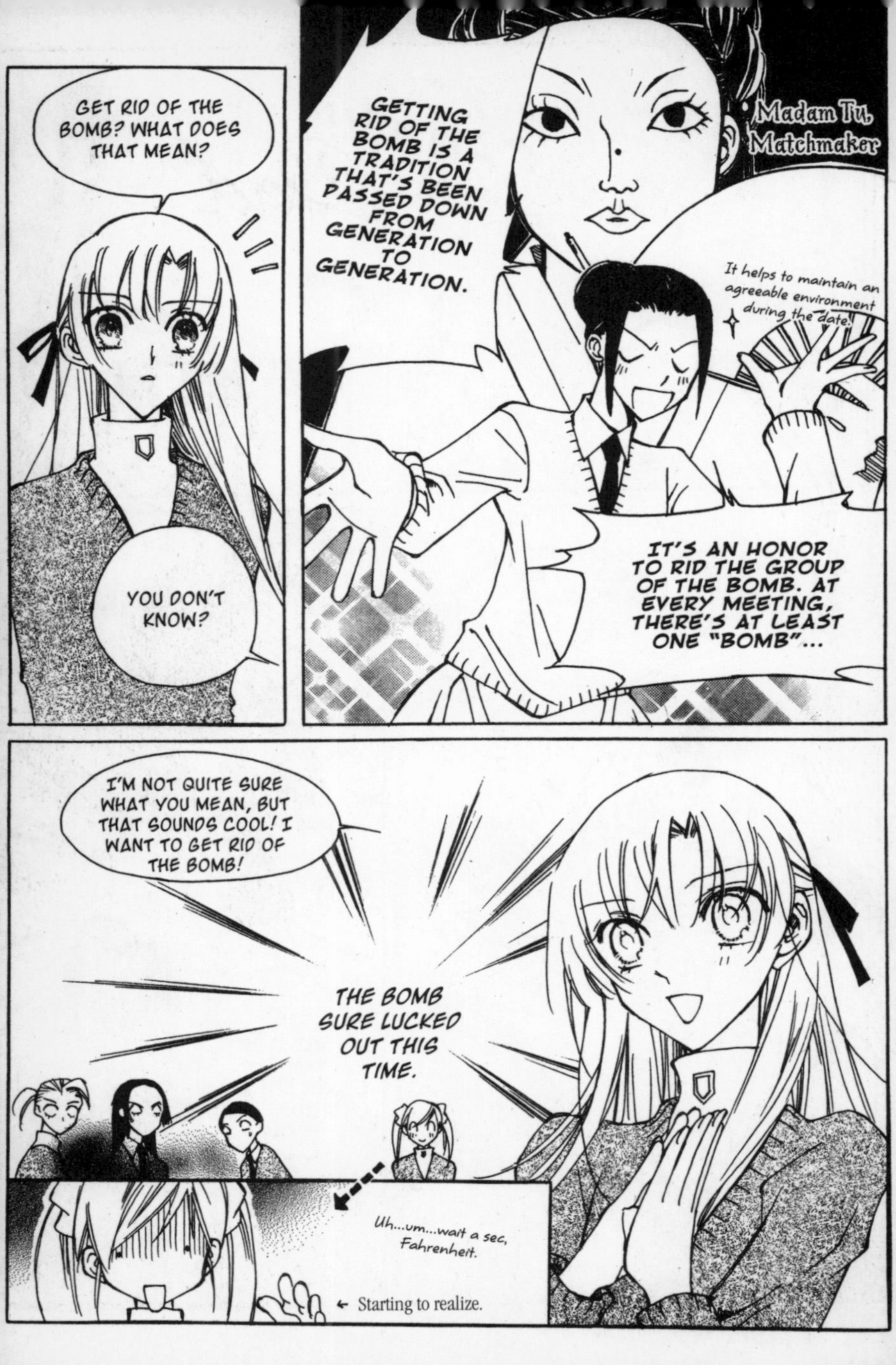
GET RID OF THE BOMB? WHAT DOES THAT MEAN?
YOU DON'T KNOW?
GETTING RID OF THE BOMB IS A TRADITION THAT'S BEEN PASSED DOWN FROM GENERATION TO GENERATION.
Madam Tu, Matchmaker
It helps to maintain an agreeable environment during the date.
IT'S AN HONOR TO RID THE GROUP OF THE BOMB. AT EVERY MEETING, THERE'S AT LEAST ONE "BOMB"...
I'M NOT QUITE SURE WHAT YOU MEAN, BUT THAT SOUNDS COOL! I WANT TO GET RID OF THE BOMB!
THE BOMB SURE LUCKED OUT THIS TIME.
Uh...um...wait a sec, Fahrenheit.
← Starting to realize.

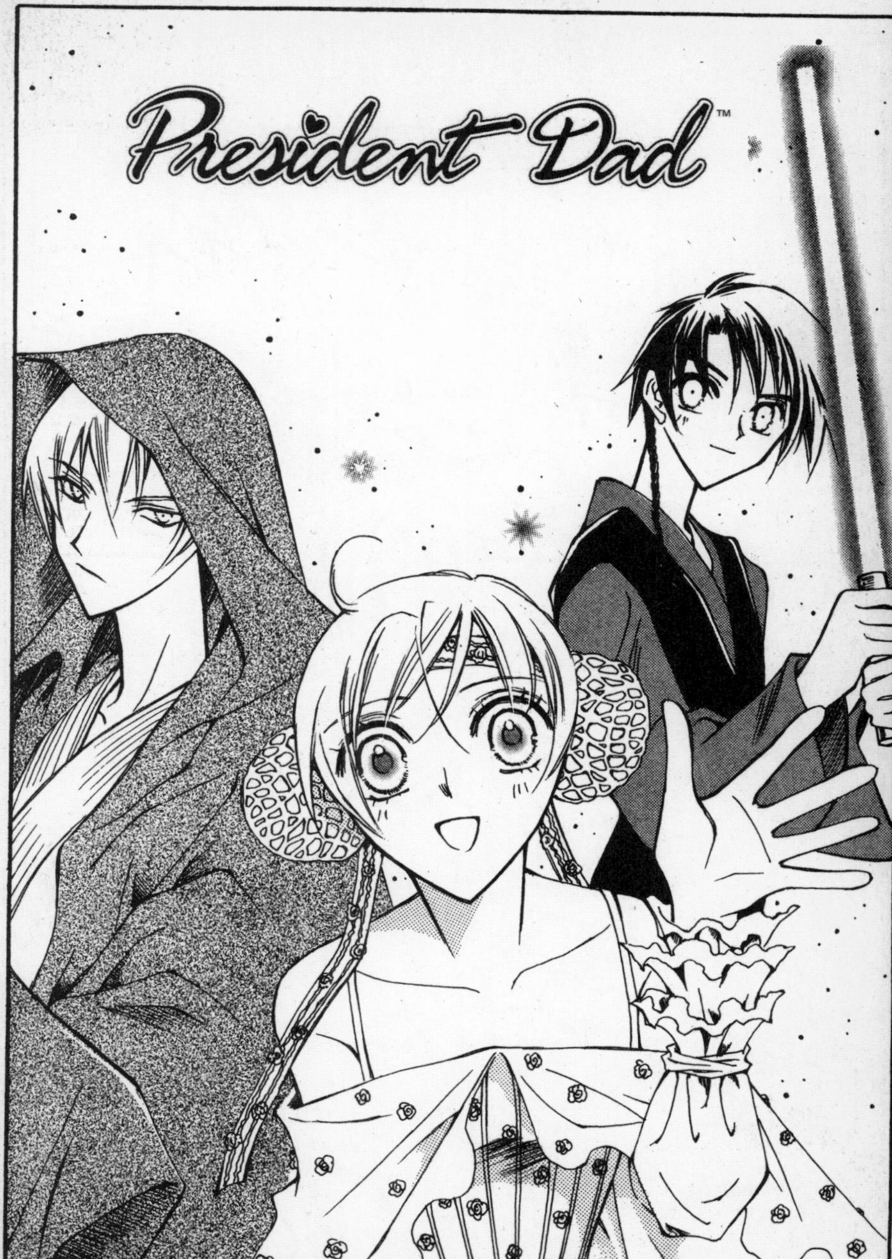
President Dad™

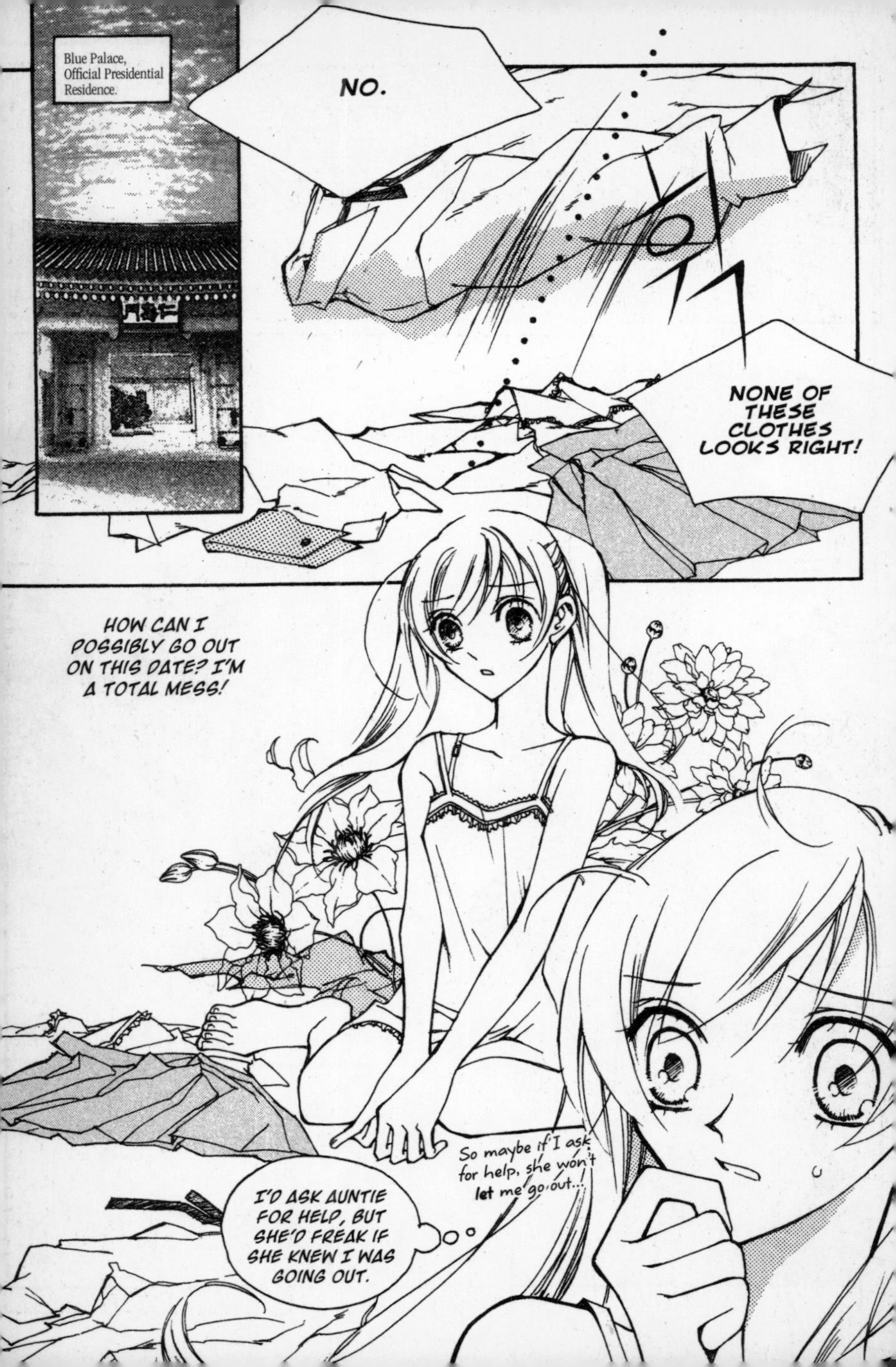

Blue Palace, Official Presidential Residence.
NO.
NONE OF THESE CLOTHES LOOKS RIGHT!
HOW CAN I POSSIBLY GO OUT ON THIS DATE? I'M A TOTAL MESS!
I'D ASK AUNTIE FOR HELP, BUT SHE'D FREAK IF SHE KNEW I WAS GOING OUT.
So maybe if I ask for help, she won't let me go out...!

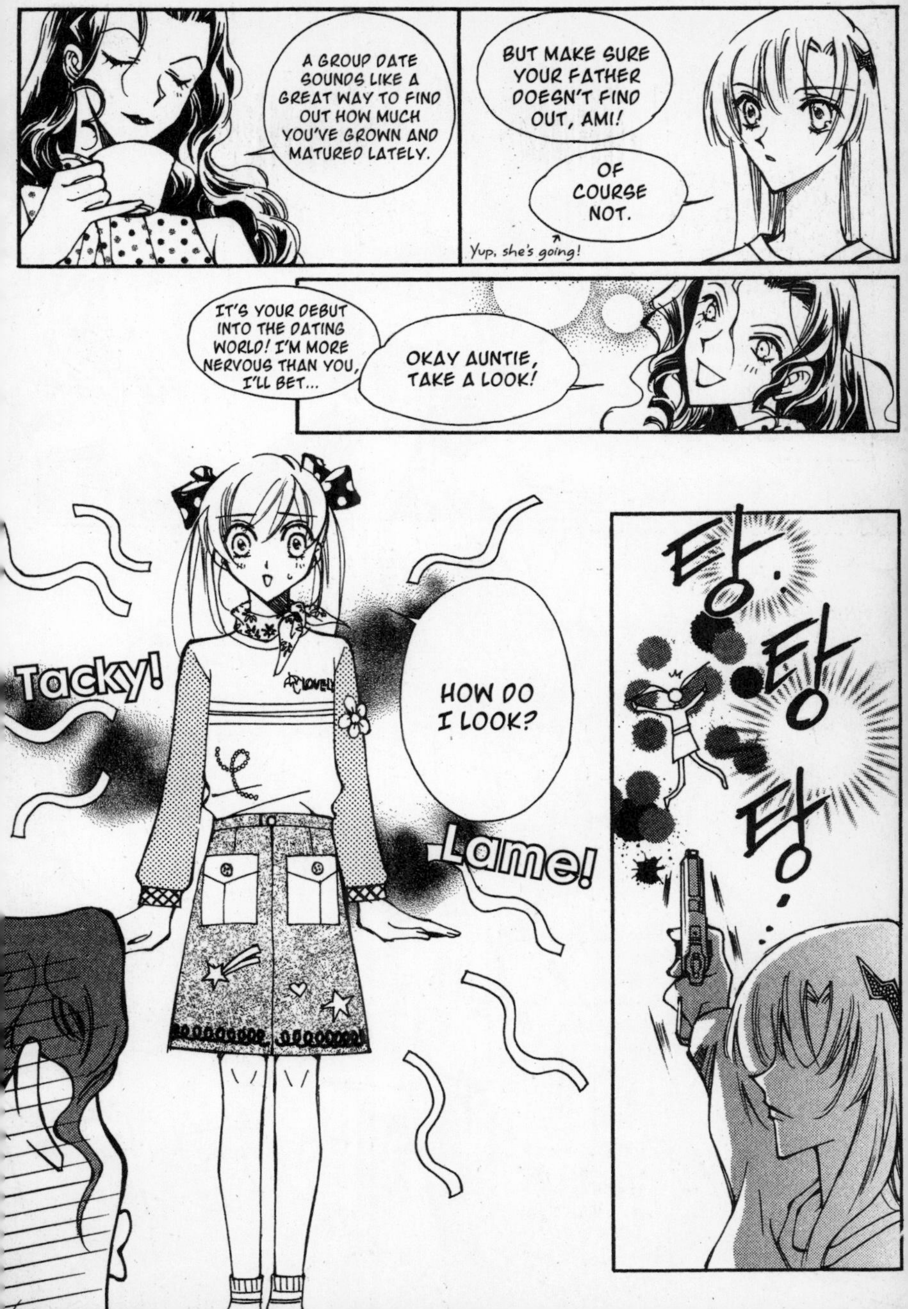
A GROUP DATE SOUNDS LIKE A GREAT WAY TO FIND OUT HOW MUCH YOU'VE GROWN AND MATURED LATELY.
BUT MAKE SURE YOUR FATHER DOESN'T FIND OUT, AMI!
OF COURSE NOT.
Yup, she's going!
IT'S YOUR DEBUT INTO THE DATING WORLD! I'M MORE NERVOUS THAN YOU, I'LL BET...
OKAY AUNTIE, TAKE A LOOK!
Tacky!
HOW DO I LOOK?
Lame!
탕.
탕
탕.

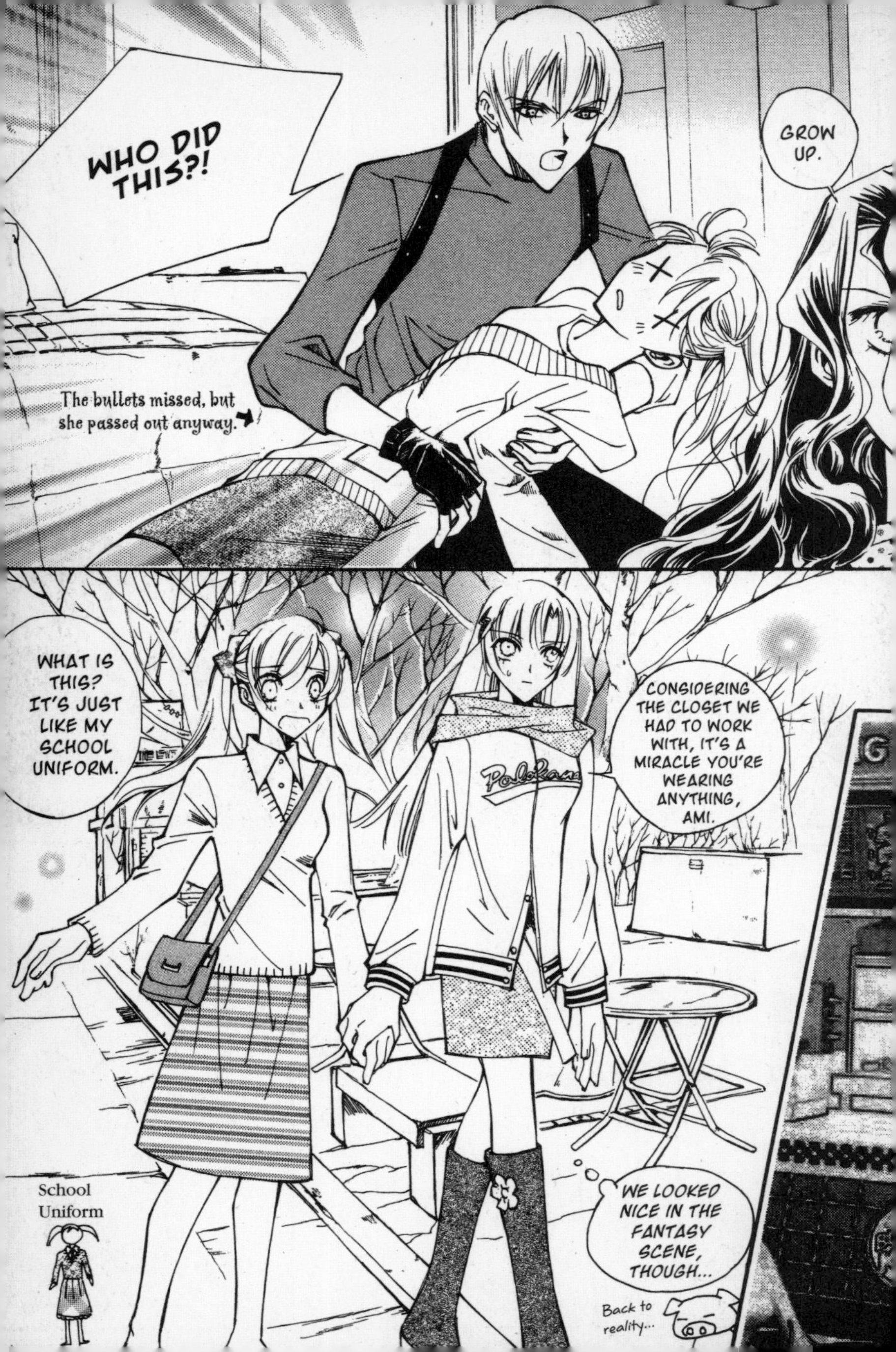
WHO DID THIS?!
The bullets missed, but she passed out anyway.
GROW UP.
WHAT IS THIS? IT'S JUST LIKE MY SCHOOL UNIFORM.
CONSIDERING THE CLOSET WE HAD TO WORK WITH, IT'S A MIRACLE YOU'RE WEARING ANYTHING, AMI.
School Uniform
WE LOOKED NICE IN THE FANTASY SCENE, THOUGH...
Back to reality...

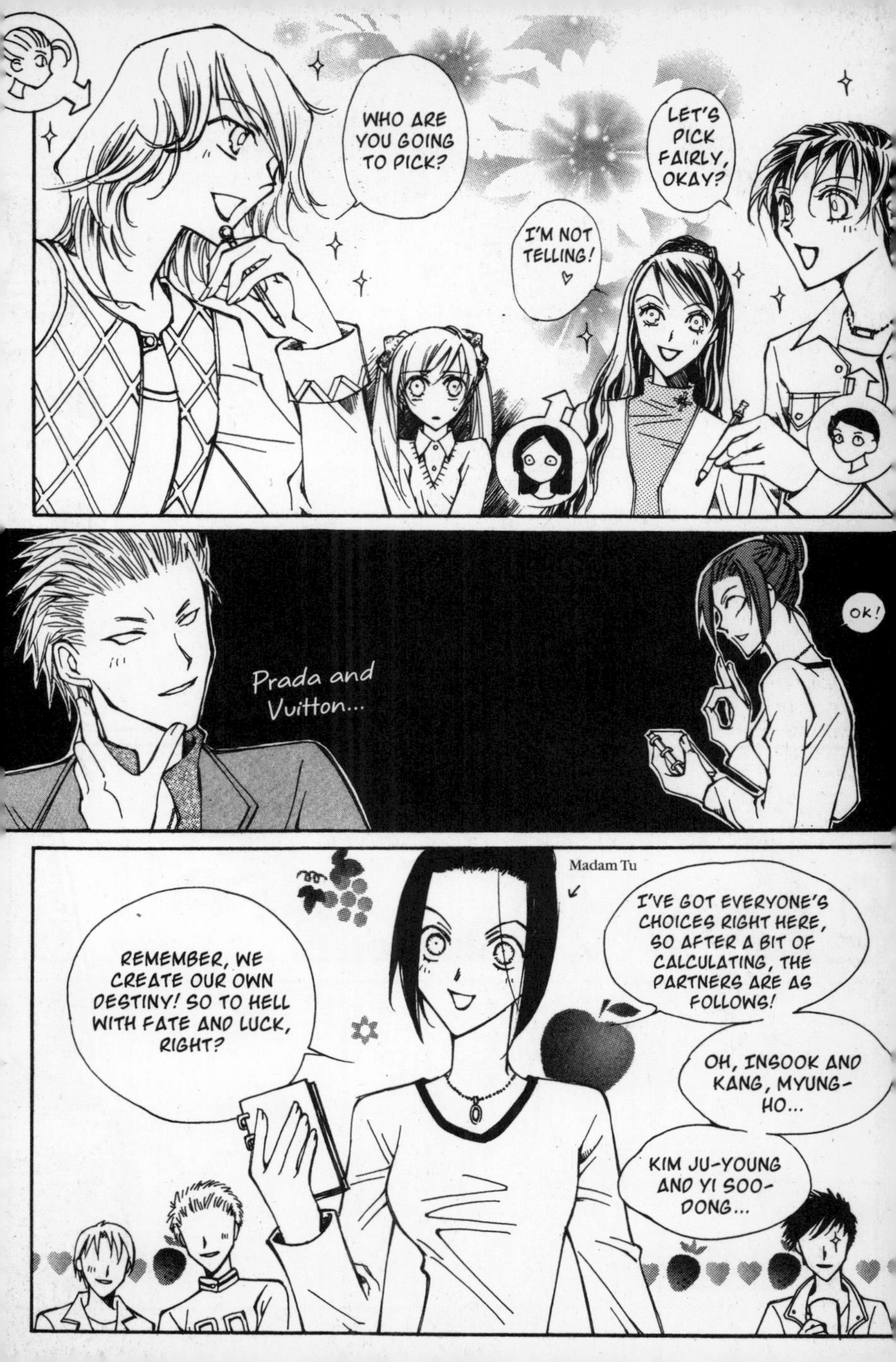
WHO ARE YOU GOING TO PICK?
I'M NOT TELLING! ♡
LET'S PICK FAIRLY, OKAY?
Prada and Vuitton...
OK!
REMEMBER, WE CREATE OUR OWN DESTINY! SO TO HELL WITH FATE AND LUCK, RIGHT?
Madam Tu
I'VE GOT EVERYONE'S CHOICES RIGHT HERE, SO AFTER A BIT OF CALCULATING, THE PARTNERS ARE AS FOLLOWS!
OH, INSOOK AND KANG, MYUNG-HO...
KIM JU-YOUNG AND YI SOO-DONG...

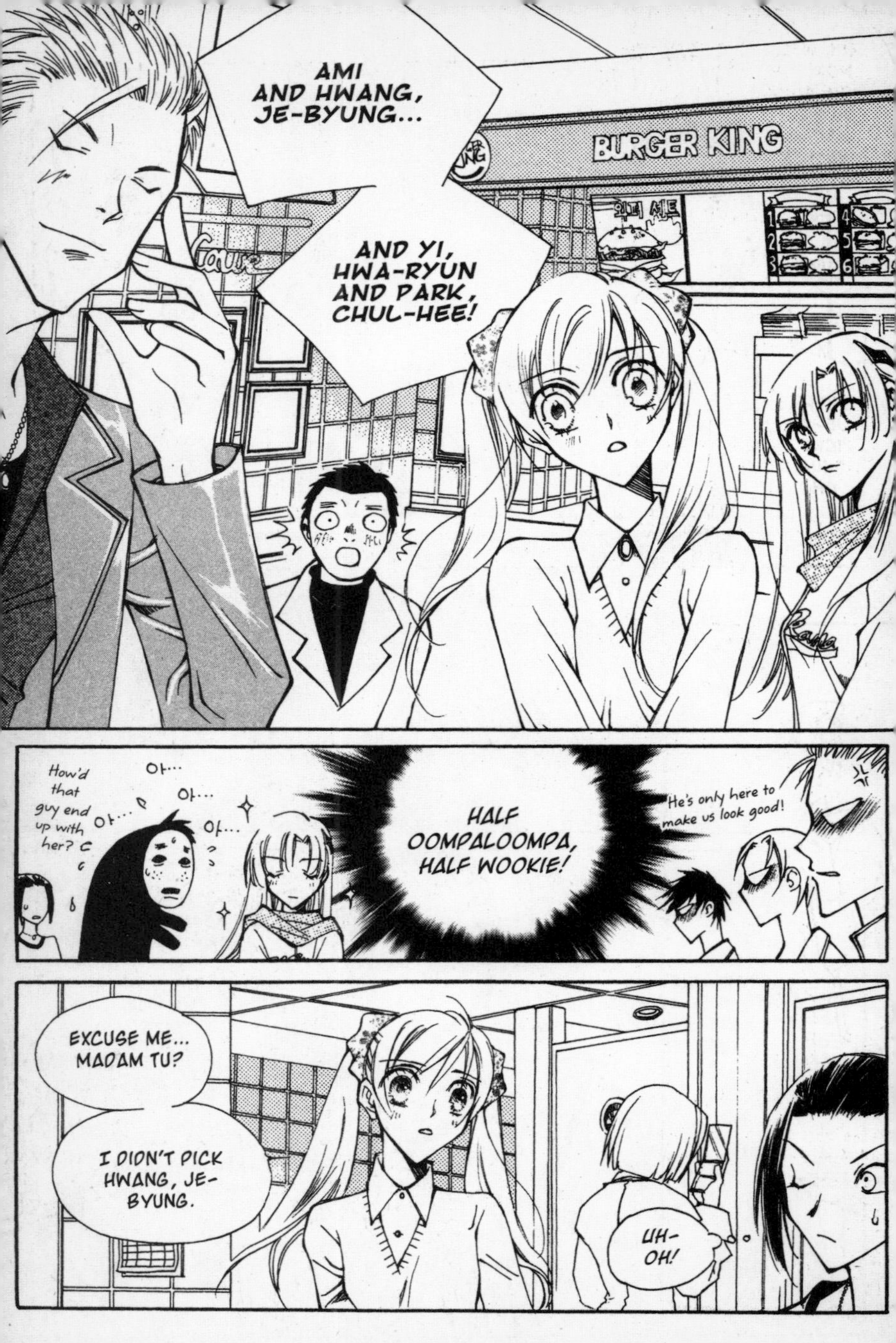
AMI AND HWANG, JE-BYUNG...
BURGER KING
AND YI, HWA-RYUN AND PARK, CHUL-HEE!
How'd that guy end up with her?
아...
아...
아...
아...
HALF OOMPALOOMPA, HALF WOOKIE!
He's only here to make us look good!
EXCUSE ME... MADAM TU?
I DIDN'T PICK HWANG, JE-BYUNG.
UH-OH!

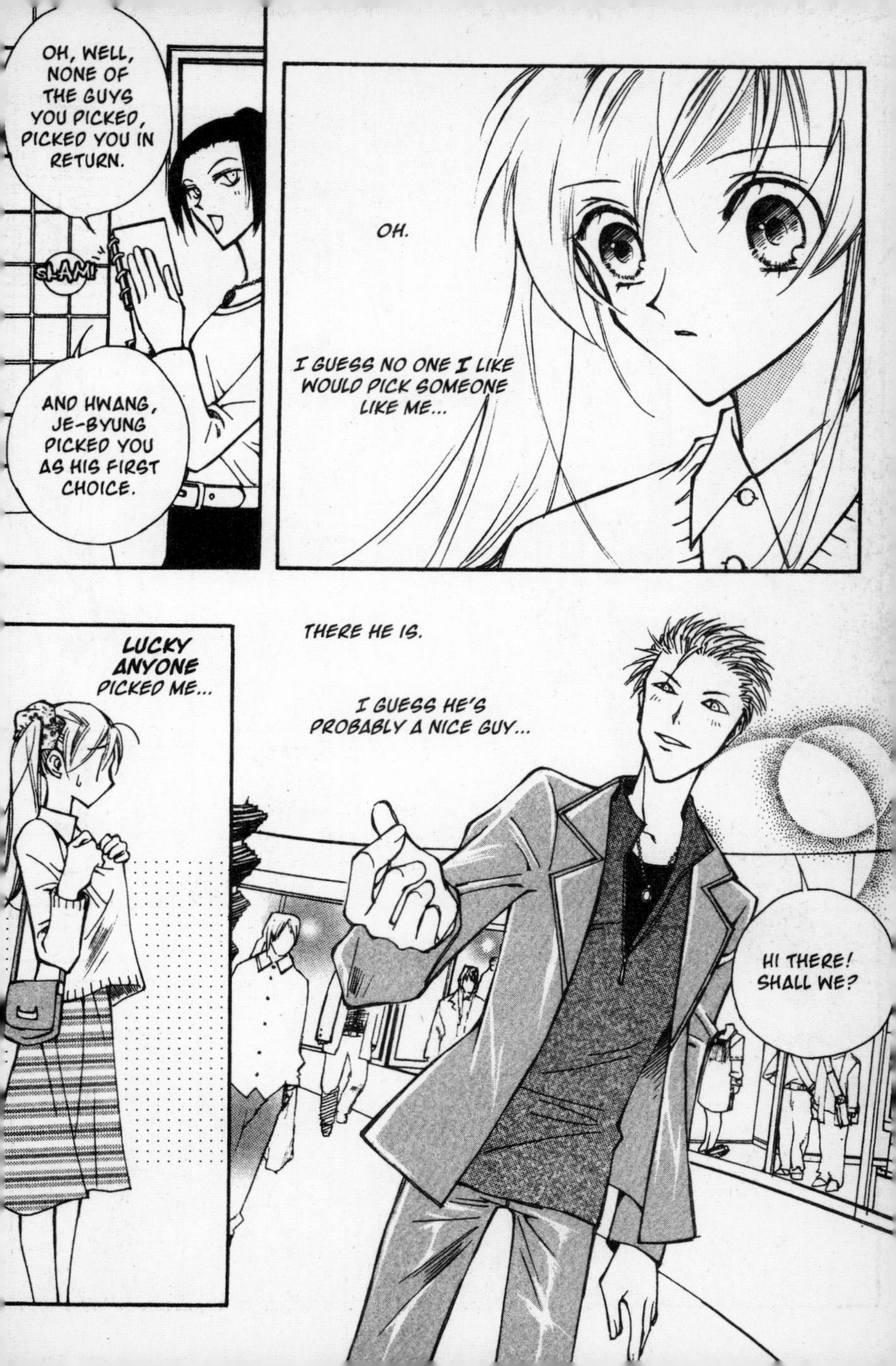
OH, WELL, NONE OF THE GUYS YOU PICKED, PICKED YOU IN RETURN.
SLAM!
AND HWANG, JE-BYUNG PICKED YOU AS HIS FIRST CHOICE.
OH.
I GUESS NO ONE I LIKE WOULD PICK SOMEONE LIKE ME...
LUCKY ANYONE PICKED ME...
THERE HE IS.
I GUESS HE'S PROBABLY A NICE GUY...
HI THERE! SHALL WE?

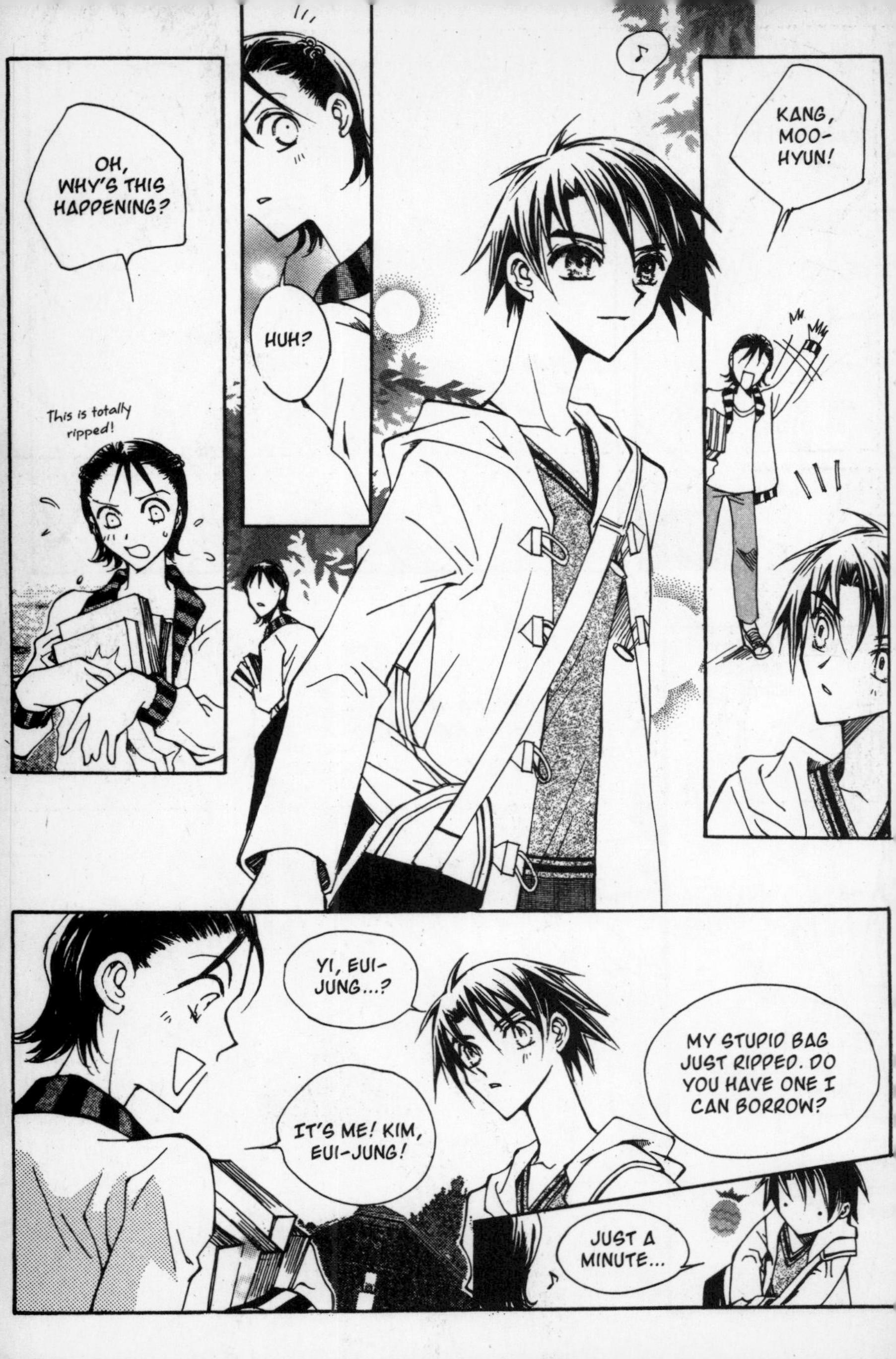
OH, WHY'S THIS HAPPENING?
This is totally ripped!
HUH?
♪
KANG, MOO-HYUN!
YI, EUI-JUNG...?
IT'S ME! KIM, EUI-JUNG!
MY STUPID BAG JUST RIPPED. DO YOU HAVE ONE I CAN BORROW?
JUST A MINUTE...
♪

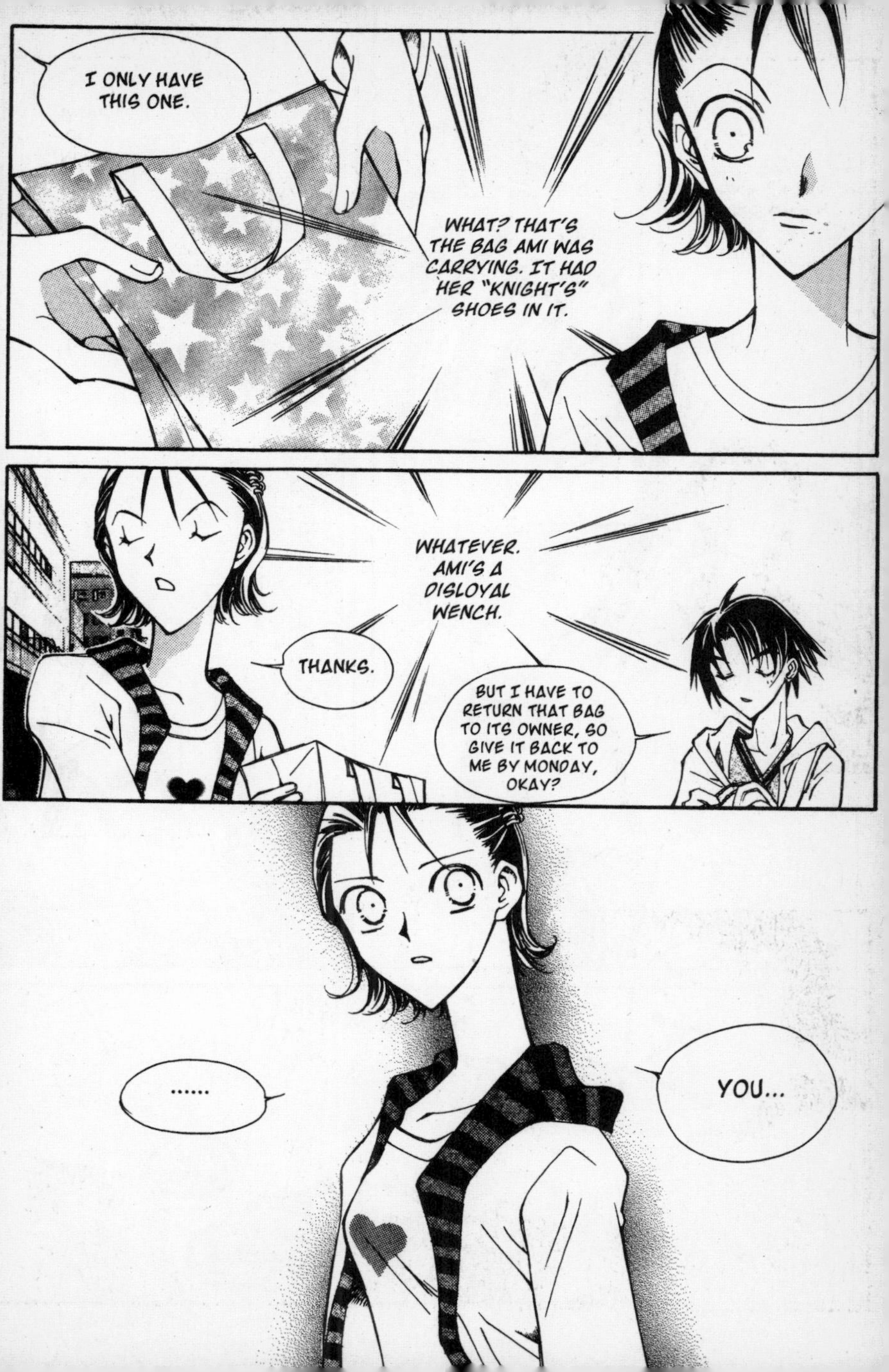
I ONLY HAVE THIS ONE.
WHAT? THAT'S THE BAG AMI WAS CARRYING. IT HAD HER "KNIGHT'S" SHOES IN IT.
WHATEVER. AMI'S A DISLOYAL WENCH.
THANKS.
BUT I HAVE TO RETURN THAT BAG TO ITS OWNER, SO GIVE IT BACK TO ME BY MONDAY, OKAY?
......
YOU...

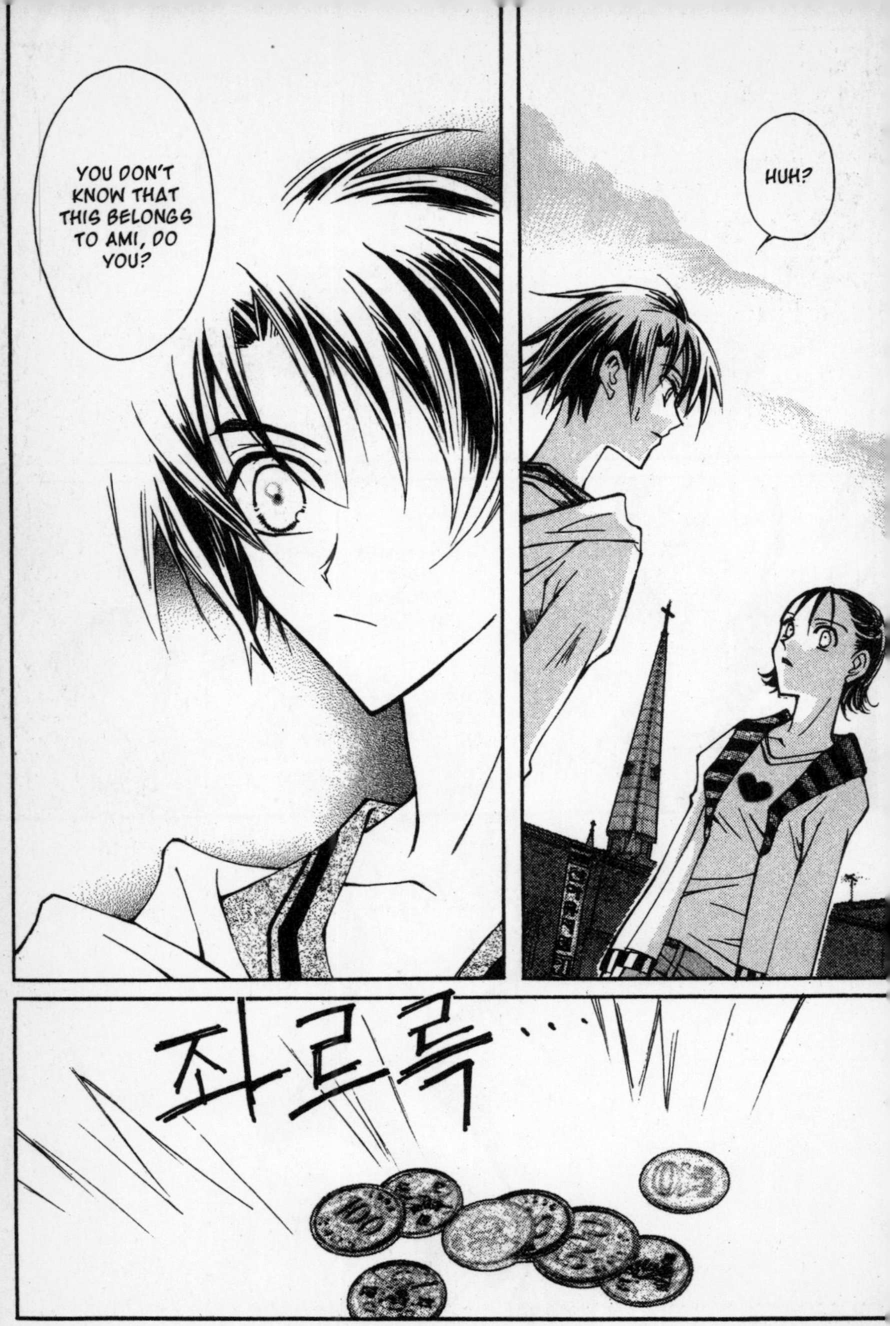
YOU DON'T KNOW THAT THIS BELONGS TO AMI, DO YOU?
HUH?
좌르륵...

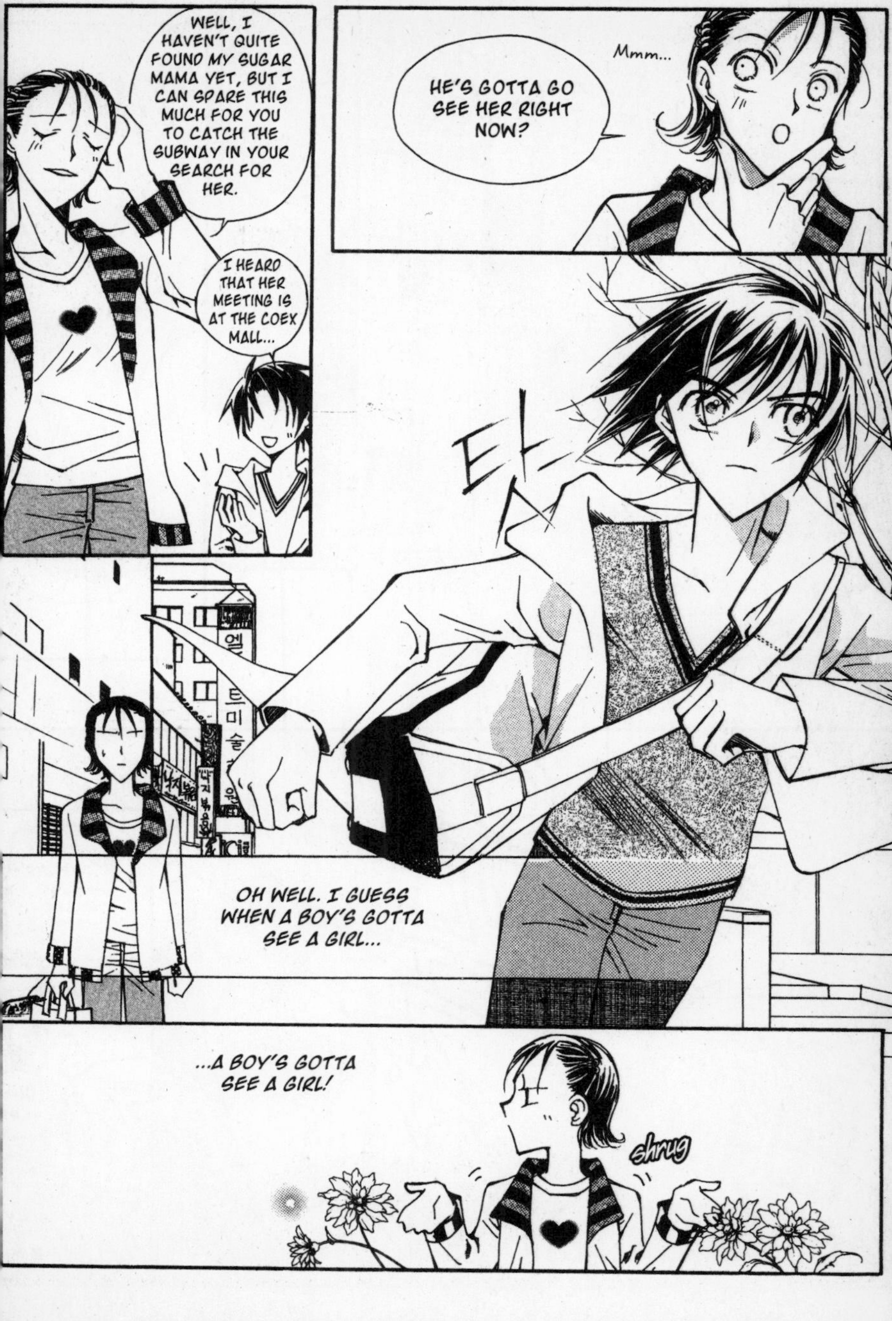
WELL, I HAVEN'T QUITE FOUND MY SUGAR MAMA YET, BUT I CAN SPARE THIS MUCH FOR YOU TO CATCH THE SUBWAY IN YOUR SEARCH FOR HER.
I HEARD THAT HER MEETING IS AT THE COEX MALL...
Mmm...
HE'S GOTTA GO SEE HER RIGHT NOW?
OH WELL. I GUESS WHEN A BOY'S GOTTA SEE A GIRL...
...A BOY'S GOTTA SEE A GIRL!
shrug

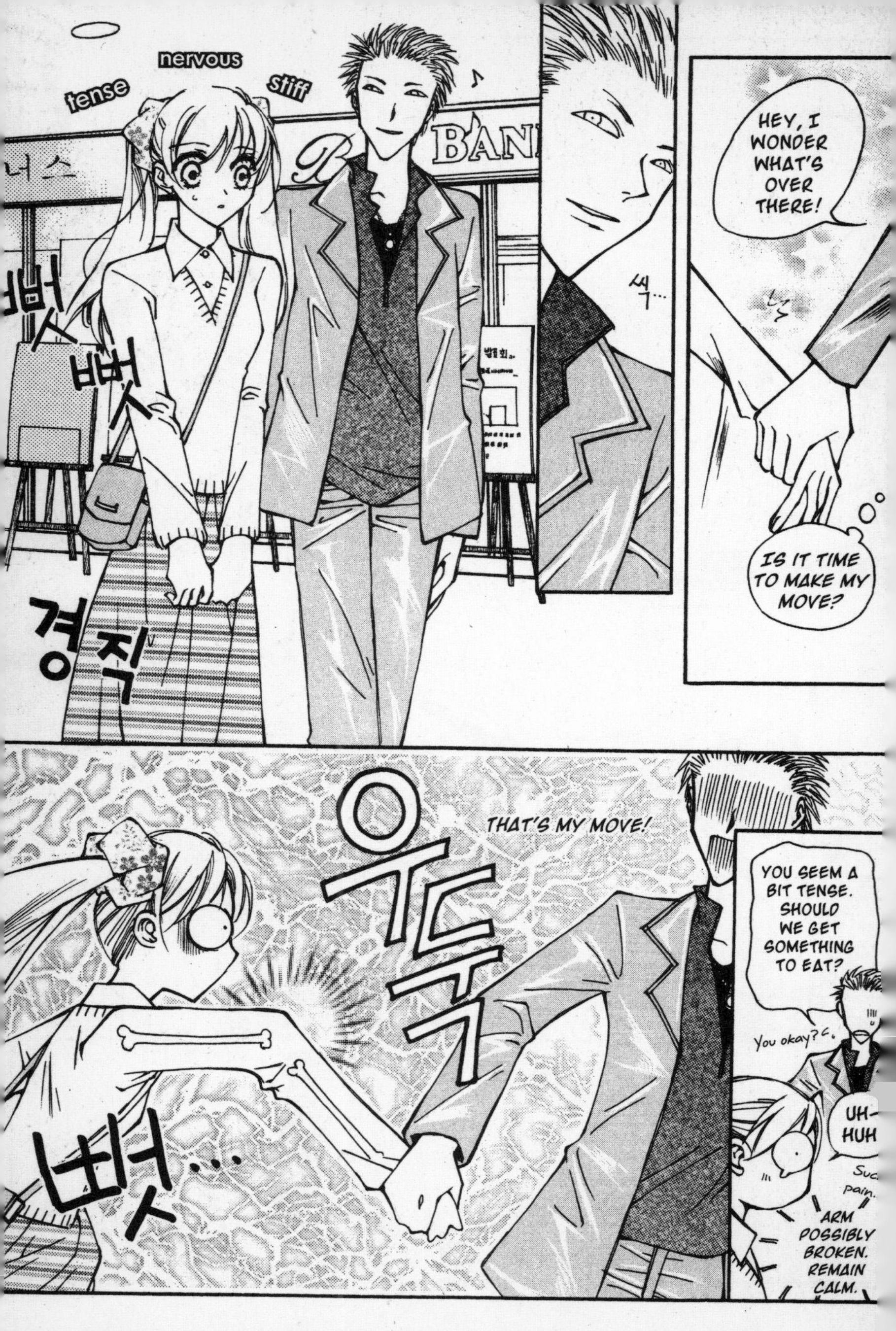
tense
nervous
stiff
경직
HEY, I WONDER WHAT'S OVER THERE!
IS IT TIME TO MAKE MY MOVE?
THAT'S MY MOVE!
YOU SEEM A BIT TENSE. SHOULD WE GET SOMETHING TO EAT?
You okay?
UH-HUH
ARM POSSIBLY BROKEN. REMAIN CALM.

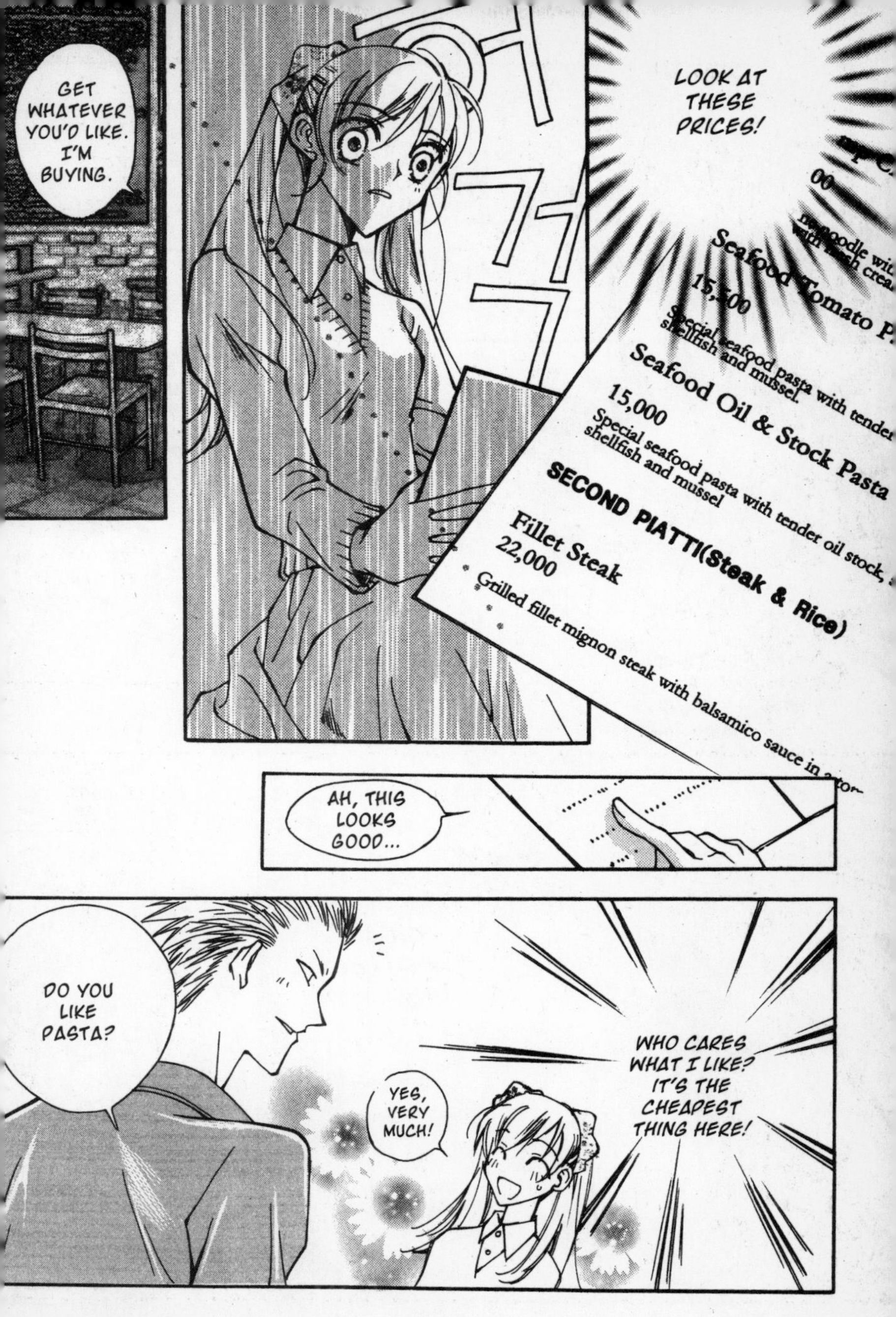
GET WHATEVER YOU'D LIKE. I'M BUYING.
LOOK AT THESE PRICES!
Special seafood pasta with tender
shellfish and mussel.
Seafood Oil & Stock Pasta
15,000
Special seafood pasta with tender oil stock,
shellfish and mussel
SECOND PIATTI(Steak & Rice)
Fillet Steak
22,000
Grilled fillet mignon steak with balsamico sauce in
AH, THIS LOOKS GOOD...
DO YOU LIKE PASTA?
YES, VERY MUCH!
WHO CARES WHAT I LIKE? IT'S THE CHEAPEST THING HERE!

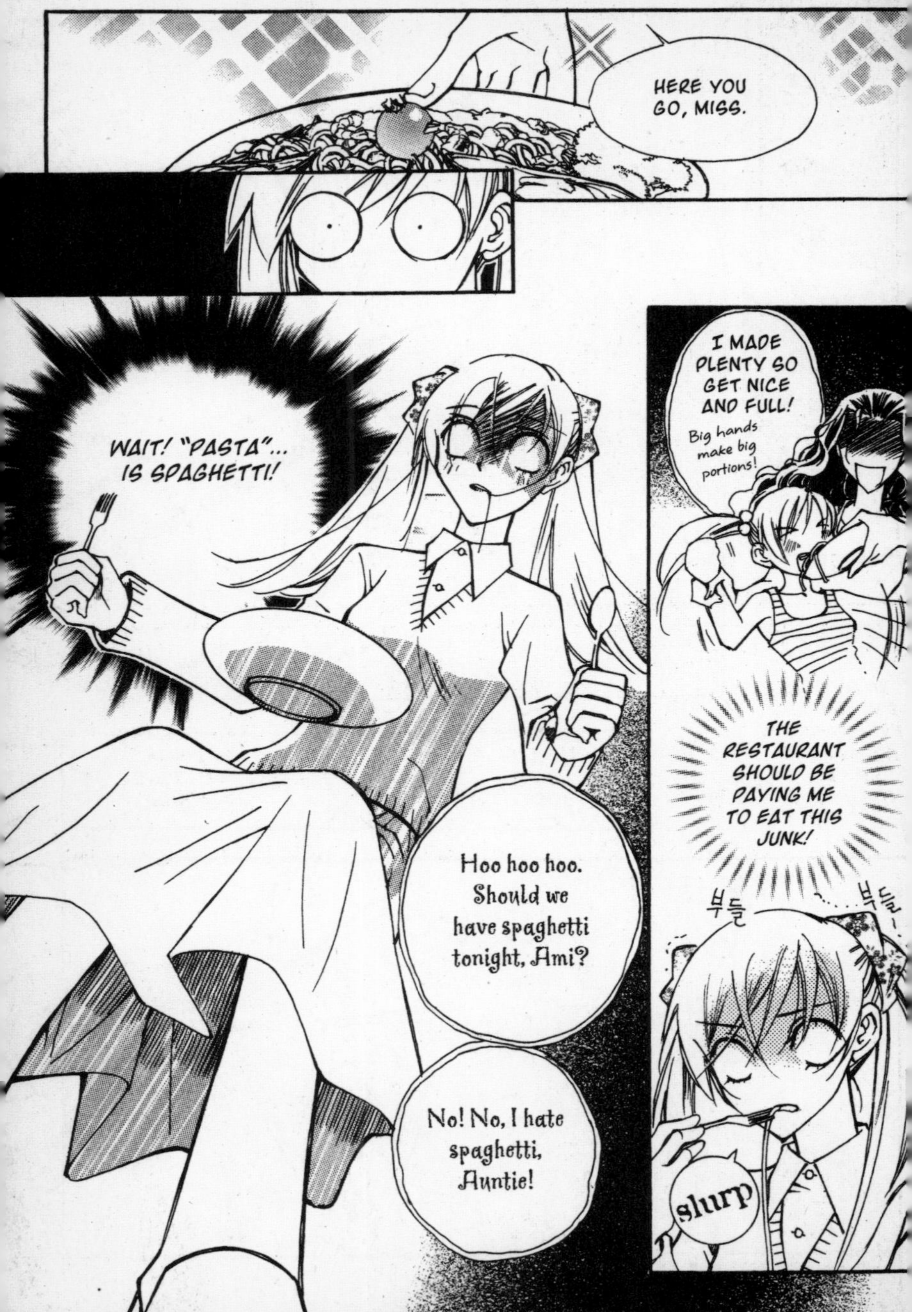
HERE YOU GO, MISS.
WAIT! "PASTA"... IS SPAGHETTI!
Hoo hoo hoo. Should we have spaghetti tonight, Ami?
No! No, I hate spaghetti, Auntie!
I MADE PLENTY SO GET NICE AND FULL!
Big hands make big portions!
THE RESTAURANT SHOULD BE PAYING ME TO EAT THIS JUNK!
부들
slurp

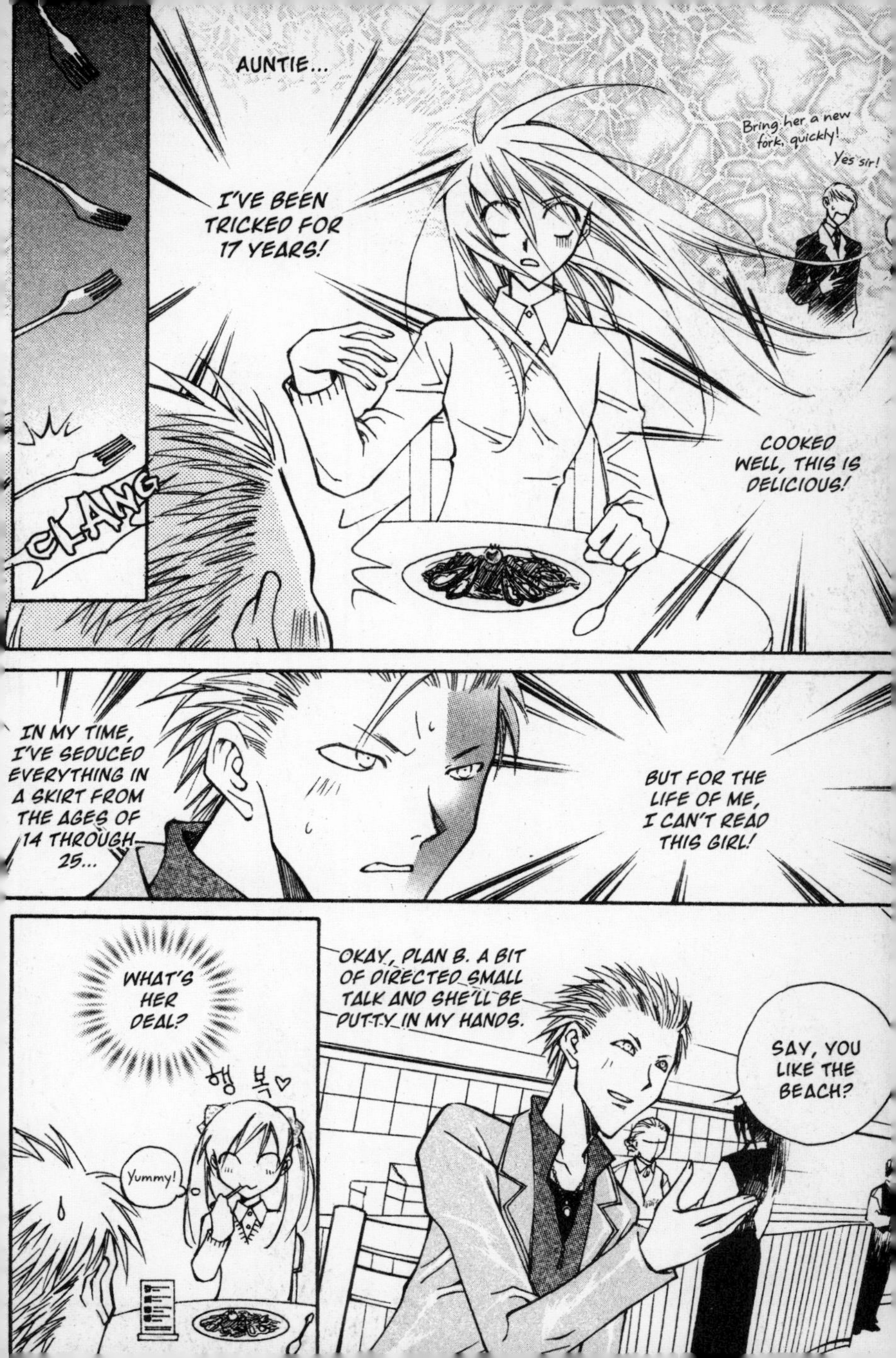

CLANG
AUNTIE...
I'VE BEEN TRICKED FOR 17 YEARS!
Bring her a new fork, quickly!
Yes sir!
COOKED WELL, THIS IS DELICIOUS!
IN MY TIME, I'VE SEDUCED EVERYTHING IN A SKIRT FROM THE AGES OF 14 THROUGH 25...
BUT FOR THE LIFE OF ME, I CAN'T READ THIS GIRL!
WHAT'S HER DEAL?
행 복♡
Yummy!
OKAY, PLAN B. A BIT OF DIRECTED SMALL TALK AND SHE'LL BE PUTTY IN MY HANDS.
SAY, YOU LIKE THE BEACH?

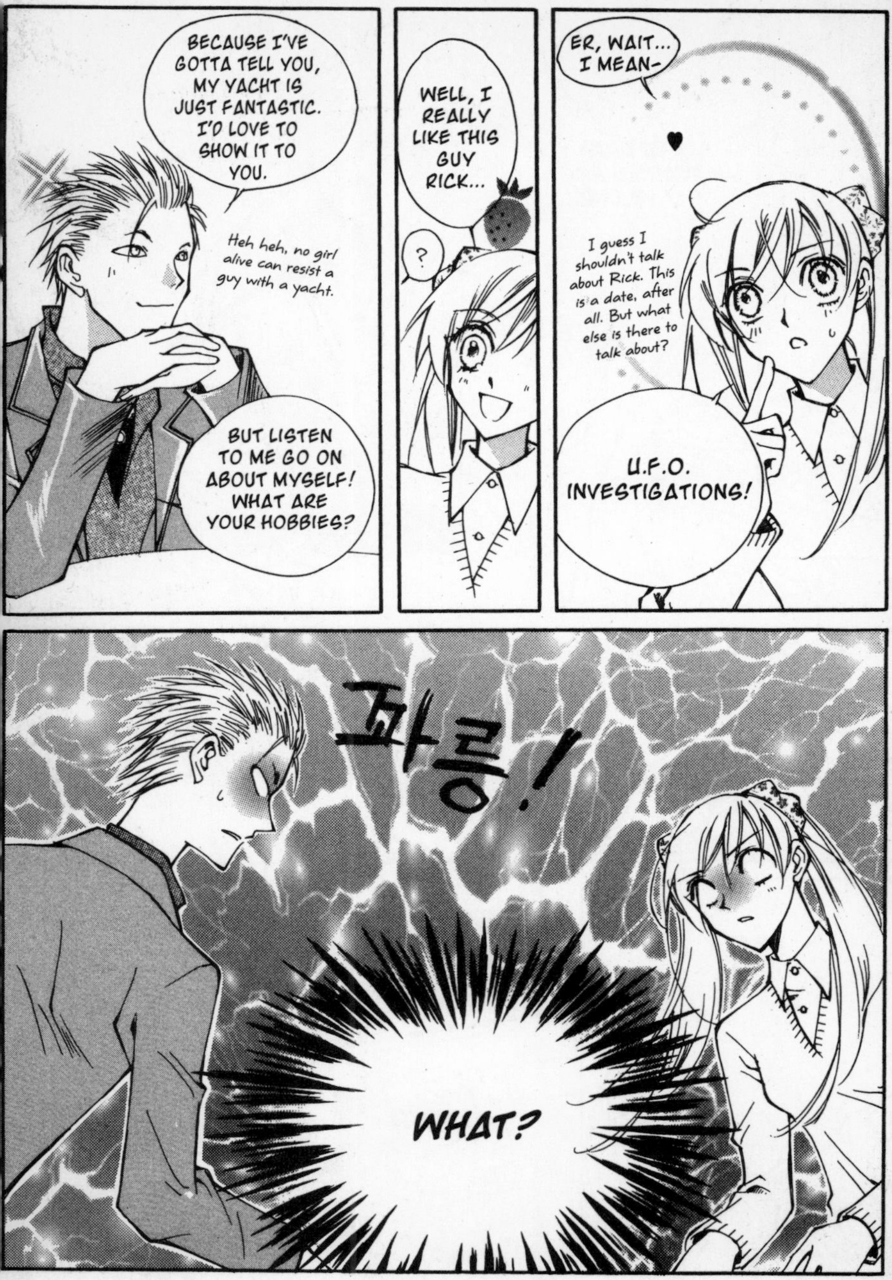

BECAUSE I'VE GOTTA TELL YOU, MY YACHT IS JUST FANTASTIC. I'D LOVE TO SHOW IT TO YOU.
Heh heh, no girl alive can resist a guy with a yacht.
BUT LISTEN TO ME GO ON ABOUT MYSELF! WHAT ARE YOUR HOBBIES?
?
WELL, I REALLY LIKE THIS GUY RICK...
ER, WAIT... I MEAN-
I guess I shouldn't talk about Rick. This is a date, after all. But what else is there to talk about?
U.F.O. INVESTIGATIONS!
파릉!
WHAT?

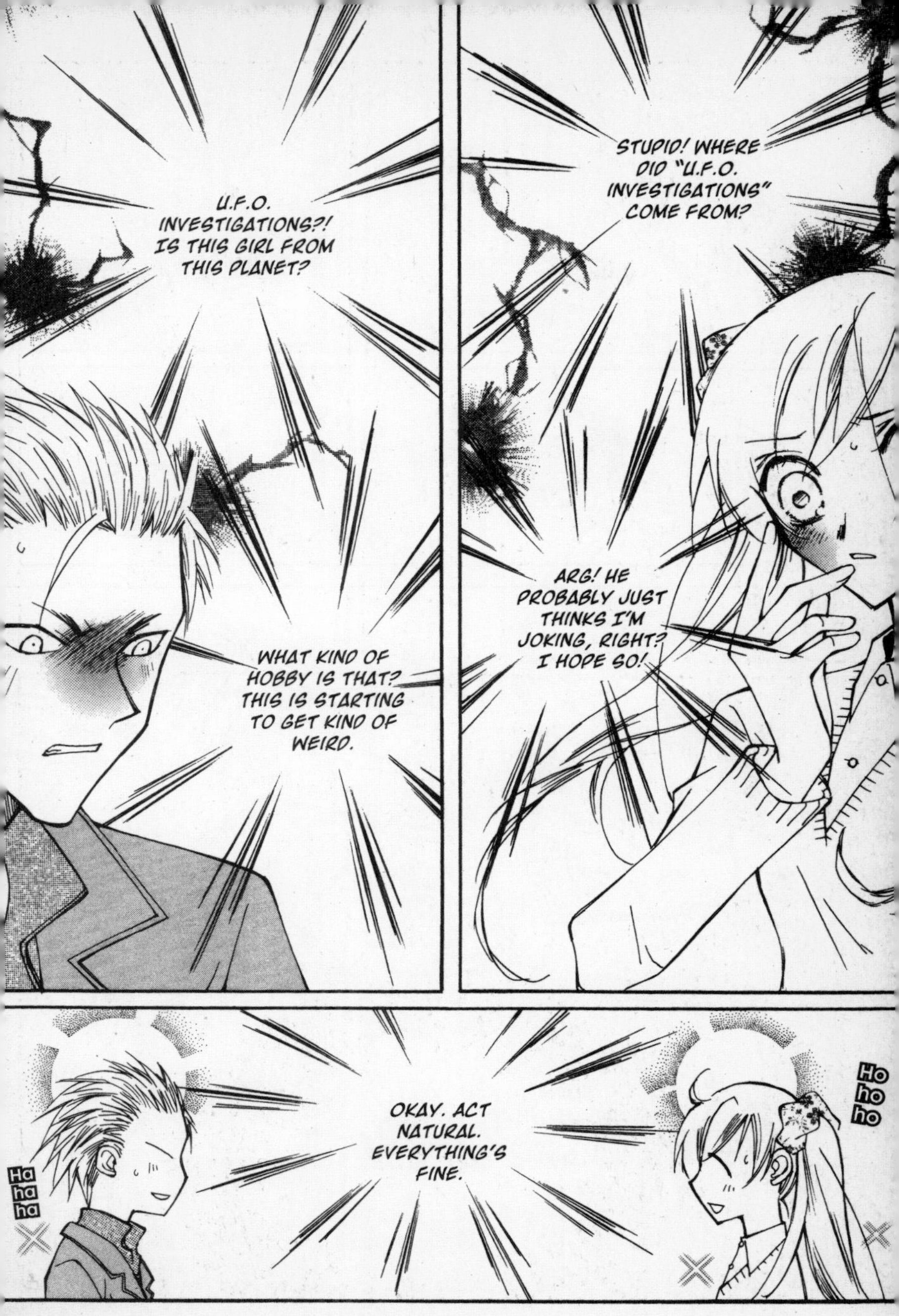
U.F.O. INVESTIGATIONS?! IS THIS GIRL FROM THIS PLANET?
WHAT KIND OF HOBBY IS THAT? THIS IS STARTING TO GET KIND OF WEIRD.
STUPID! WHERE DID "U.F.O. INVESTIGATIONS" COME FROM?
ARG! HE PROBABLY JUST THINKS I'M JOKING, RIGHT? I HOPE SO!
Ha ha ha
OKAY. ACT NATURAL. EVERYTHING'S FINE.
Ho ho ho

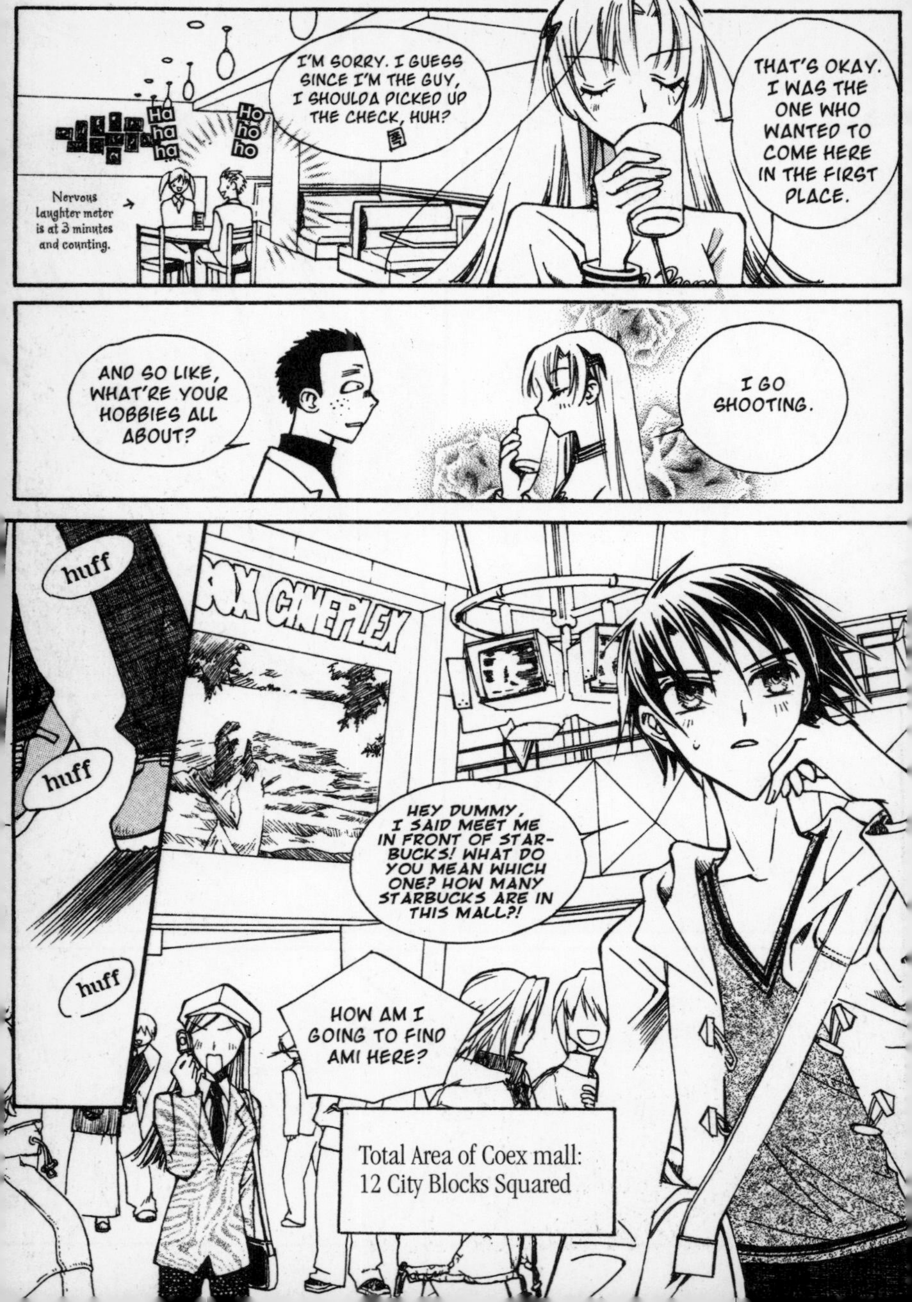
Ha ha ha
Ho ho ho
Nervous laughter meter is at 3 minutes and counting.
I'M SORRY. I GUESS SINCE I'M THE GUY, I SHOULDA PICKED UP THE CHECK, HUH?
THAT'S OKAY. I WAS THE ONE WHO WANTED TO COME HERE IN THE FIRST PLACE.
AND SO LIKE, WHAT'RE YOUR HOBBIES ALL ABOUT?
I GO SHOOTING.
huff
huff
huff
COEX CINEPLEX
HEY DUMMY, I SAID MEET ME IN FRONT OF STARBUCKS! WHAT DO YOU MEAN WHICH ONE? HOW MANY STARBUCKS ARE IN THIS MALL?!
HOW AM I GOING TO FIND AMI HERE?
Total Area of Coex mall: 12 City Blocks Squared

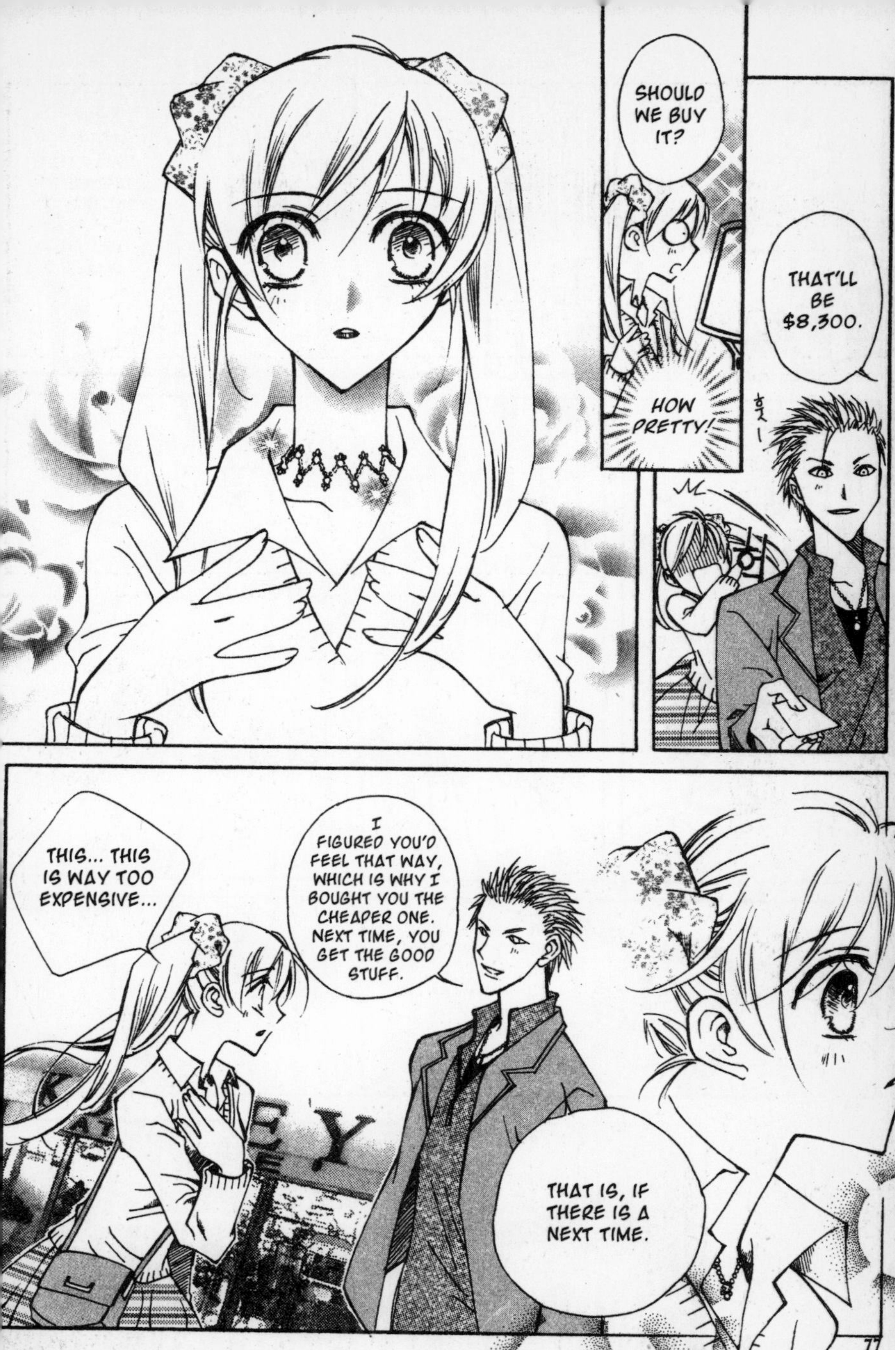
SHOULD WE BUY IT?
HOW PRETTY!
THAT'LL BE $8,300.
THIS... THIS IS WAY TOO EXPENSIVE...
I FIGURED YOU'D FEEL THAT WAY, WHICH IS WHY I BOUGHT YOU THE CHEAPER ONE. NEXT TIME, YOU GET THE GOOD STUFF.
THAT IS, IF THERE IS A NEXT TIME.

UM...
EXCUSE ME...
MA'AM...?

I, UH,
BOUGHT
THIS FOR
YOU...
ER...

At the store we were just at...

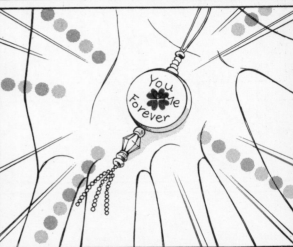

You
Me
Forever

AH! THAT WAS
ALREADY WRITTEN
ON THERE! IT
DOESN'T MEAN
ANYTHING! ARG!!

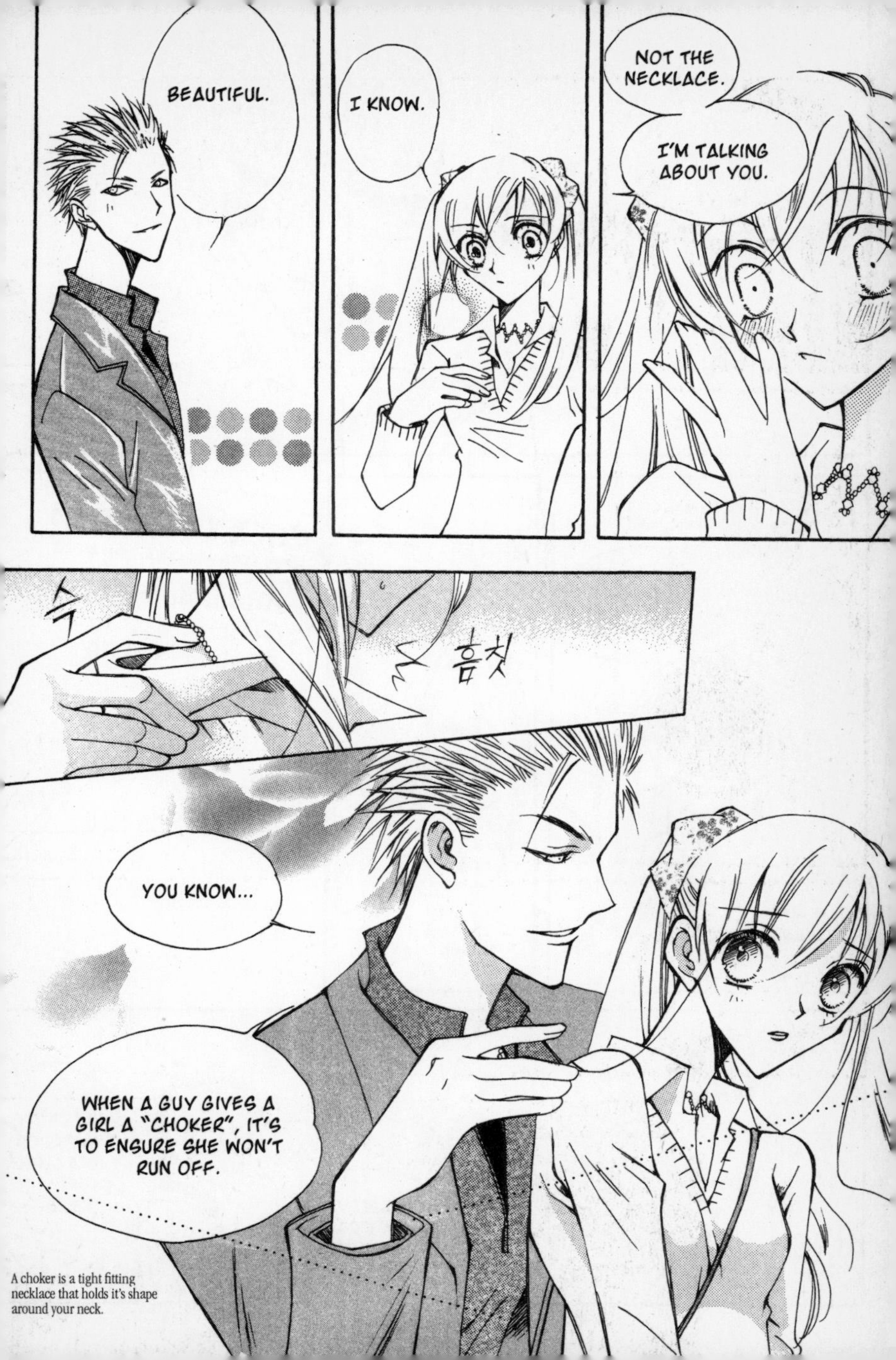
BEAUTIFUL.
I KNOW.
NOT THE NECKLACE.
I'M TALKING ABOUT YOU.
흠칫
YOU KNOW...
WHEN A GUY GIVES A GIRL A "CHOKER", IT'S TO ENSURE SHE WON'T RUN OFF.

A choker is a tight fitting necklace that holds it's shape around your neck.

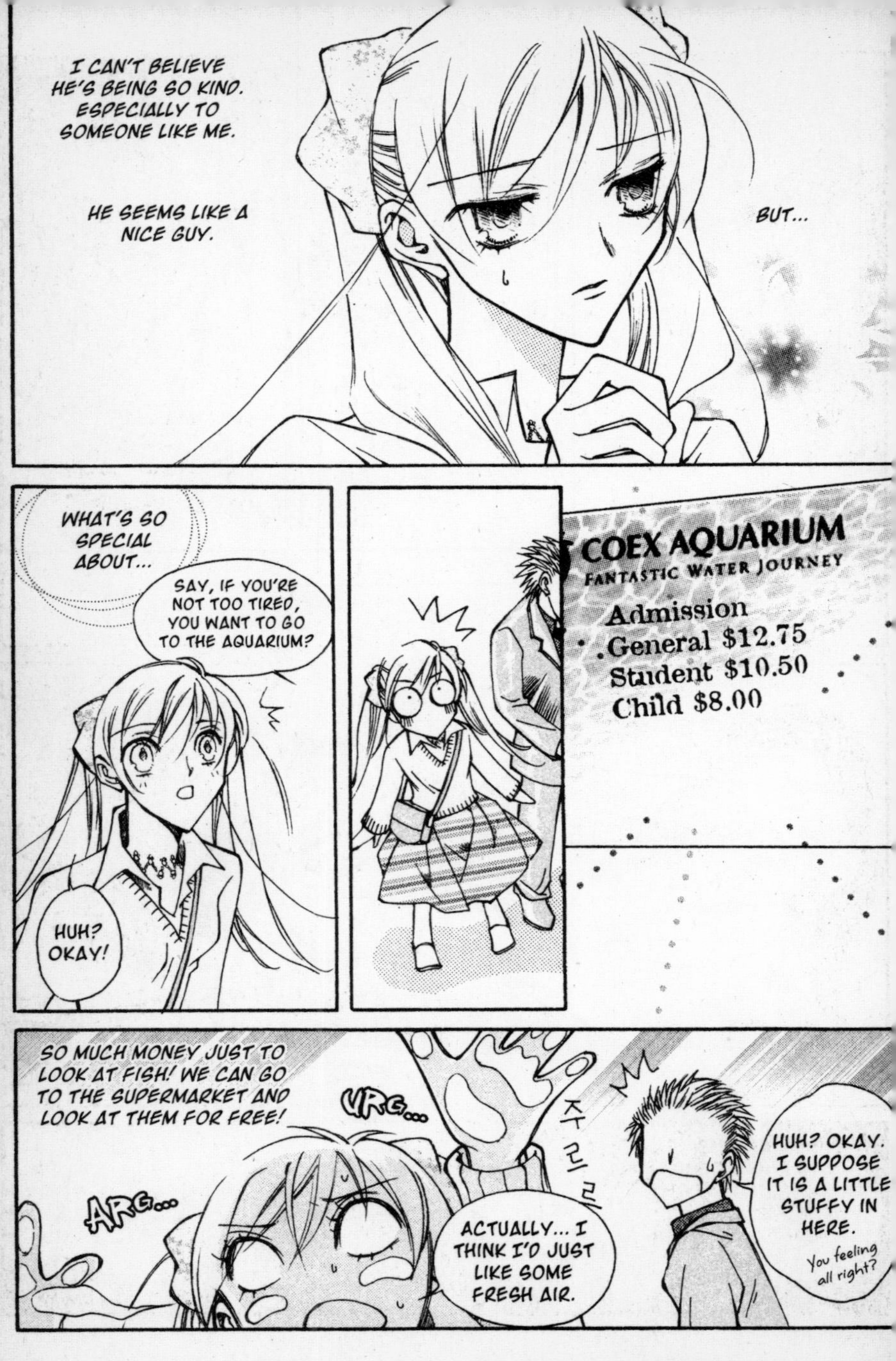

I CAN'T BELIEVE HE'S BEING SO KIND. ESPECIALLY TO SOMEONE LIKE ME.
HE SEEMS LIKE A NICE GUY.
BUT...
WHAT'S SO SPECIAL ABOUT...
SAY, IF YOU'RE NOT TOO TIRED, YOU WANT TO GO TO THE AQUARIUM?
HUH? OKAY!
COEX AQUARIUM
FANTASTIC WATER JOURNEY
Admission
General $12.75
Student $10.50
Child $8.00
SO MUCH MONEY JUST TO LOOK AT FISH! WE CAN GO TO THE SUPERMARKET AND LOOK AT THEM FOR FREE!
URG...
ARG...
ACTUALLY... I THINK I'D JUST LIKE SOME FRESH AIR.
HUH? OKAY. I SUPPOSE IT IS A LITTLE STUFFY IN HERE.
You feeling all right?

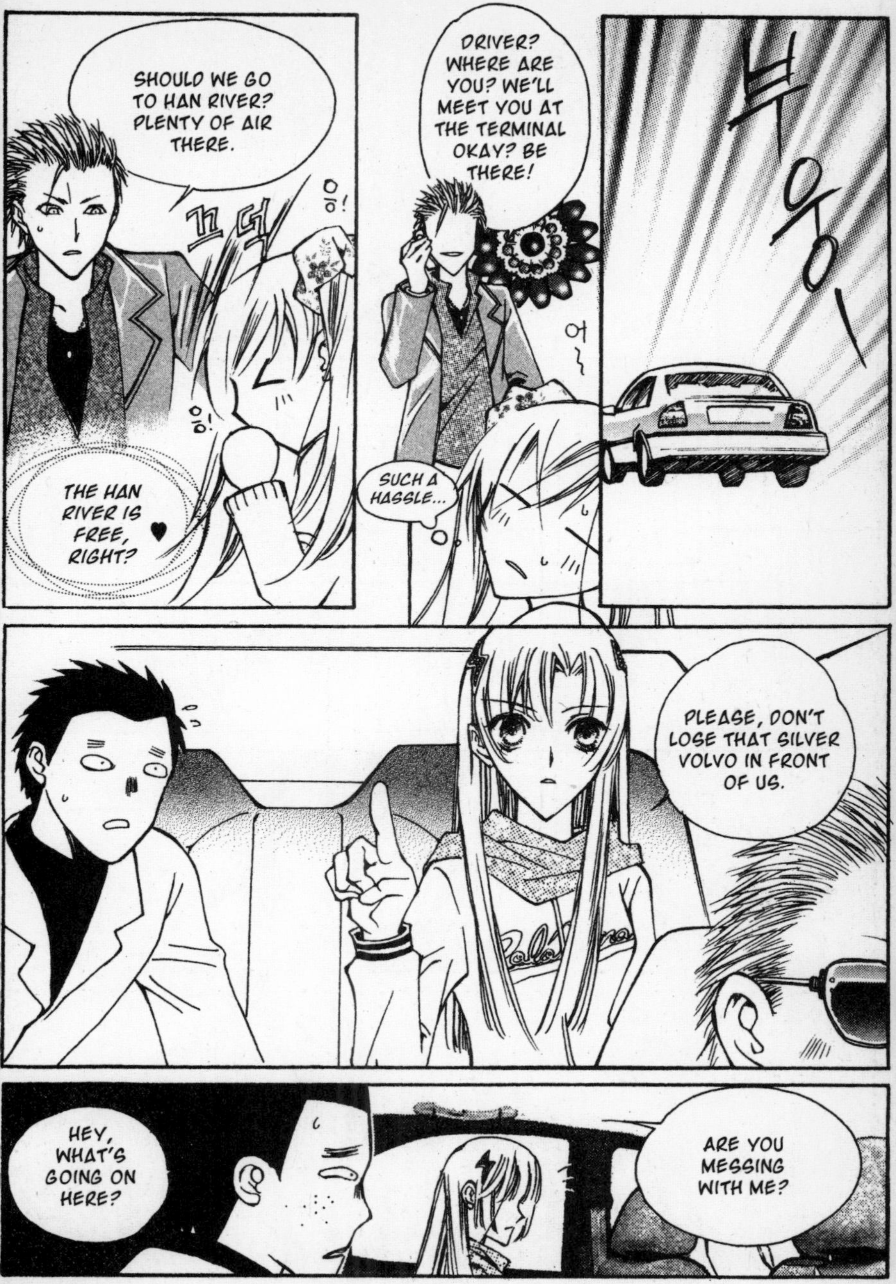
SHOULD WE GO TO HAN RIVER? PLENTY OF AIR THERE.
THE HAN RIVER IS FREE, RIGHT? ♥
DRIVER? WHERE ARE YOU? WE'LL MEET YOU AT THE TERMINAL OKAY? BE THERE!
SUCH A HASSLE...
PLEASE, DON'T LOSE THAT SILVER VOLVO IN FRONT OF US.
HEY, WHAT'S GOING ON HERE?
ARE YOU MESSING WITH ME?

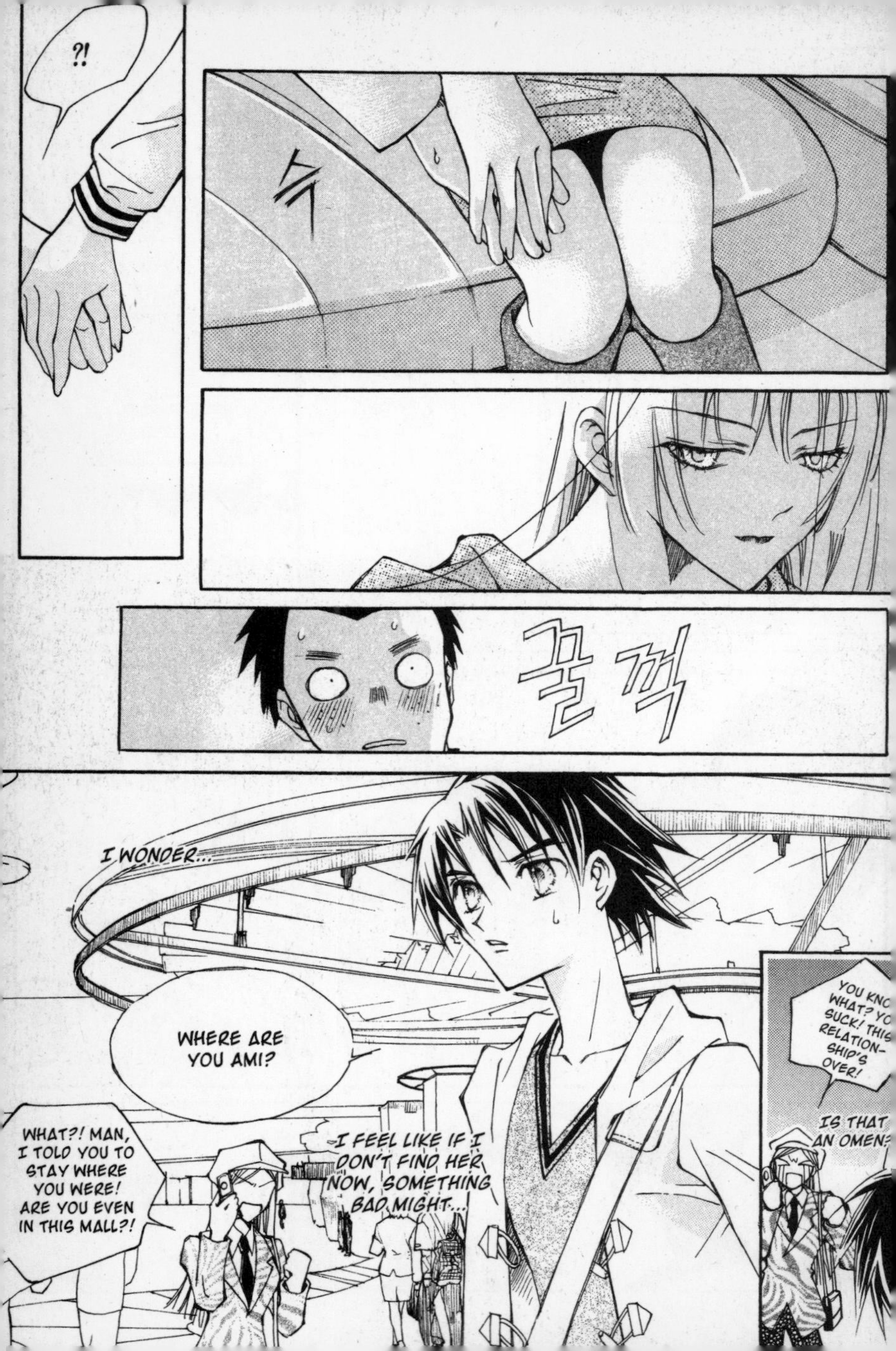
?!
슥
꿀꺽
I WONDER...
WHERE ARE YOU AMI?
WHAT?! MAN, I TOLD YOU TO STAY WHERE YOU WERE! ARE YOU EVEN IN THIS MALL?!
-I FEEL LIKE IF I DON'T FIND HER NOW, SOMETHING BAD MIGHT...
YOU KNO WHAT? YO SUCK! THIS RELATION-SHIP'S OVER!
IS THAT AN OMEN?

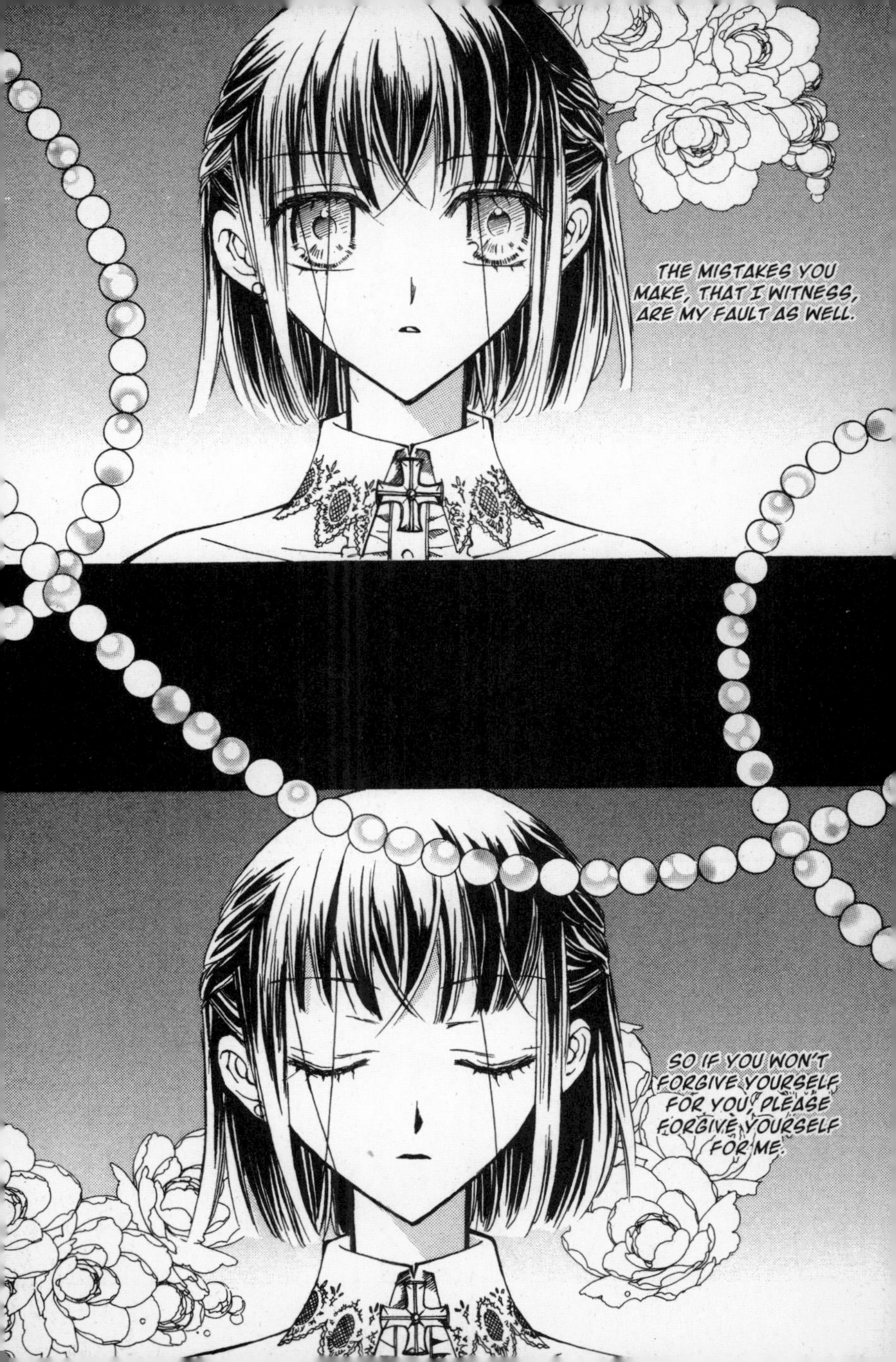
THE MISTAKES YOU MAKE, THAT I WITNESS, ARE MY FAULT AS WELL.
SO IF YOU WON'T FORGIVE YOURSELF FOR YOU, PLEASE FORGIVE YOURSELF FOR ME.

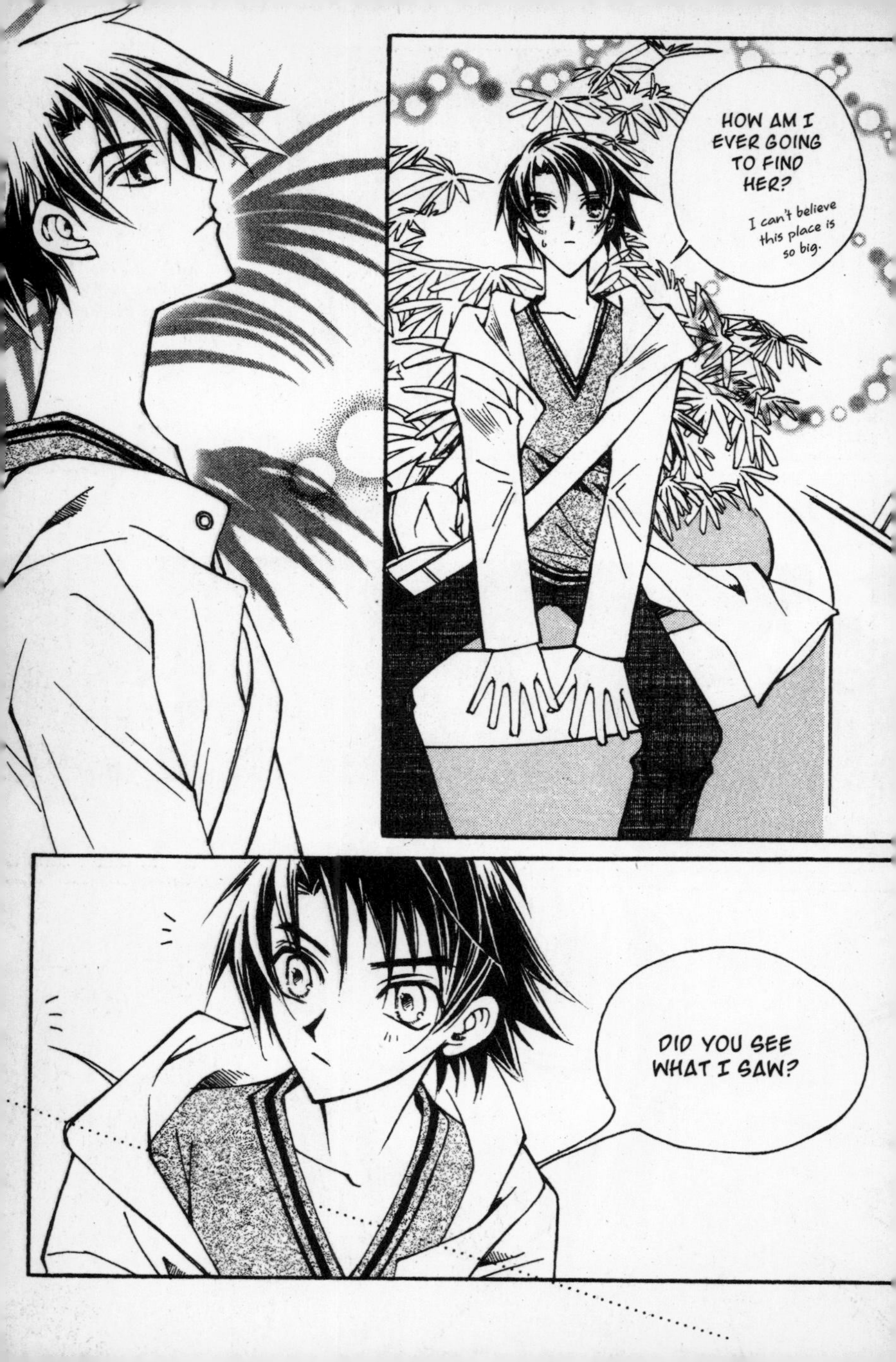
HOW AM I EVER GOING TO FIND HER?
I can't believe this place is so big.
DID YOU SEE WHAT I SAW?

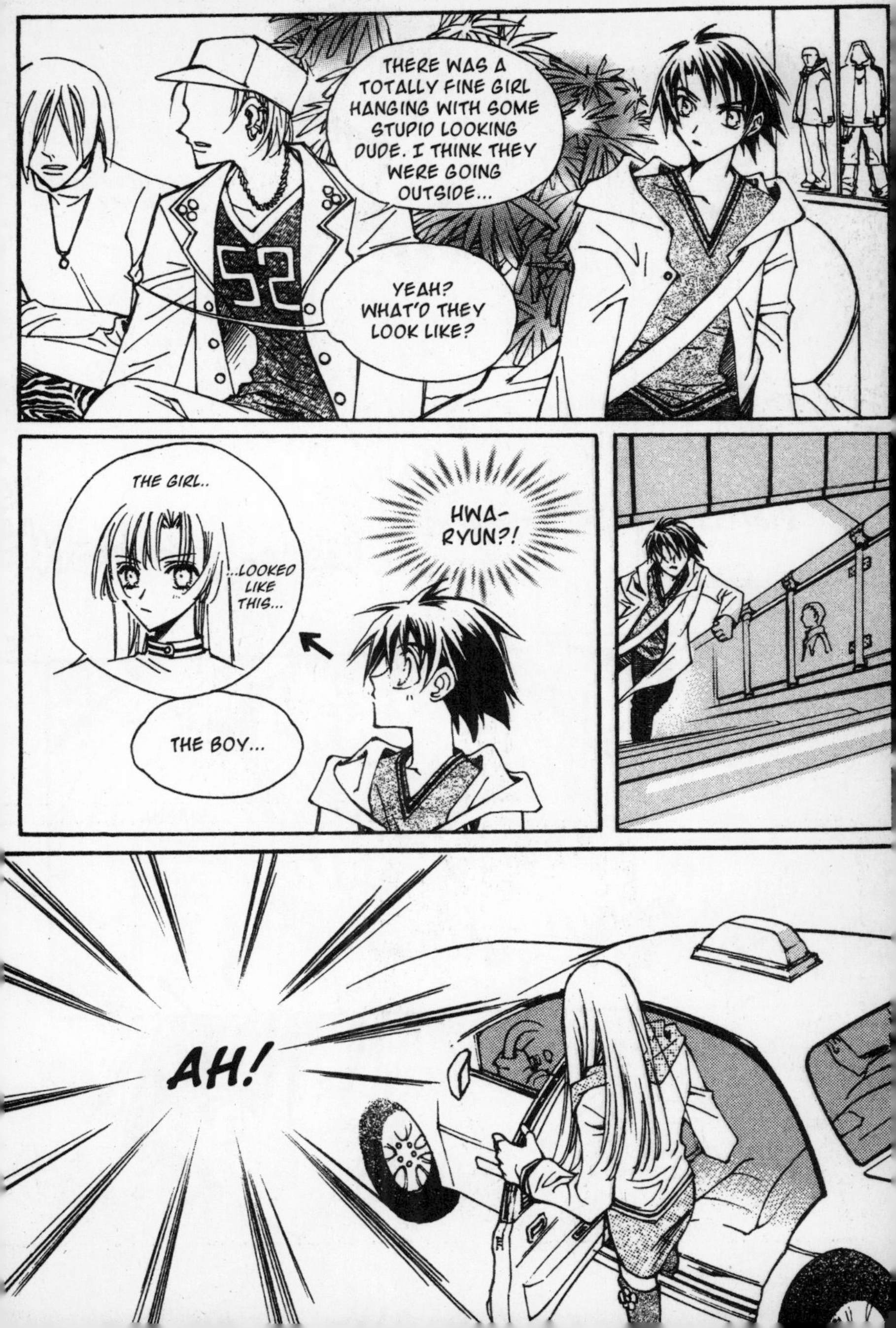
THERE WAS A TOTALLY FINE GIRL HANGING WITH SOME STUPID LOOKING DUDE. I THINK THEY WERE GOING OUTSIDE...
YEAH? WHAT'D THEY LOOK LIKE?
THE GIRL..
...LOOKED LIKE THIS...
THE BOY...
HWA-RYUN?!
AH!

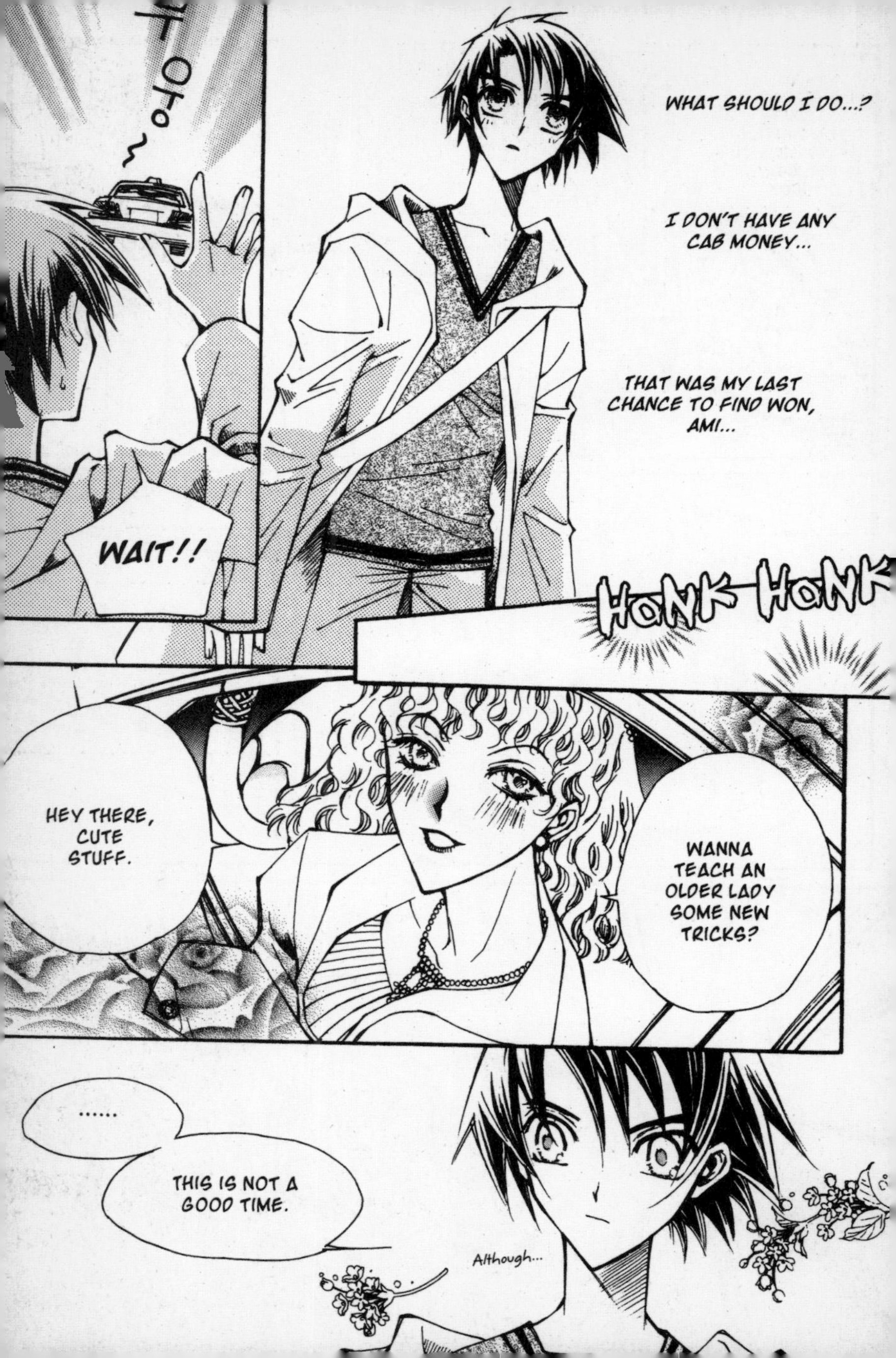
WAIT!!
WHAT SHOULD I DO...?
I DON'T HAVE ANY CAB MONEY...
THAT WAS MY LAST CHANCE TO FIND WON, AMI...
HONK HONK
HEY THERE, CUTE STUFF.
WANNA TEACH AN OLDER LADY SOME NEW TRICKS?
......
THIS IS NOT A GOOD TIME.
Although...

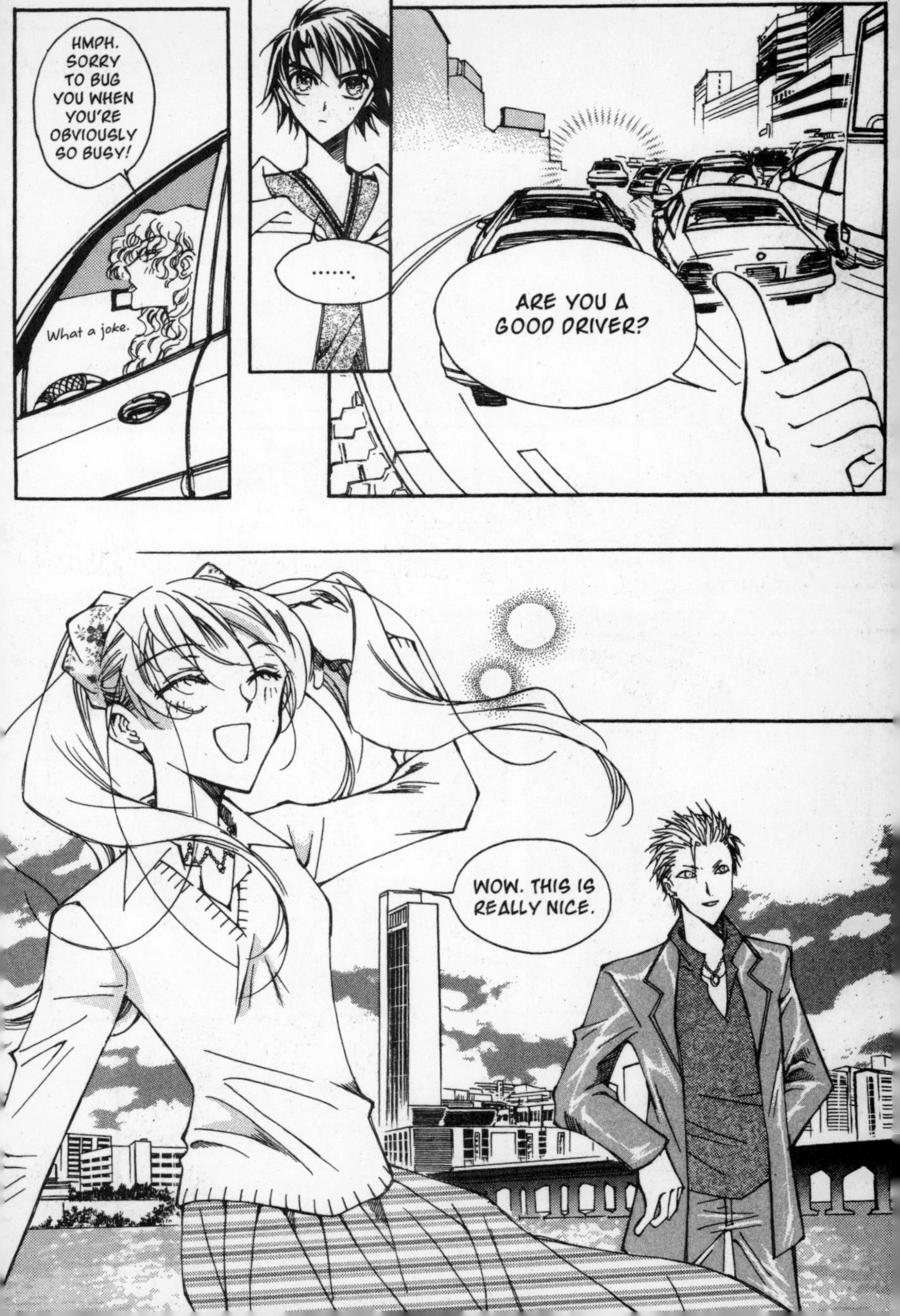
HMPH. SORRY TO BUG YOU WHEN YOU'RE OBVIOUSLY SO BUSY!
What a joke.
......
ARE YOU A GOOD DRIVER?
WOW. THIS IS REALLY NICE.

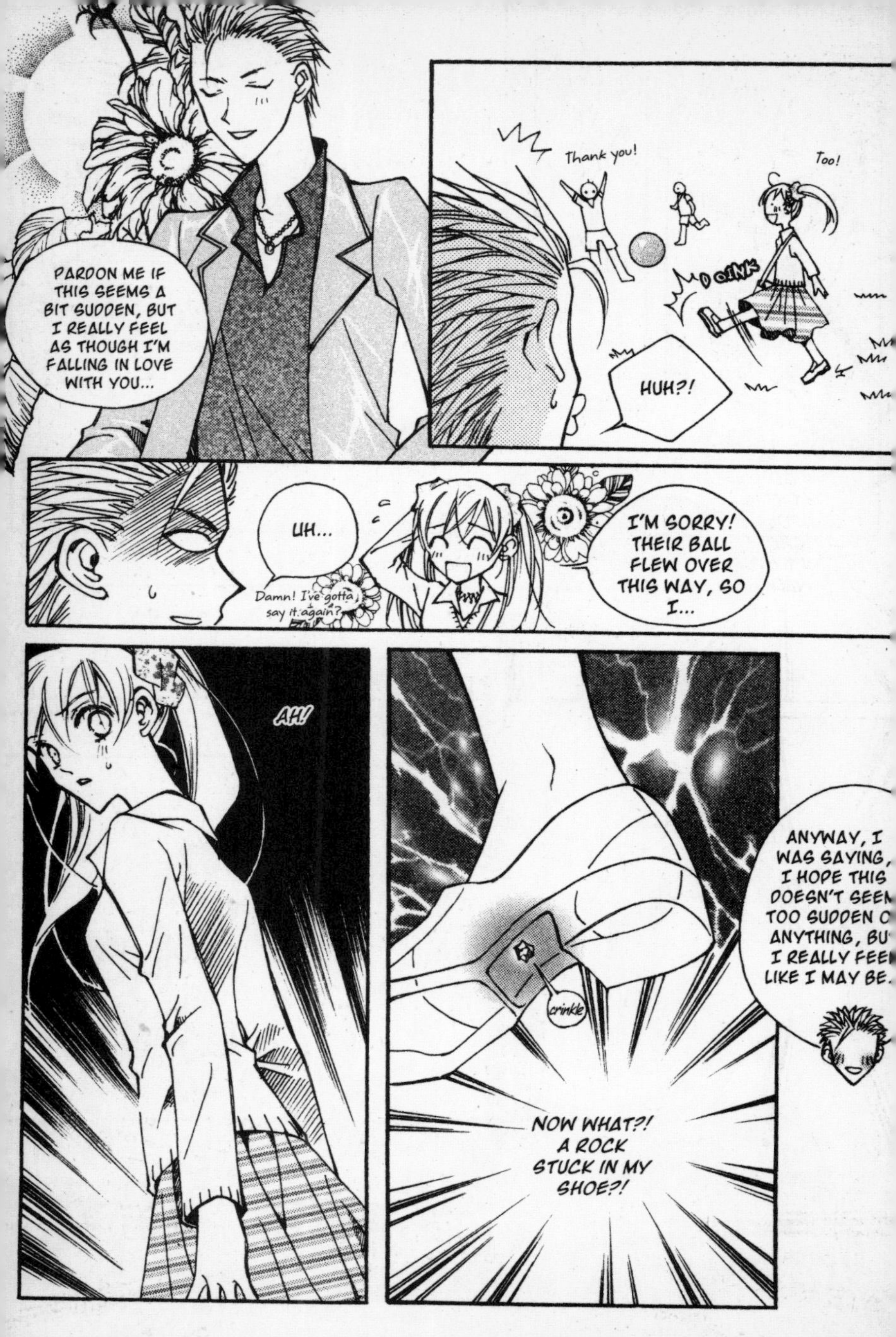

PARDON ME IF THIS SEEMS A BIT SUDDEN, BUT I REALLY FEEL AS THOUGH I'M FALLING IN LOVE WITH YOU...
Thank you!
Too!
DOINK
HUH?!
UH...
Damn! I've gotta say it again?
I'M SORRY! THEIR BALL FLEW OVER THIS WAY, SO I...
AH!
ANYWAY, I WAS SAYING, I HOPE THIS DOESN'T SEEM TOO SUDDEN O ANYTHING, BU I REALLY FEE LIKE I MAY BE.
crinkle
NOW WHAT?! A ROCK STUCK IN MY SHOE?!

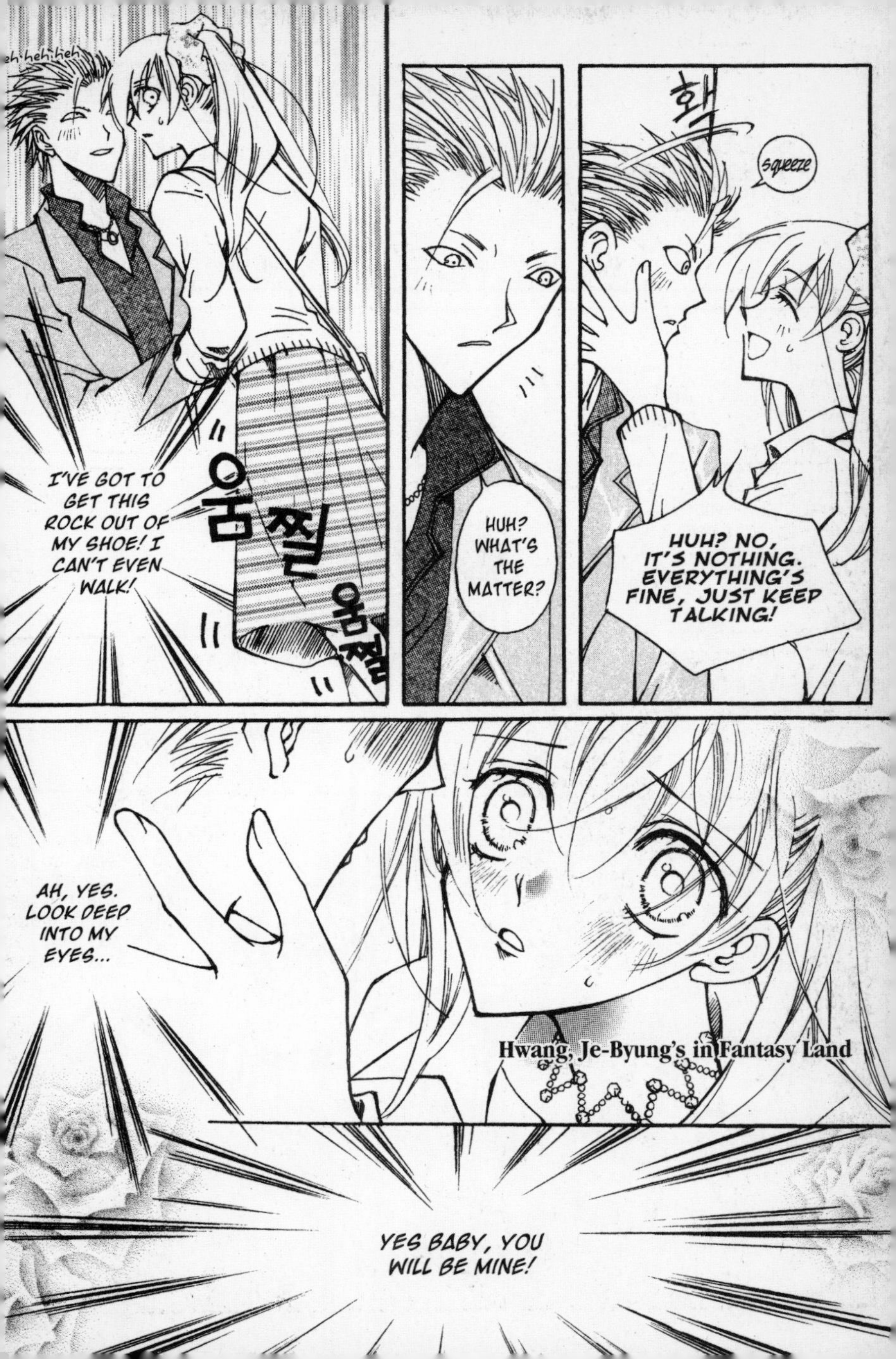
heh heh heh
I'VE GOT TO GET THIS ROCK OUT OF MY SHOE! I CAN'T EVEN WALK!
움찔
움찔
HUH? WHAT'S THE MATTER?
확
squeeze
HUH? NO, IT'S NOTHING. EVERYTHING'S FINE, JUST KEEP TALKING!
AH, YES. LOOK DEEP INTO MY EYES...
Hwang, Je-Byung's in Fantasy Land
YES BABY, YOU WILL BE MINE!

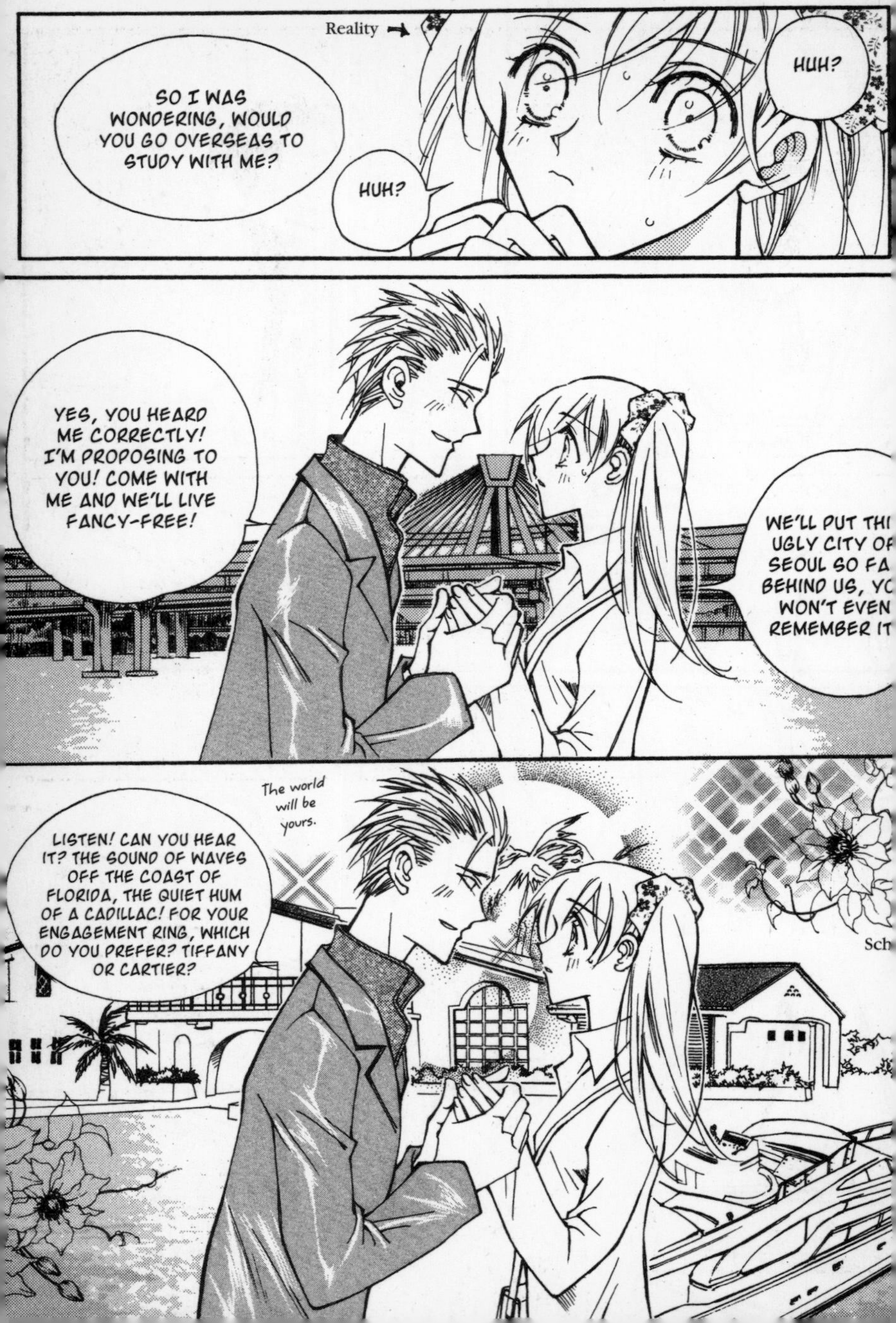
Reality →
SO I WAS WONDERING, WOULD YOU GO OVERSEAS TO STUDY WITH ME?
HUH?
HUH?
YES, YOU HEARD ME CORRECTLY! I'M PROPOSING TO YOU! COME WITH ME AND WE'LL LIVE FANCY-FREE!
WE'LL PUT THI UGLY CITY OF SEOUL SO FA BEHIND US, YO WON'T EVEN REMEMBER IT
The world will be yours.
LISTEN! CAN YOU HEAR IT? THE SOUND OF WAVES OFF THE COAST OF FLORIDA, THE QUIET HUM OF A CADILLAC! FOR YOUR ENGAGEMENT RING, WHICH DO YOU PREFER? TIFFANY OR CARTIER?
Sch

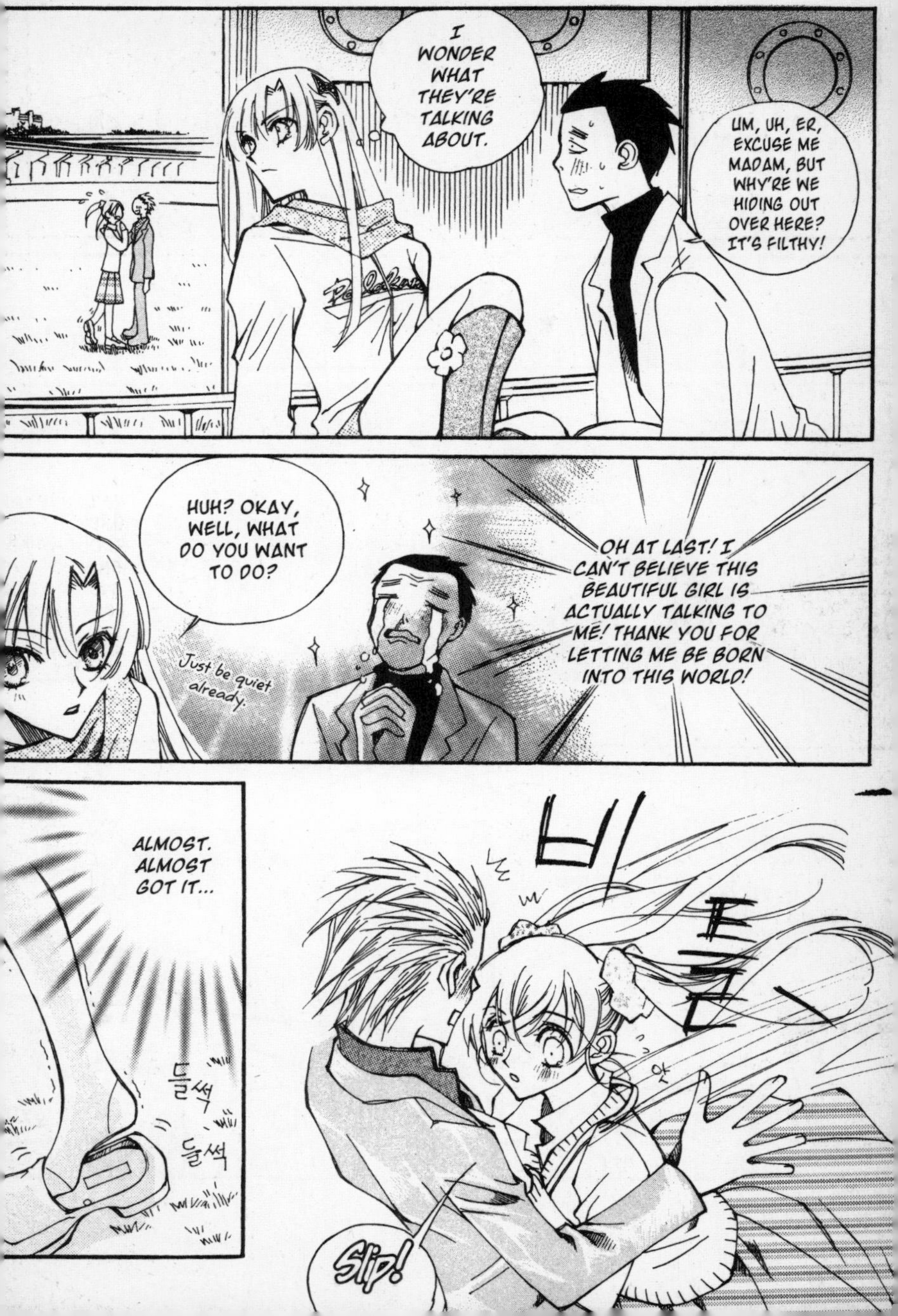

I WONDER WHAT THEY'RE TALKING ABOUT.
UM, UH, ER, EXCUSE ME MADAM, BUT WHY'RE WE HIDING OUT OVER HERE? IT'S FILTHY!
HUH? OKAY, WELL, WHAT DO YOU WANT TO DO?
Just be quiet already.
OH AT LAST! I CAN'T BELIEVE THIS BEAUTIFUL GIRL IS ACTUALLY TALKING TO ME! THANK YOU FOR LETTING ME BE BORN INTO THIS WORLD!
ALMOST. ALMOST GOT IT...
들썩
들썩
앗
Slip!

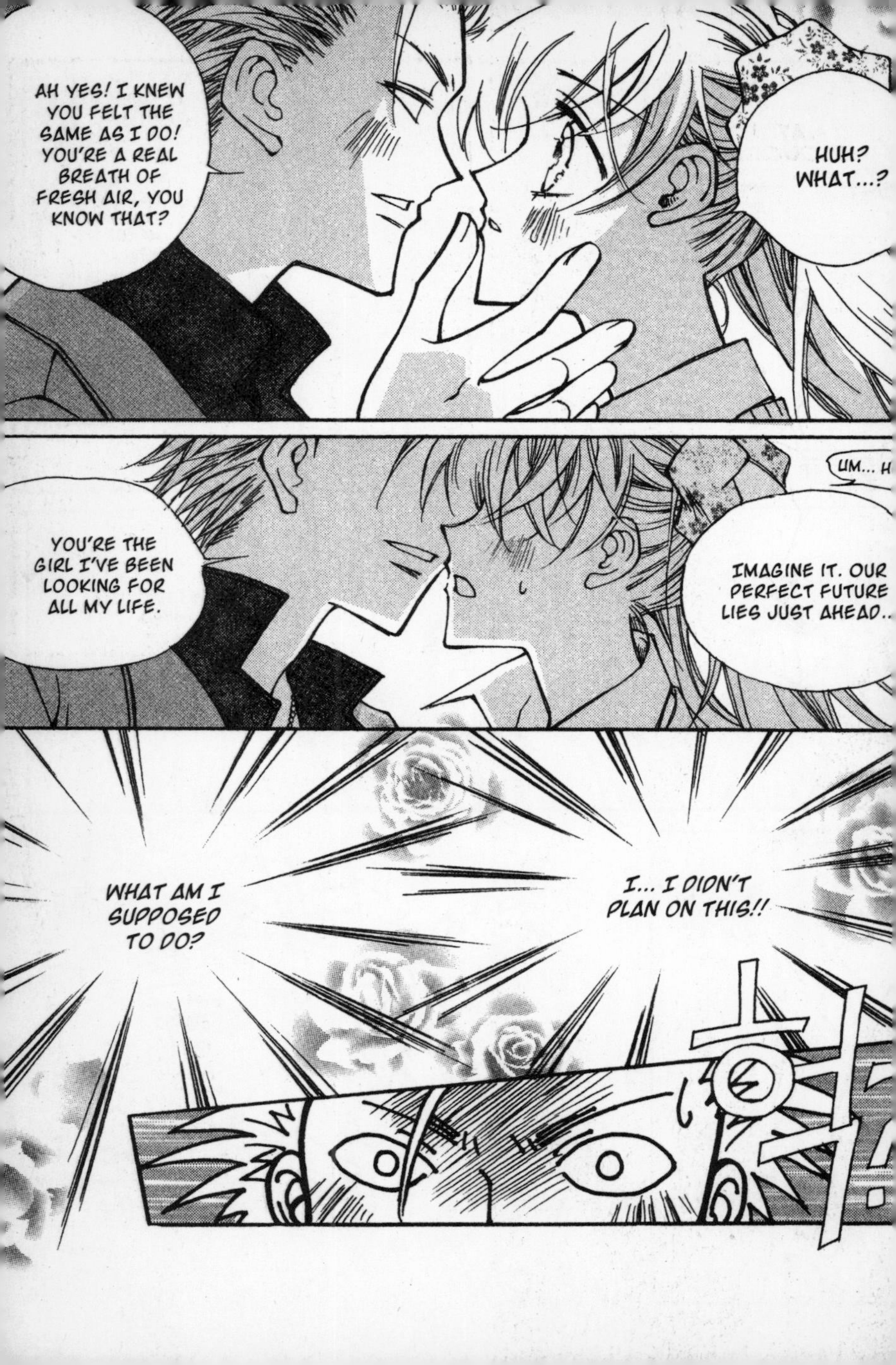
AH YES! I KNEW YOU FELT THE SAME AS I DO! YOU'RE A REAL BREATH OF FRESH AIR, YOU KNOW THAT?
HUH? WHAT...?
YOU'RE THE GIRL I'VE BEEN LOOKING FOR ALL MY LIFE.
UM... H
IMAGINE IT. OUR PERFECT FUTURE LIES JUST AHEAD...
WHAT AM I SUPPOSED TO DO?
I... I DIDN'T PLAN ON THIS!!

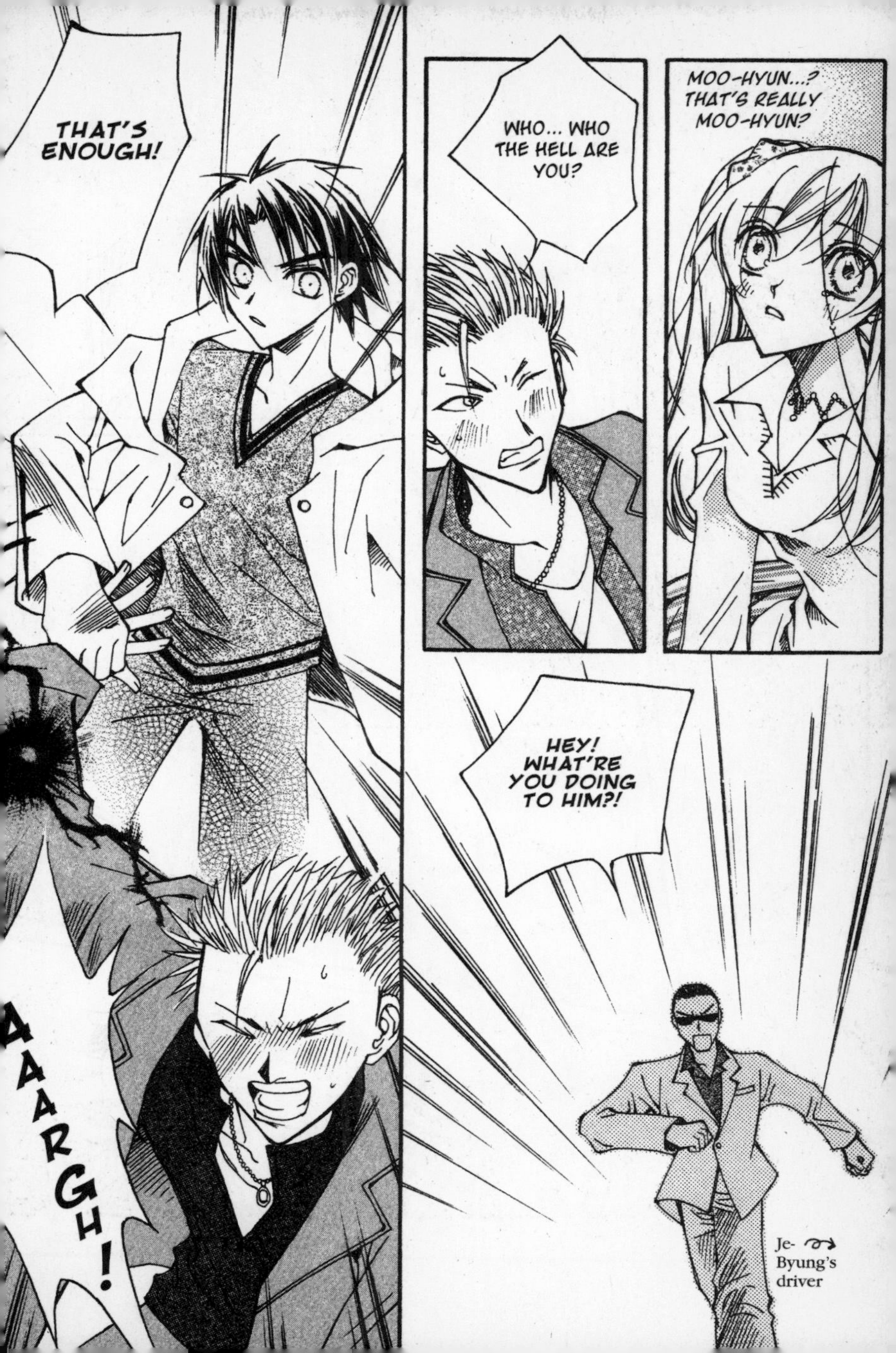
THAT'S ENOUGH!
AAARGH!
WHO... WHO THE HELL ARE YOU?
MOO-HYUN...? THAT'S REALLY MOO-HYUN?
HEY! WHAT'RE YOU DOING TO HIM?!
Je-Byung's driver

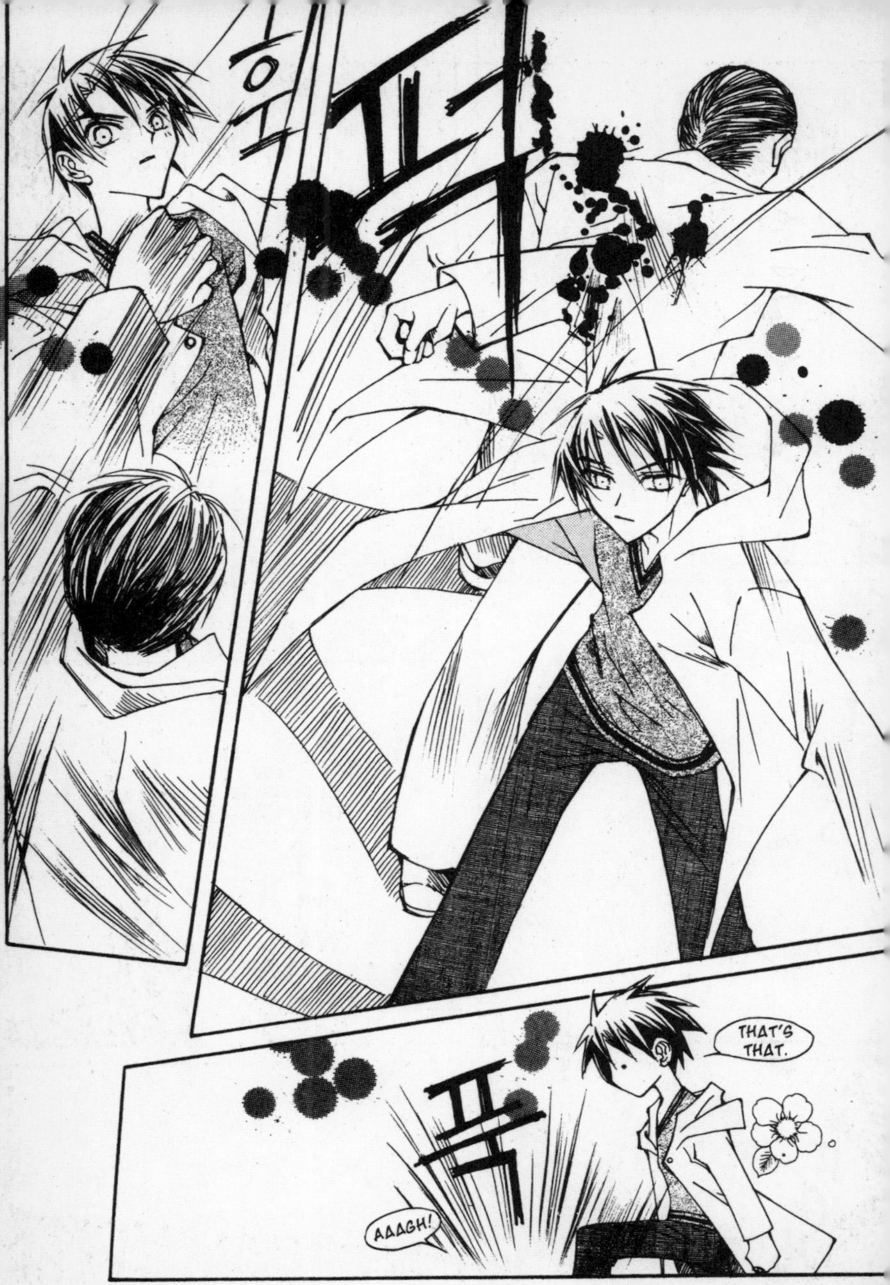
푹
AAAGH!
THAT'S THAT.

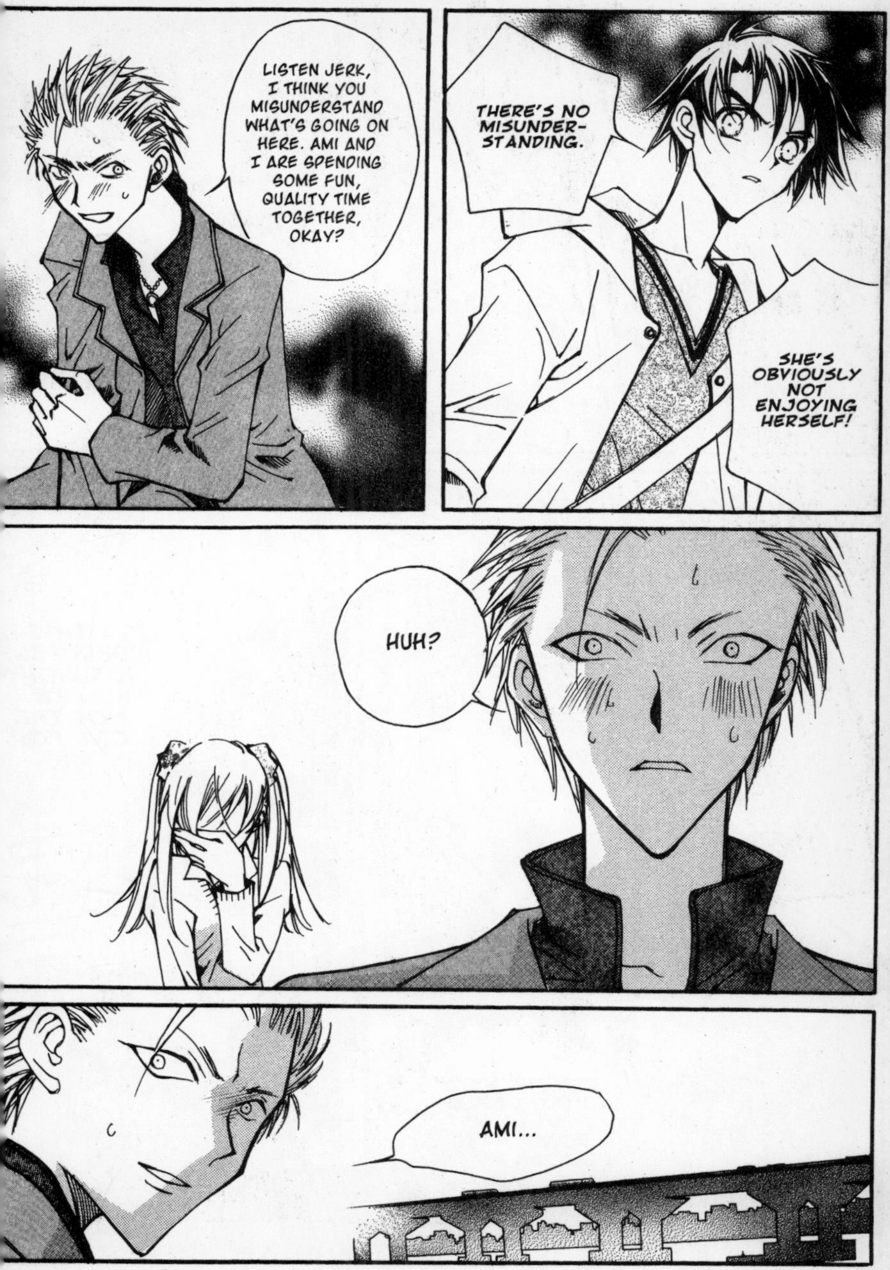
LISTEN JERK, I THINK YOU MISUNDERSTAND WHAT'S GOING ON HERE. AMI AND I ARE SPENDING SOME FUN, QUALITY TIME TOGETHER, OKAY?
THERE'S NO MISUNDER-STANDING.
SHE'S OBVIOUSLY NOT ENJOYING HERSELF!
HUH?
AMI...

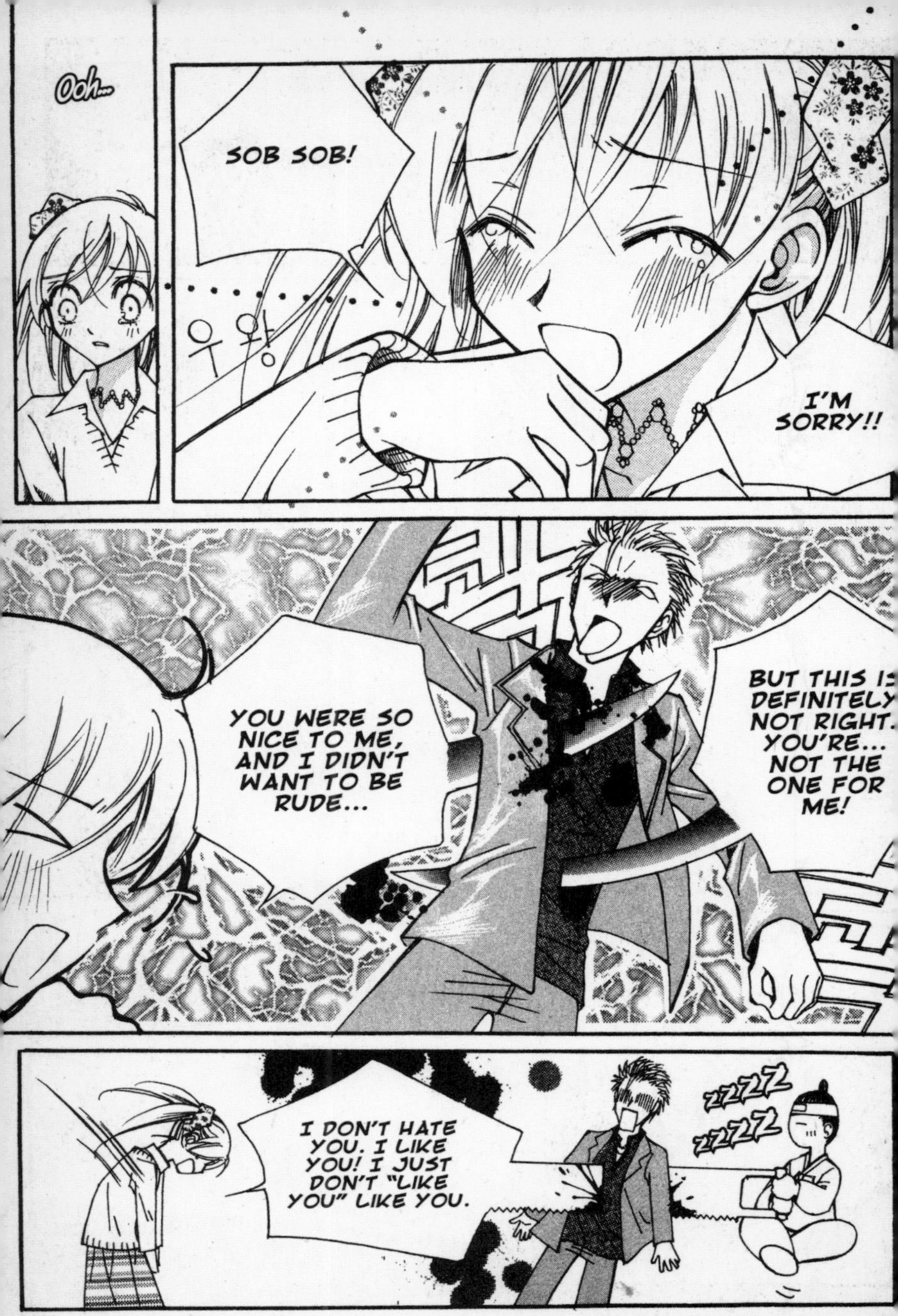
Ooh...
SOB SOB!
I'M SORRY!!
YOU WERE SO NICE TO ME, AND I DIDN'T WANT TO BE RUDE...
BUT THIS IS DEFINITELY NOT RIGHT. YOU'RE... NOT THE ONE FOR ME!
I DON'T HATE YOU. I LIKE YOU! I JUST DON'T "LIKE YOU" LIKE YOU.
ZZZZZ
ZZZZZ

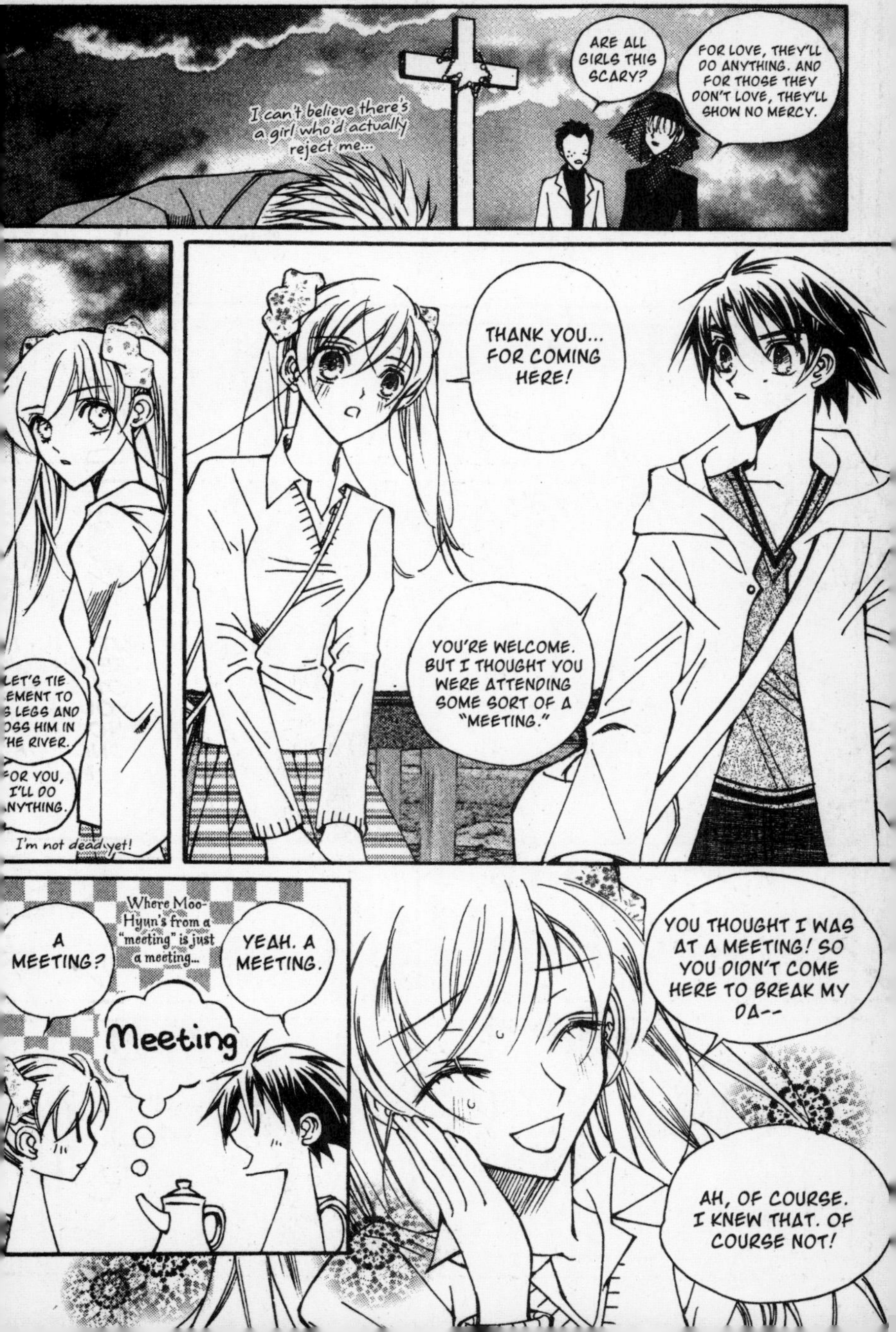
I can't believe there's a girl who'd actually reject me...
ARE ALL GIRLS THIS SCARY?
FOR LOVE, THEY'LL DO ANYTHING. AND FOR THOSE THEY DON'T LOVE, THEY'LL SHOW NO MERCY.
LET'S TIE EMENT TO S LEGS AND OSS HIM IN THE RIVER.
FOR YOU, I'LL DO NYTHING.
I'm not dead yet!
THANK YOU... FOR COMING HERE!
YOU'RE WELCOME. BUT I THOUGHT YOU WERE ATTENDING SOME SORT OF A "MEETING."
A MEETING?
Where Moo-Hyun's from a "meeting" is just a meeting...
YEAH. A MEETING.
Meeting
YOU THOUGHT I WAS AT A MEETING! SO YOU DIDN'T COME HERE TO BREAK MY DA--
AH, OF COURSE. I KNEW THAT. OF COURSE NOT!

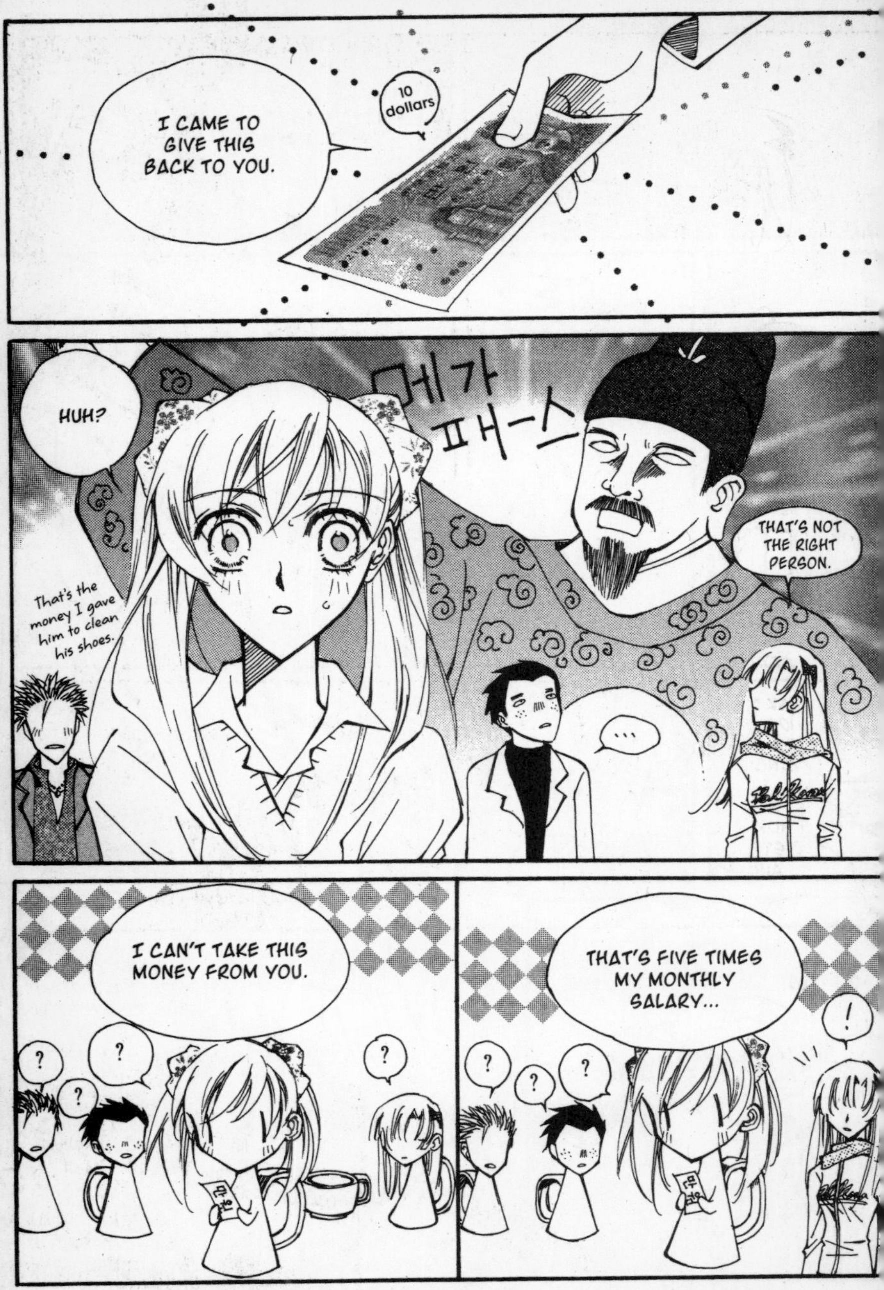
I CAME TO GIVE THIS BACK TO YOU.
10 dollars
HUH?
메가 패스
That's the money I gave him to clean his shoes.
THAT'S NOT THE RIGHT PERSON.
...
I CAN'T TAKE THIS MONEY FROM YOU.
?
?
?
?
THAT'S FIVE TIMES MY MONTHLY SALARY...
?
?
?
!

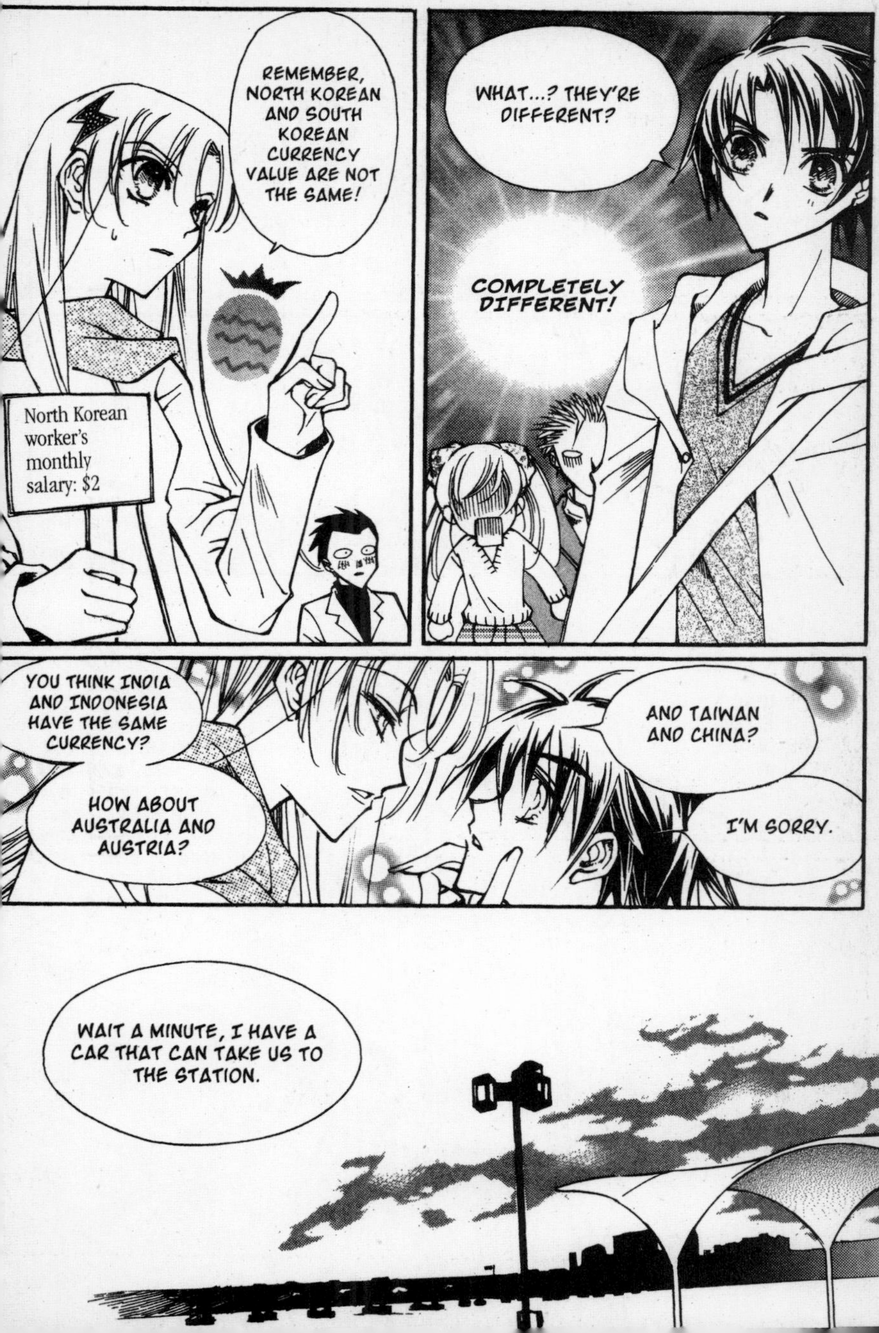
REMEMBER, NORTH KOREAN AND SOUTH KOREAN CURRENCY VALUE ARE NOT THE SAME!
North Korean worker's monthly salary: $2
WHAT...? THEY'RE DIFFERENT?
COMPLETELY DIFFERENT!
YOU THINK INDIA AND INDONESIA HAVE THE SAME CURRENCY?
HOW ABOUT AUSTRALIA AND AUSTRIA?
AND TAIWAN AND CHINA?
I'M SORRY.
WAIT A MINUTE, I HAVE A CAR THAT CAN TAKE US TO THE STATION.

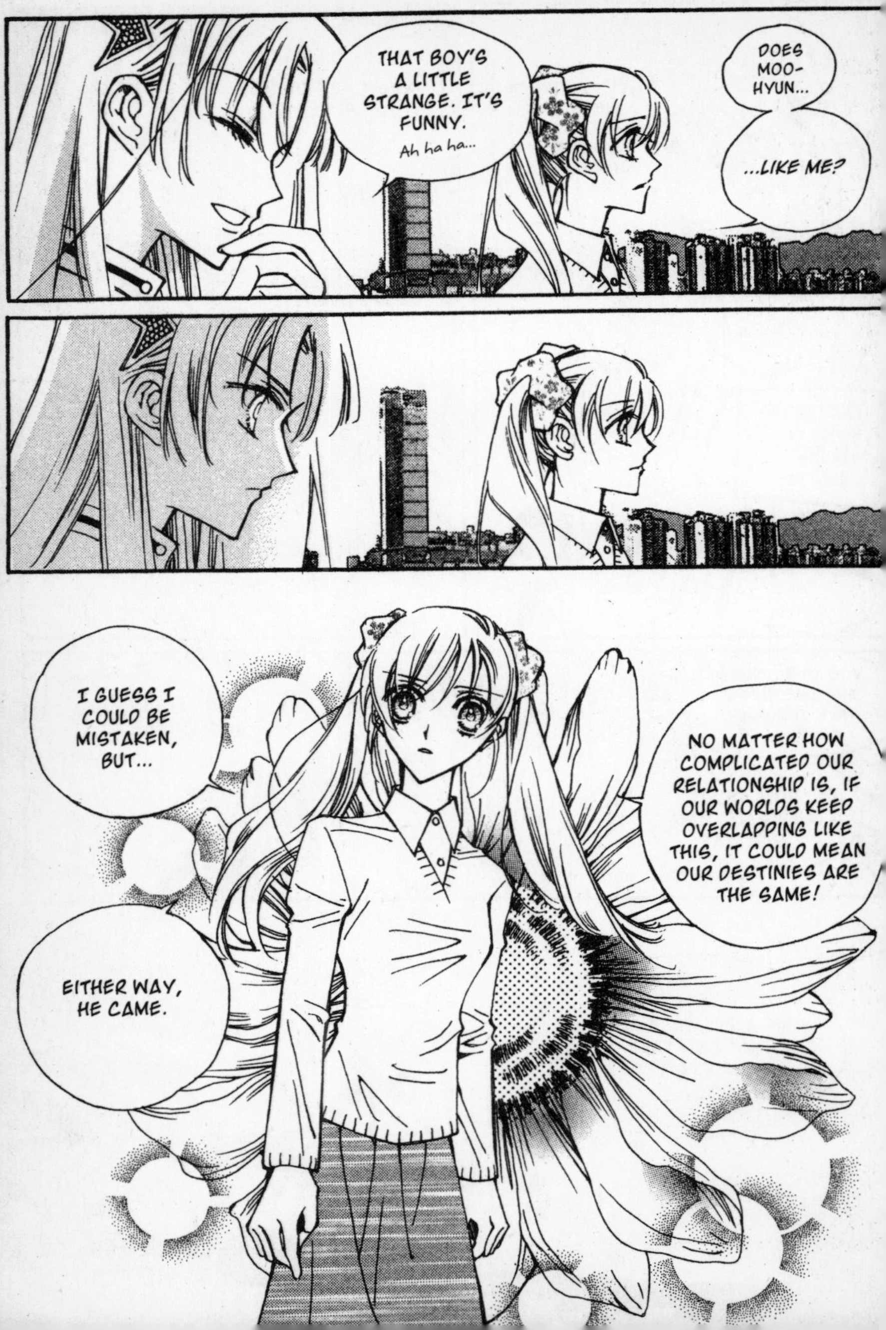
THAT BOY'S A LITTLE STRANGE. IT'S FUNNY.
Ah ha ha...
DOES MOO-HYUN...
...LIKE ME?
I GUESS I COULD BE MISTAKEN, BUT...
NO MATTER HOW COMPLICATED OUR RELATIONSHIP IS, IF OUR WORLDS KEEP OVERLAPPING LIKE THIS, IT COULD MEAN OUR DESTINIES ARE THE SAME!
EITHER WAY, HE CAME.

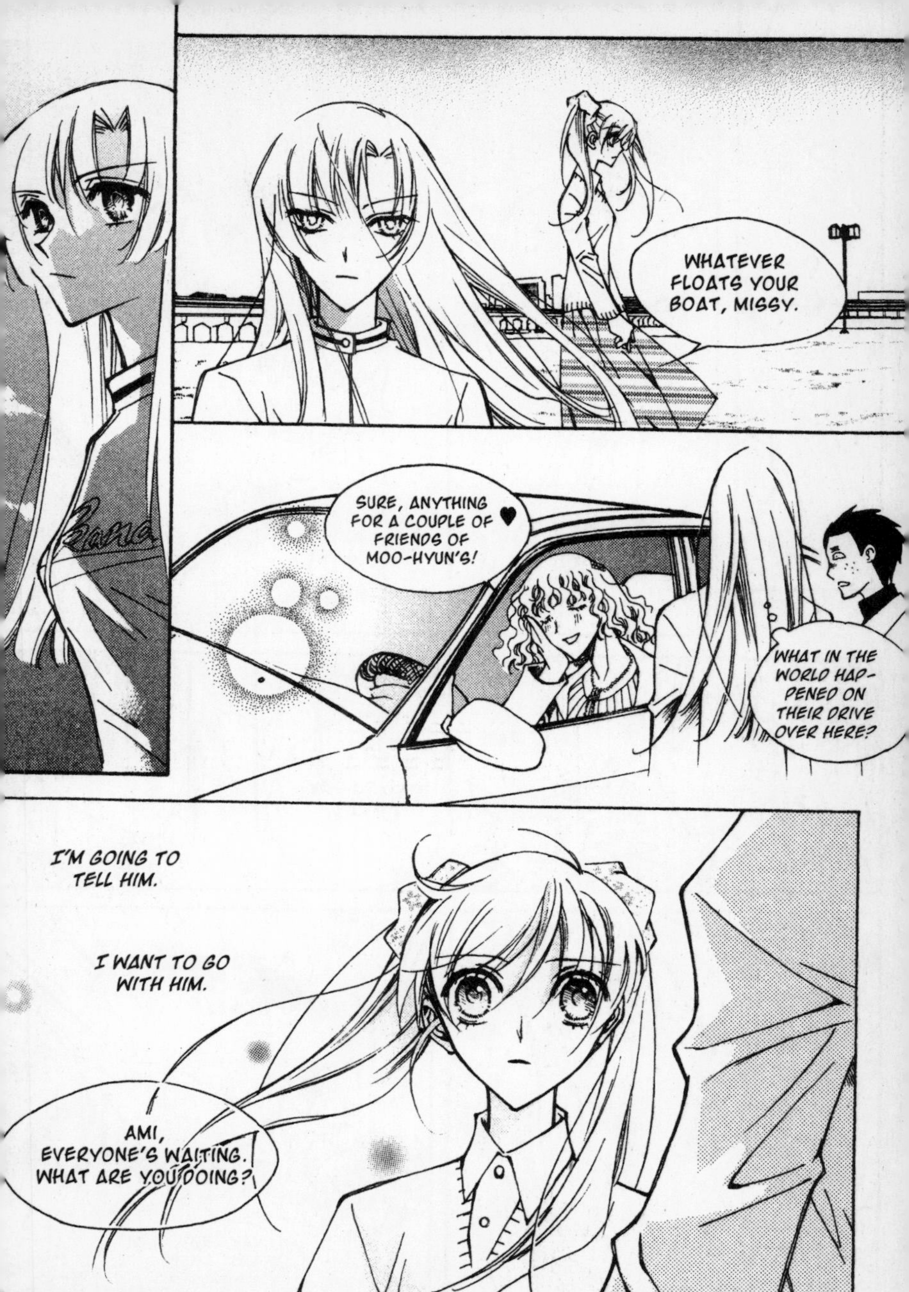
WHATEVER FLOATS YOUR BOAT, MISSY.
SURE, ANYTHING FOR A COUPLE OF FRIENDS OF MOO-HYUN'S! ♥
WHAT IN THE WORLD HAP-PENED ON THEIR DRIVE OVER HERE?
I'M GOING TO TELL HIM.
I WANT TO GO WITH HIM.
AMI, EVERYONE'S WAITING. WHAT ARE YOU DOING?

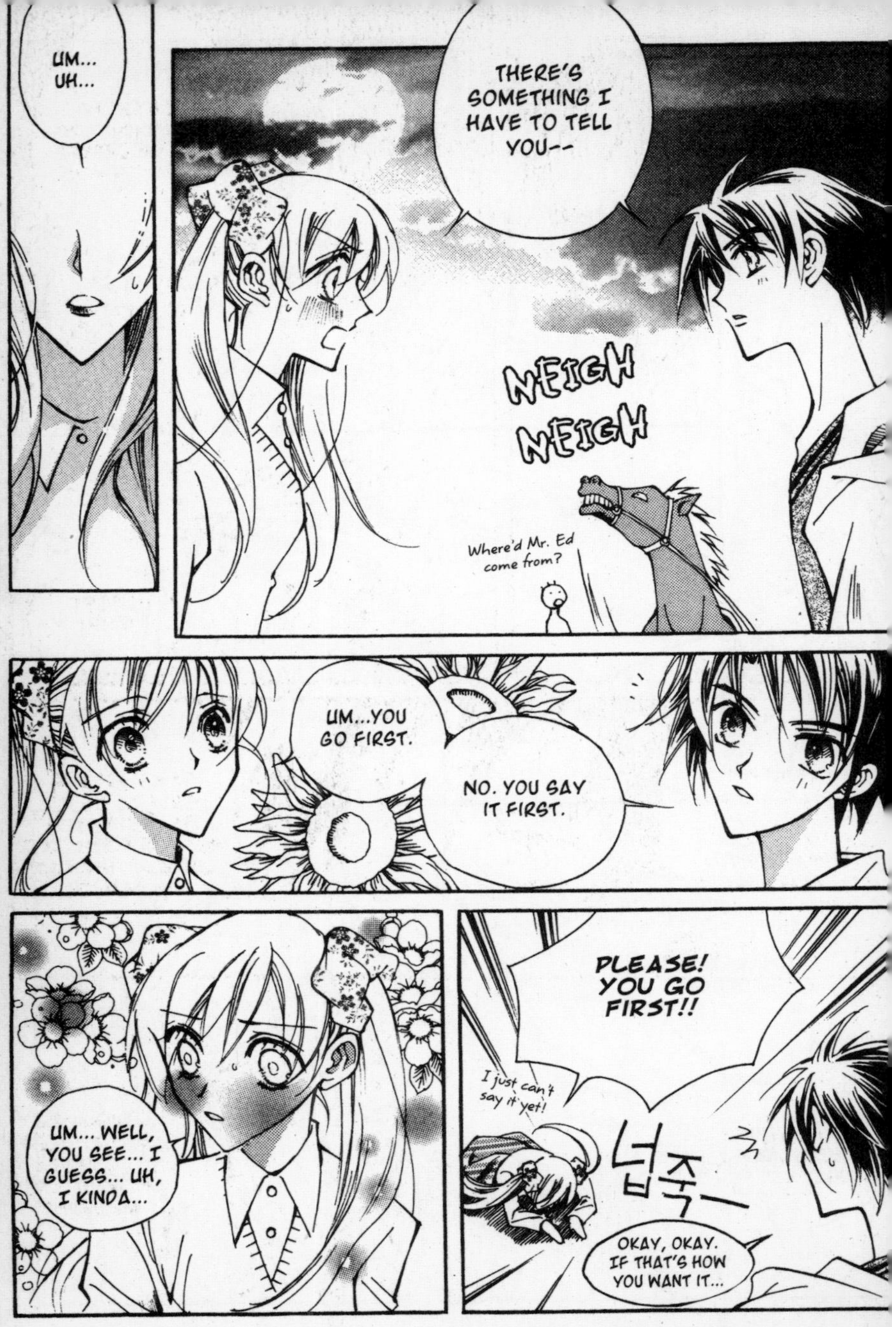
UM...
UH...
THERE'S SOMETHING I HAVE TO TELL YOU--
NEIGH
NEIGH
Where'd Mr. Ed come from?
UM...YOU GO FIRST.
NO. YOU SAY IT FIRST.
UM... WELL, YOU SEE... I GUESS... UH, I KINDA...
PLEASE! YOU GO FIRST!!
I just can't say it yet!
넙죽
OKAY, OKAY. IF THAT'S HOW YOU WANT IT...

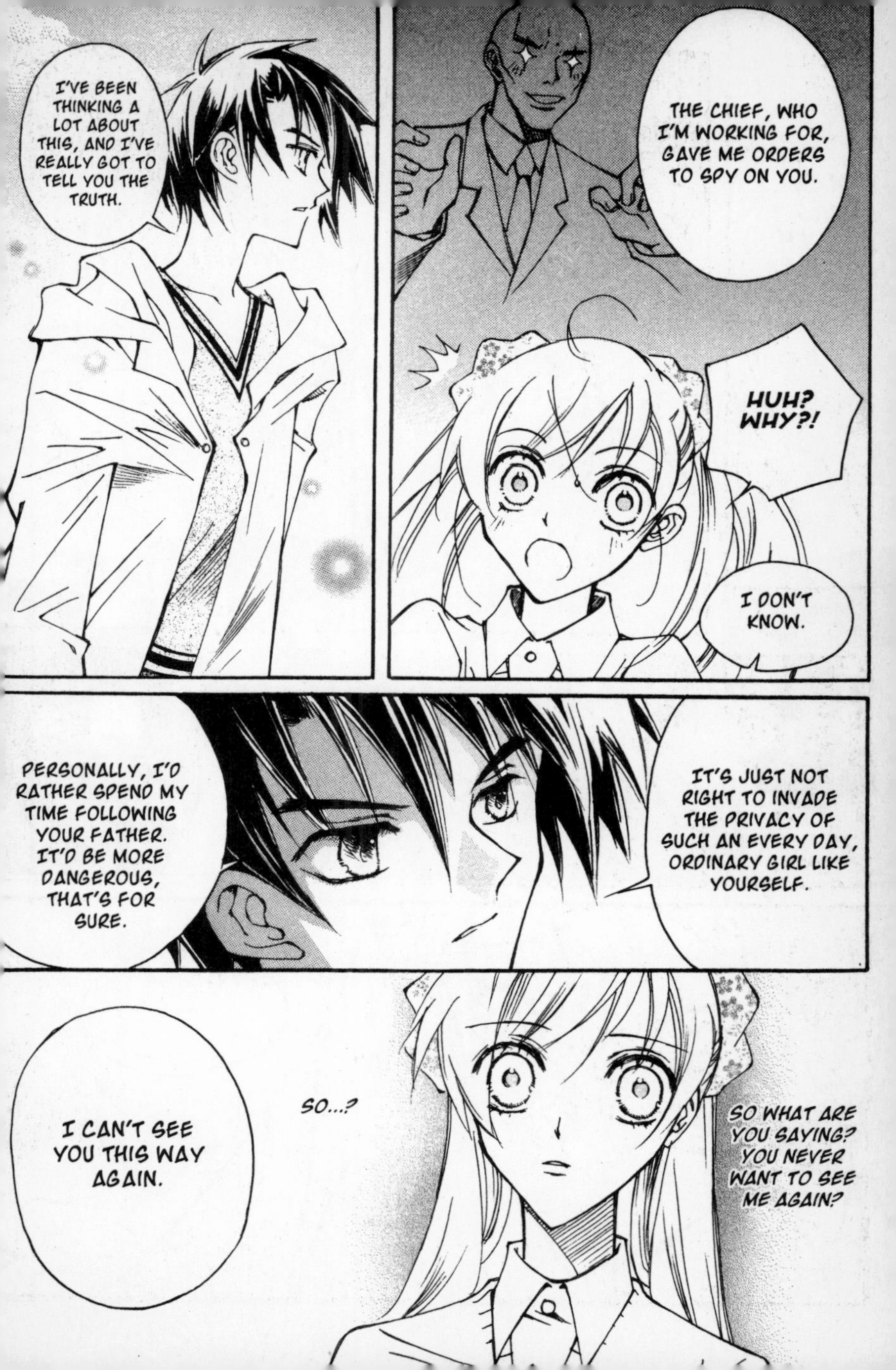
I'VE BEEN THINKING A LOT ABOUT THIS, AND I'VE REALLY GOT TO TELL YOU THE TRUTH.
THE CHIEF, WHO I'M WORKING FOR, GAVE ME ORDERS TO SPY ON YOU.
HUH? WHY?!
I DON'T KNOW.
PERSONALLY, I'D RATHER SPEND MY TIME FOLLOWING YOUR FATHER. IT'D BE MORE DANGEROUS, THAT'S FOR SURE.
IT'S JUST NOT RIGHT TO INVADE THE PRIVACY OF SUCH AN EVERY DAY, ORDINARY GIRL LIKE YOURSELF.
I CAN'T SEE YOU THIS WAY AGAIN.
SO...?
SO WHAT ARE YOU SAYING? YOU NEVER WANT TO SEE ME AGAIN?

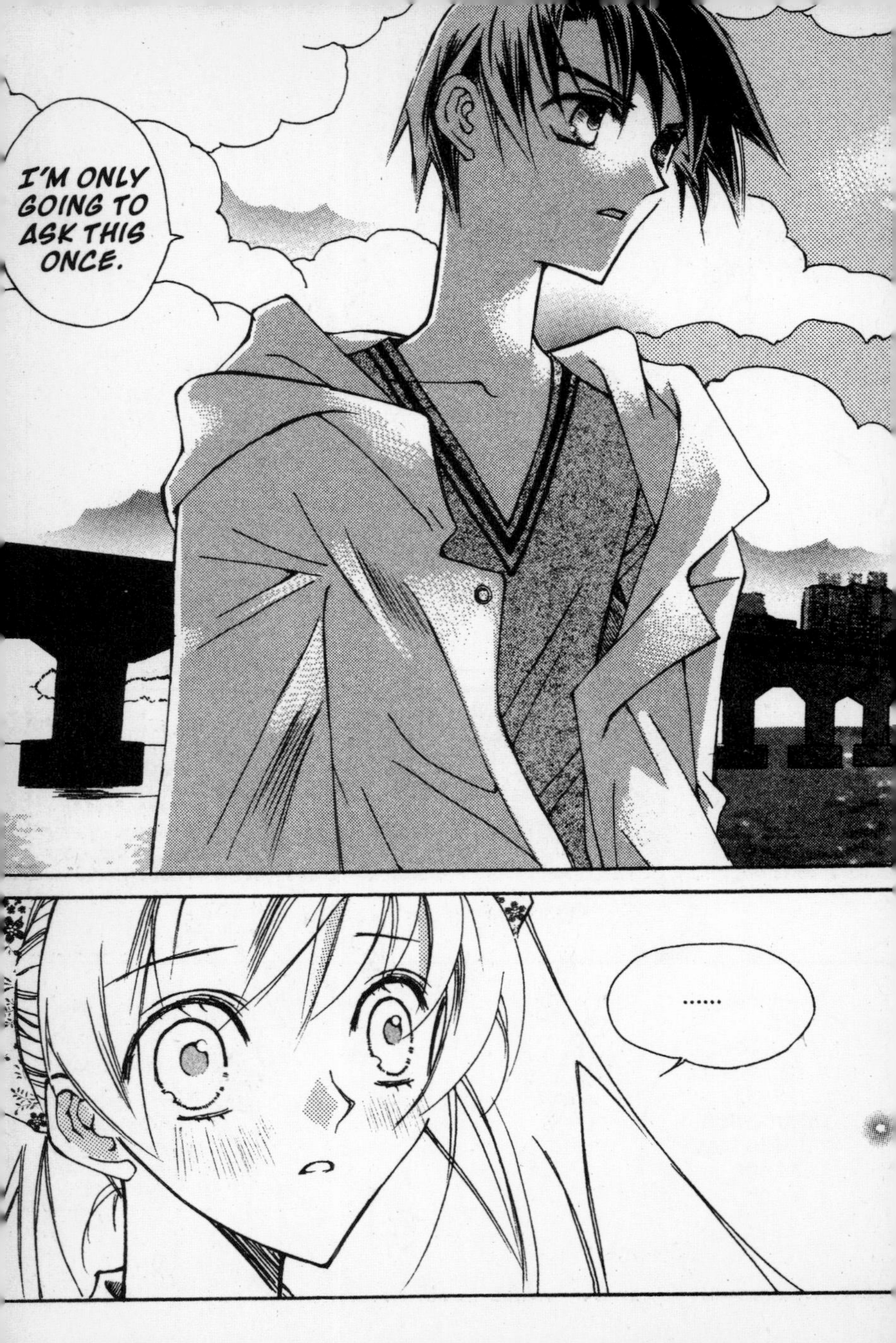
I'M ONLY GOING TO ASK THIS ONCE.
......

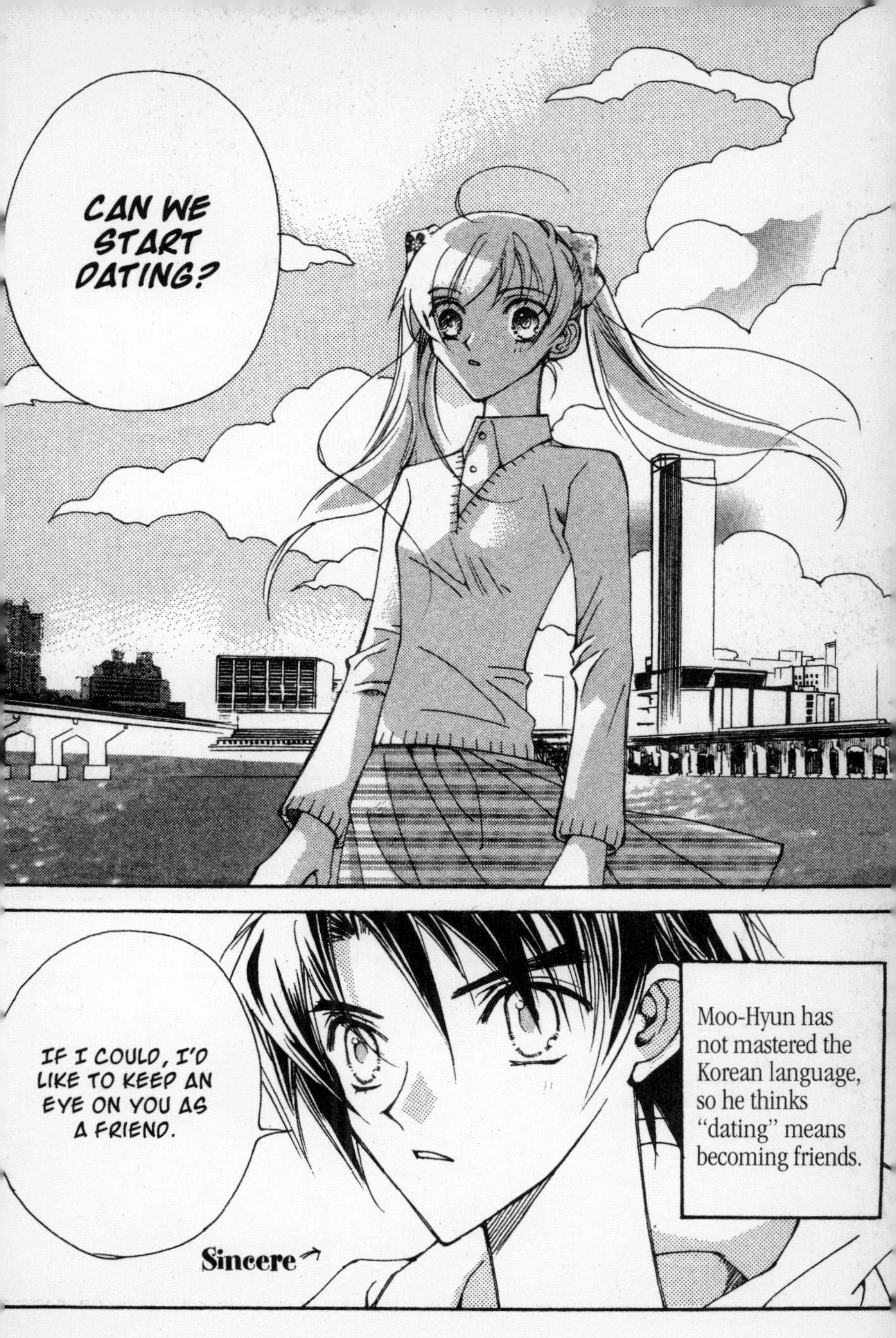
CAN WE START DATING?
IF I COULD, I'D LIKE TO KEEP AN EYE ON YOU AS A FRIEND.
Moo-Hyun has not mastered the Korean language, so he thinks "dating" means becoming friends.
Sincere

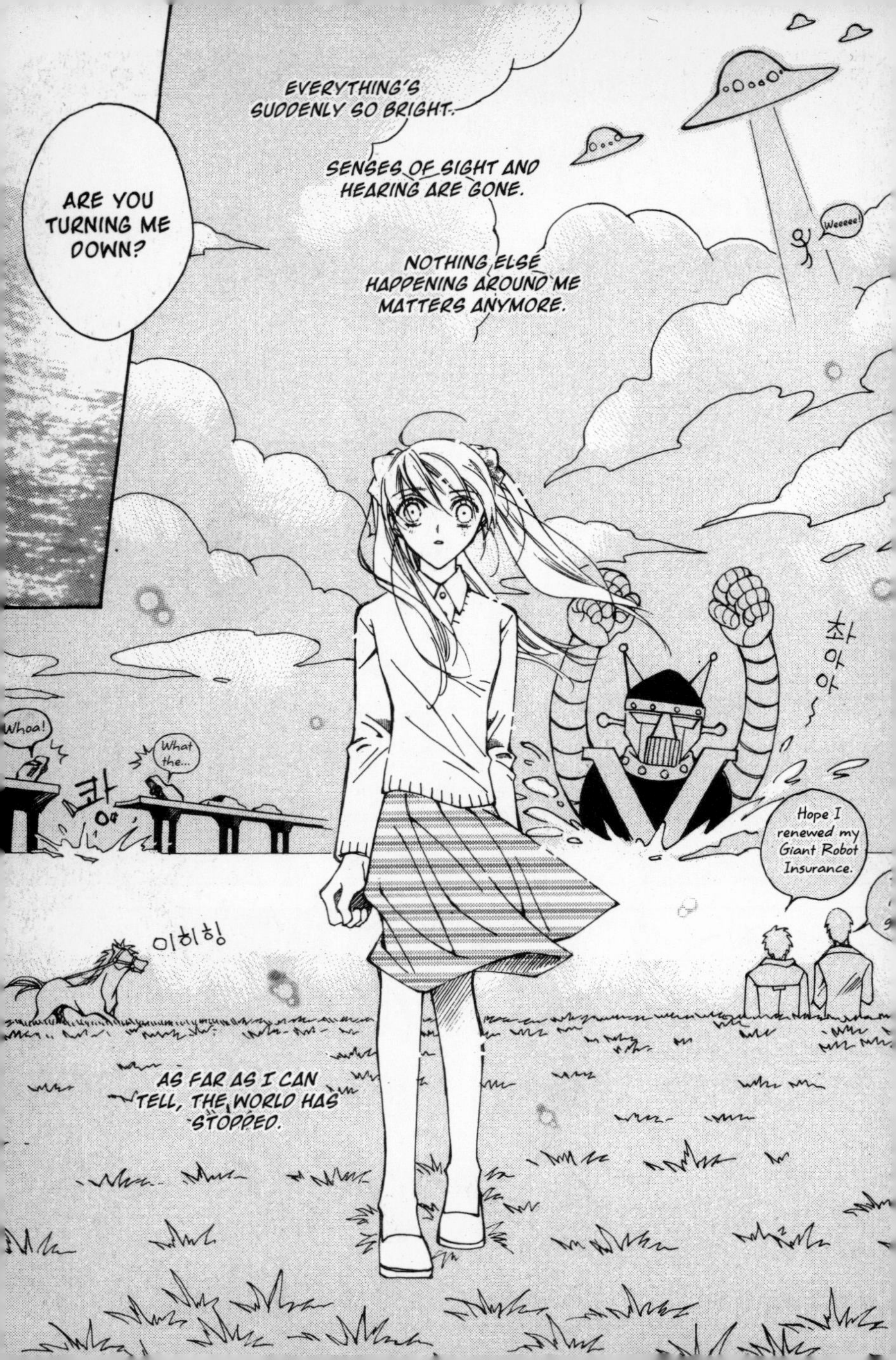
ARE YOU TURNING ME DOWN?
EVERYTHING'S SUDDENLY SO BRIGHT.
SENSES OF SIGHT AND HEARING ARE GONE.
Weeeee!
NOTHING ELSE HAPPENING AROUND ME MATTERS ANYMORE.
Whoa!
What the...
콰아
촤아아
Hope I renewed my Giant Robot Insurance.
이히힝
AS FAR AS I CAN TELL, THE WORLD HAS STOPPED.

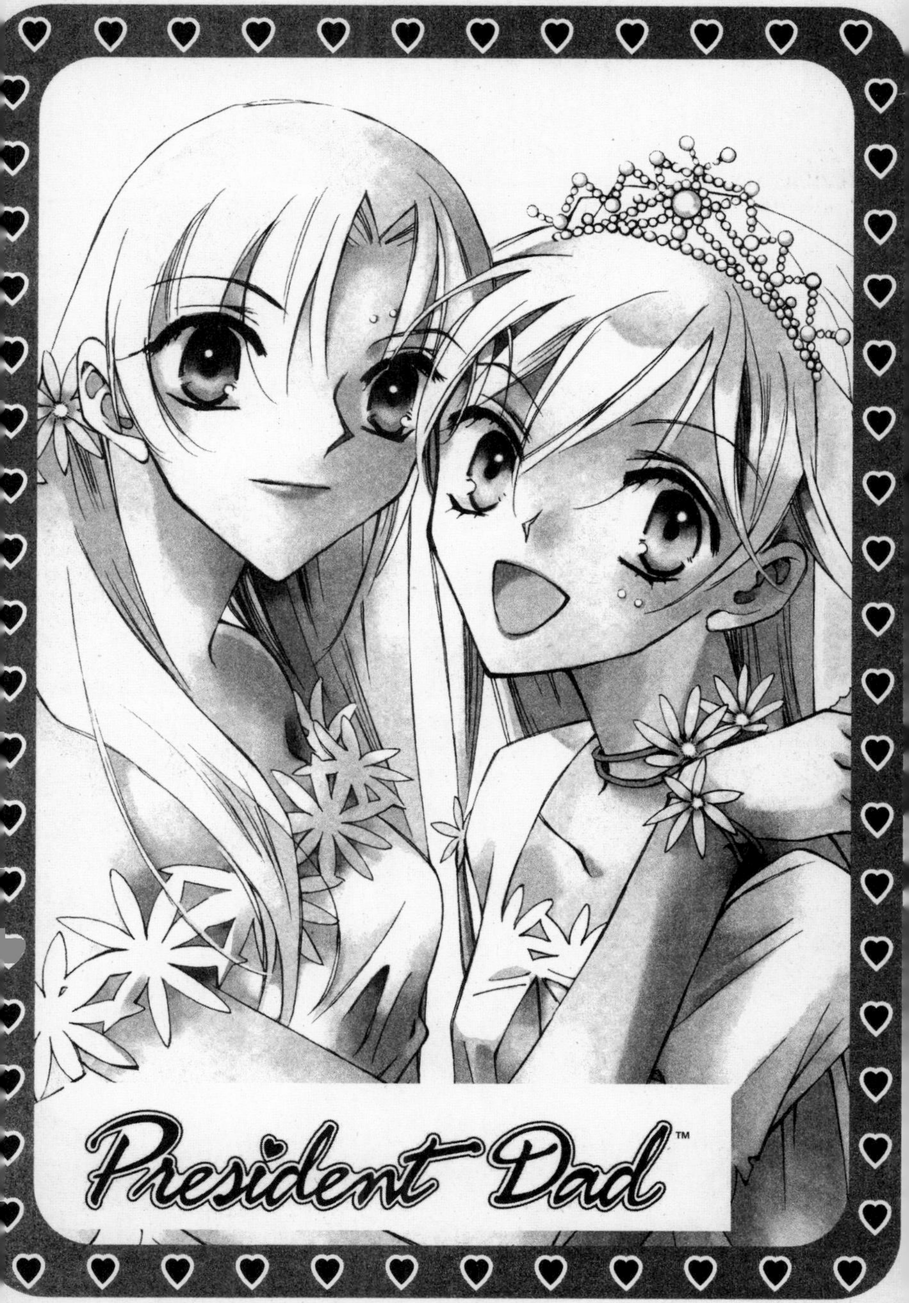
President Dad™

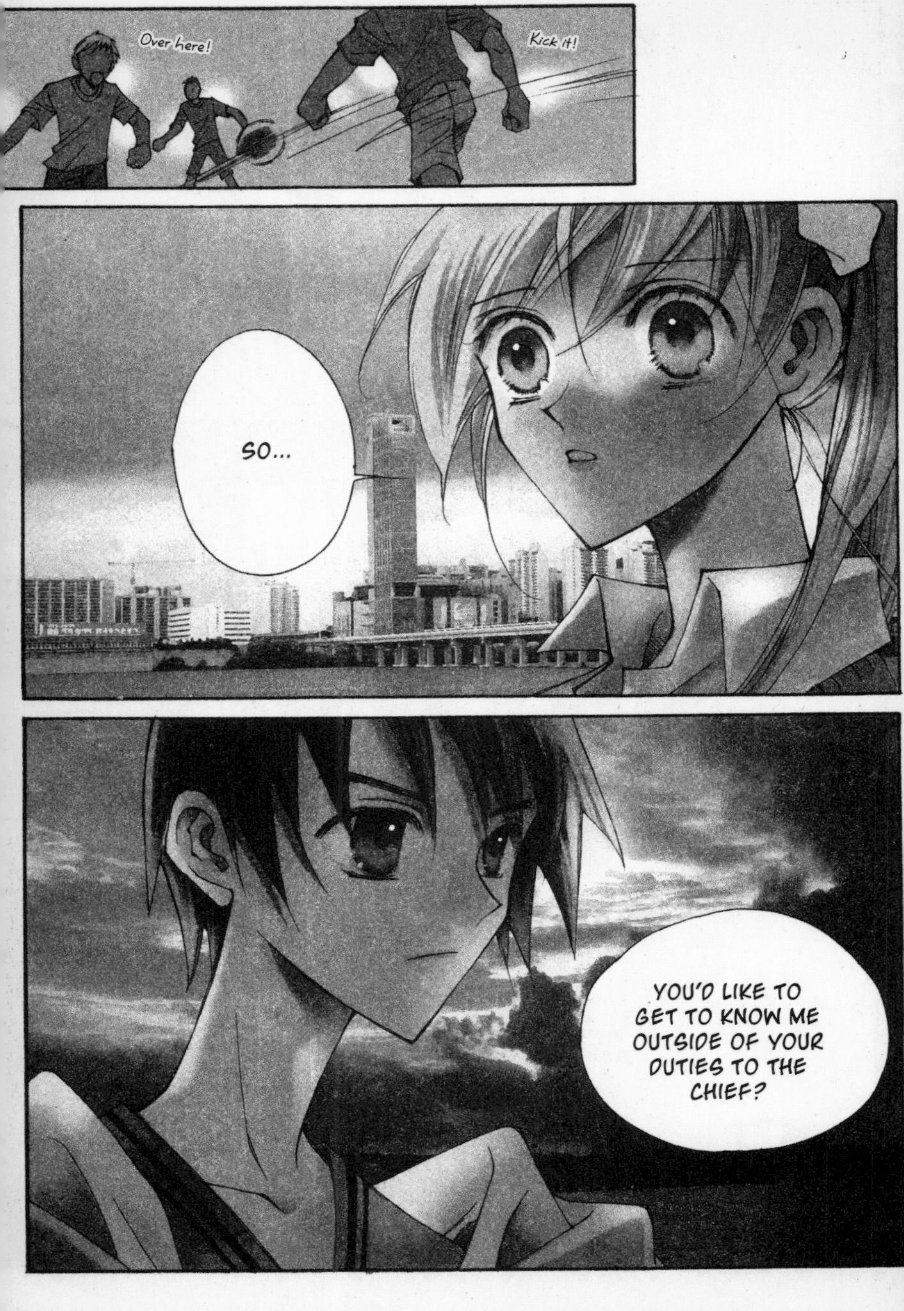
Over here!
Kick it!
SO...
YOU'D LIKE TO GET TO KNOW ME OUTSIDE OF YOUR DUTIES TO THE CHIEF?

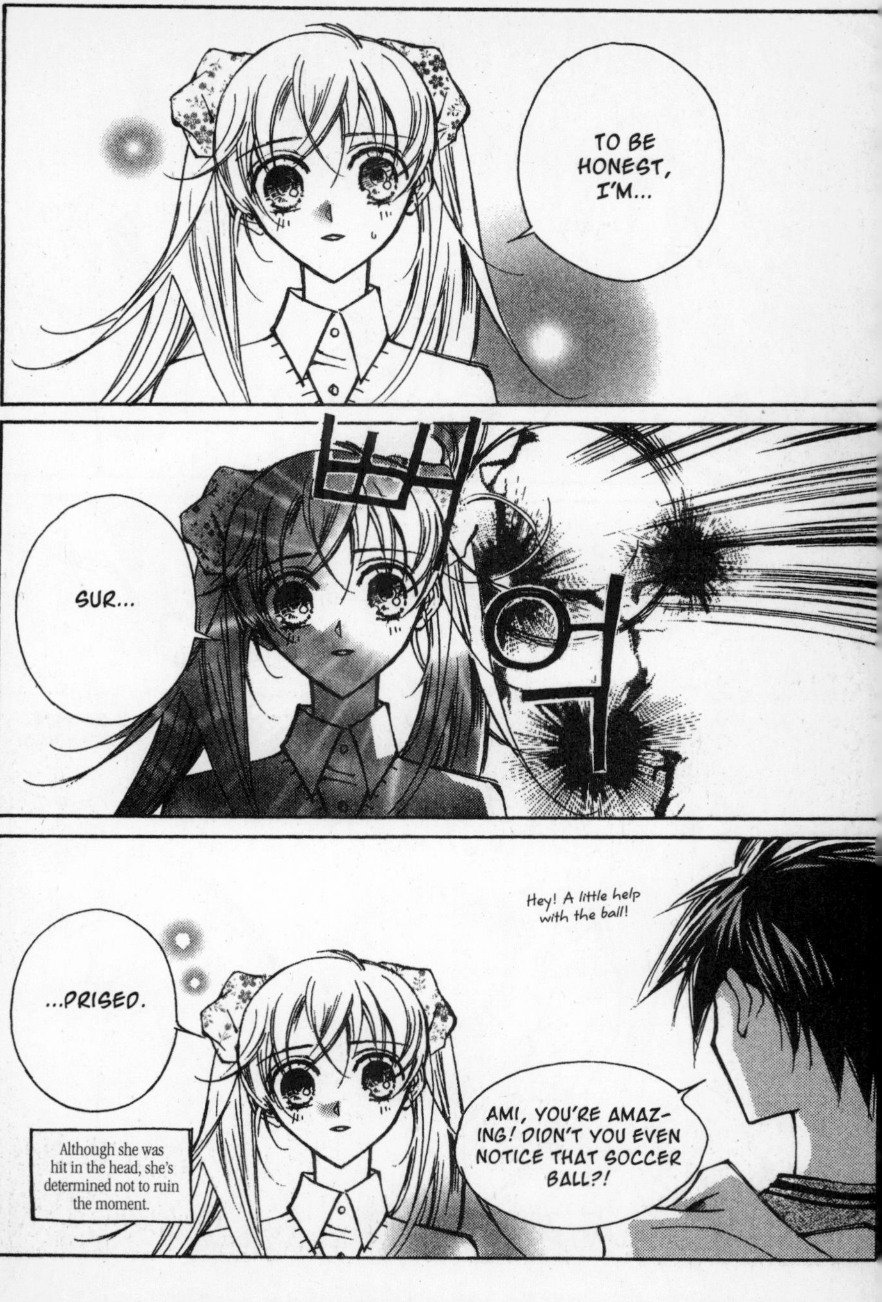
TO BE HONEST, I'M...
SUR...
...PRISED.
Hey! A little help with the ball!
AMI, YOU'RE AMAZ-ING! DIDN'T YOU EVEN NOTICE THAT SOCCER BALL?!
Although she was hit in the head, she's determined not to ruin the moment.

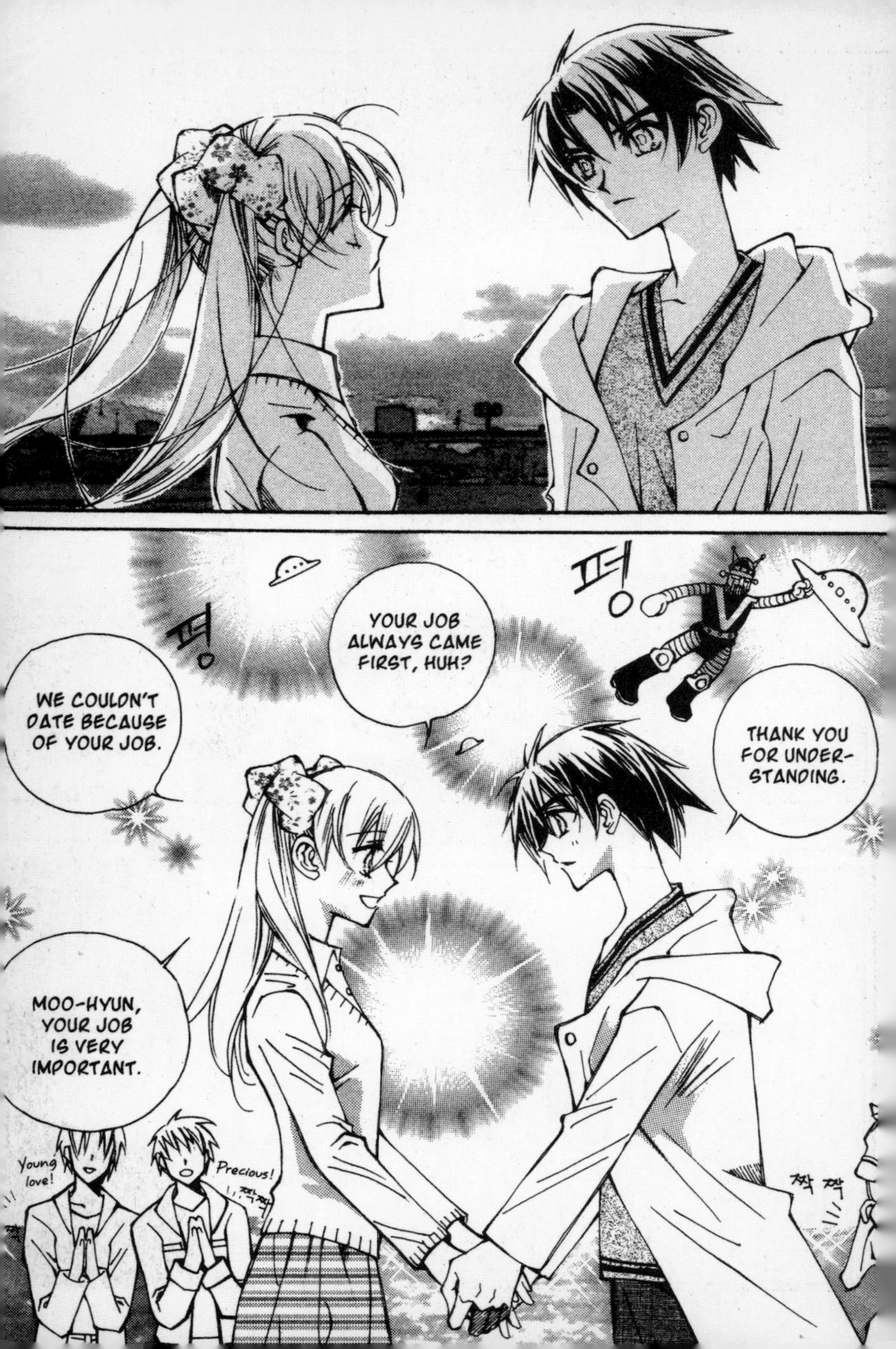

펑
WE COULDN'T DATE BECAUSE OF YOUR JOB.
YOUR JOB ALWAYS CAME FIRST, HUH?
펑
THANK YOU FOR UNDER-STANDING.
MOO-HYUN, YOUR JOB IS VERY IMPORTANT.
Young love!
Precious!
짝짝
짝 짝

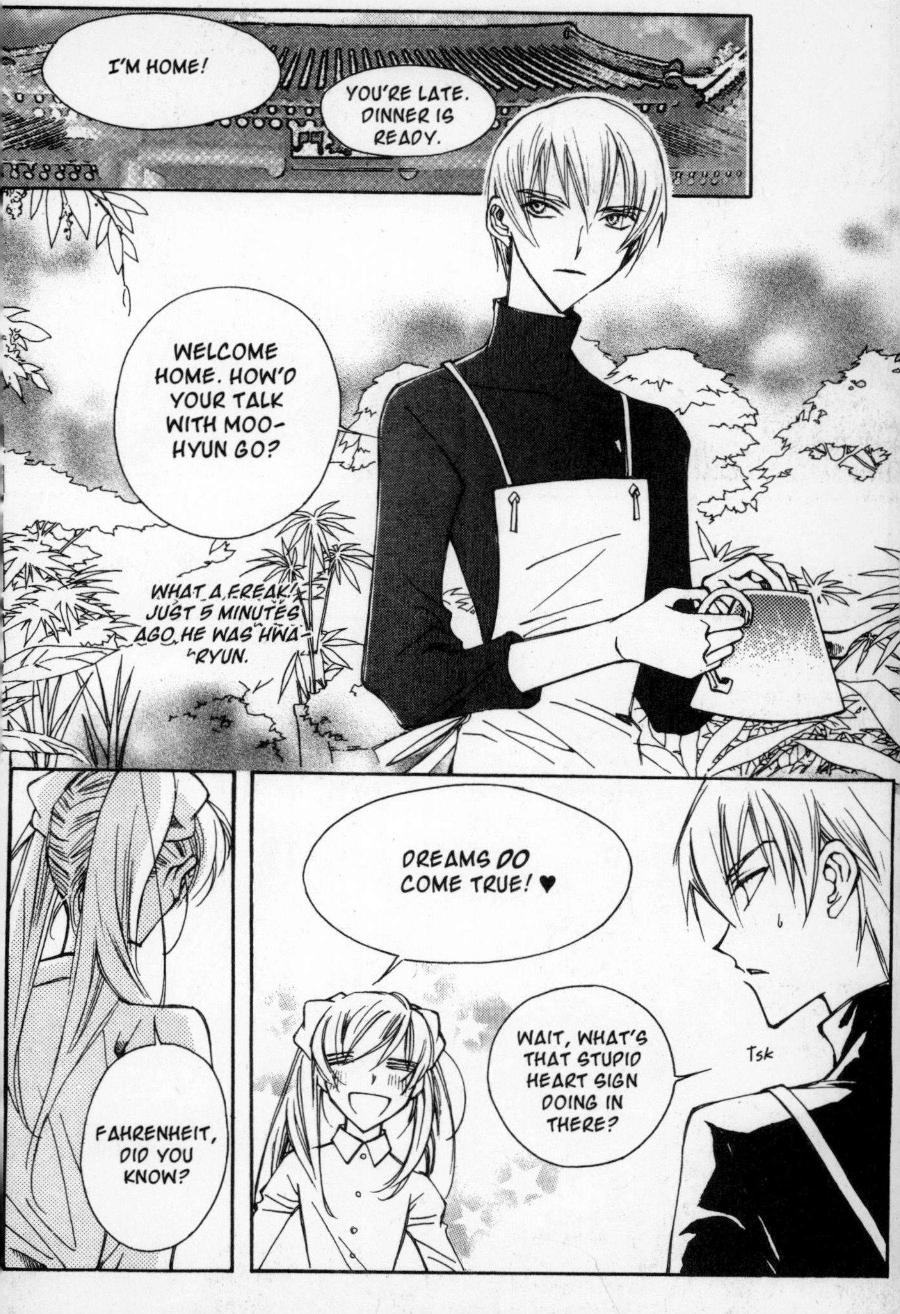
I'M HOME!
YOU'RE LATE. DINNER IS READY.
WELCOME HOME. HOW'D YOUR TALK WITH MOO-HYUN GO?
WHAT A FREAK! JUST 5 MINUTES AGO HE WAS HWA-RYUN.
FAHRENHEIT, DID YOU KNOW?
DREAMS DO COME TRUE! ♥
WAIT, WHAT'S THAT STUPID HEART SIGN DOING IN THERE?
Tsk

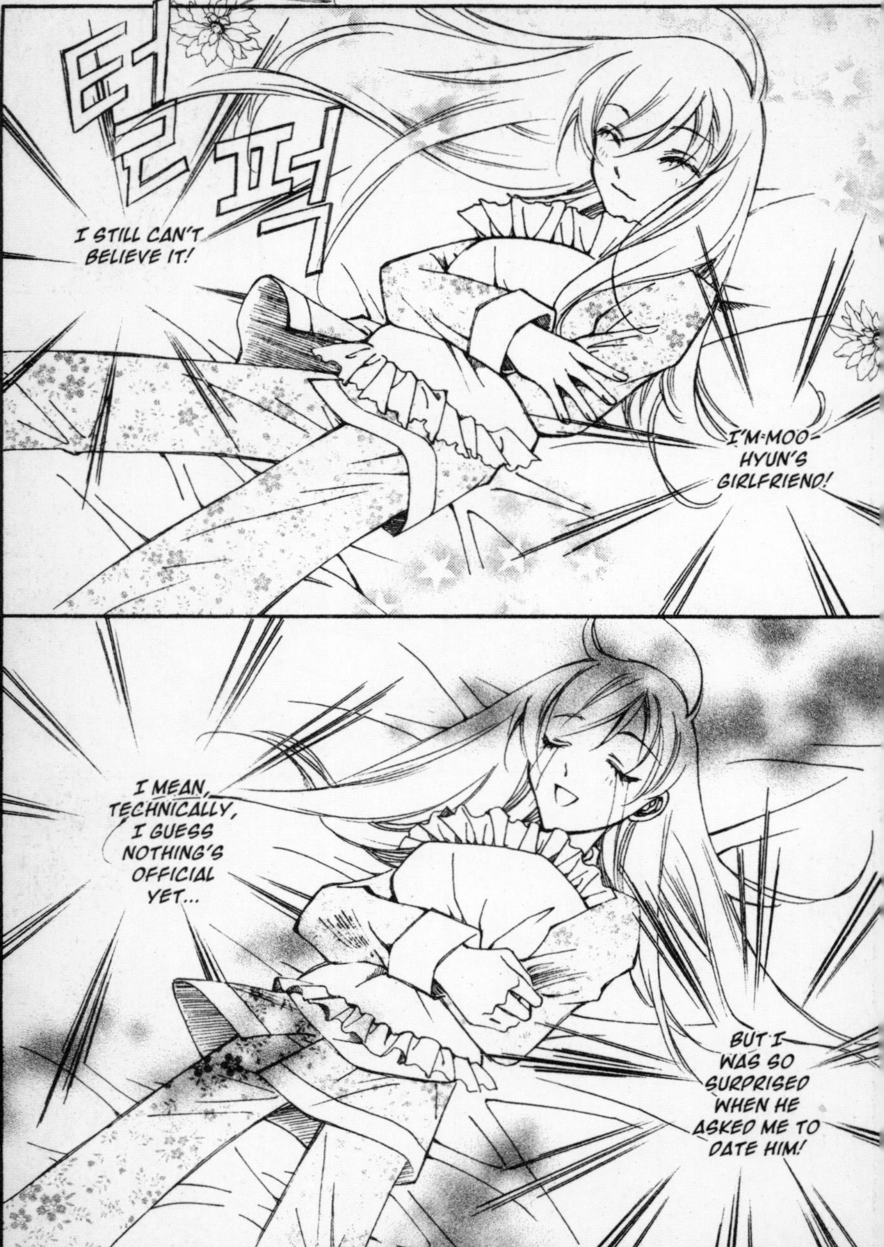
털퍽
I STILL CAN'T BELIEVE IT!
I'M MOO-HYUN'S GIRLFRIEND!
I MEAN, TECHNICALLY, I GUESS NOTHING'S OFFICIAL YET...
BUT I WAS SO SURPRISED WHEN HE ASKED ME TO DATE HIM!

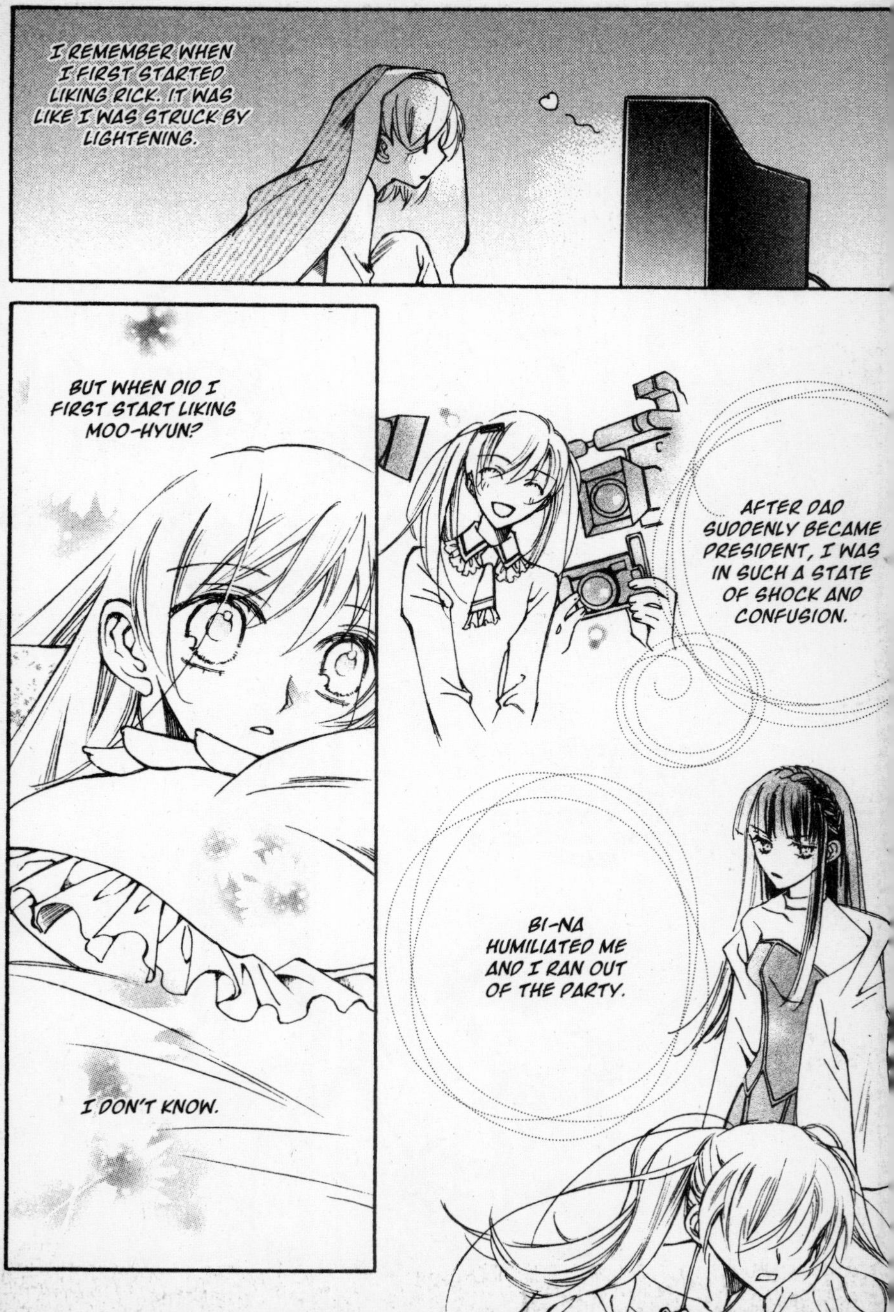

I REMEMBER WHEN I FIRST STARTED LIKING RICK. IT WAS LIKE I WAS STRUCK BY LIGHTENING.
BUT WHEN DID I FIRST START LIKING MOO-HYUN?
I DON'T KNOW.
AFTER DAD SUDDENLY BECAME PRESIDENT, I WAS IN SUCH A STATE OF SHOCK AND CONFUSION.
BI-NA HUMILIATED ME AND I RAN OUT OF THE PARTY.

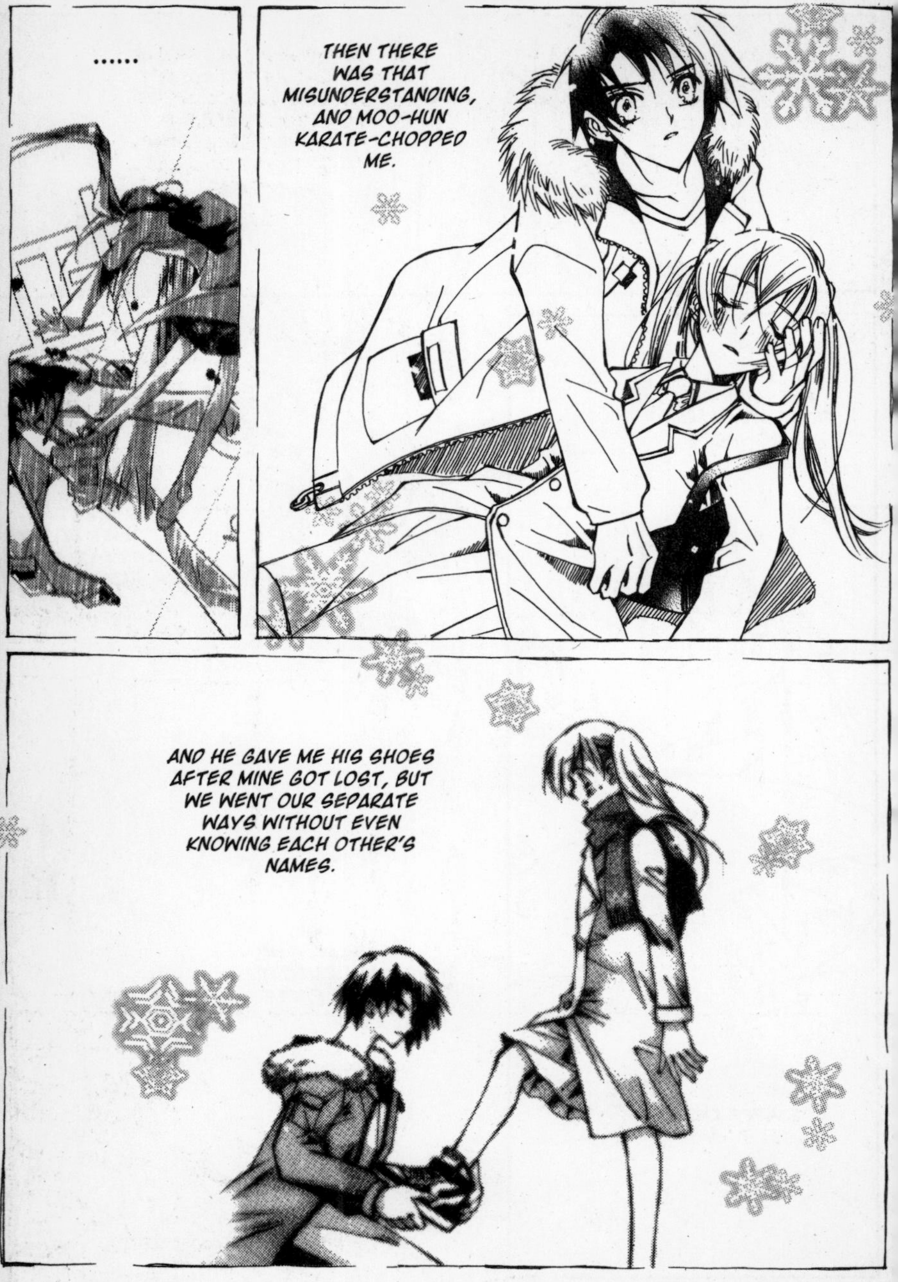
......
THEN THERE WAS THAT MISUNDERSTANDING, AND MOO-HUN KARATE-CHOPPED ME.
AND HE GAVE ME HIS SHOES AFTER MINE GOT LOST, BUT WE WENT OUR SEPARATE WAYS WITHOUT EVEN KNOWING EACH OTHER'S NAMES.

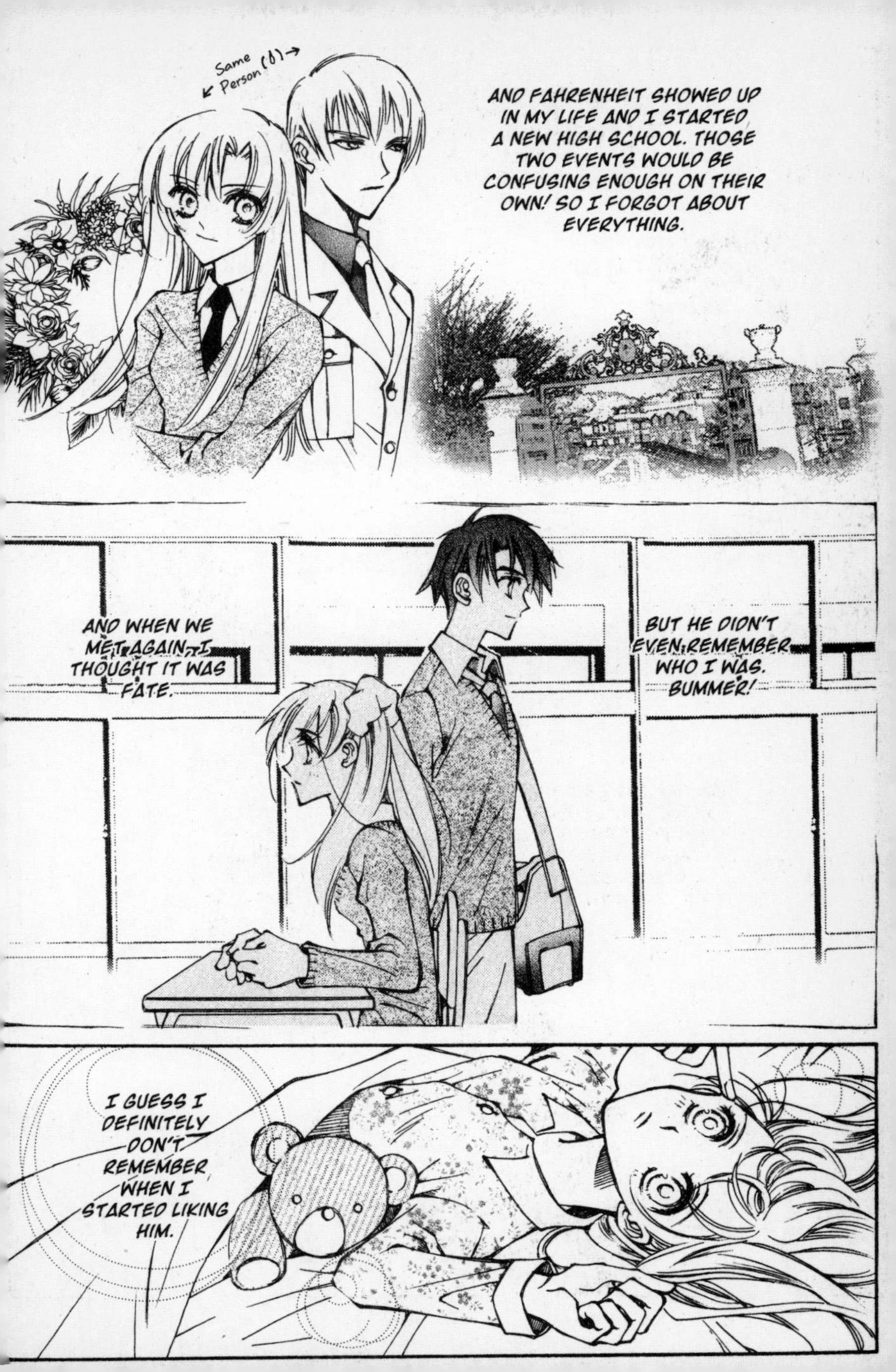
Same Person (♪)
AND FAHRENHEIT SHOWED UP IN MY LIFE AND I STARTED A NEW HIGH SCHOOL. THOSE TWO EVENTS WOULD BE CONFUSING ENOUGH ON THEIR OWN! SO I FORGOT ABOUT EVERYTHING.
AND WHEN WE MET AGAIN, I THOUGHT IT WAS FATE.
BUT HE DIDN'T EVEN REMEMBER WHO I WAS. BUMMER!
I GUESS I DEFINITELY DON'T REMEMBER WHEN I STARTED LIKING HIM.

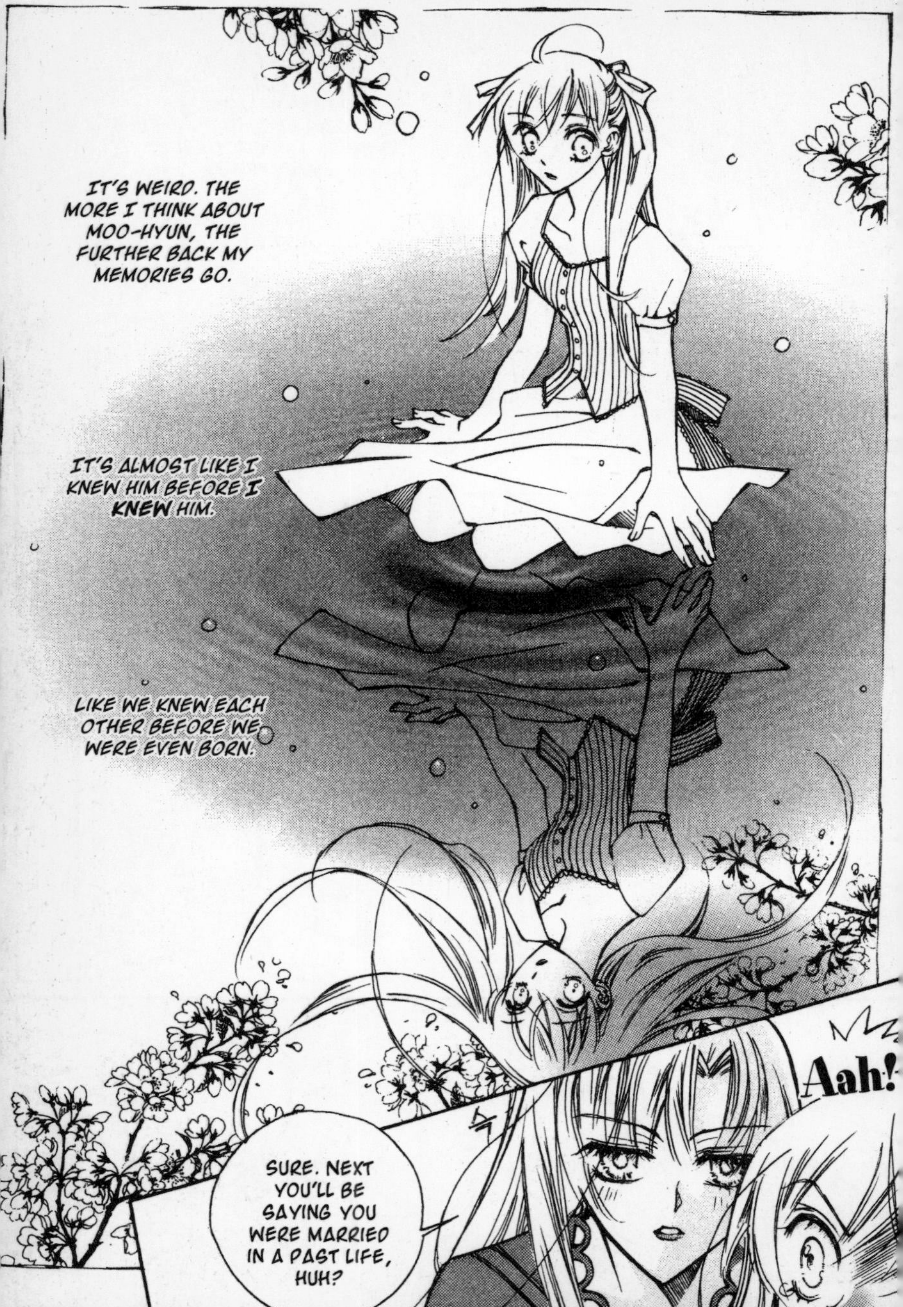
IT'S WEIRD. THE MORE I THINK ABOUT MOO-HYUN, THE FURTHER BACK MY MEMORIES GO.
IT'S ALMOST LIKE I KNEW HIM BEFORE I KNEW HIM.
LIKE WE KNEW EACH OTHER BEFORE WE WERE EVEN BORN.
SURE. NEXT YOU'LL BE SAYING YOU WERE MARRIED IN A PAST LIFE, HUH?
Aah!

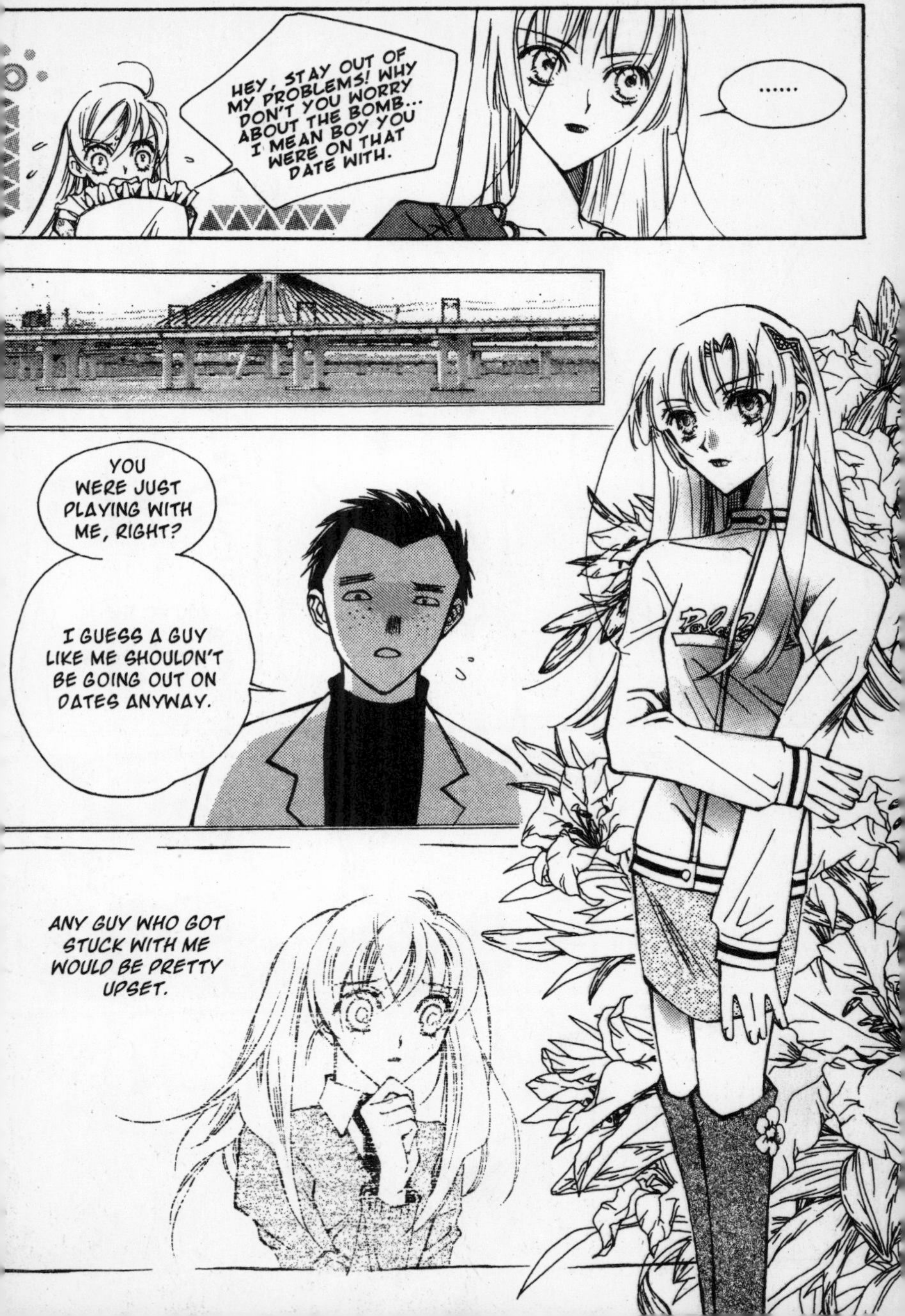
HEY, STAY OUT OF MY PROBLEMS! WHY DON'T YOU WORRY ABOUT THE BOMB... I MEAN BOY YOU WERE ON THAT DATE WITH.
......
YOU WERE JUST PLAYING WITH ME, RIGHT?
I GUESS A GUY LIKE ME SHOULDN'T BE GOING OUT ON DATES ANYWAY.
ANY GUY WHO GOT STUCK WITH ME WOULD BE PRETTY UPSET.

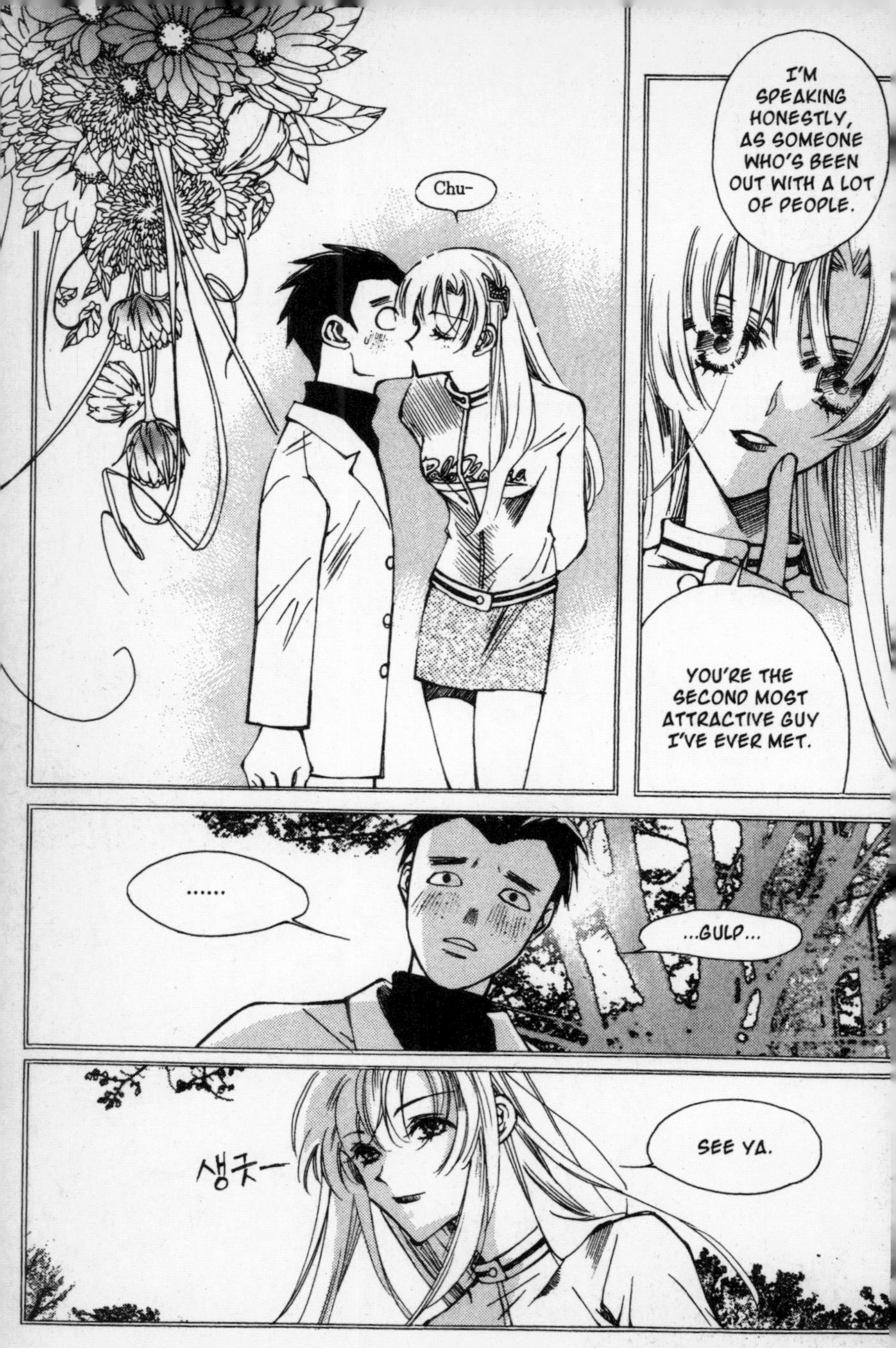
Chu-
I'M SPEAKING HONESTLY, AS SOMEONE WHO'S BEEN OUT WITH A LOT OF PEOPLE.
YOU'RE THE SECOND MOST ATTRACTIVE GUY I'VE EVER MET.
......
...GULP...
생긋—
SEE YA.

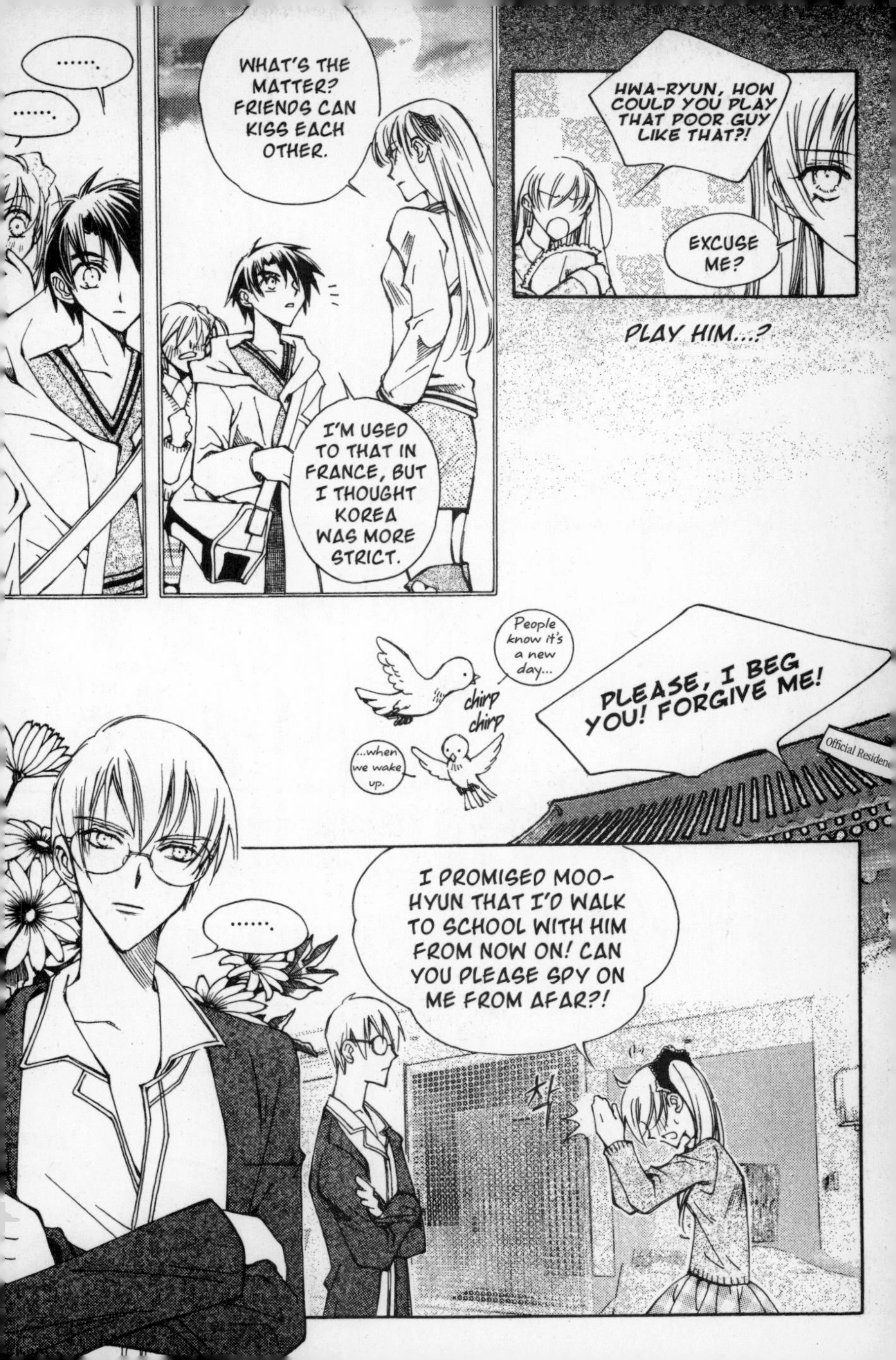

......
......
WHAT'S THE MATTER? FRIENDS CAN KISS EACH OTHER.
I'M USED TO THAT IN FRANCE, BUT I THOUGHT KOREA WAS MORE STRICT.
HWA-RYUN, HOW COULD YOU PLAY THAT POOR GUY LIKE THAT?!
EXCUSE ME?
PLAY HIM...?
People know it's a new day...
chirp chirp
...when we wake up.
PLEASE, I BEG YOU! FORGIVE ME!
Official Residen
......
I PROMISED MOO-HYUN THAT I'D WALK TO SCHOOL WITH HIM FROM NOW ON! CAN YOU PLEASE SPY ON ME FROM AFAR?!

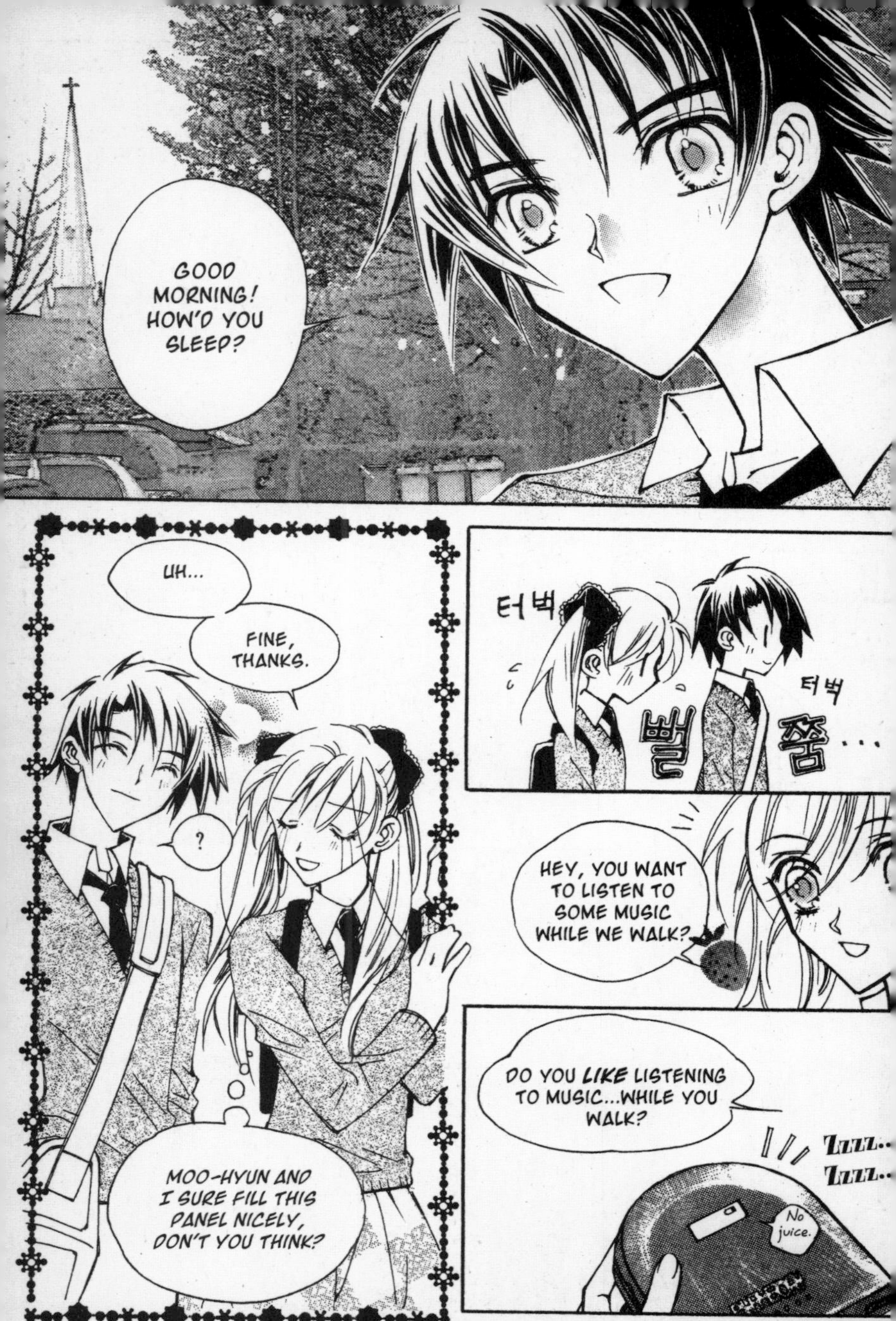
GOOD MORNING! HOW'D YOU SLEEP?
UH...
FINE, THANKS.
?
MOO-HYUN AND I SURE FILL THIS PANEL NICELY, DON'T YOU THINK?
터벅
터벅
뻘쭘...
HEY, YOU WANT TO LISTEN TO SOME MUSIC WHILE WE WALK?
DO YOU ***LIKE*** LISTENING TO MUSIC...WHILE YOU WALK?
Zzzz...
Zzzz...
No juice.

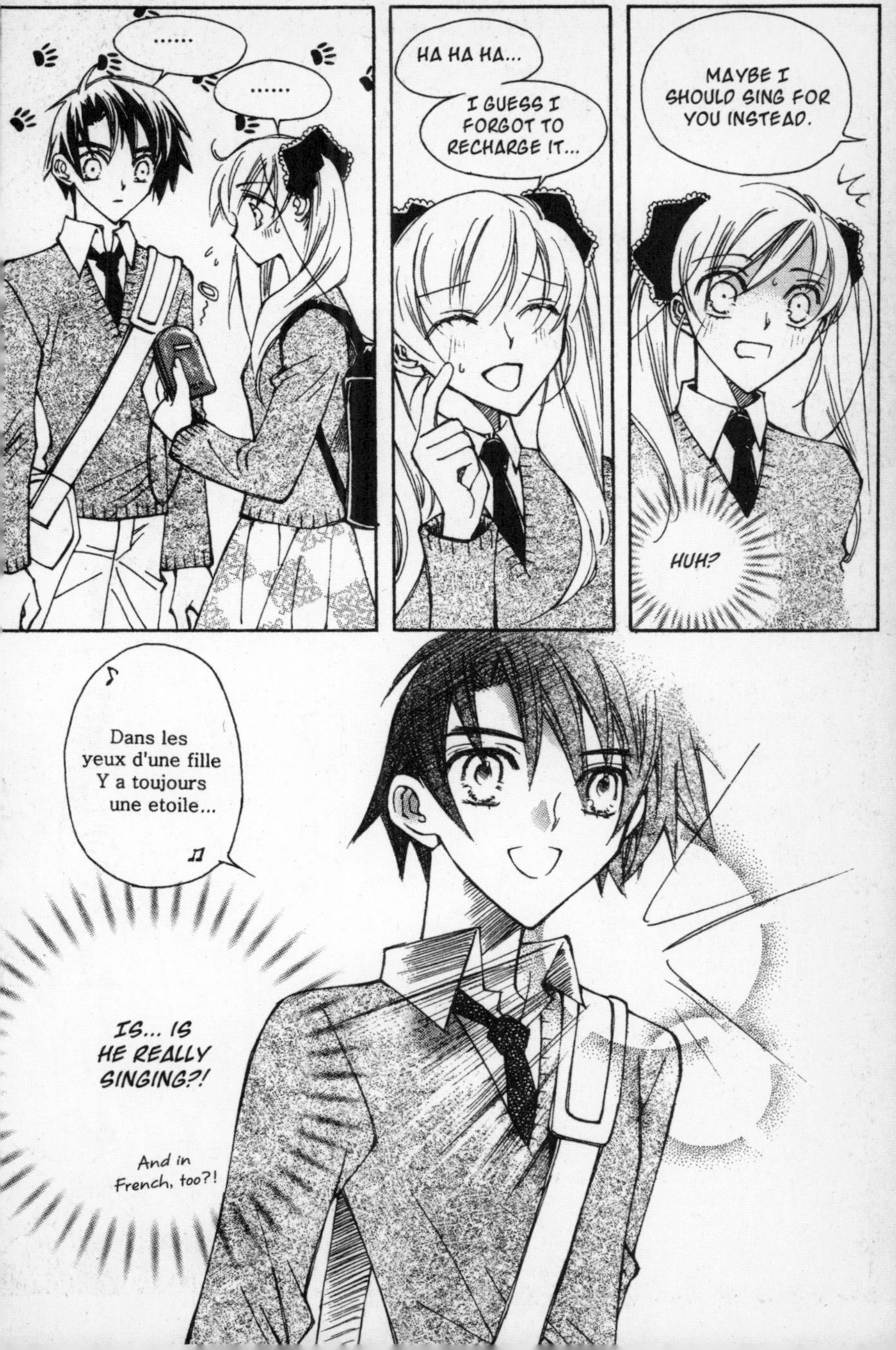

......
......
HA HA HA...
I GUESS I FORGOT TO RECHARGE IT...
MAYBE I SHOULD SING FOR YOU INSTEAD.
HUH?
Dans les yeux d'une fille Y a toujours une etoile...
IS... IS HE REALLY SINGING?!
And in French, too?!

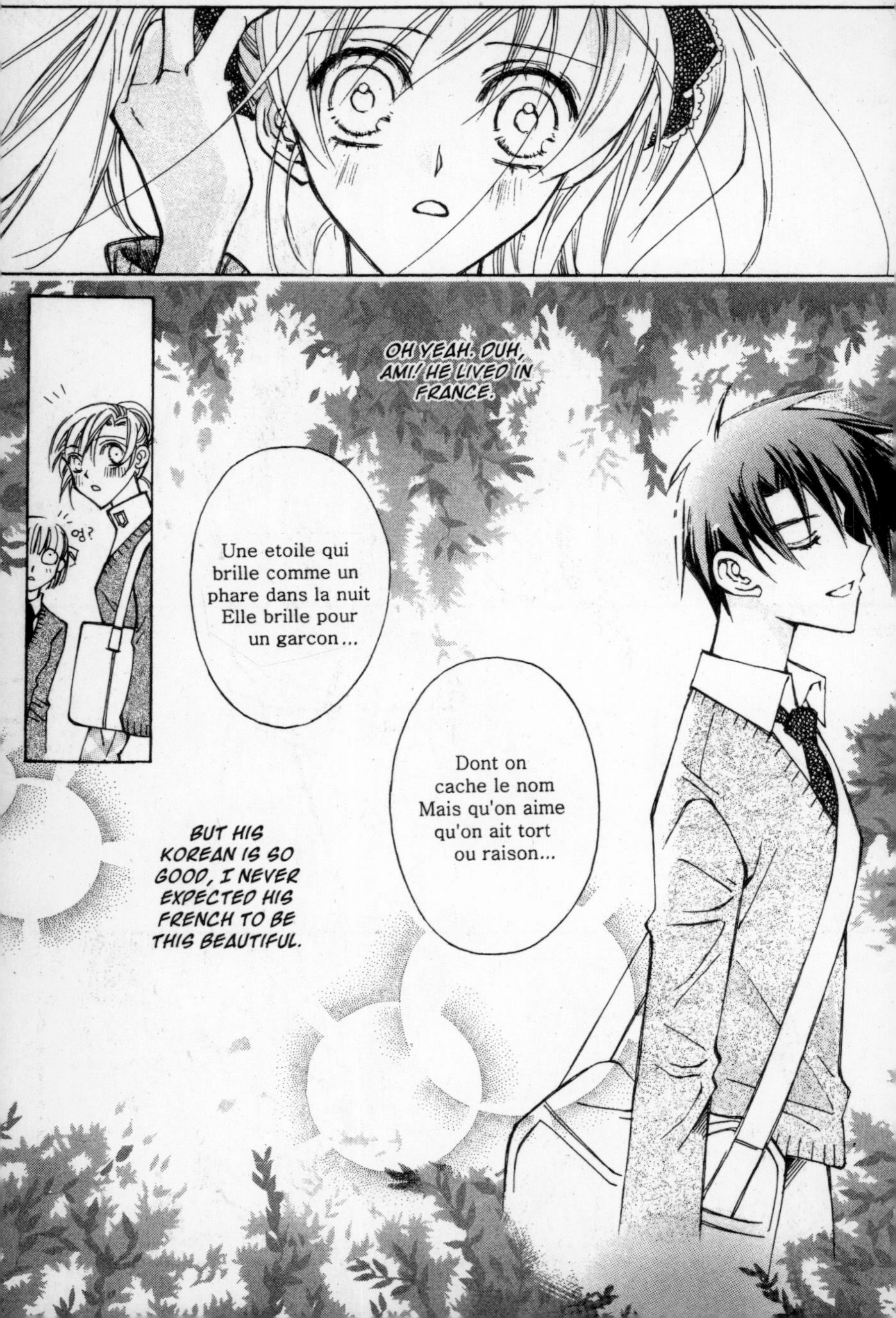
엉?
OH YEAH. DUH, AMI! HE LIVED IN FRANCE.
Une etoile qui brille comme un phare dans la nuit Elle brille pour un garcon...
Dont on cache le nom Mais qu'on aime qu'on ait tort ou raison...
BUT HIS KOREAN IS SO GOOD, I NEVER EXPECTED HIS FRENCH TO BE THIS BEAUTIFUL.

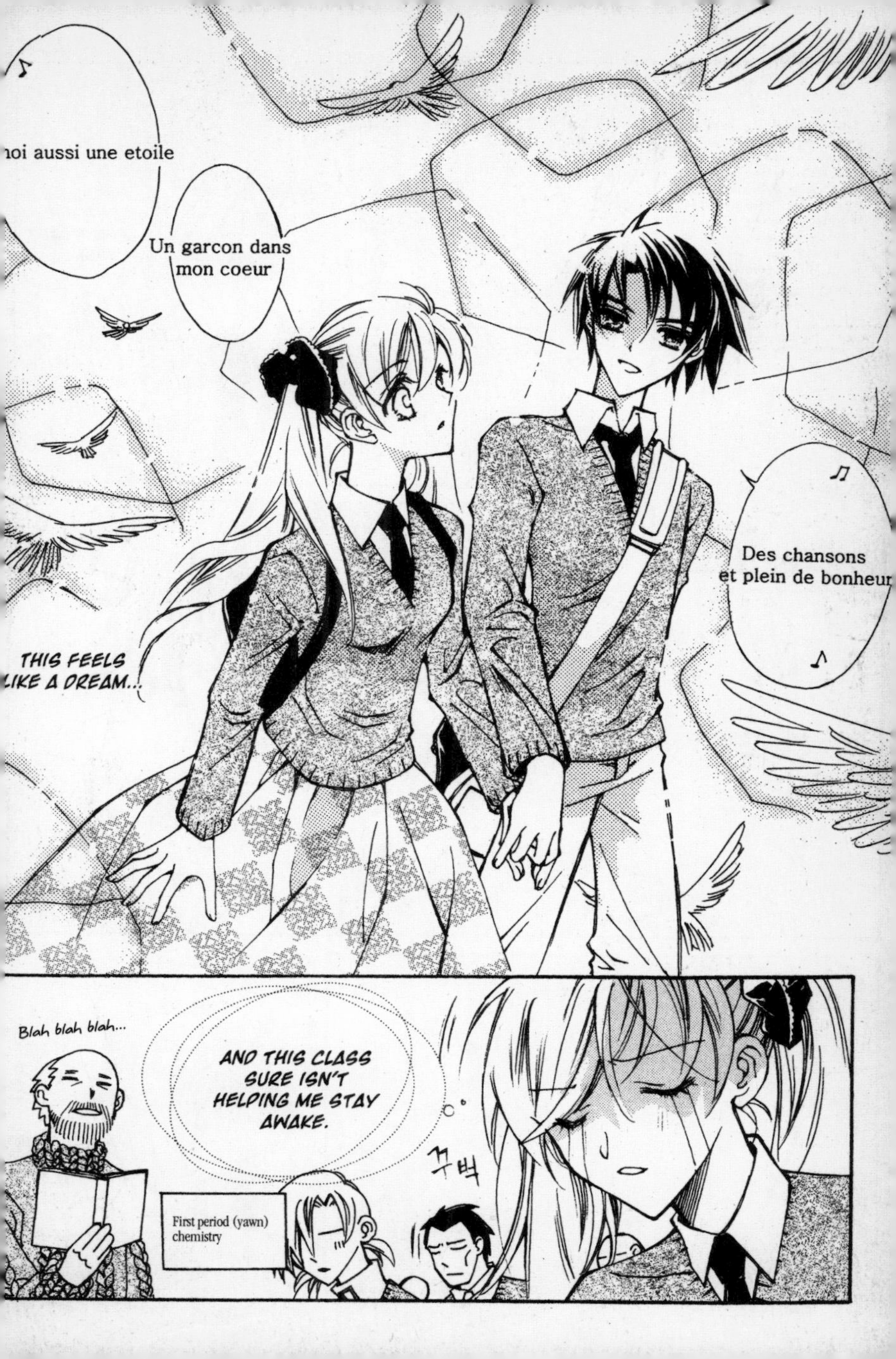
♪
noi aussi une etoile
Un garcon dans mon coeur
IKE A DREAM...
THIS FEELS
♫
Des chansons et plein de bonheur
♪
Blah blah blah...
AND THIS CLASS SURE ISN'T HELPING ME STAY AWAKE.
First period (yawn) chemistry
꾸벅

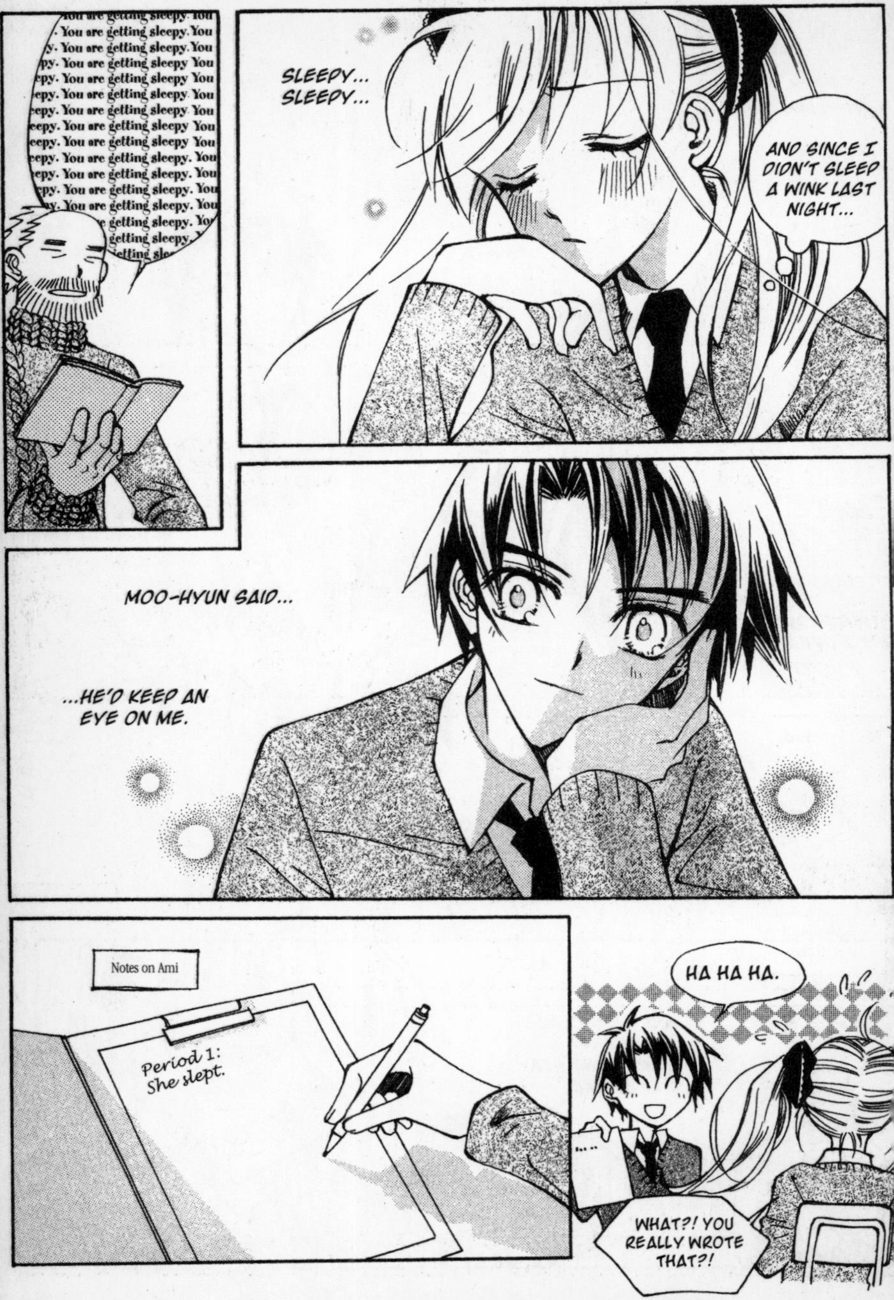
You are getting sleepy. You
. You are getting sleepy. You
y. You are getting sleepy. You
py. You are getting sleepy You
epy. You are getting sleepy You
epy. You are getting sleepy. You
eepy. You are getting sleepy. You
eepy. You are getting sleepy You
eepy. You are getting sleepy. You
eepy. You are getting sleepy. You
eepy. You are getting sleepy. You
epy. You are getting sleepy. You
y. You are getting sleepy. You
getting sleepy. You
getting sleepy. You
SLEEPY... SLEEPY...
AND SINCE I DIDN'T SLEEP A WINK LAST NIGHT...
MOO-HYUN SAID...
...HE'D KEEP AN EYE ON ME.
Notes on Ami
Period 1: She slept.
HA HA HA.
WHAT?! YOU REALLY WROTE THAT?!

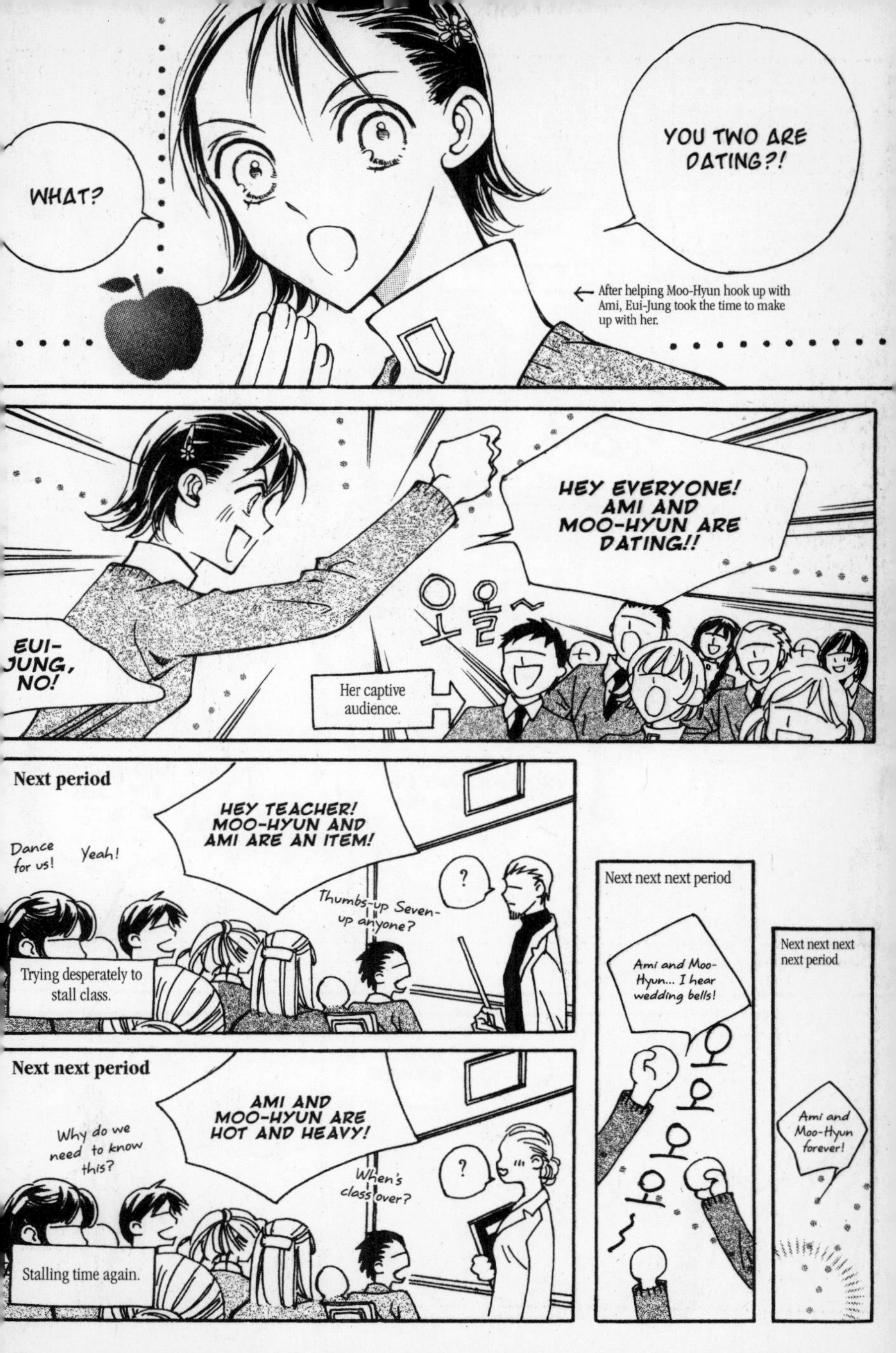

WHAT?
YOU TWO ARE DATING?!
← After helping Moo-Hyun hook up with Ami, Eui-Jung took the time to make up with her.
EUI-JUNG, NO!
HEY EVERYONE! AMI AND MOO-HYUN ARE DATING!!
오올~
Her captive audience.
Next period
Dance for us!
Yeah!
HEY TEACHER! MOO-HYUN AND AMI ARE AN ITEM!
?
Thumbs-up Seven-up anyone?
Trying desperately to stall class.
Next next period
Why do we need to know this?
AMI AND MOO-HYUN ARE HOT AND HEAVY!
?
When's class over?
Stalling time again.
Next next next period
Ami and Moo-Hyun... I hear wedding bells!
오오오오~
Next next next next period
Ami and Moo-Hyun forever!

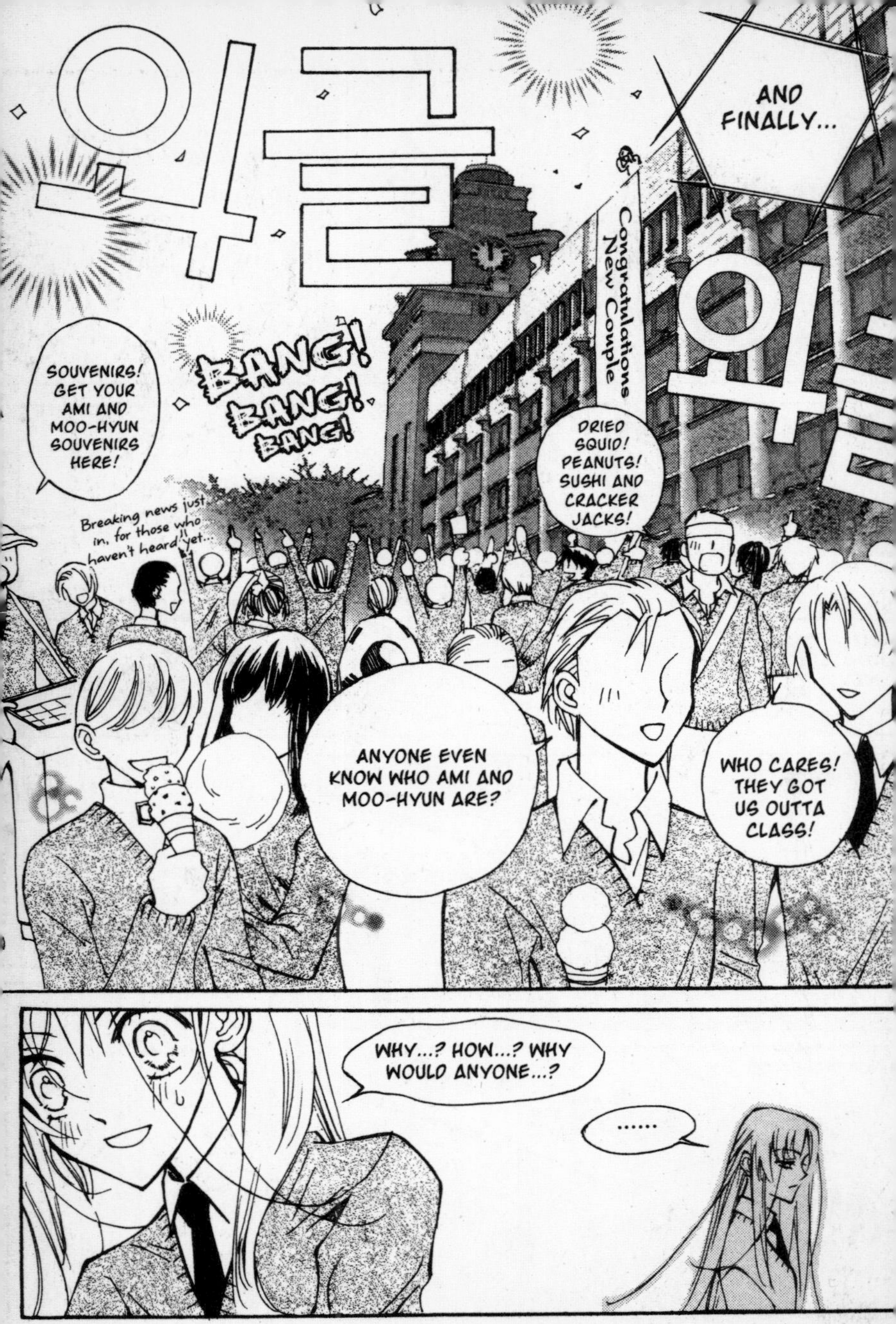
와글
AND FINALLY...
Congratulations New Couple
SOUVENIRS! GET YOUR AMI AND MOO-HYUN SOUVENIRS HERE!
BANG! BANG! BANG!
DRIED SQUID! PEANUTS! SUSHI AND CRACKER JACKS!
Breaking news just in, for those who haven't heard yet...
ANYONE EVEN KNOW WHO AMI AND MOO-HYUN ARE?
WHO CARES! THEY GOT US OUTTA CLASS!
WHY...? HOW...? WHY WOULD ANYONE...?
......

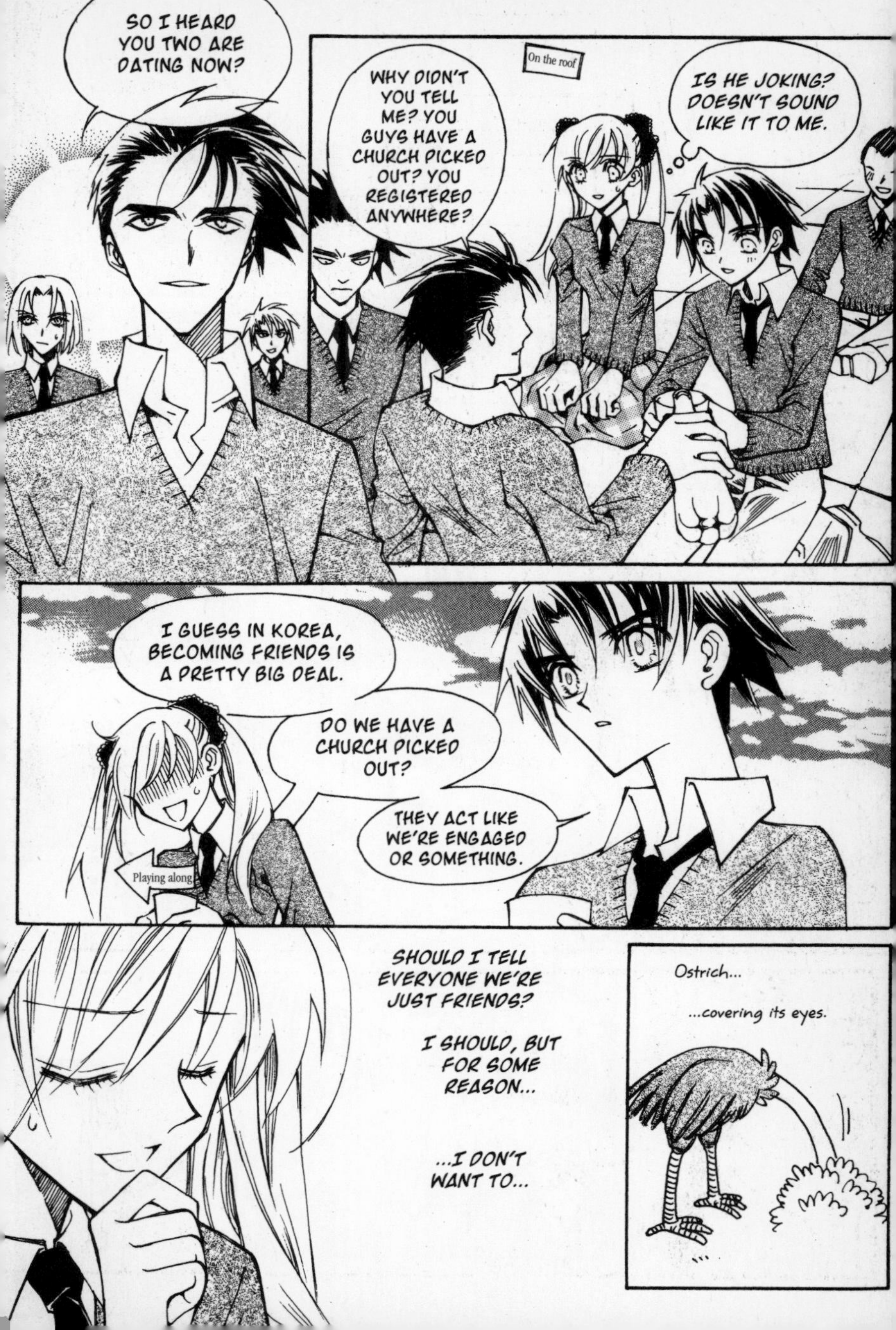
SO I HEARD YOU TWO ARE DATING NOW?
On the roof
WHY DIDN'T YOU TELL ME? YOU GUYS HAVE A CHURCH PICKED OUT? YOU REGISTERED ANYWHERE?
IS HE JOKING? DOESN'T SOUND LIKE IT TO ME.
I GUESS IN KOREA, BECOMING FRIENDS IS A PRETTY BIG DEAL.
Playing along
DO WE HAVE A CHURCH PICKED OUT?
THEY ACT LIKE WE'RE ENGAGED OR SOMETHING.
SHOULD I TELL EVERYONE WE'RE JUST FRIENDS?
I SHOULD, BUT FOR SOME REASON...
...I DON'T WANT TO...
Ostrich...
...covering its eyes.

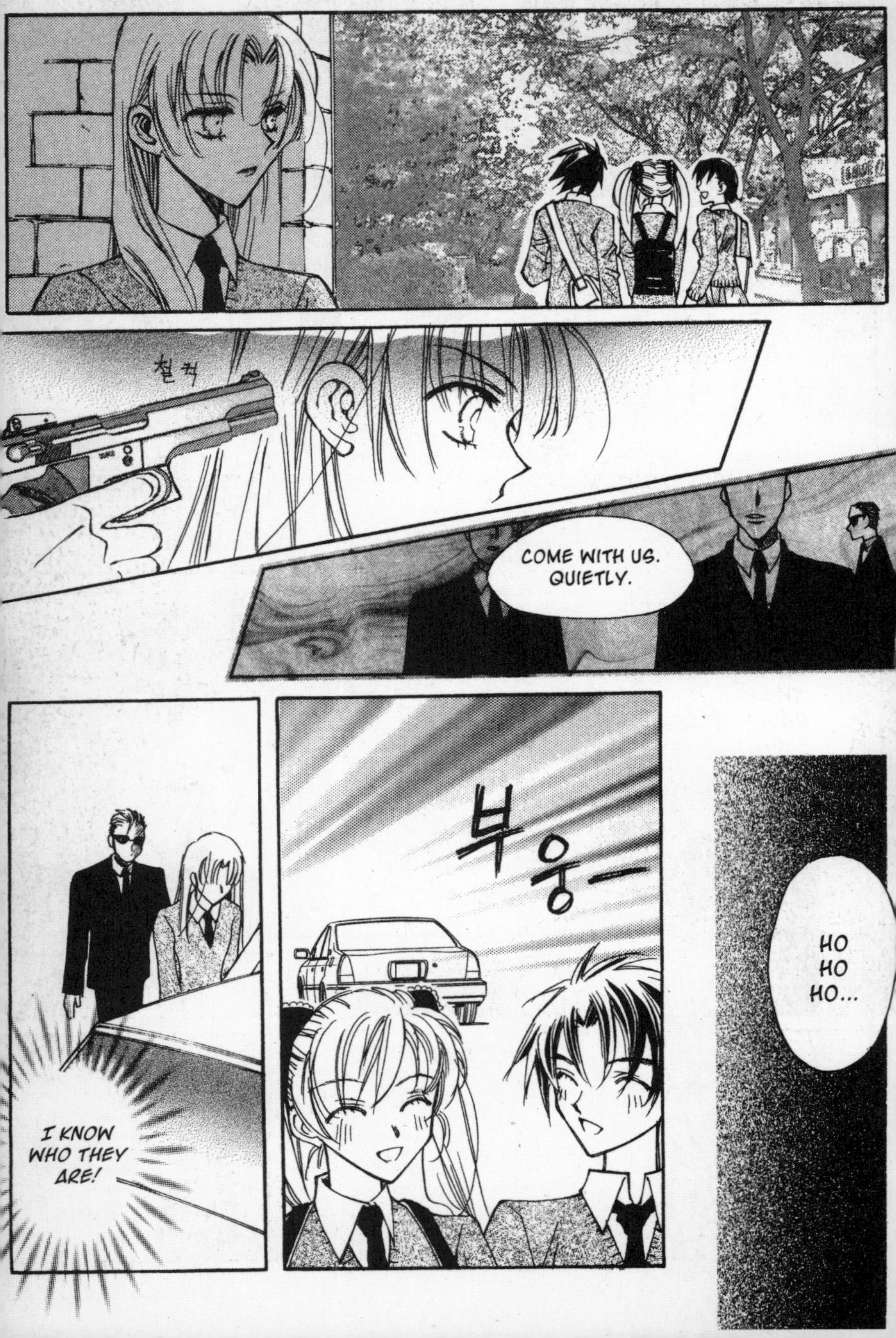
철컥
COME WITH US. QUIETLY.
I KNOW WHO THEY ARE!
부웅ㅡ
HO HO HO...

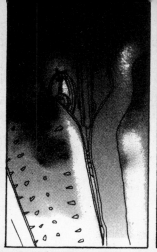

......

Ami's Father, President Won, Ho-Chan

NOW, WOULD YOU KINDLY TELL ME ABOUT THE BOY MY DAUGHTER IS DATING?

YEAH, THEY WERE DEFINITELY SECRET SERVICE MEN.

YOU NEVER TOLD ME YOU COLLECTED WEAPONS BEFORE!

DON'T TRY AND CHANGE THE SUBJECT! MY PRIVATE LIFE IS NONE OF YOUR BUSINESS!

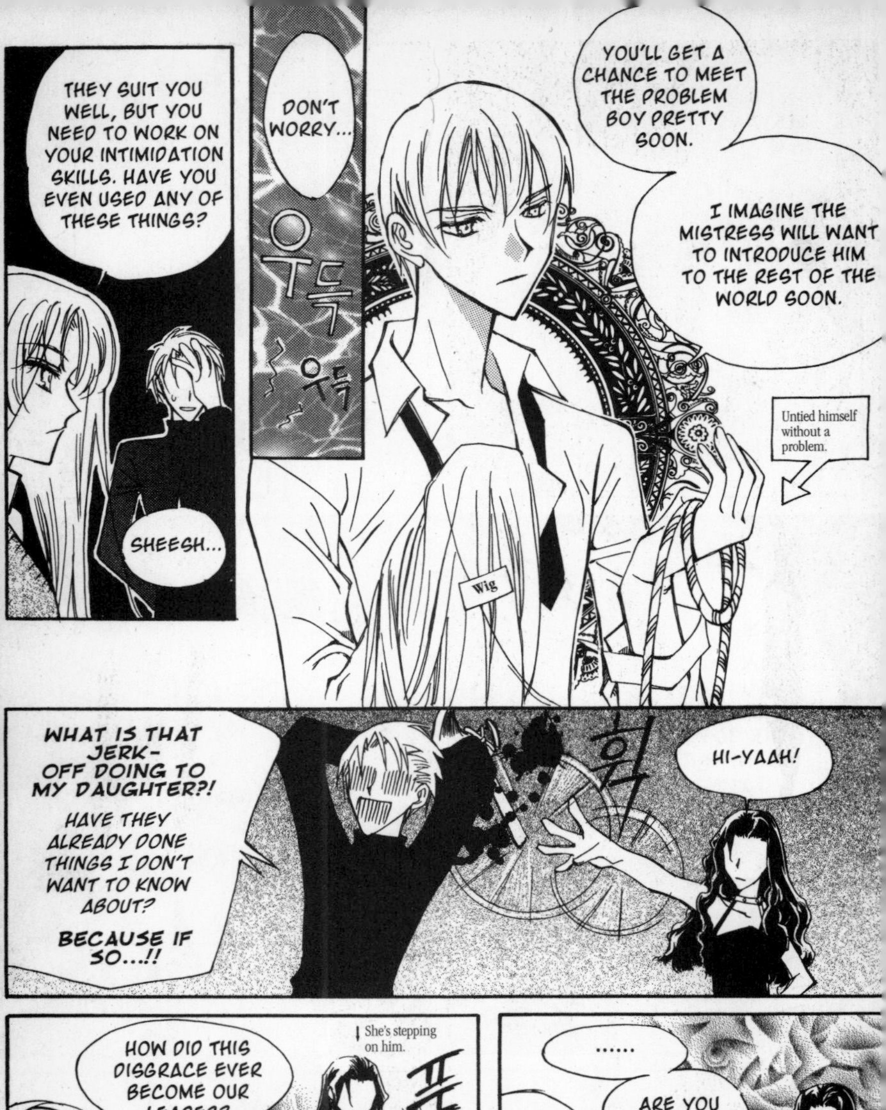
THEY SUIT YOU WELL, BUT YOU NEED TO WORK ON YOUR INTIMIDATION SKILLS. HAVE YOU EVEN USED ANY OF THESE THINGS?
SHEESH...
DON'T WORRY...
우드득
우득
YOU'LL GET A CHANCE TO MEET THE PROBLEM BOY PRETTY SOON.
I IMAGINE THE MISTRESS WILL WANT TO INTRODUCE HIM TO THE REST OF THE WORLD SOON.
Untied himself without a problem.
Wig
WHAT IS THAT JERK-OFF DOING TO MY DAUGHTER?!
HAVE THEY ALREADY DONE THINGS I DON'T WANT TO KNOW ABOUT?
BECAUSE IF SO...!!
휙
HI-YAAH!
HOW DID THIS DISGRACE EVER BECOME OUR LEADER?
She's stepping on him.
푹
HEY, HE'S FUNNY!
......
ARE YOU SERIOUS?
ARE YOU SERIOUSLY ASKING?

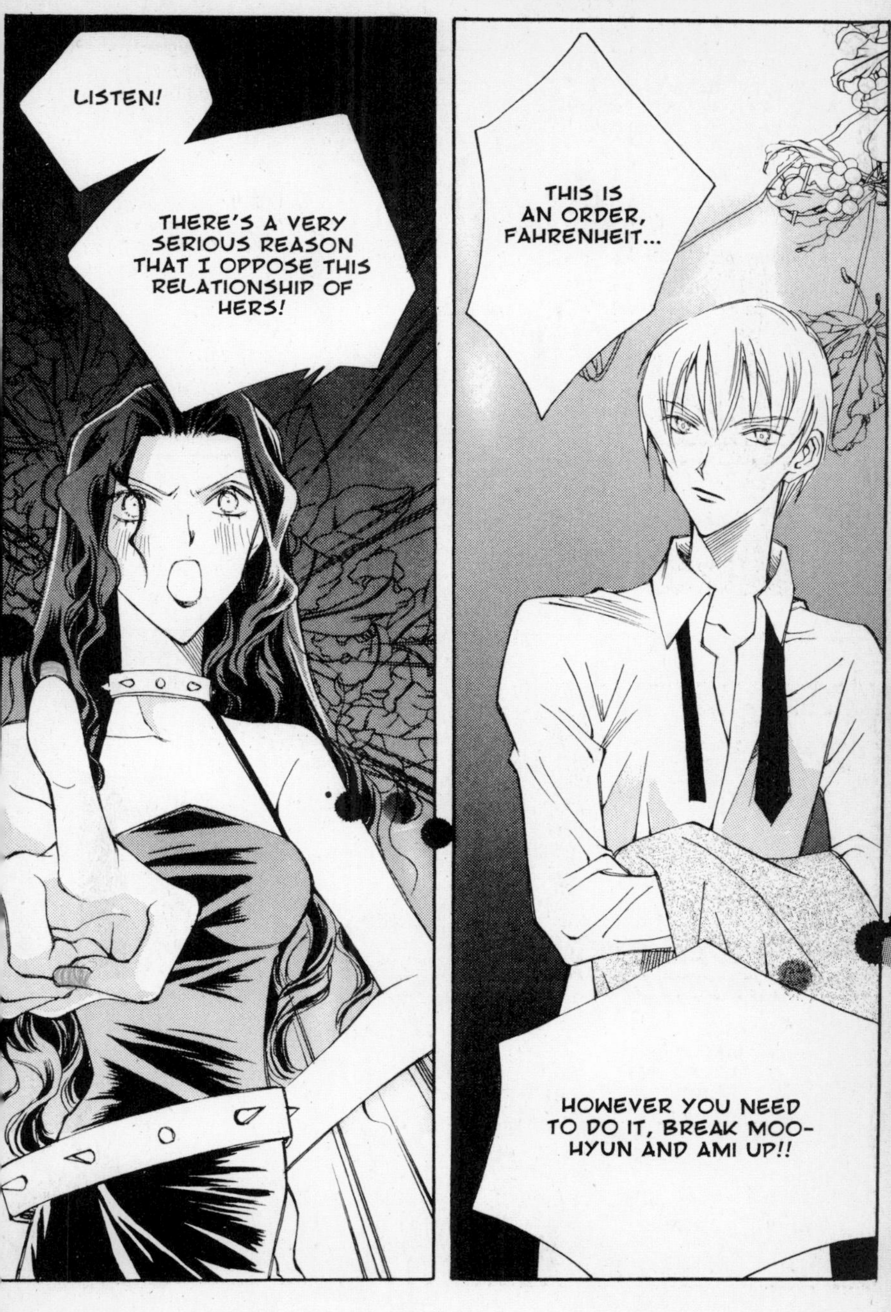

LISTEN!
THERE'S A VERY SERIOUS REASON THAT I OPPOSE THIS RELATIONSHIP OF HERS!
THIS IS AN ORDER, FAHRENHEIT...
HOWEVER YOU NEED TO DO IT, BREAK MOO-HYUN AND AMI UP!!

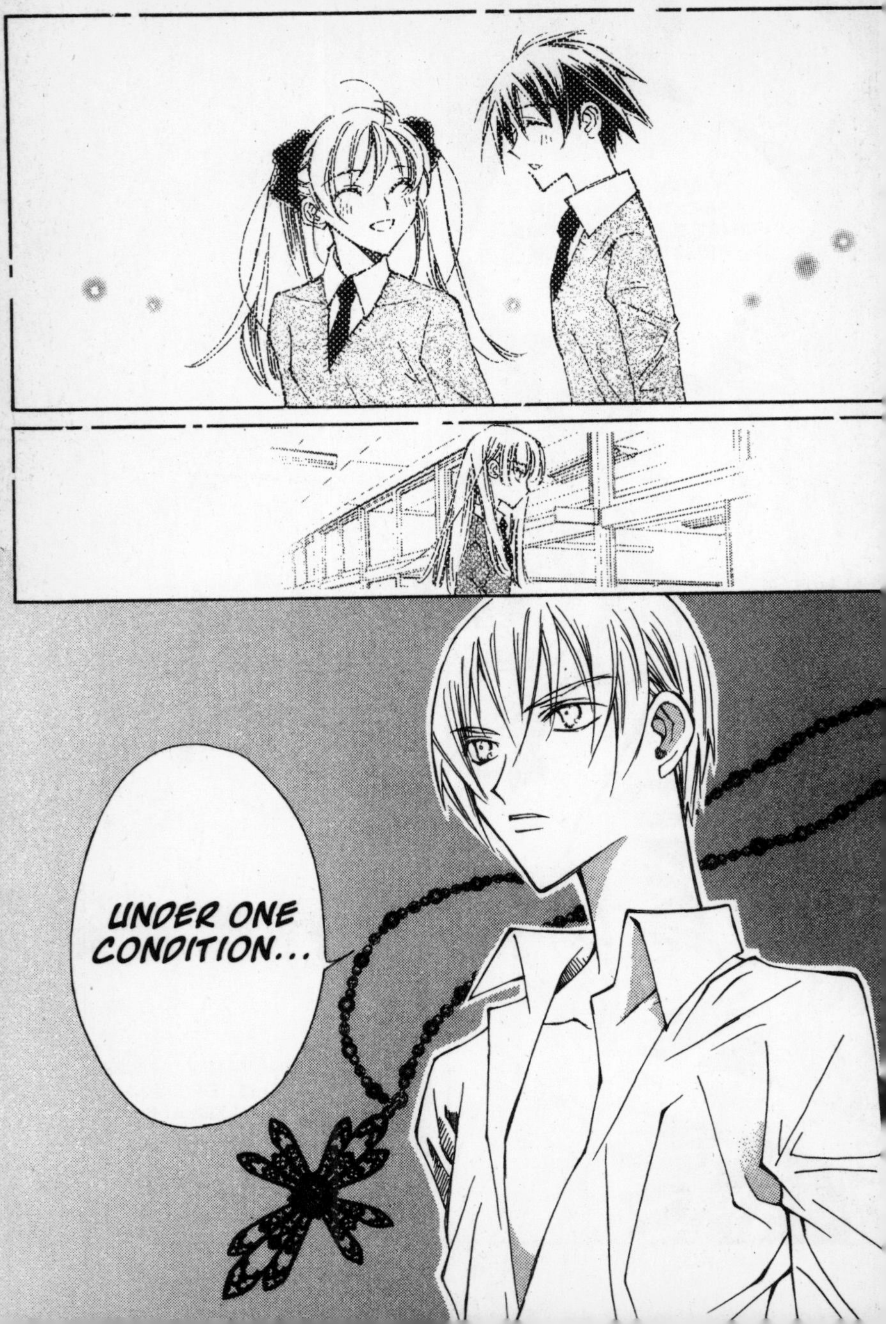
UNDER ONE CONDITION...

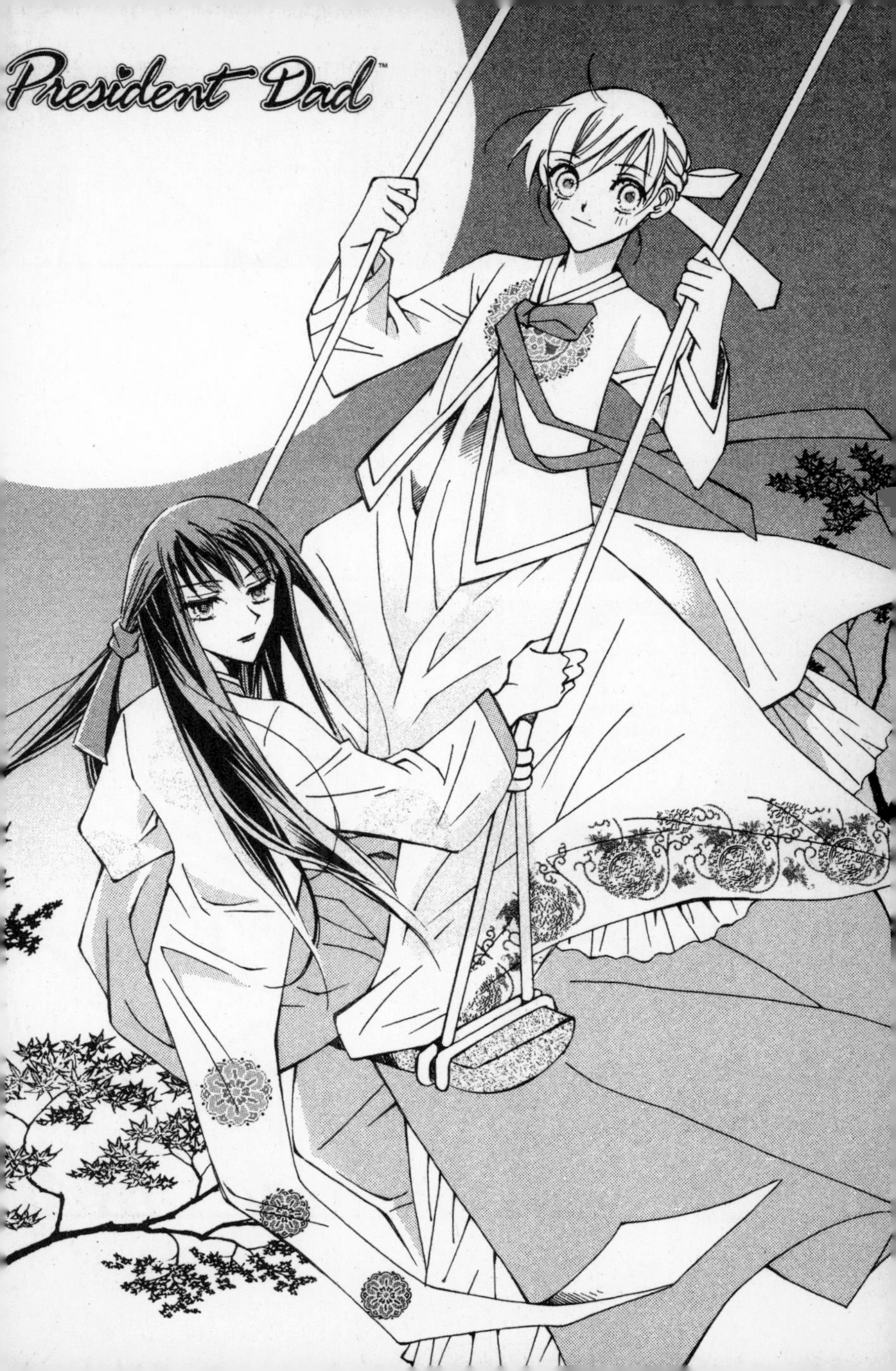
President Dad™

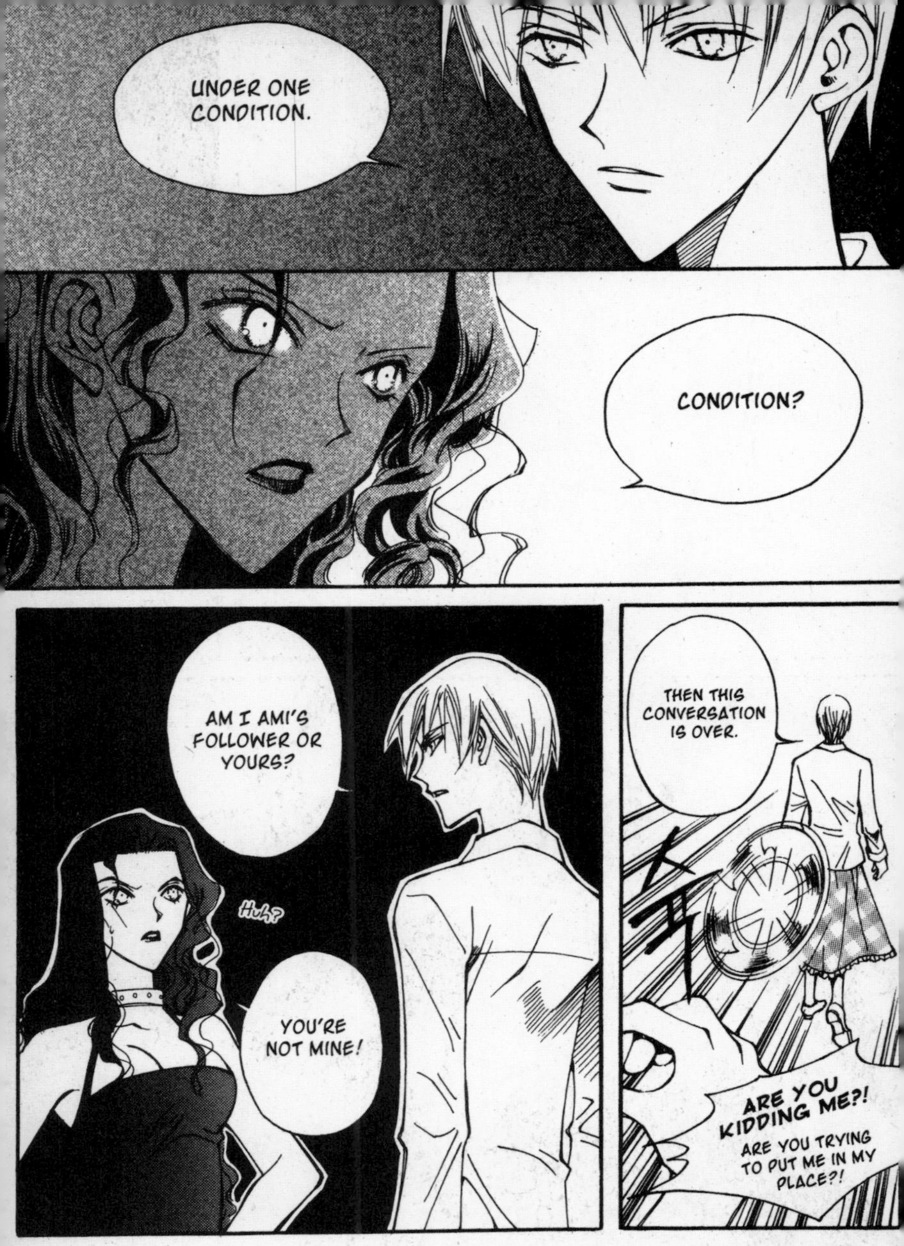
UNDER ONE CONDITION.
CONDITION?
AM I AMI'S FOLLOWER OR YOURS?
Huh?
YOU'RE NOT MINE!
THEN THIS CONVERSATION IS OVER.
ARE YOU KIDDING ME?!
ARE YOU TRYING TO PUT ME IN MY PLACE?!

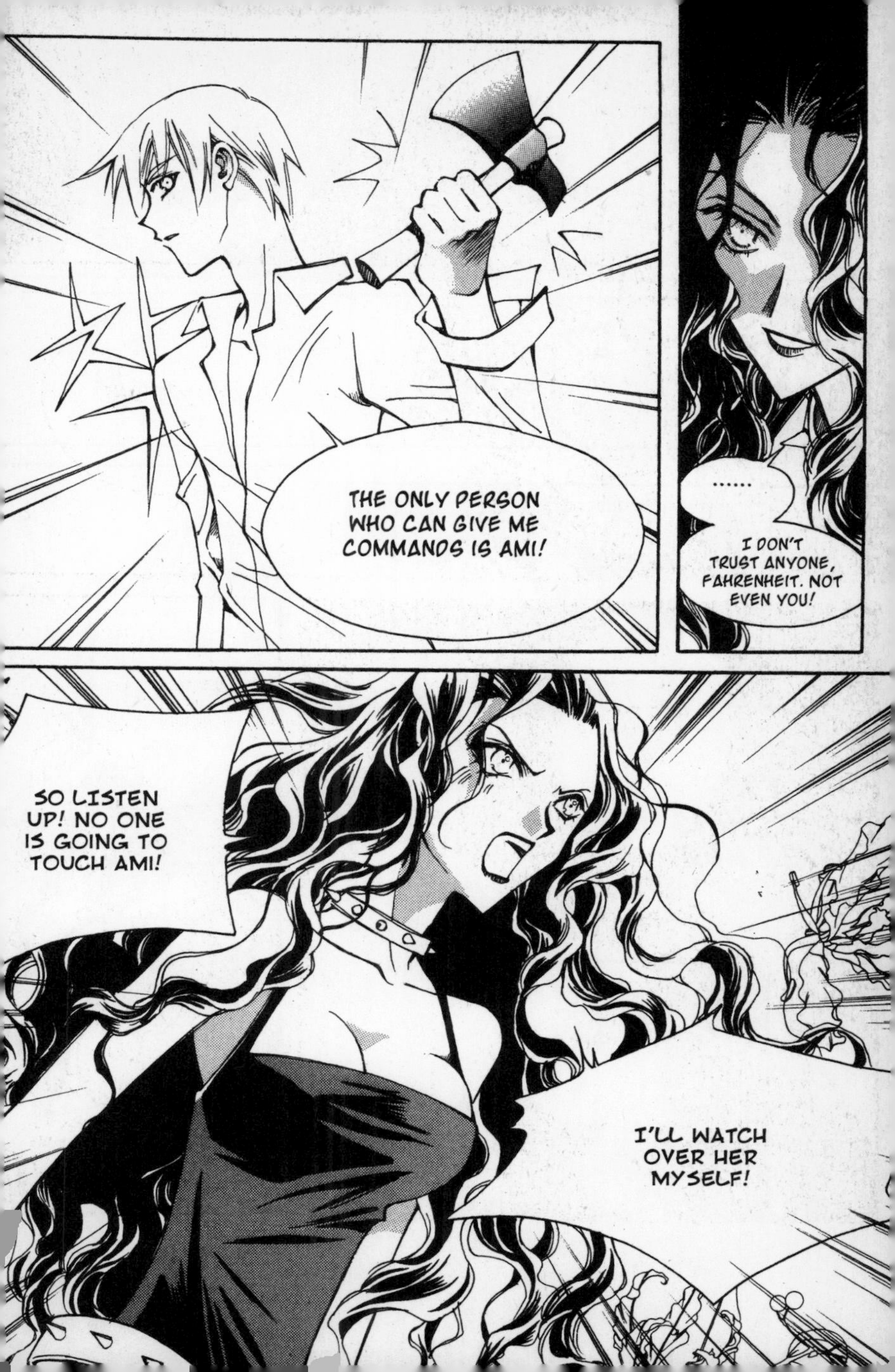
THE ONLY PERSON WHO CAN GIVE ME COMMANDS IS AMI!
......
I DON'T TRUST ANYONE, FAHRENHEIT. NOT EVEN YOU!
SO LISTEN UP! NO ONE IS GOING TO TOUCH AMI!
I'LL WATCH OVER HER MYSELF!

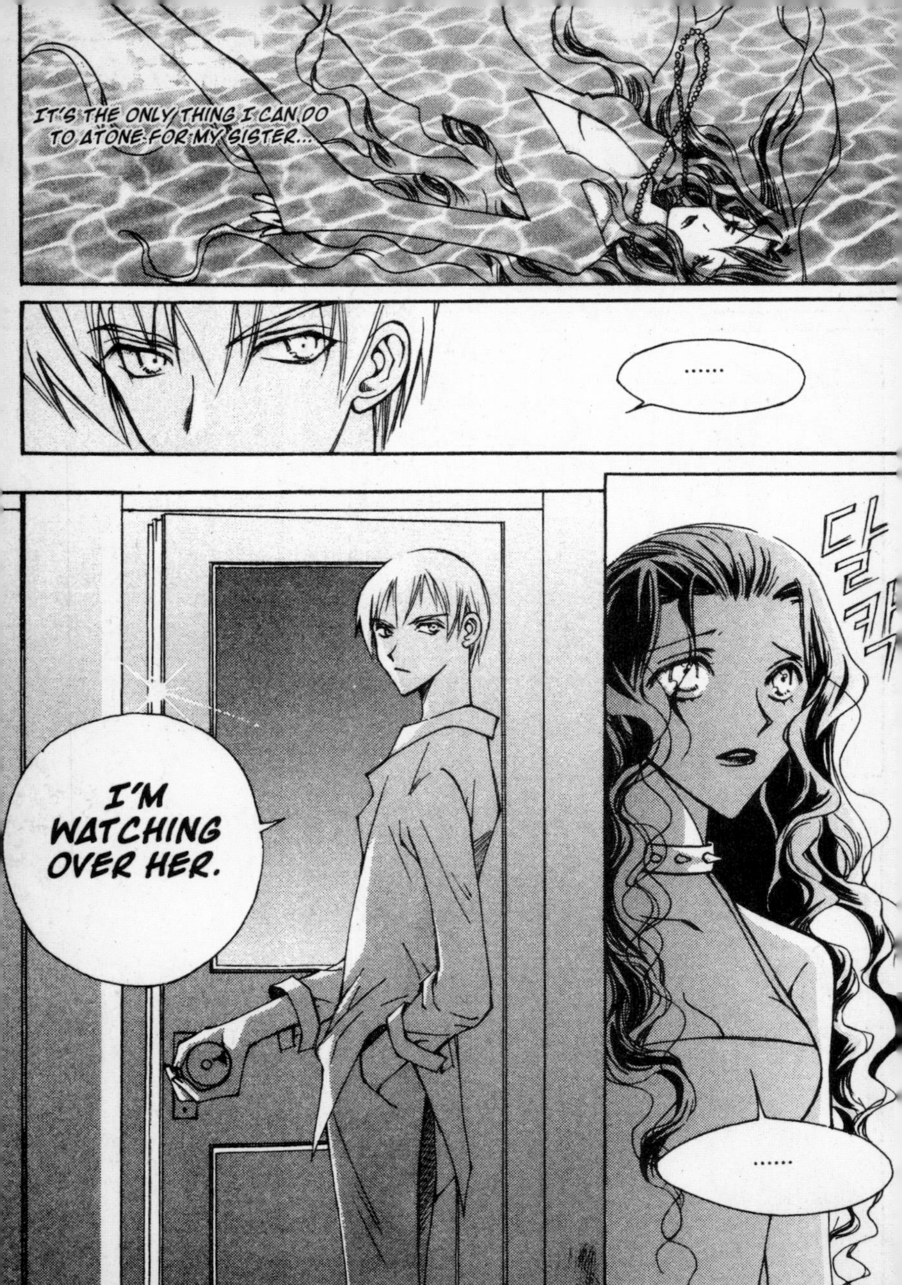
IT'S THE ONLY THING I CAN DO TO ATONE FOR MY SISTER...
......
I'M WATCHING OVER HER.
달칵
......

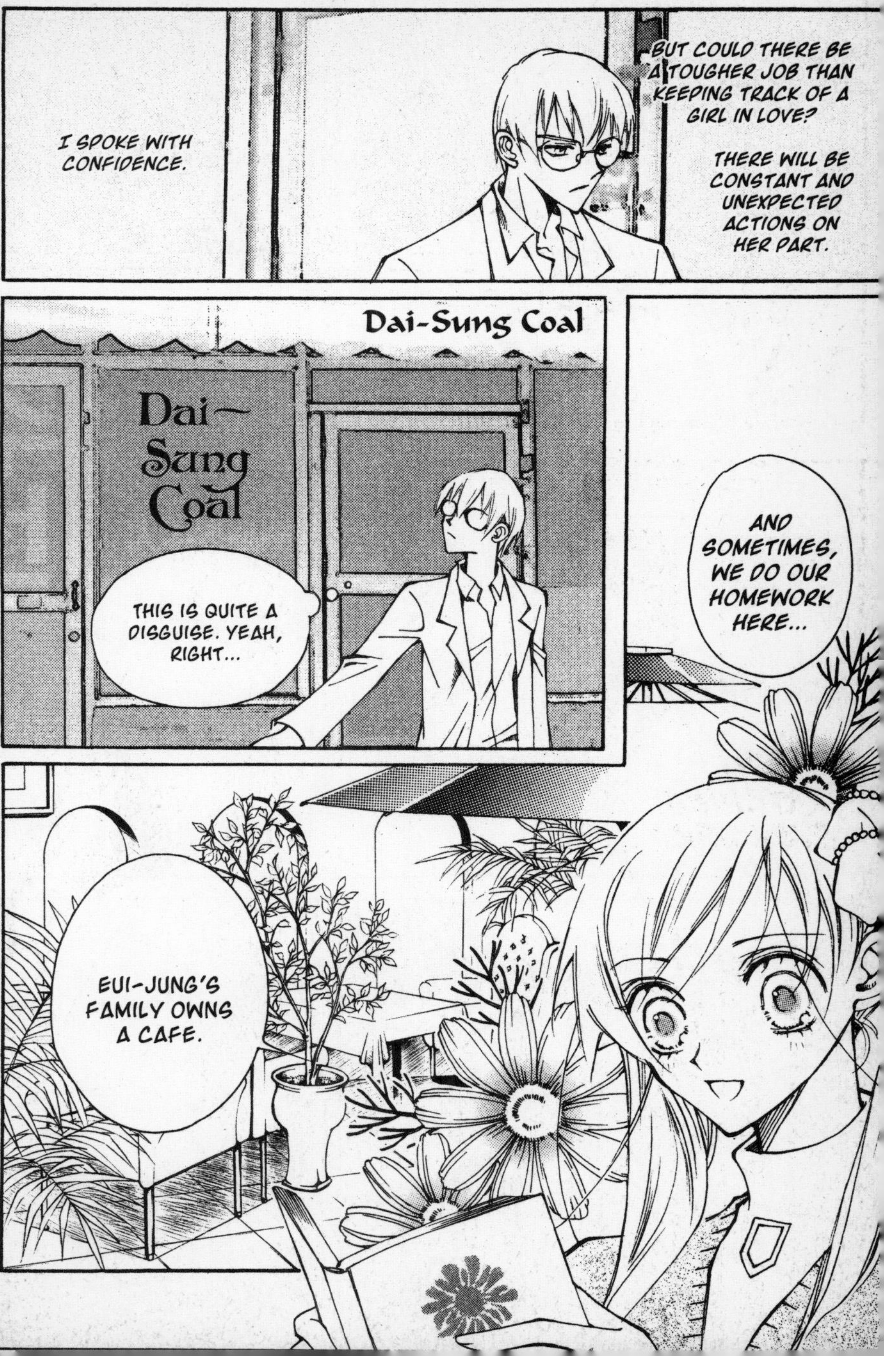
I SPOKE WITH CONFIDENCE.
BUT COULD THERE BE A TOUGHER JOB THAN KEEPING TRACK OF A GIRL IN LOVE?
THERE WILL BE CONSTANT AND UNEXPECTED ACTIONS ON HER PART.
Dai-Sung Coal
Dai-Sung Coal
THIS IS QUITE A DISGUISE. YEAH, RIGHT...
AND SOMETIMES, WE DO OUR HOMEWORK HERE...
EUI-JUNG'S FAMILY OWNS A CAFE.

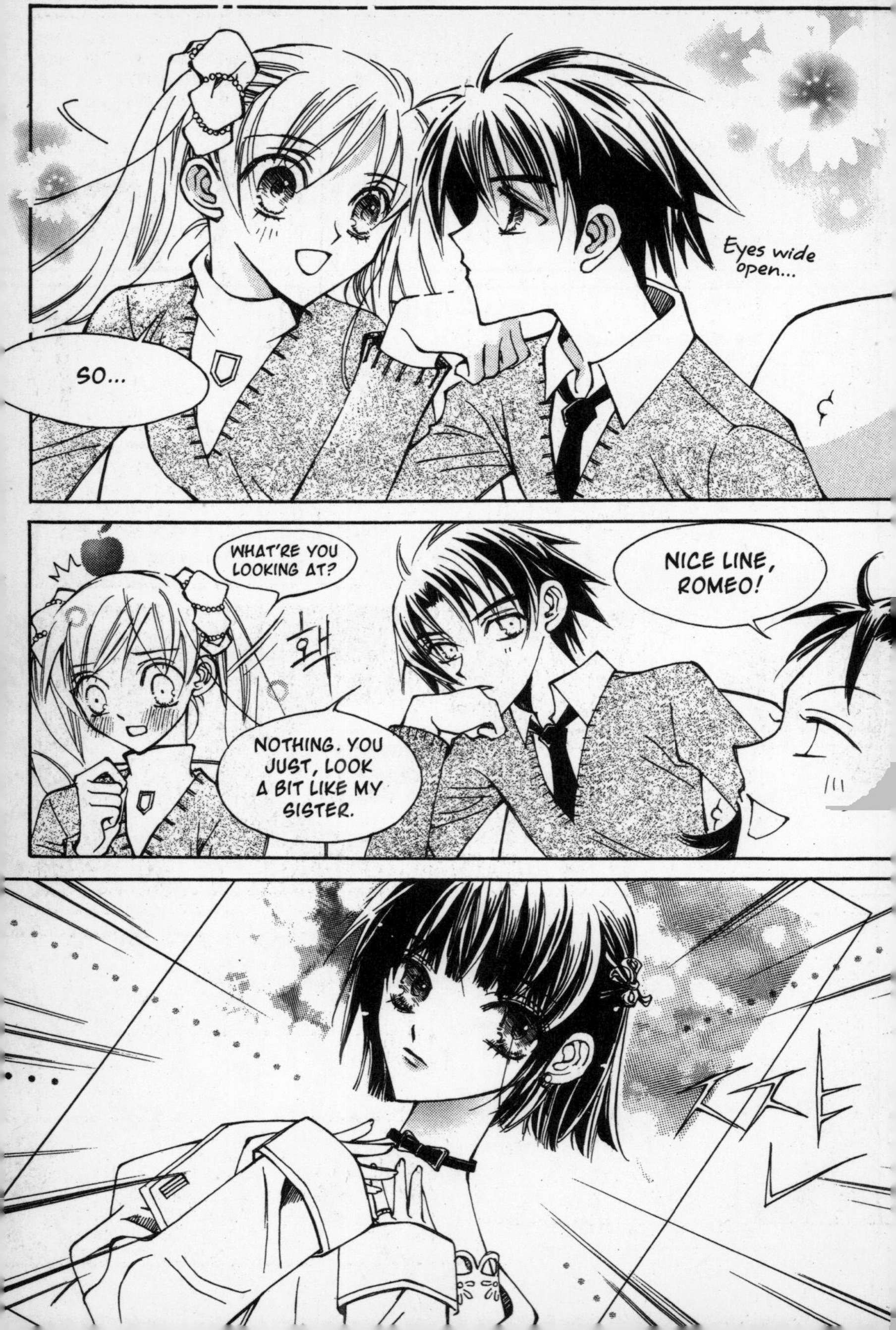
SO...
Eyes wide open...
WHAT'RE YOU LOOKING AT?
홱
NICE LINE, ROMEO!
NOTHING. YOU JUST, LOOK A BIT LIKE MY SISTER.

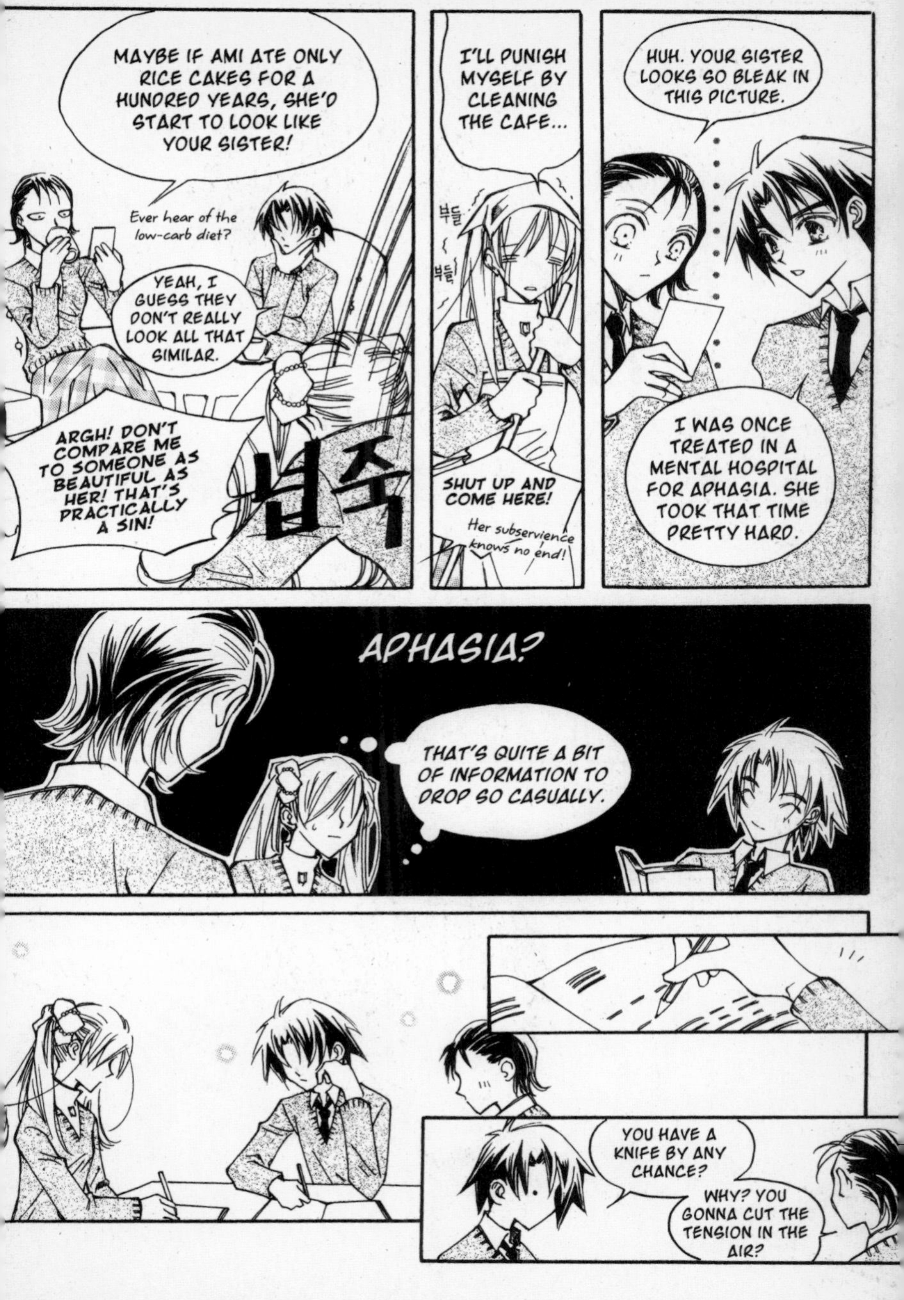
MAYBE IF AMI ATE ONLY RICE CAKES FOR A HUNDRED YEARS, SHE'D START TO LOOK LIKE YOUR SISTER!
Ever hear of the low-carb diet?
YEAH, I GUESS THEY DON'T REALLY LOOK ALL THAT SIMILAR.
ARGH! DON'T COMPARE ME TO SOMEONE AS BEAUTIFUL AS HER! THAT'S PRACTICALLY A SIN!
넙죽
I'LL PUNISH MYSELF BY CLEANING THE CAFE...
부들 부들
SHUT UP AND COME HERE!
Her subservience knows no end!
HUH. YOUR SISTER LOOKS SO BLEAK IN THIS PICTURE.
I WAS ONCE TREATED IN A MENTAL HOSPITAL FOR APHASIA. SHE TOOK THAT TIME PRETTY HARD.
APHASIA?
THAT'S QUITE A BIT OF INFORMATION TO DROP SO CASUALLY.
YOU HAVE A KNIFE BY ANY CHANCE?
WHY? YOU GONNA CUT THE TENSION IN THE AIR?

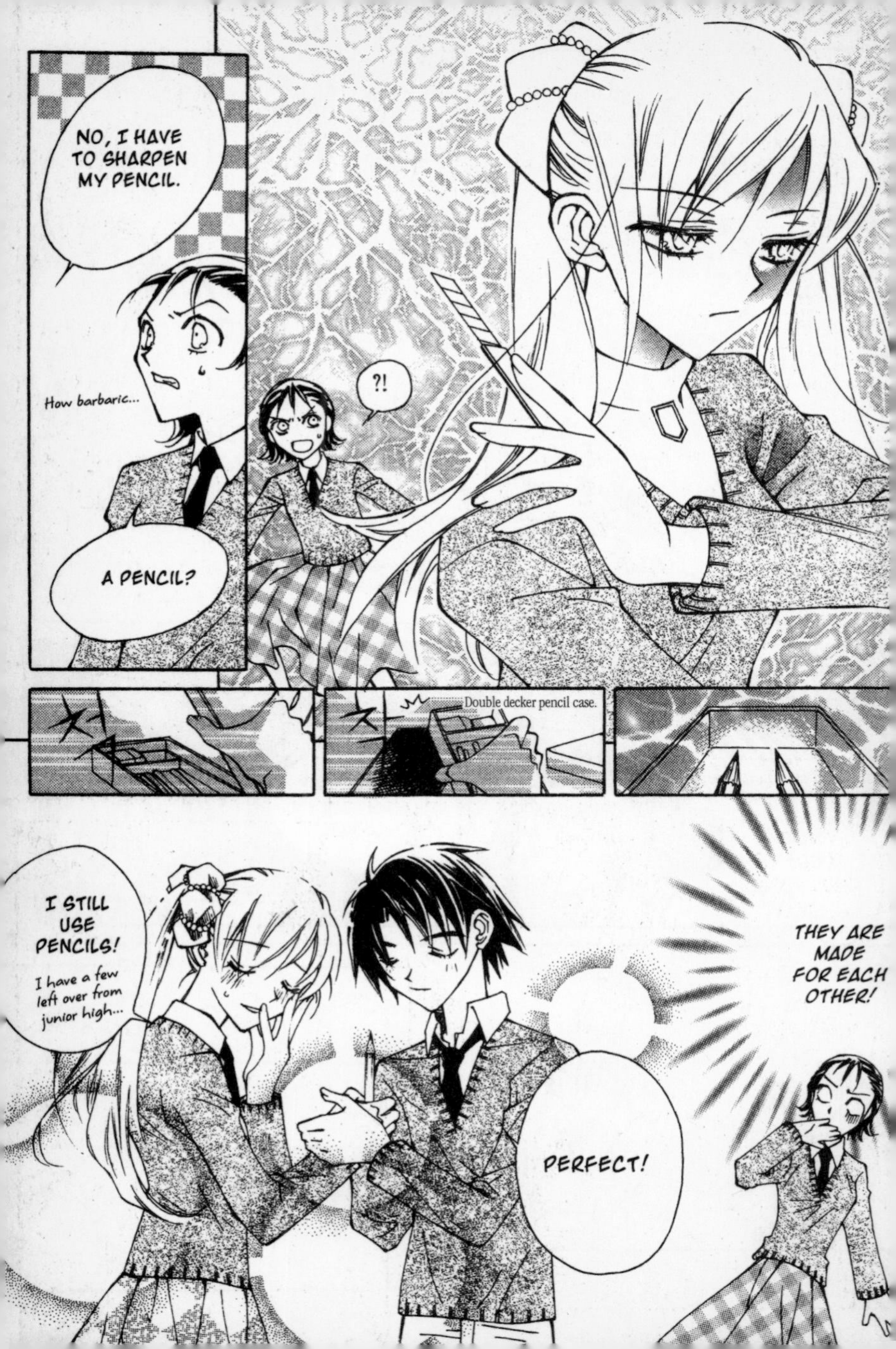
NO, I HAVE TO SHARPEN MY PENCIL.
How barbaric...
A PENCIL?
?!
Double decker pencil case.
I STILL USE PENCILS!
I have a few left over from junior high...
PERFECT!
THEY ARE MADE FOR EACH OTHER!

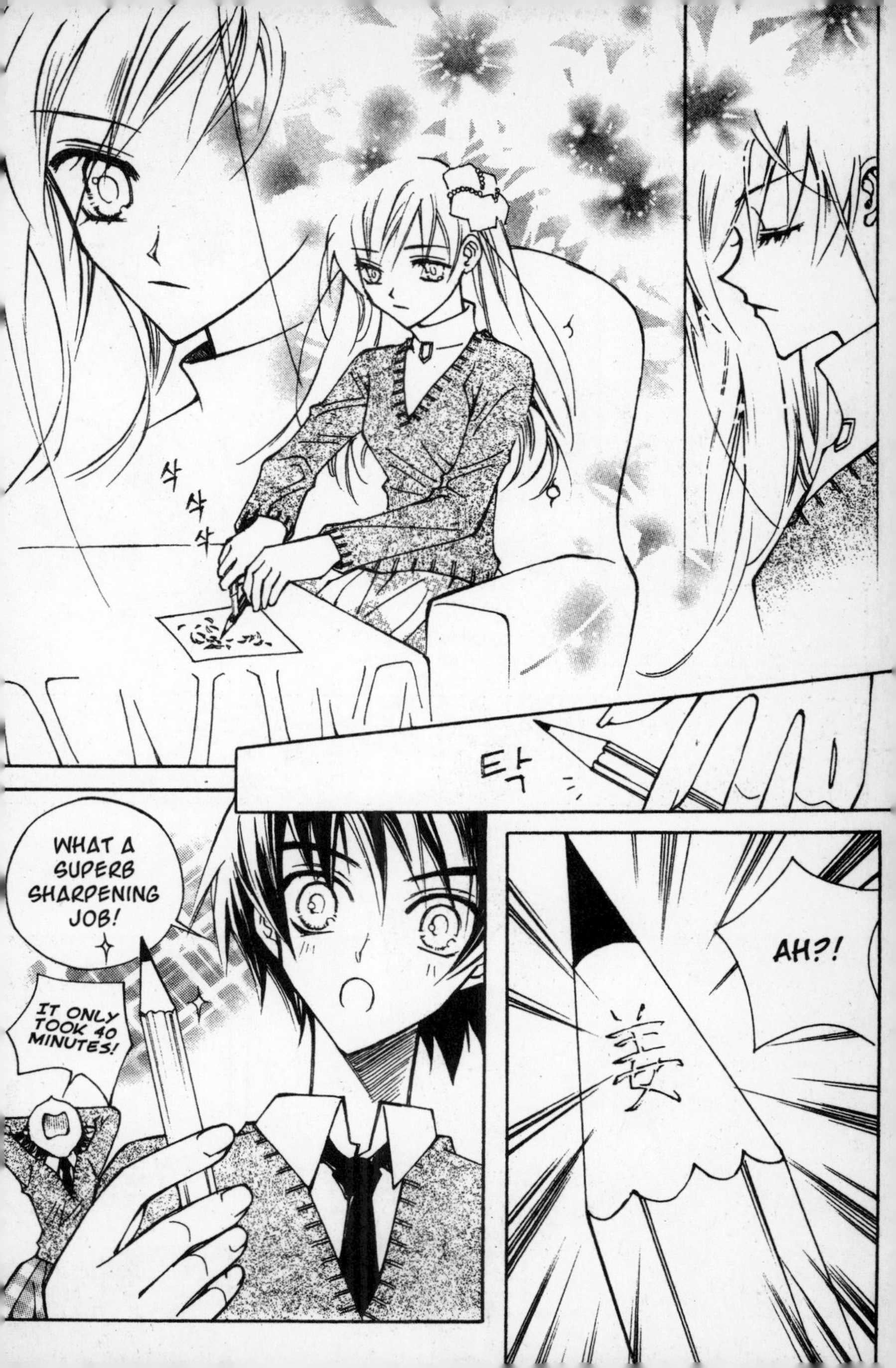

삭
삭
삭
탁
WHAT A SUPERB SHARPENING JOB!
IT ONLY TOOK 40 MINUTES!
AH?!

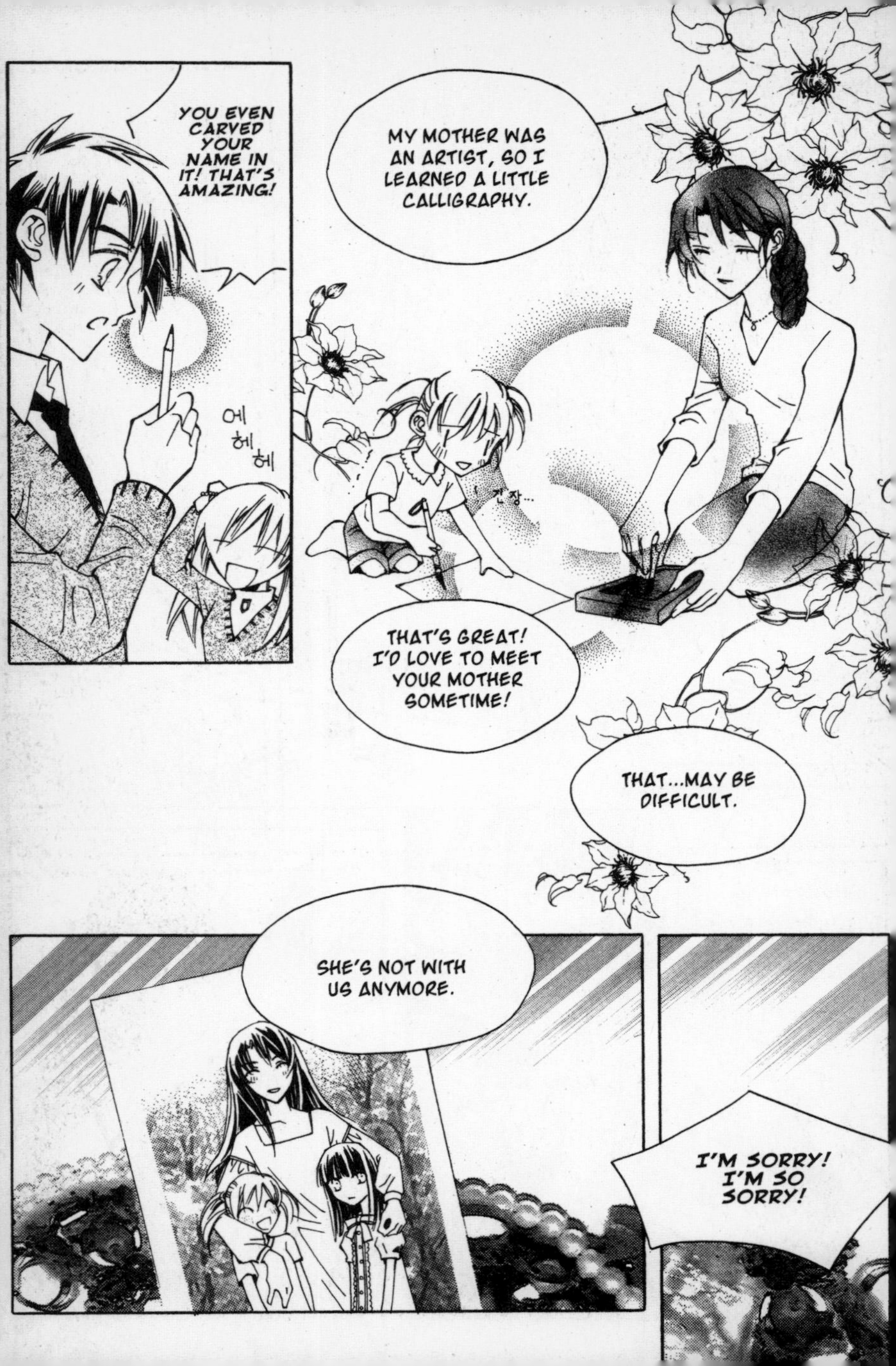
YOU EVEN CARVED YOUR NAME IN IT! THAT'S AMAZING!
에헤헤
MY MOTHER WAS AN ARTIST, SO I LEARNED A LITTLE CALLIGRAPHY.
긴장...
THAT'S GREAT! I'D LOVE TO MEET YOUR MOTHER SOMETIME!
THAT...MAY BE DIFFICULT.
SHE'S NOT WITH US ANYMORE.
I'M SORRY! I'M SO SORRY!

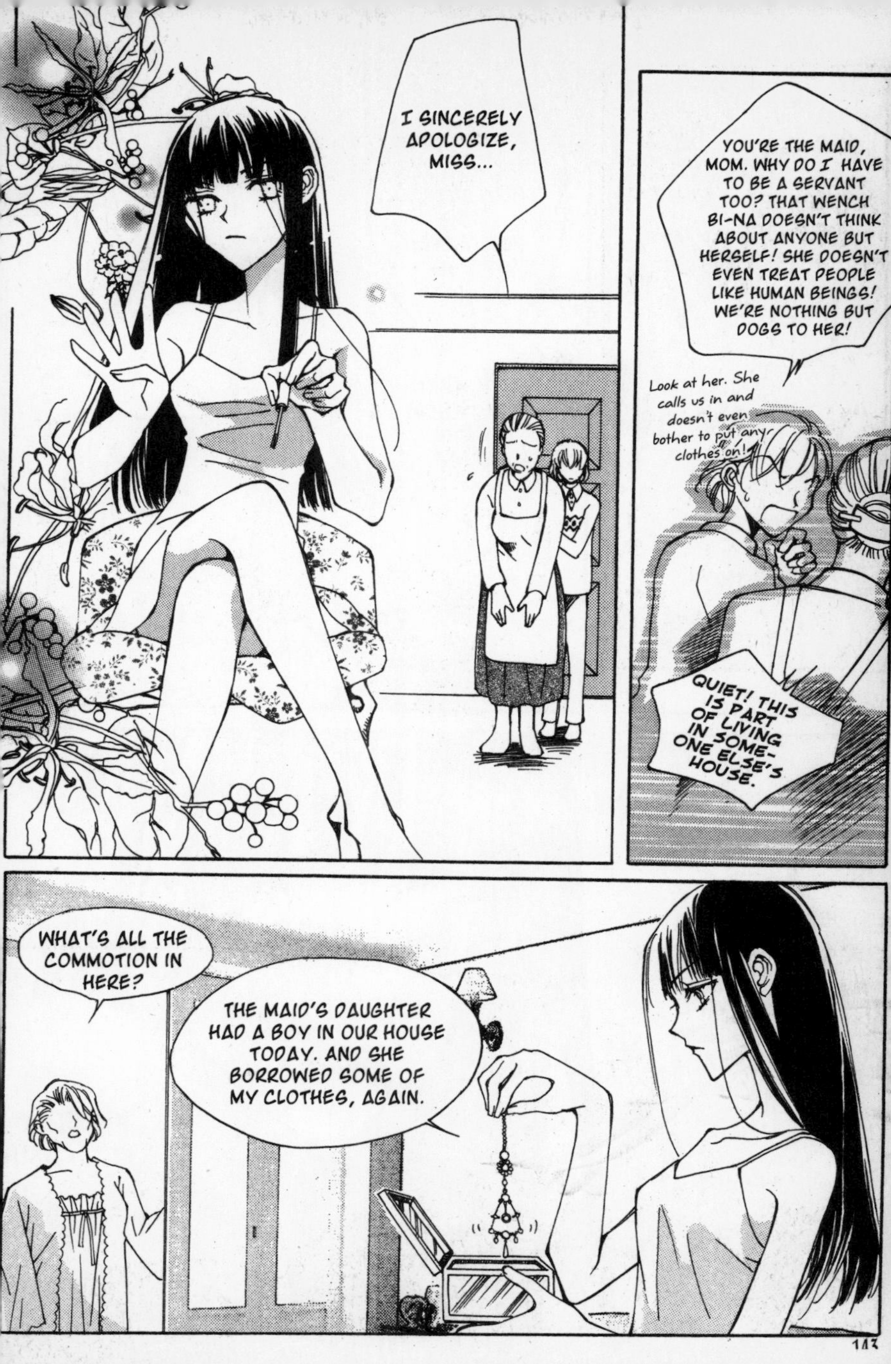
I SINCERELY APOLOGIZE, MISS...
YOU'RE THE MAID, MOM. WHY DO I HAVE TO BE A SERVANT TOO? THAT WENCH BI-NA DOESN'T THINK ABOUT ANYONE BUT HERSELF! SHE DOESN'T EVEN TREAT PEOPLE LIKE HUMAN BEINGS! WE'RE NOTHING BUT DOGS TO HER!
Look at her. She calls us in and doesn't even bother to put any clothes on!
QUIET! THIS IS PART OF LIVING IN SOMEONE ELSE'S HOUSE.
WHAT'S ALL THE COMMOTION IN HERE?
THE MAID'S DAUGHTER HAD A BOY IN OUR HOUSE TODAY. AND SHE BORROWED SOME OF MY CLOTHES, AGAIN.

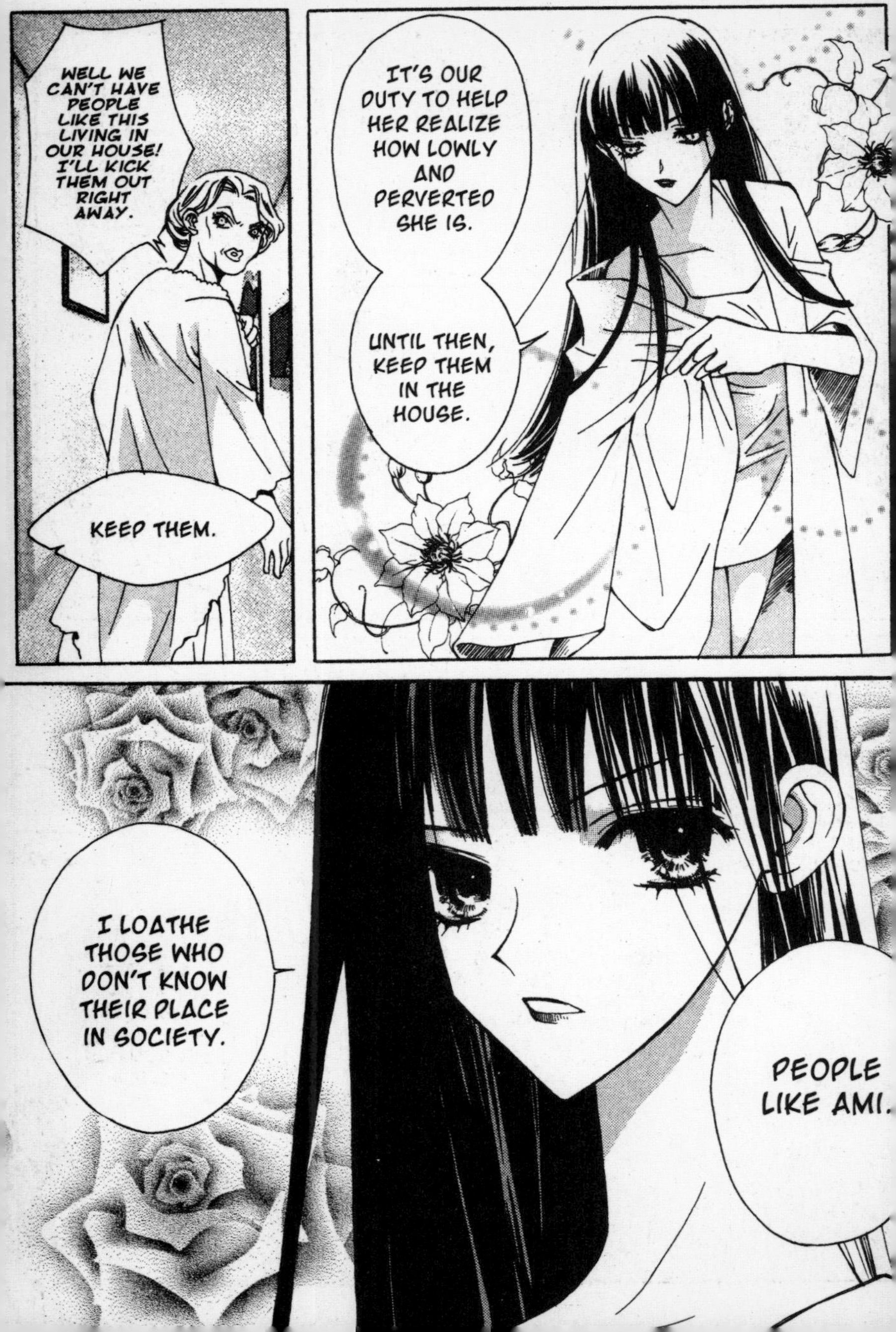
WELL WE CAN'T HAVE PEOPLE LIKE THIS LIVING IN OUR HOUSE! I'LL KICK THEM OUT RIGHT AWAY.
KEEP THEM.
IT'S OUR DUTY TO HELP HER REALIZE HOW LOWLY AND PERVERTED SHE IS.
UNTIL THEN, KEEP THEM IN THE HOUSE.
I LOATHE THOSE WHO DON'T KNOW THEIR PLACE IN SOCIETY.
PEOPLE LIKE AMI.

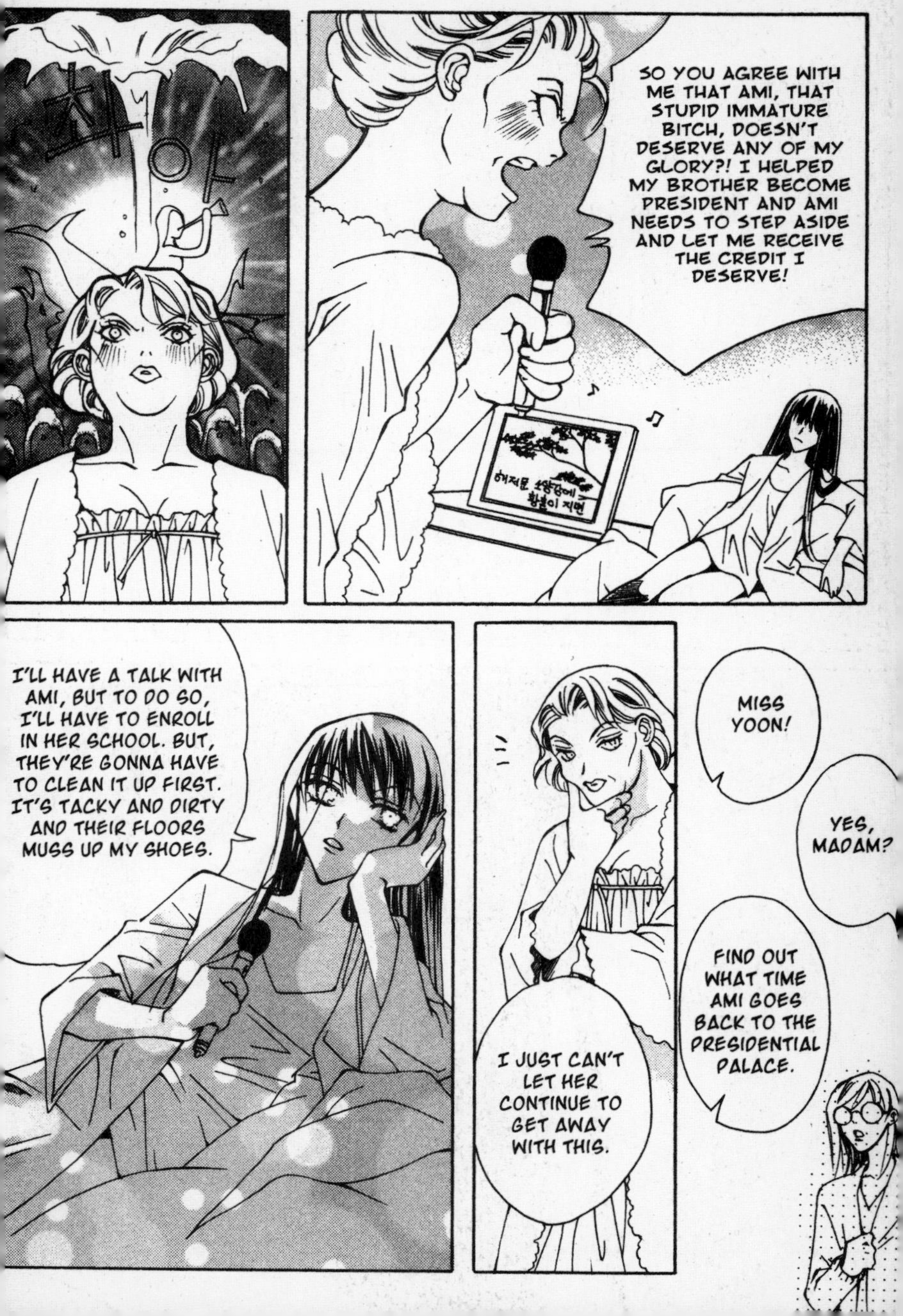
SO YOU AGREE WITH ME THAT AMI, THAT STUPID IMMATURE BITCH, DOESN'T DESERVE ANY OF MY GLORY?! I HELPED MY BROTHER BECOME PRESIDENT AND AMI NEEDS TO STEP ASIDE AND LET ME RECEIVE THE CREDIT I DESERVE!
해저문 소양강에 황혼이 지면
I'LL HAVE A TALK WITH AMI, BUT TO DO SO, I'LL HAVE TO ENROLL IN HER SCHOOL. BUT, THEY'RE GONNA HAVE TO CLEAN IT UP FIRST. IT'S TACKY AND DIRTY AND THEIR FLOORS MUSS UP MY SHOES.
MISS YOON!
YES, MADAM?
FIND OUT WHAT TIME AMI GOES BACK TO THE PRESIDENTIAL PALACE.
I JUST CAN'T LET HER CONTINUE TO GET AWAY WITH THIS.

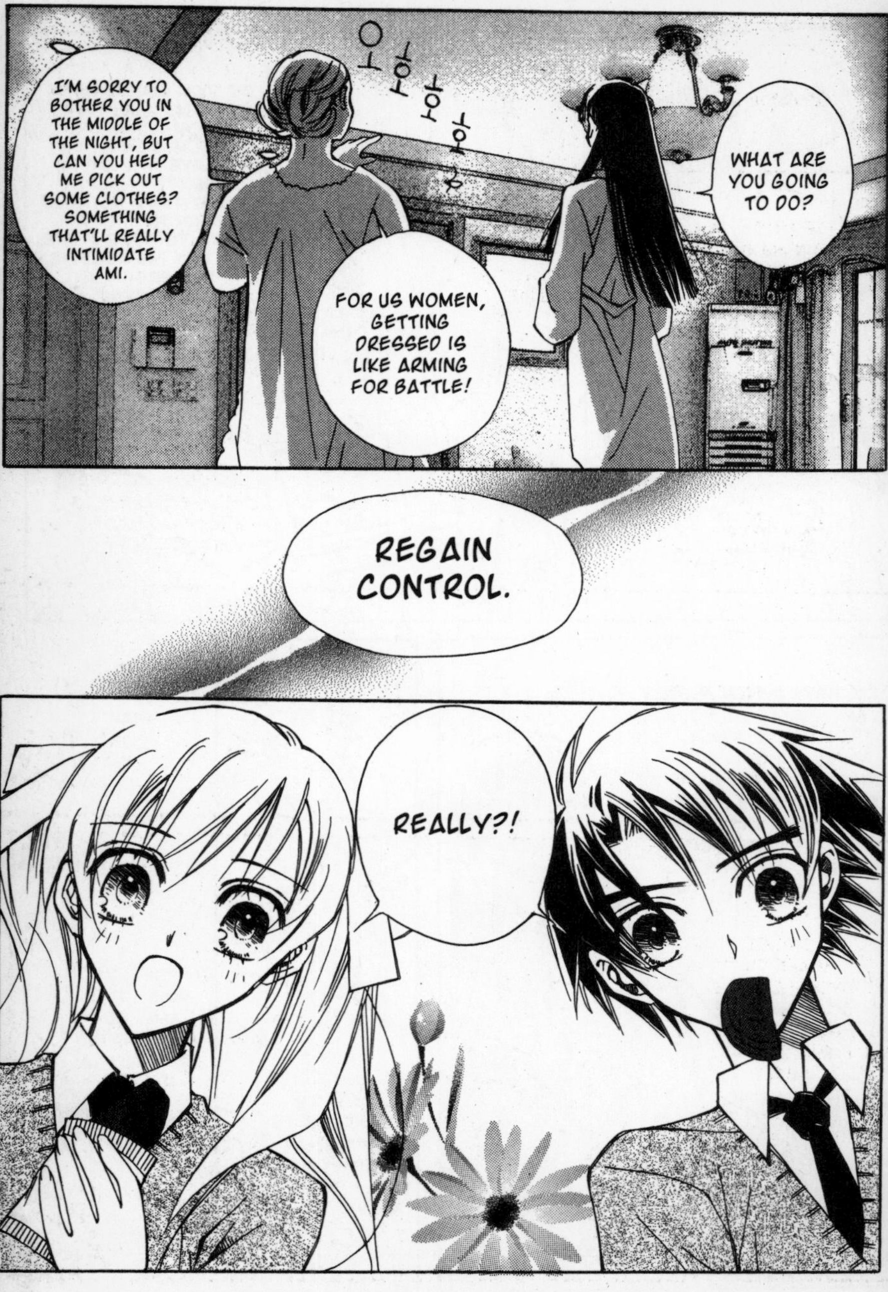
I'M SORRY TO BOTHER YOU IN THE MIDDLE OF THE NIGHT, BUT CAN YOU HELP ME PICK OUT SOME CLOTHES? SOMETHING THAT'LL REALLY INTIMIDATE AMI.
오호호호호
WHAT ARE YOU GOING TO DO?
FOR US WOMEN, GETTING DRESSED IS LIKE ARMING FOR BATTLE!
REGAIN CONTROL.
REALLY?!

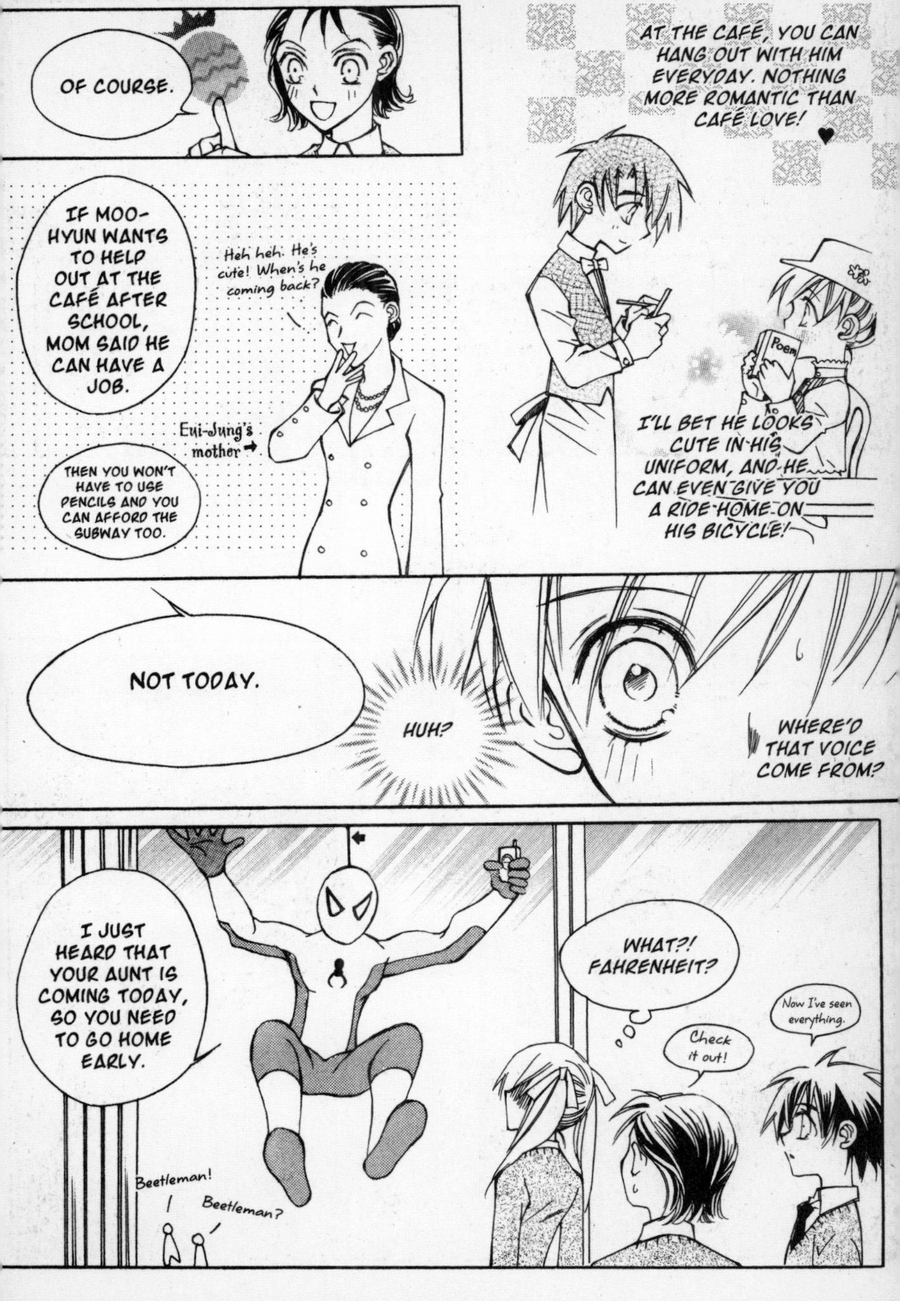
OF COURSE.
IF MOO-HYUN WANTS TO HELP OUT AT THE CAFÉ AFTER SCHOOL, MOM SAID HE CAN HAVE A JOB.
Heh heh. He's cute! When's he coming back?
Eui-Jung's mother
THEN YOU WON'T HAVE TO USE PENCILS AND YOU CAN AFFORD THE SUBWAY TOO.
AT THE CAFÉ, YOU CAN HANG OUT WITH HIM EVERYDAY. NOTHING MORE ROMANTIC THAN CAFÉ LOVE!
Poem
I'LL BET HE LOOKS CUTE IN HIS UNIFORM, AND HE CAN EVEN GIVE YOU A RIDE HOME ON HIS BICYCLE!
NOT TODAY.
HUH?
WHERE'D THAT VOICE COME FROM?
I JUST HEARD THAT YOUR AUNT IS COMING TODAY, SO YOU NEED TO GO HOME EARLY.
Beetleman!
Beetleman?
WHAT?! FAHRENHEIT?
Check it out!
Now I've seen everything.

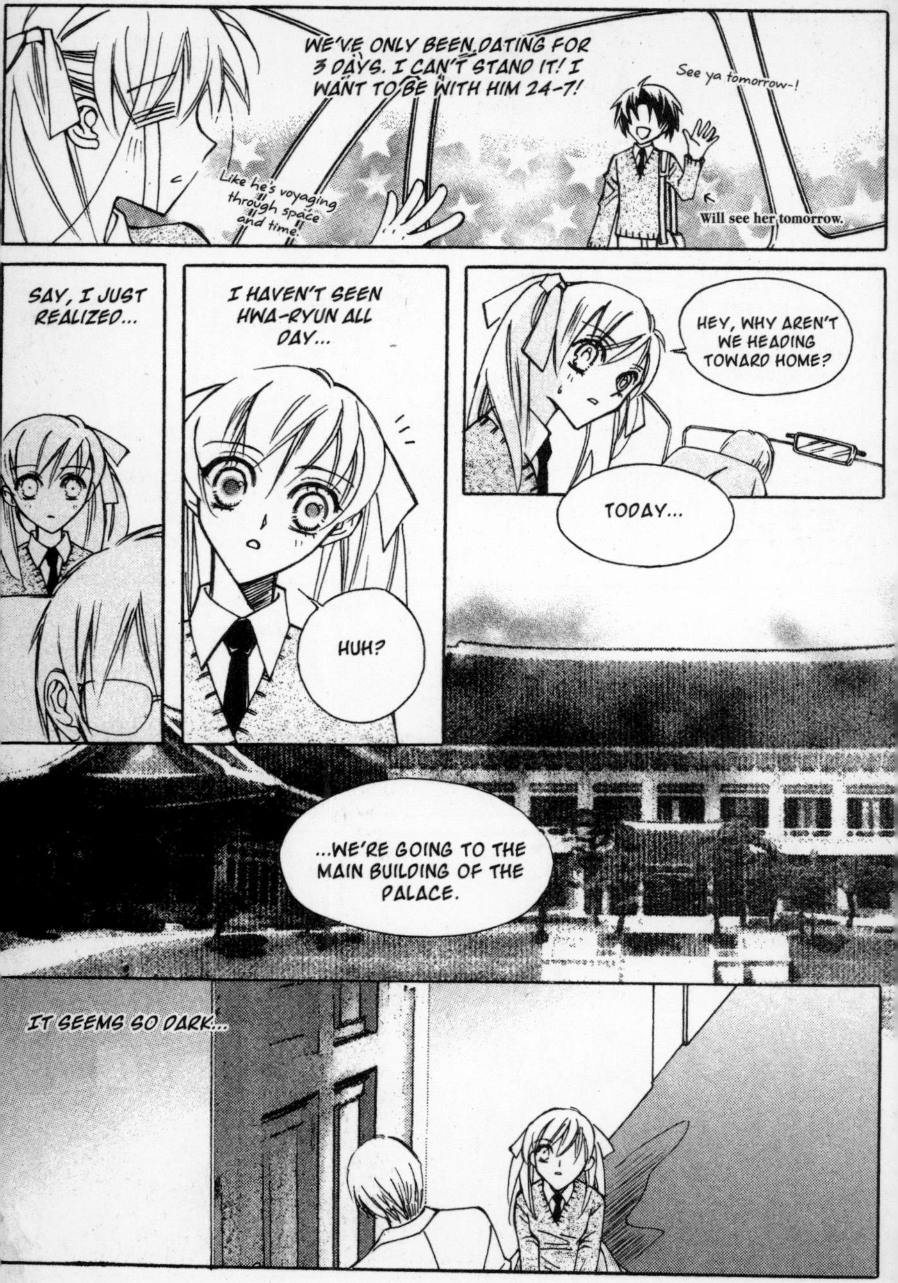
WE'VE ONLY BEEN DATING FOR 3 DAYS. I CAN'T STAND IT! I WANT TO BE WITH HIM 24-7!
See ya tomorrow-!
Like he's voyaging through space and time.
Will see her tomorrow.
SAY, I JUST REALIZED...
I HAVEN'T SEEN HWA-RYUN ALL DAY...
HUH?
HEY, WHY AREN'T WE HEADING TOWARD HOME?
TODAY...
...WE'RE GOING TO THE MAIN BUILDING OF THE PALACE.
IT SEEMS SO DARK...

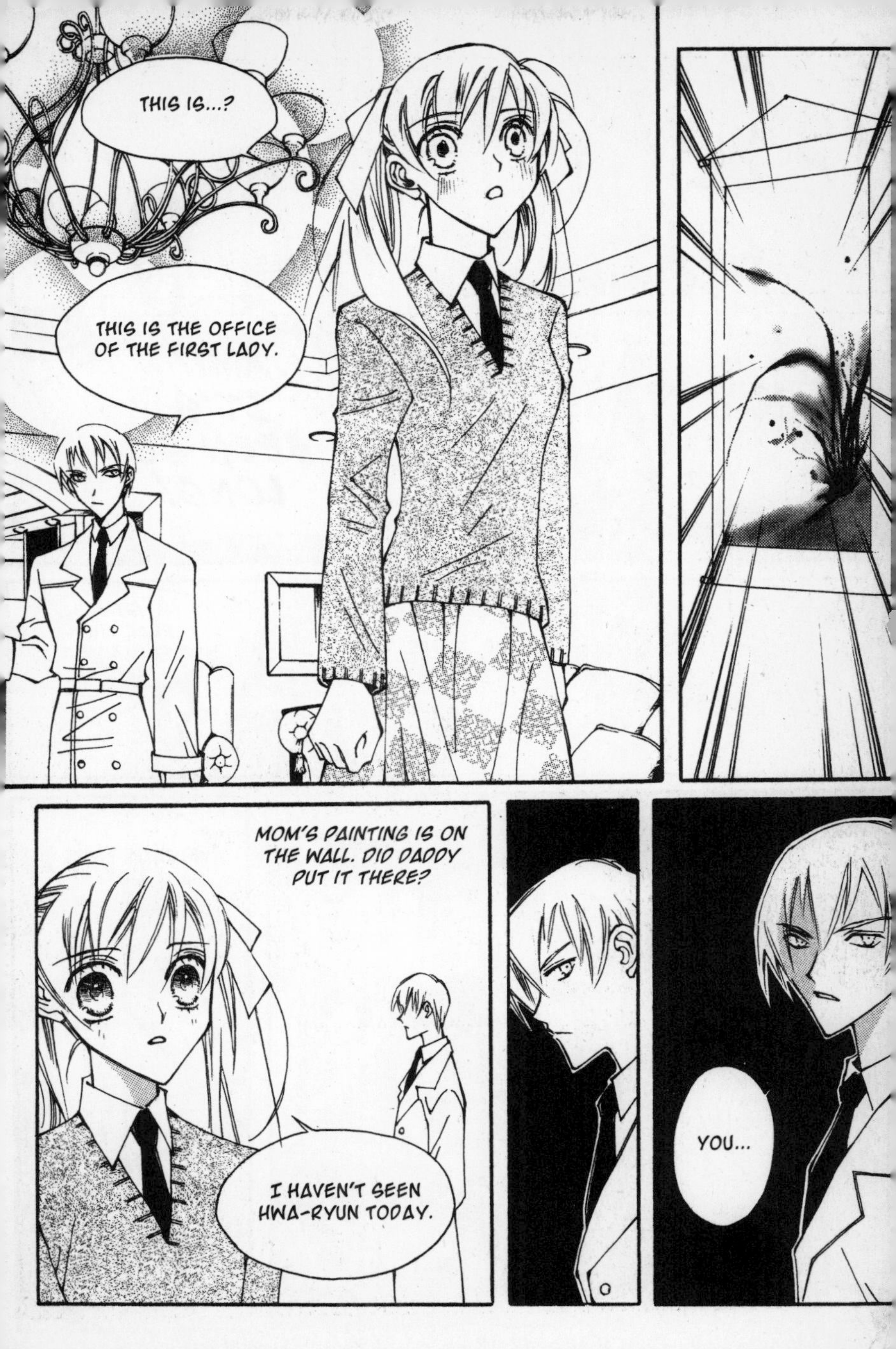
THIS IS...?
THIS IS THE OFFICE OF THE FIRST LADY.
MOM'S PAINTING IS ON THE WALL. DID DADDY PUT IT THERE?
I HAVEN'T SEEN HWA-RYUN TODAY.
YOU...

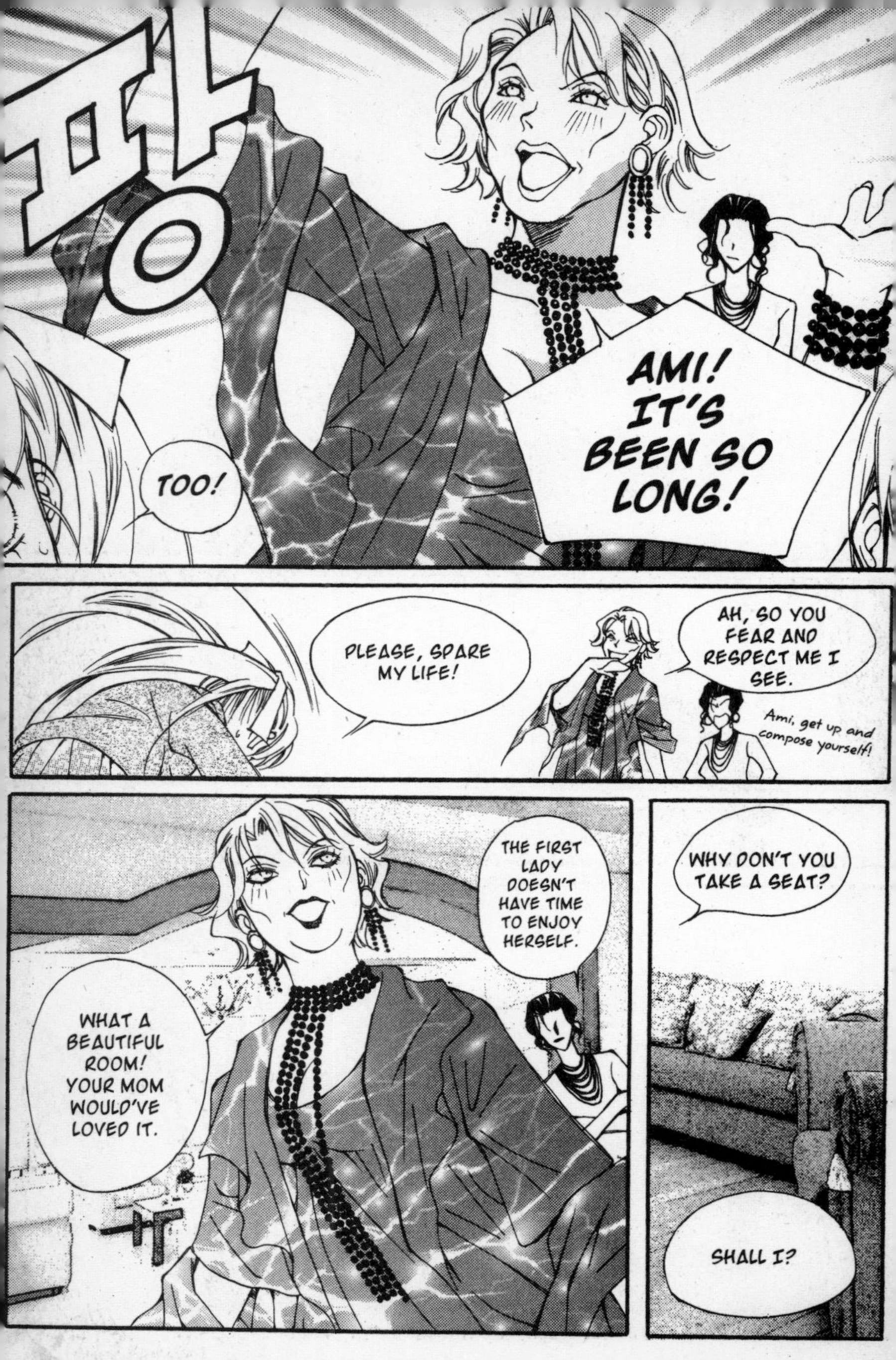
TOO!
AMI! IT'S BEEN SO LONG!
PLEASE, SPARE MY LIFE!
AH, SO YOU FEAR AND RESPECT ME I SEE.
Ami, get up and compose yourself!
THE FIRST LADY DOESN'T HAVE TIME TO ENJOY HERSELF.
WHAT A BEAUTIFUL ROOM! YOUR MOM WOULD'VE LOVED IT.
WHY DON'T YOU TAKE A SEAT?
SHALL I?

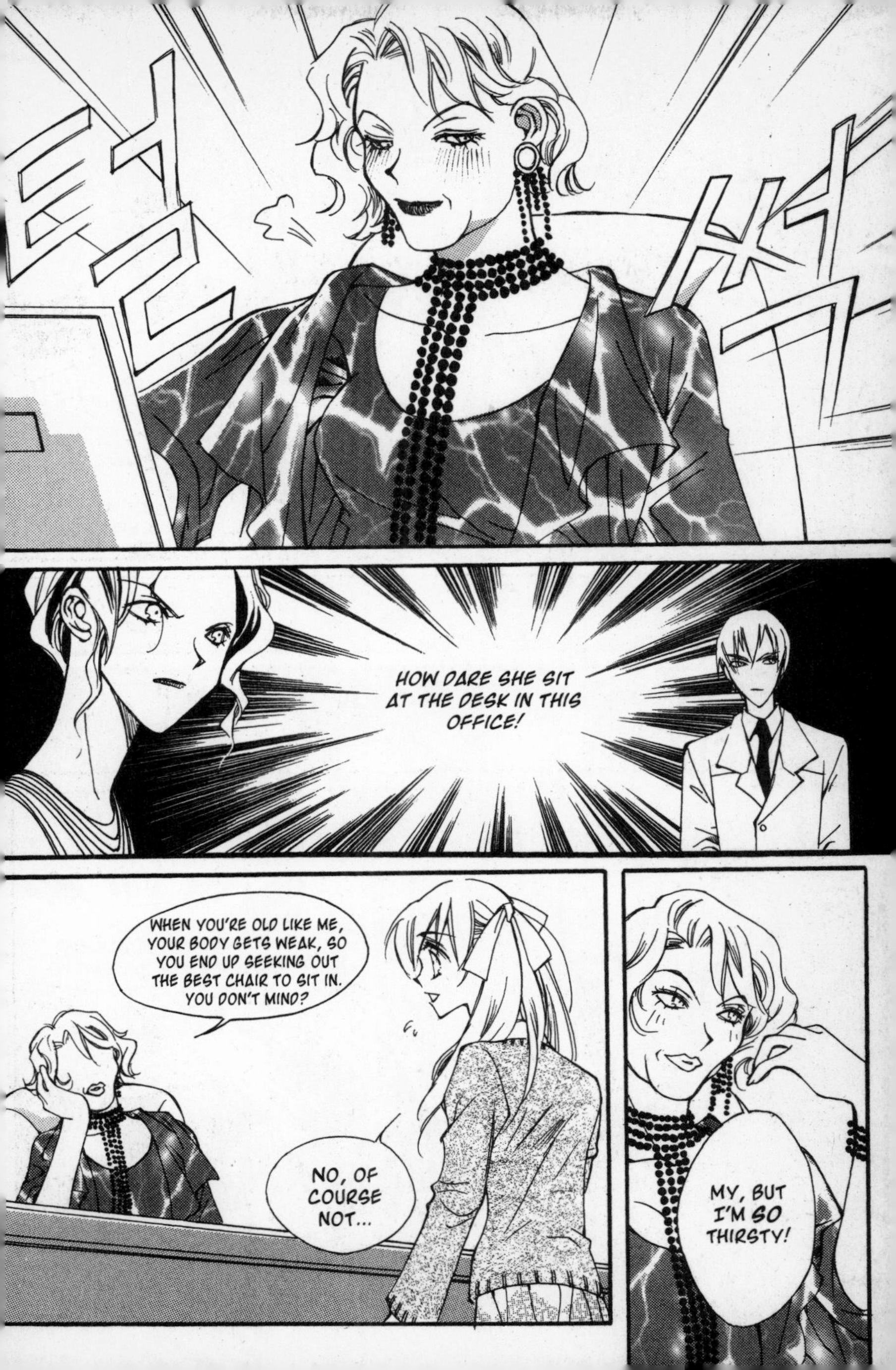
HOW DARE SHE SIT AT THE DESK IN THIS OFFICE!
WHEN YOU'RE OLD LIKE ME, YOUR BODY GETS WEAK, SO YOU END UP SEEKING OUT THE BEST CHAIR TO SIT IN. YOU DON'T MIND?
NO, OF COURSE NOT...
MY, BUT I'M SO THIRSTY!

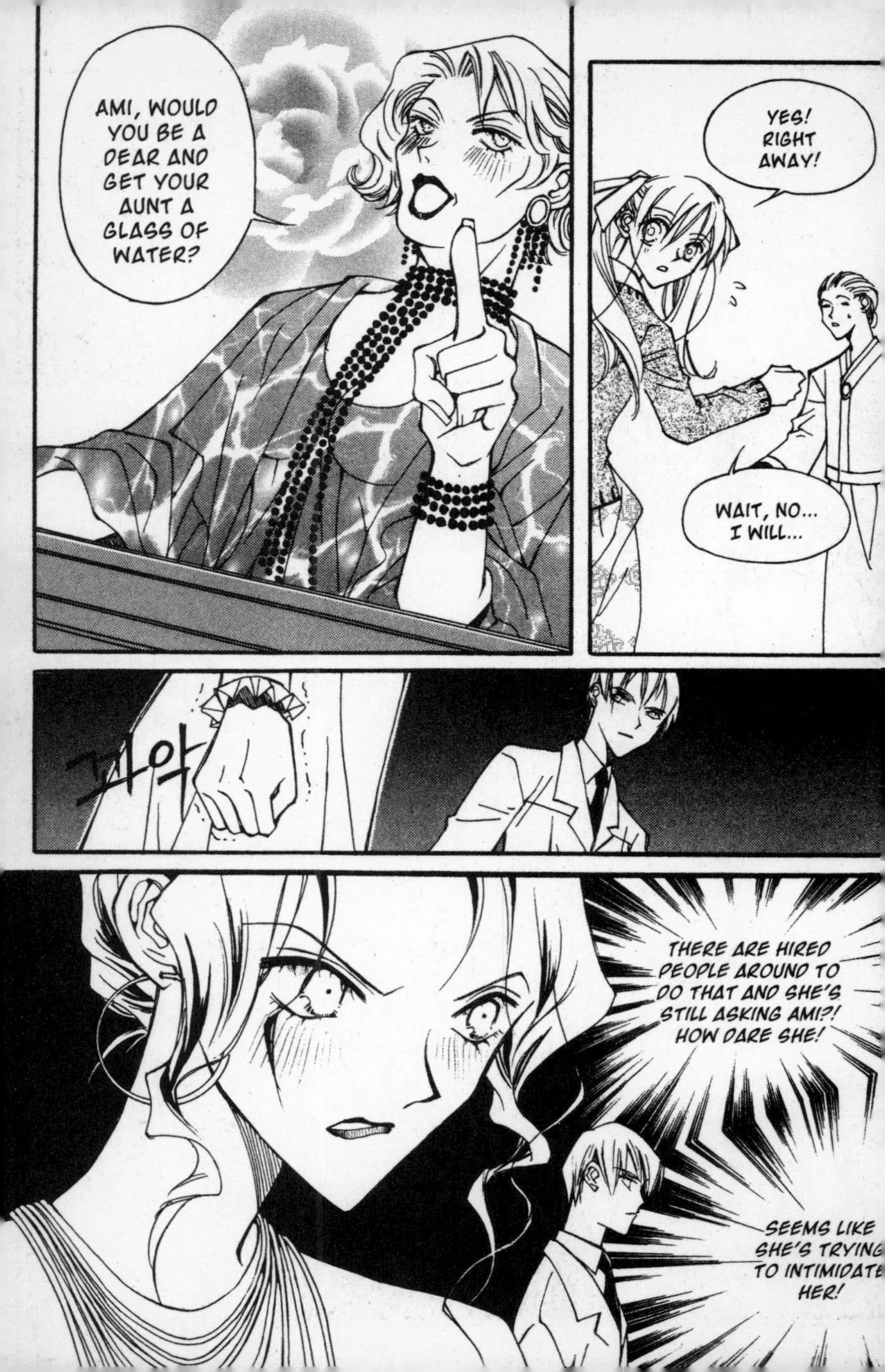
AMI, WOULD YOU BE A DEAR AND GET YOUR AUNT A GLASS OF WATER?
YES! RIGHT AWAY!
WAIT, NO... I WILL...
THERE ARE HIRED PEOPLE AROUND TO DO THAT AND SHE'S STILL ASKING AMI?! HOW DARE SHE!
SEEMS LIKE SHE'S TRYING TO INTIMIDATE HER!

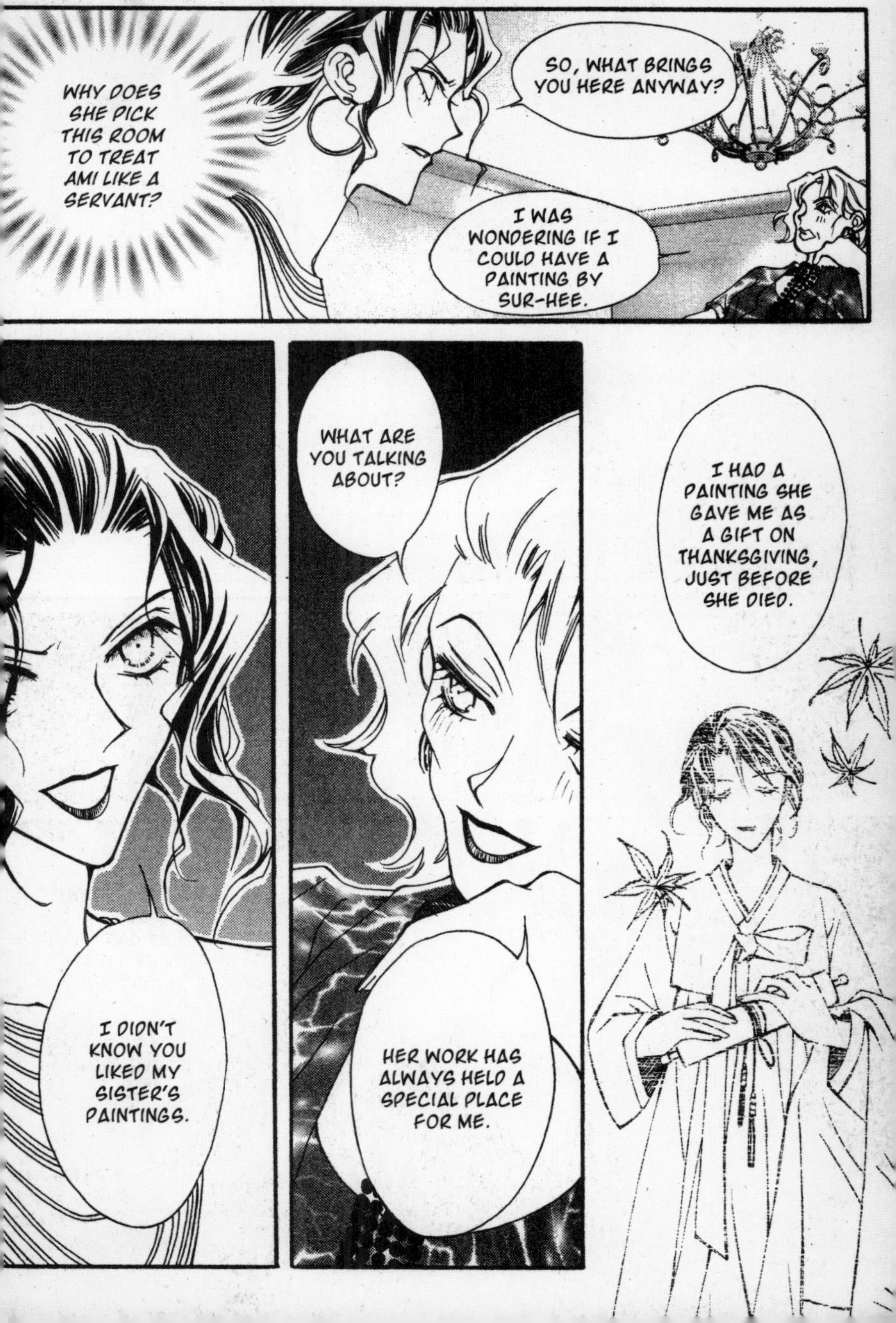
WHY DOES SHE PICK THIS ROOM TO TREAT AMI LIKE A SERVANT?
SO, WHAT BRINGS YOU HERE ANYWAY?
I WAS WONDERING IF I COULD HAVE A PAINTING BY SUR-HEE.
I DIDN'T KNOW YOU LIKED MY SISTER'S PAINTINGS.
WHAT ARE YOU TALKING ABOUT?
HER WORK HAS ALWAYS HELD A SPECIAL PLACE FOR ME.
I HAD A PAINTING SHE GAVE ME AS A GIFT ON THANKSGIVING, JUST BEFORE SHE DIED.

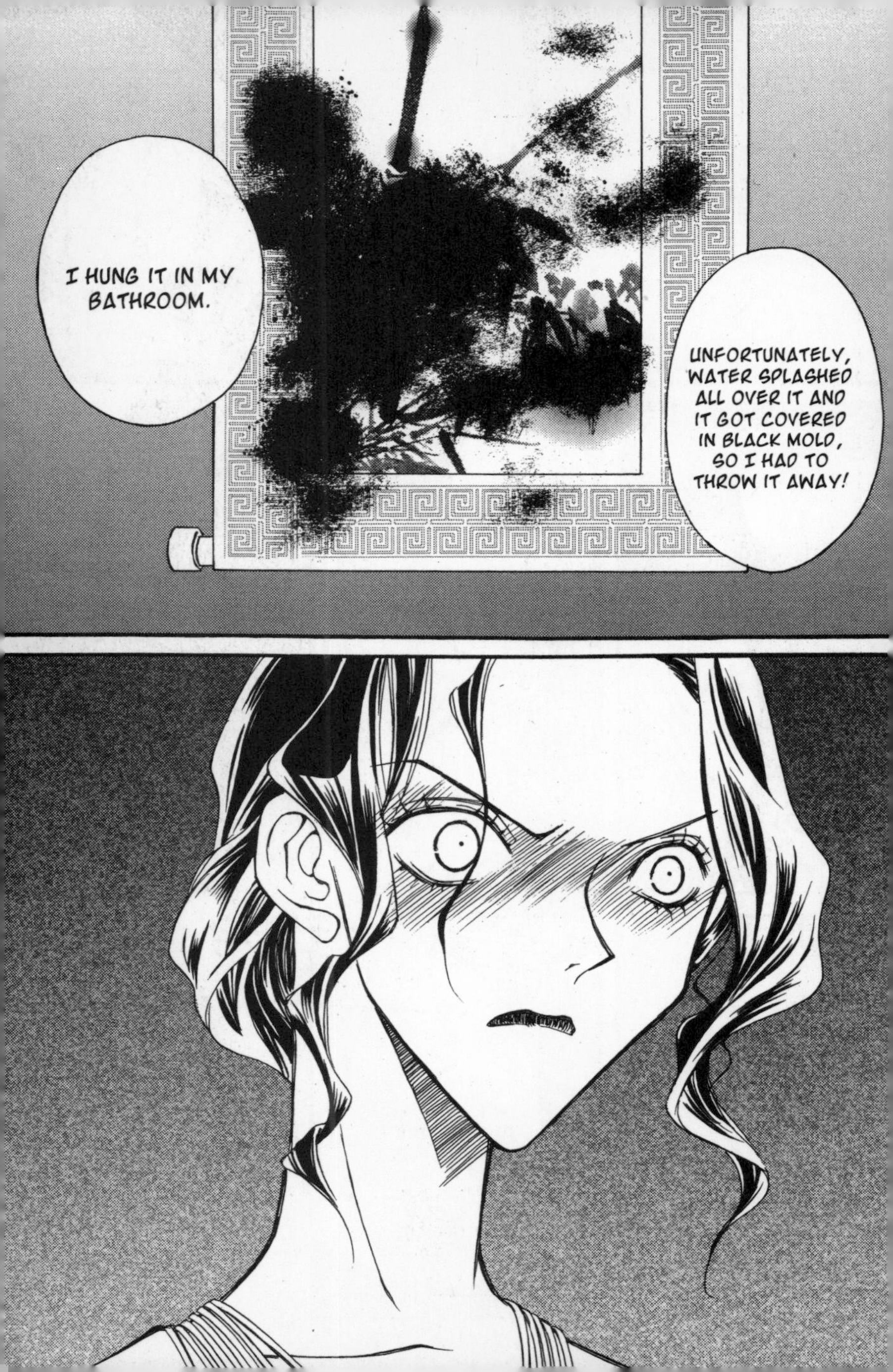
I HUNG IT IN MY BATHROOM.
UNFORTUNATELY, WATER SPLASHED ALL OVER IT AND IT GOT COVERED IN BLACK MOLD, SO I HAD TO THROW IT AWAY!

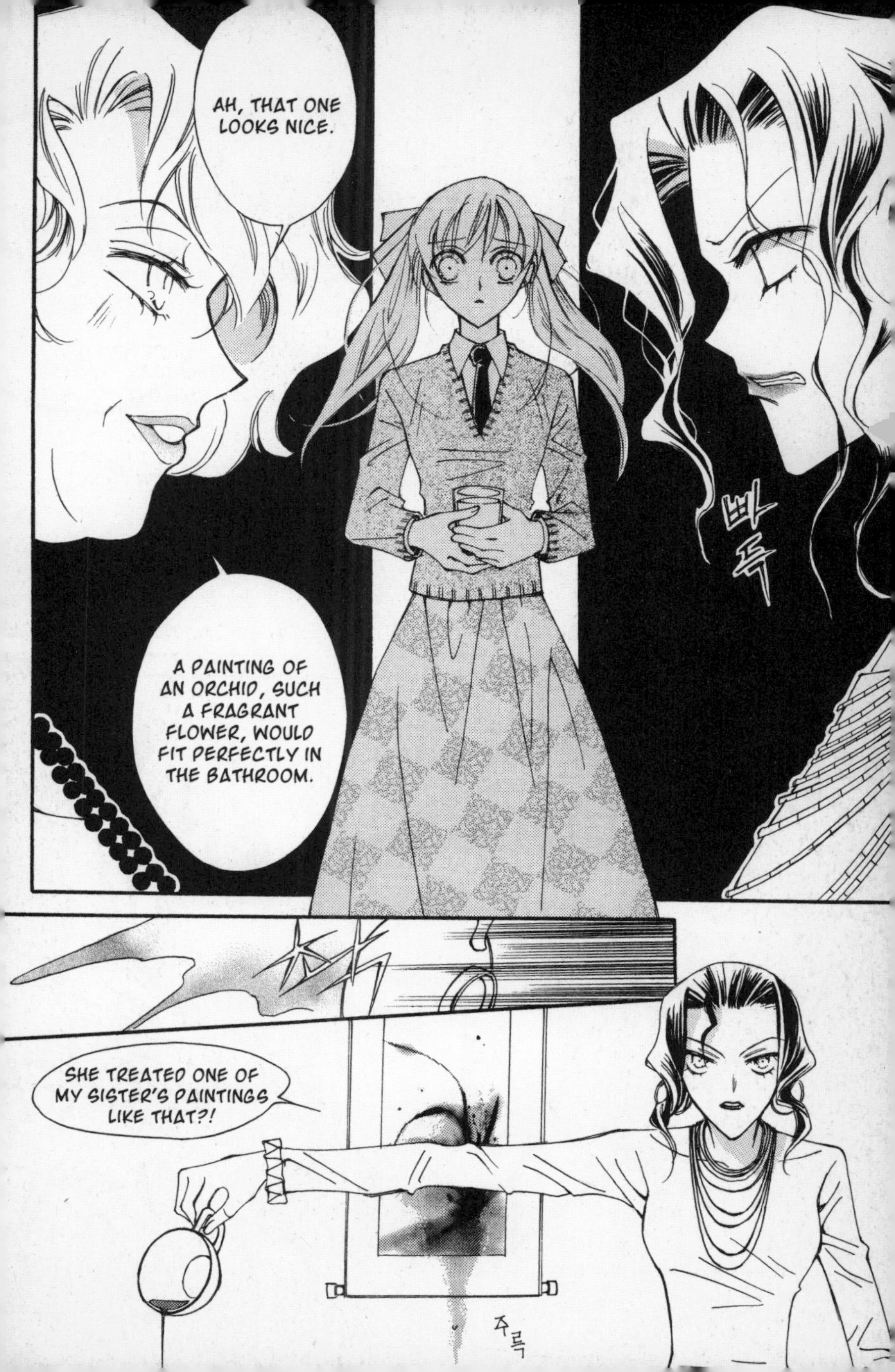
AH, THAT ONE LOOKS NICE.
A PAINTING OF AN ORCHID, SUCH A FRAGRANT FLOWER, WOULD FIT PERFECTLY IN THE BATHROOM.
빠득
SHE TREATED ONE OF MY SISTER'S PAINTINGS LIKE THAT?!
주륵

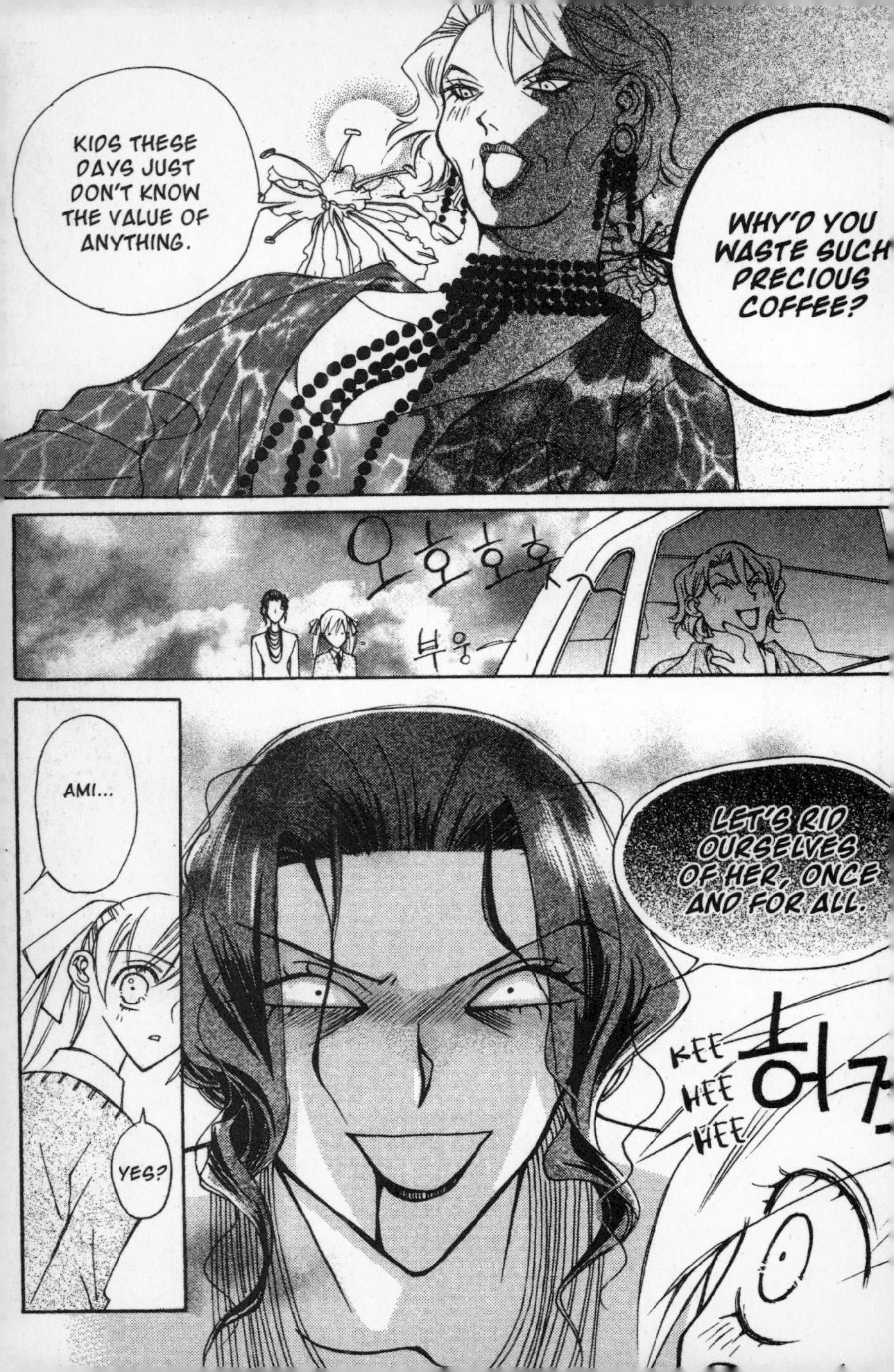
KIDS THESE DAYS JUST DON'T KNOW THE VALUE OF ANYTHING.
WHY'D YOU WASTE SUCH PRECIOUS COFFEE?
오호호홋~
부웅~
AMI...
YES?
LET'S RID OURSELVES OF HER, ONCE AND FOR ALL.
KEE HEE HEE
히

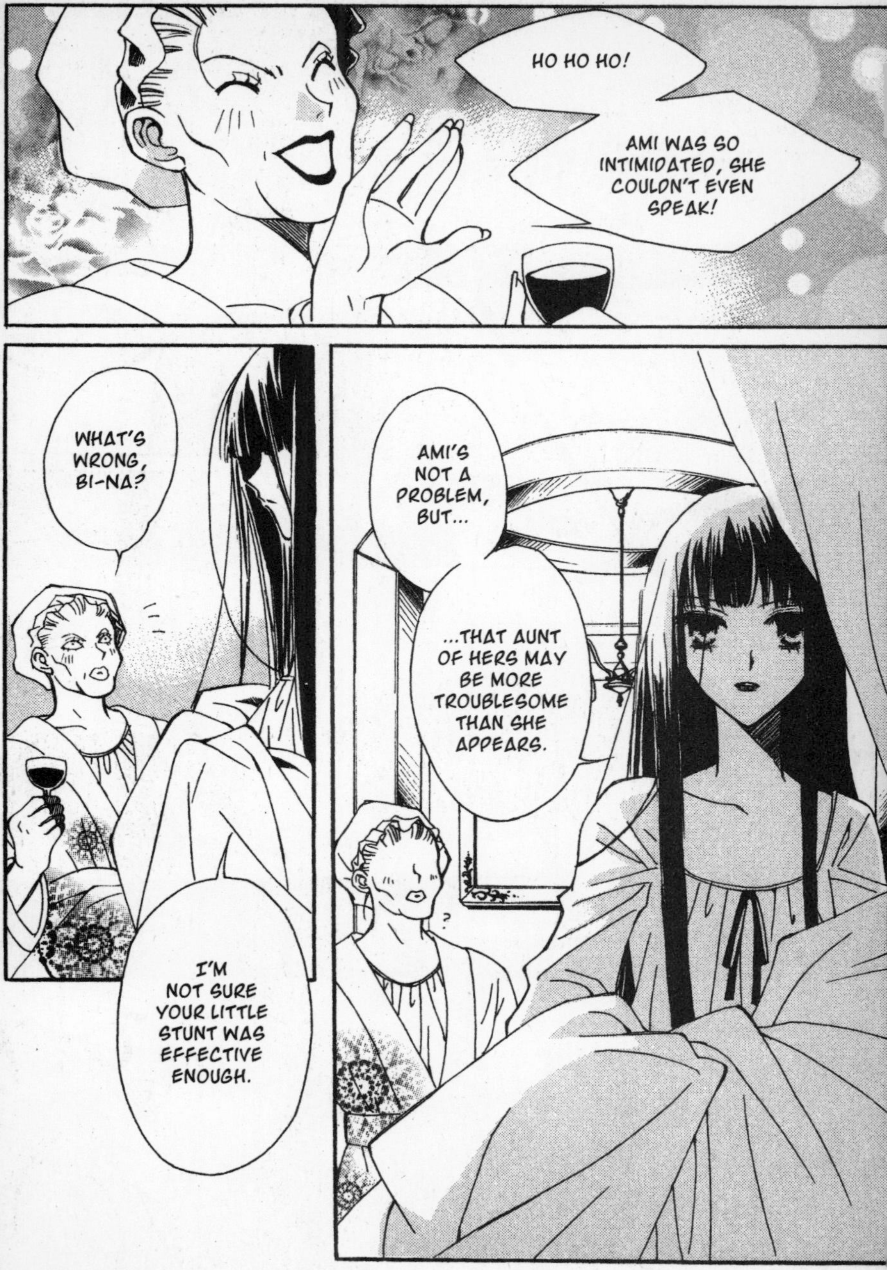
HO HO HO!
AMI WAS SO INTIMIDATED, SHE COULDN'T EVEN SPEAK!
WHAT'S WRONG, BI-NA?
I'M NOT SURE YOUR LITTLE STUNT WAS EFFECTIVE ENOUGH.
AMI'S NOT A PROBLEM, BUT...
...THAT AUNT OF HERS MAY BE MORE TROUBLESOME THAN SHE APPEARS.
?

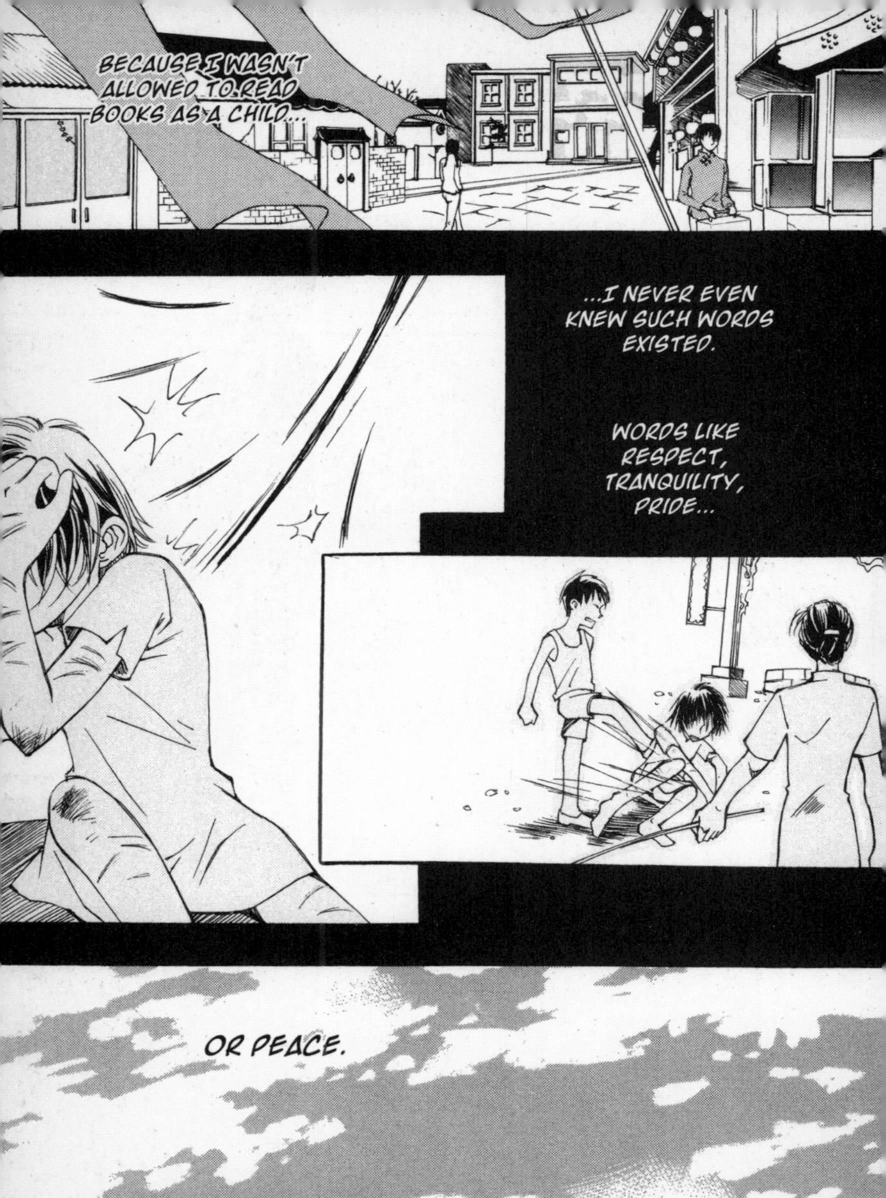
BECAUSE I WASN'T ALLOWED TO READ BOOKS AS A CHILD...
...I NEVER EVEN KNEW SUCH WORDS EXISTED.
WORDS LIKE RESPECT, TRANQUILITY, PRIDE...
OR PEACE.

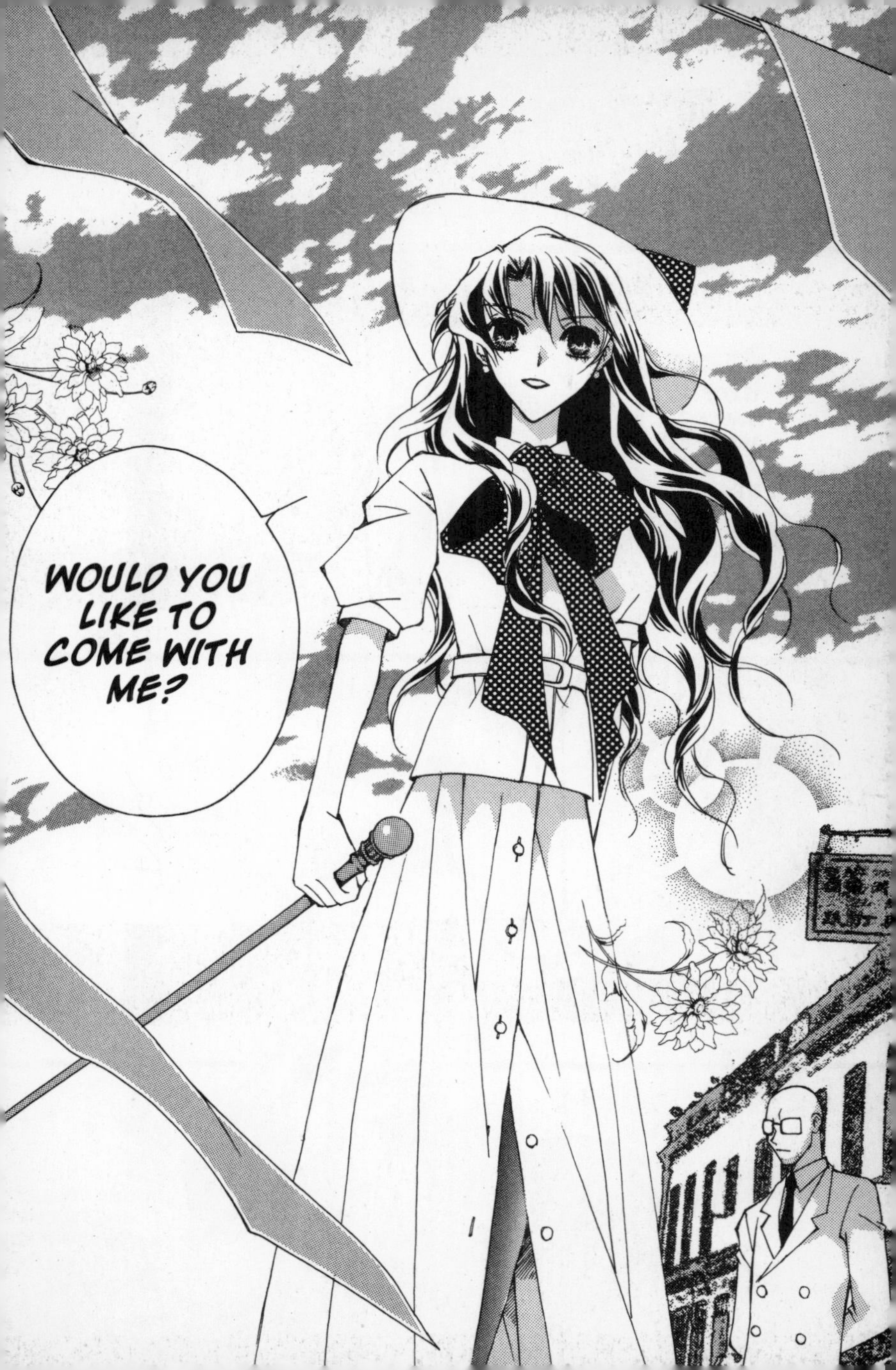
WOULD YOU LIKE TO COME WITH ME?

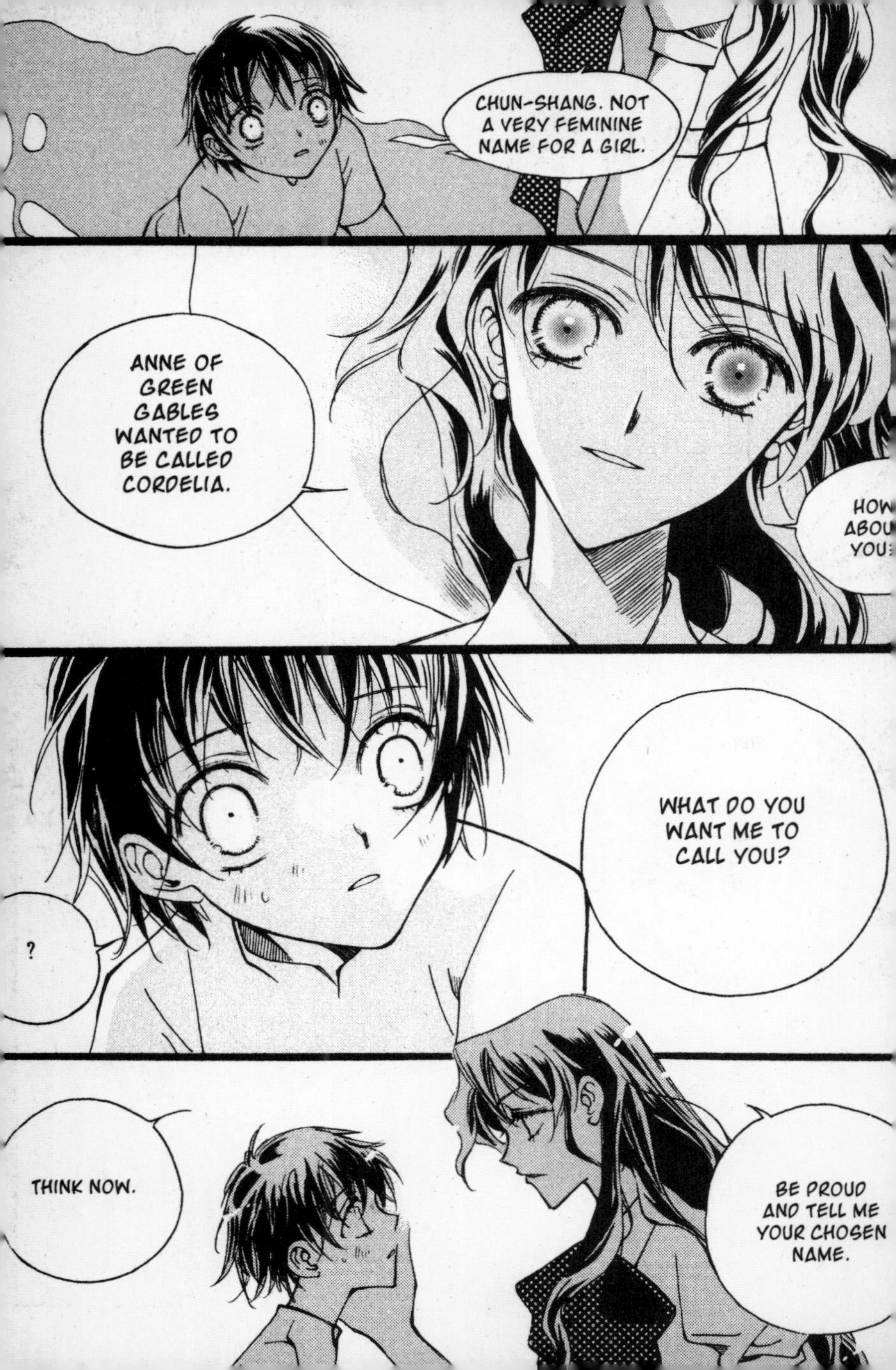
CHUN-SHANG. NOT A VERY FEMININE NAME FOR A GIRL.
ANNE OF GREEN GABLES WANTED TO BE CALLED CORDELIA.
HOW ABOU YOU
?
WHAT DO YOU WANT ME TO CALL YOU?
THINK NOW.
BE PROUD AND TELL ME YOUR CHOSEN NAME.

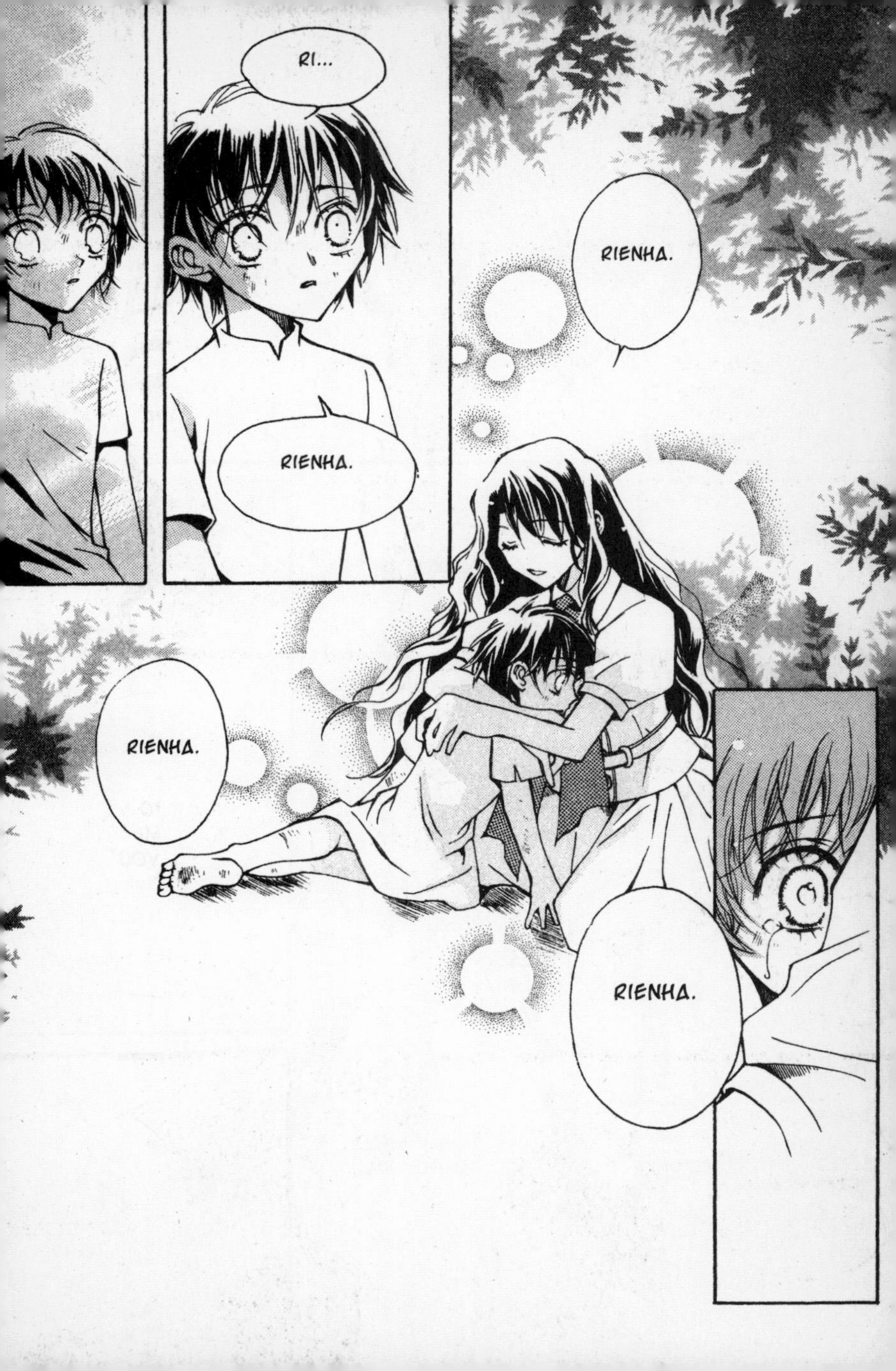
RI...
RIENHA.
RIENHA.
RIENHA.
RIENHA.

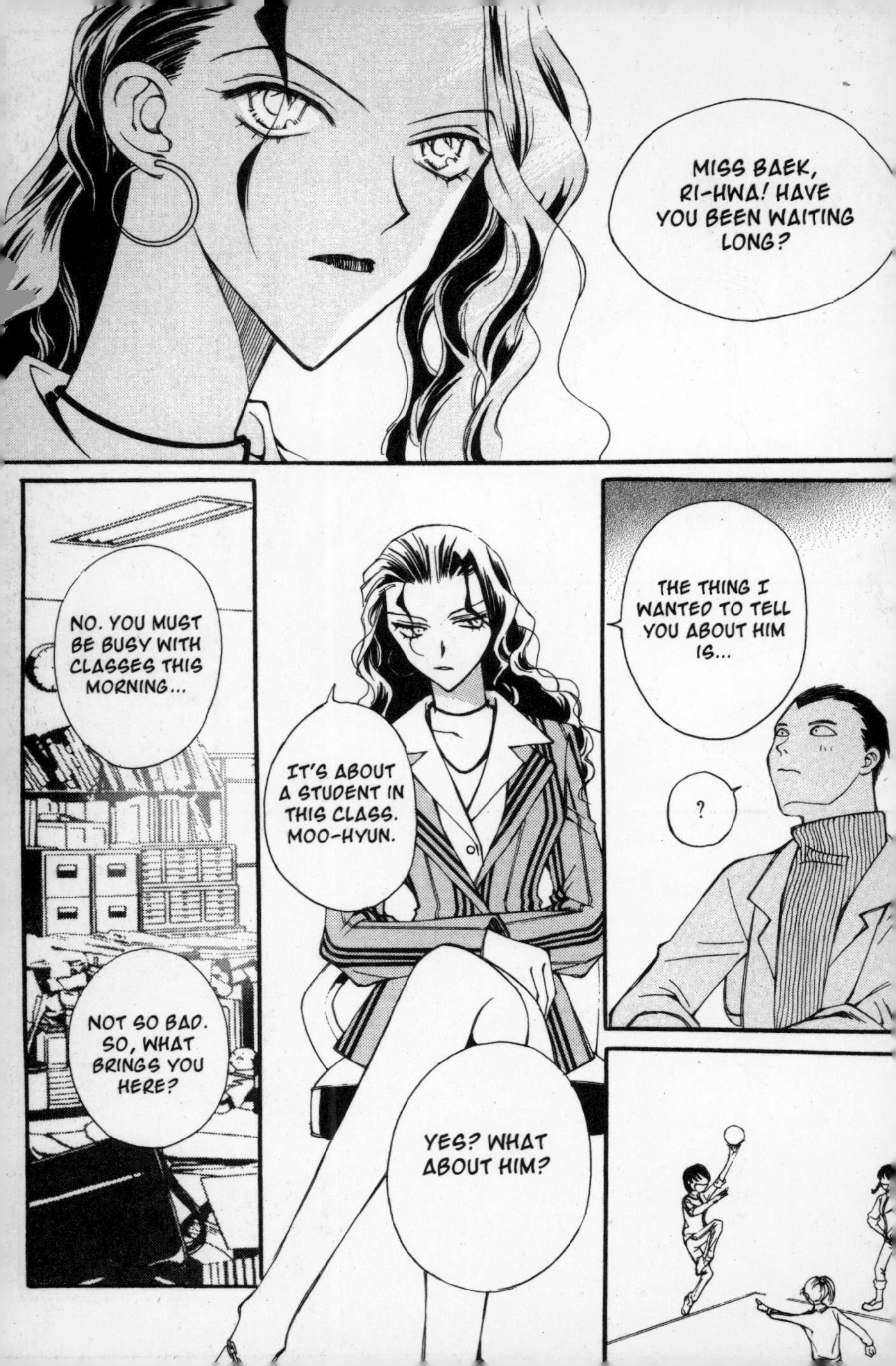
MISS BAEK, RI-HWA! HAVE YOU BEEN WAITING LONG?
NO. YOU MUST BE BUSY WITH CLASSES THIS MORNING...
NOT SO BAD. SO, WHAT BRINGS YOU HERE?
IT'S ABOUT A STUDENT IN THIS CLASS. MOO-HYUN.
YES? WHAT ABOUT HIM?
THE THING I WANTED TO TELL YOU ABOUT HIM IS...
?

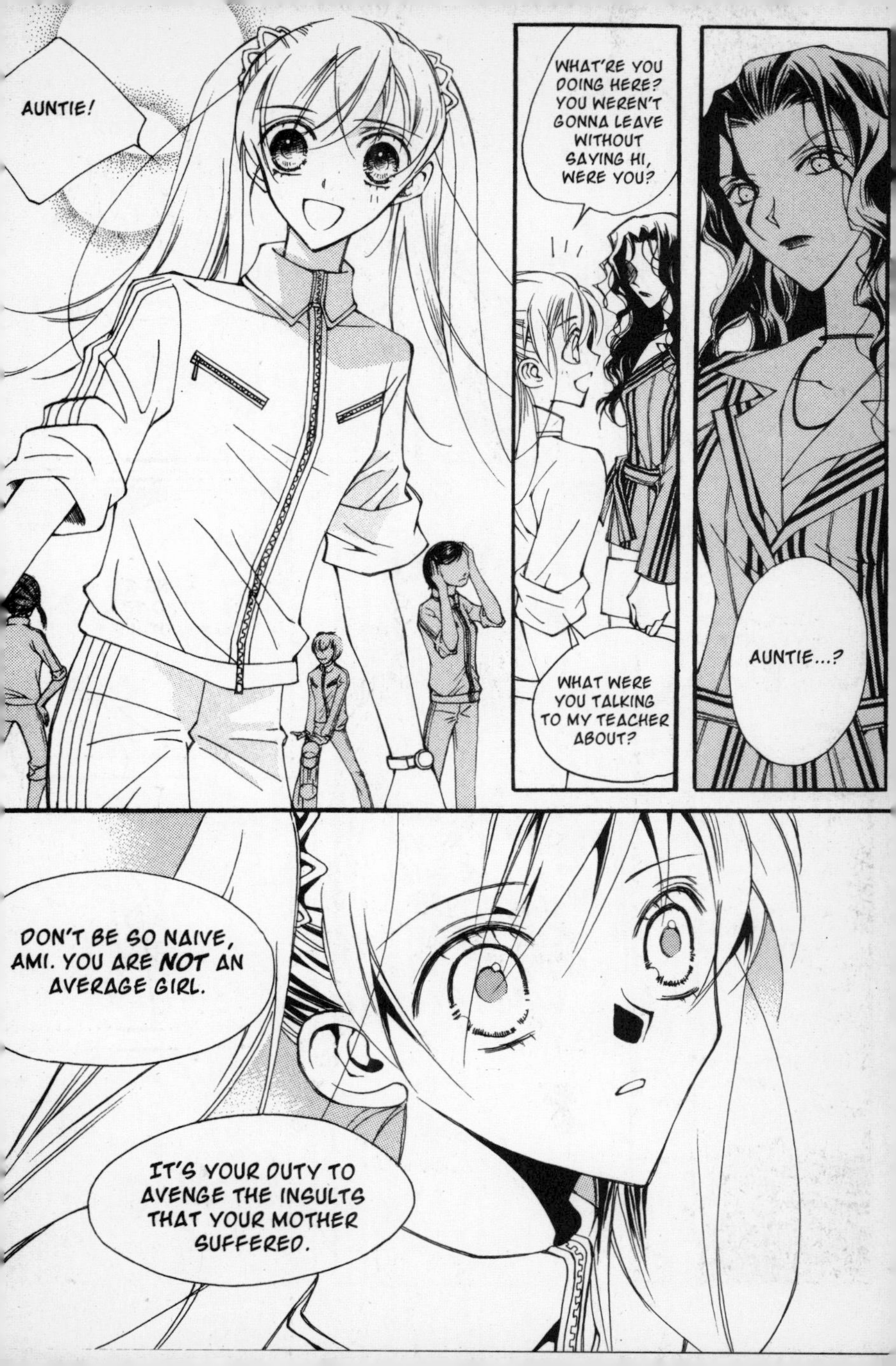
AUNTIE!
WHAT'RE YOU DOING HERE? YOU WEREN'T GONNA LEAVE WITHOUT SAYING HI, WERE YOU?
WHAT WERE YOU TALKING TO MY TEACHER ABOUT?
AUNTIE...?
DON'T BE SO NAIVE, AMI. YOU ARE **NOT** AN AVERAGE GIRL.
IT'S YOUR DUTY TO AVENGE THE INSULTS THAT YOUR MOTHER SUFFERED.

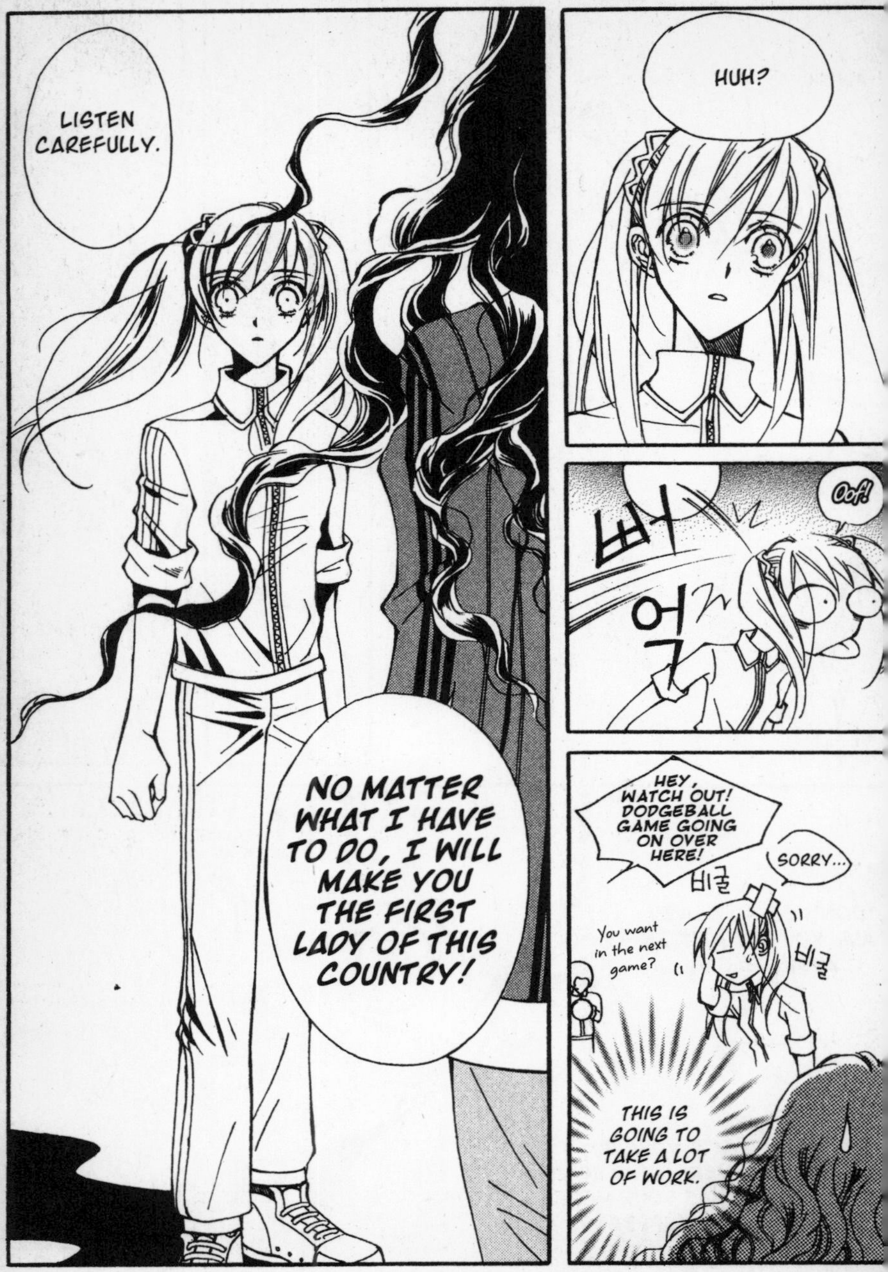
LISTEN CAREFULLY.
NO MATTER WHAT I HAVE TO DO, I WILL MAKE YOU THE FIRST LADY OF THIS COUNTRY!
HUH?
빠
억
Oof!
HEY, WATCH OUT! DODGEBALL GAME GOING ON OVER HERE!
SORRY...
비굴
You want in the next game?
비굴
THIS IS GOING TO TAKE A LOT OF WORK.

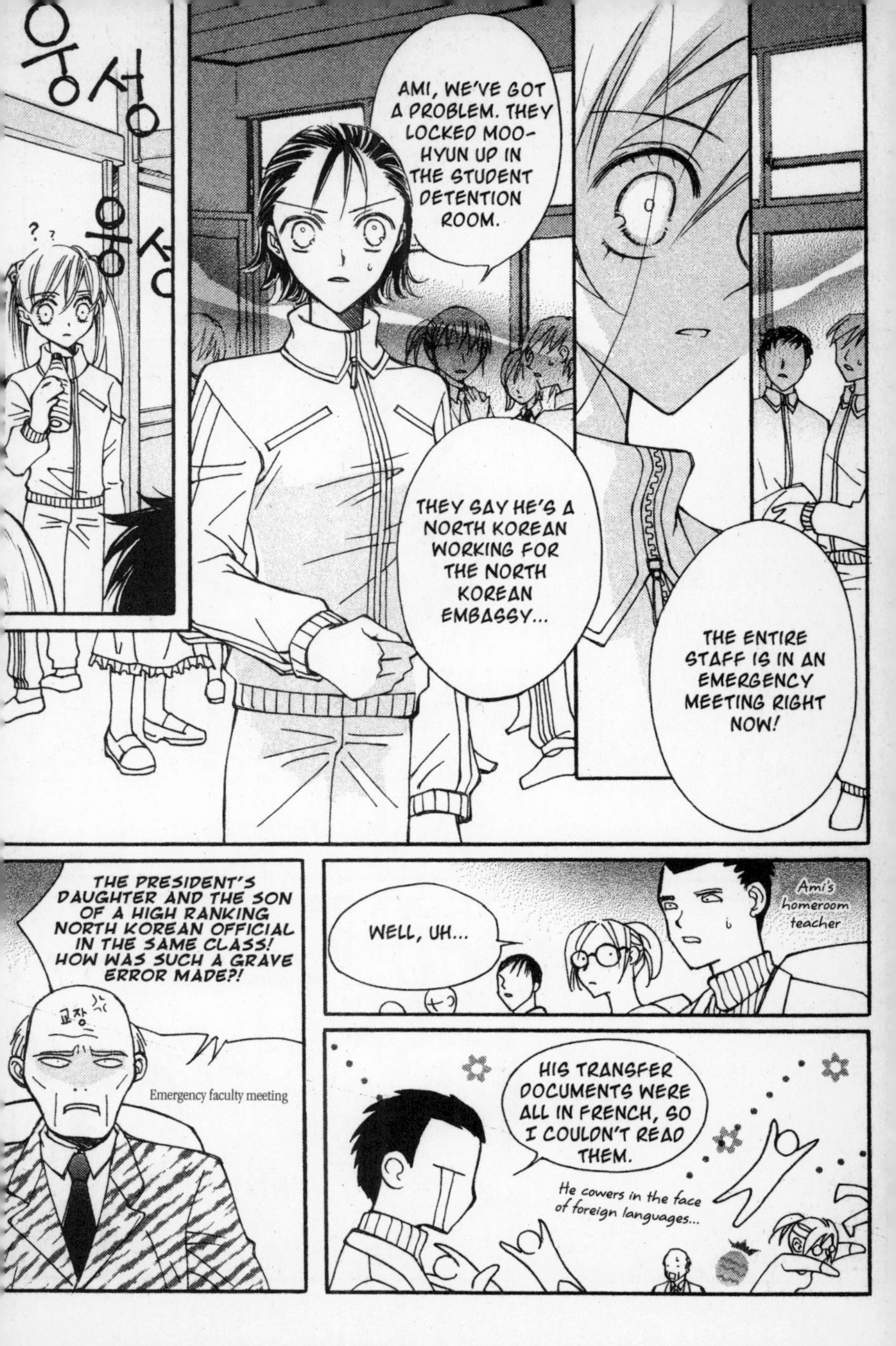

웅성 웅성
? ?
AMI, WE'VE GOT A PROBLEM. THEY LOCKED MOO-HYUN UP IN THE STUDENT DETENTION ROOM.
THEY SAY HE'S A NORTH KOREAN WORKING FOR THE NORTH KOREAN EMBASSY...
THE ENTIRE STAFF IS IN AN EMERGENCY MEETING RIGHT NOW!
THE PRESIDENT'S DAUGHTER AND THE SON OF A HIGH RANKING NORTH KOREAN OFFICIAL IN THE SAME CLASS! HOW WAS SUCH A GRAVE ERROR MADE?!
교장
Emergency faculty meeting
WELL, UH...
Ami's homeroom teacher
HIS TRANSFER DOCUMENTS WERE ALL IN FRENCH, SO I COULDN'T READ THEM.
He cowers in the face of foreign languages...

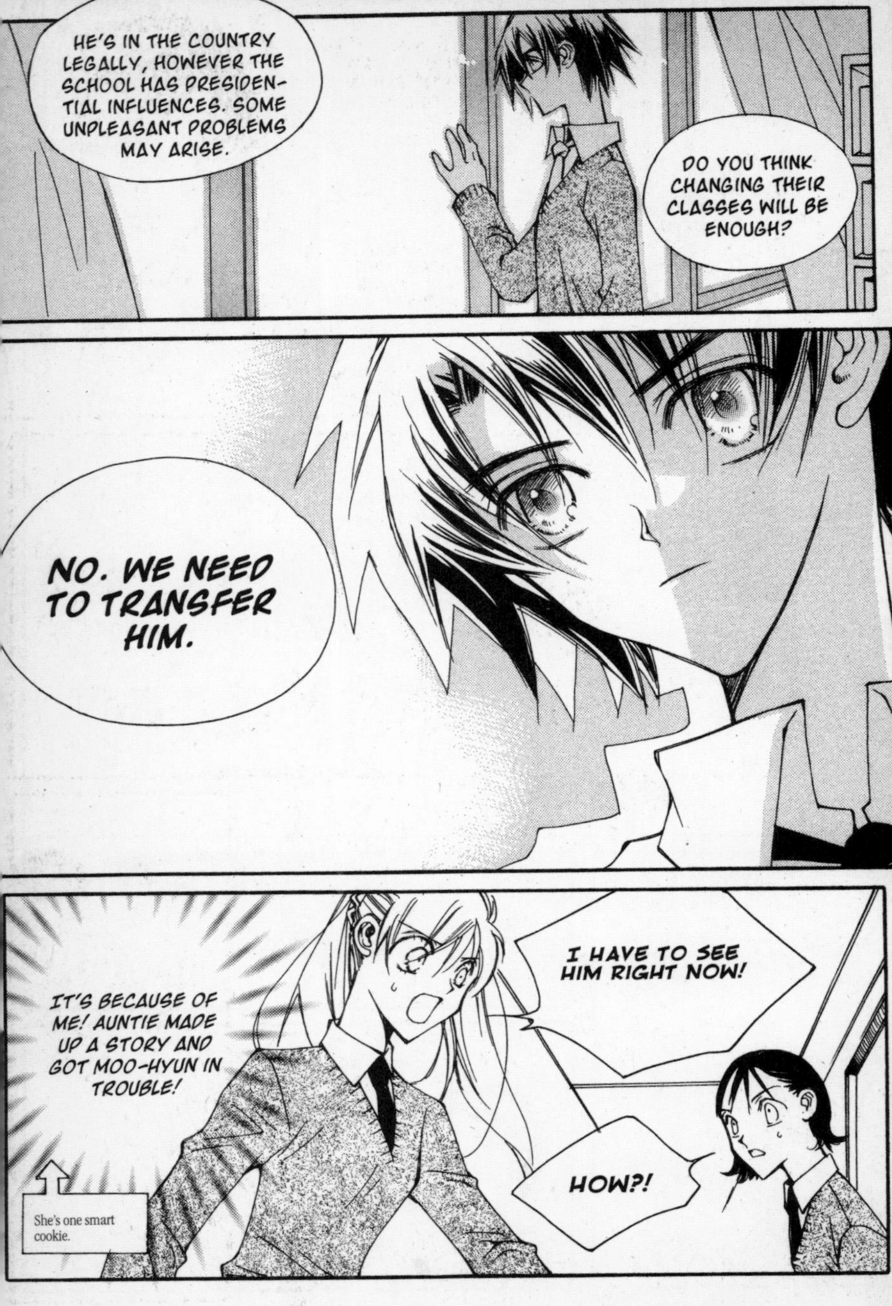
HE'S IN THE COUNTRY LEGALLY, HOWEVER THE SCHOOL HAS PRESIDENTIAL INFLUENCES. SOME UNPLEASANT PROBLEMS MAY ARISE.
DO YOU THINK CHANGING THEIR CLASSES WILL BE ENOUGH?
NO. WE NEED TO TRANSFER HIM.
IT'S BECAUSE OF ME! AUNTIE MADE UP A STORY AND GOT MOO-HYUN IN TROUBLE!
She's one smart cookie.
I HAVE TO SEE HIM RIGHT NOW!
HOW?!

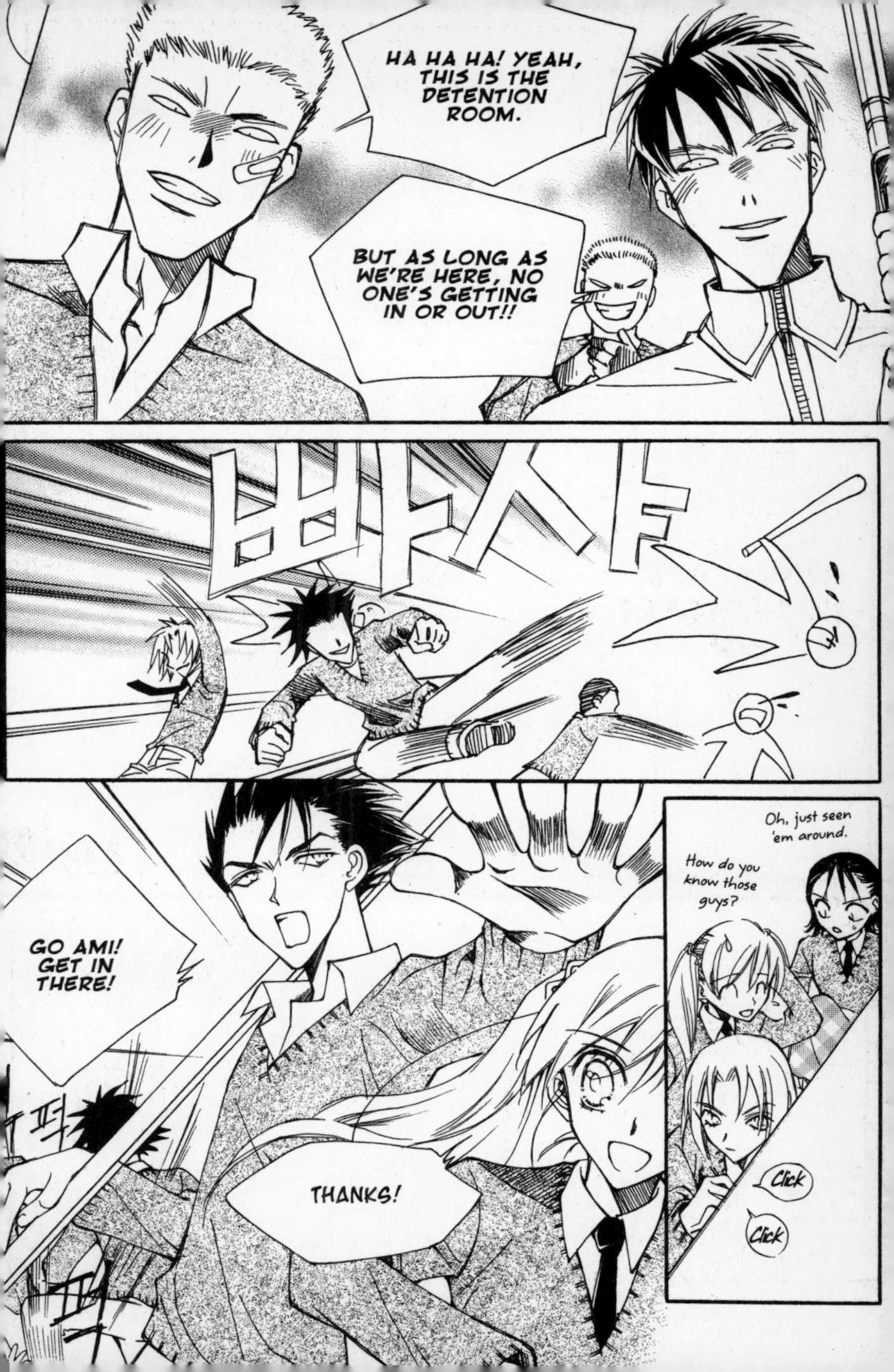
HA HA HA! YEAH, THIS IS THE DETENTION ROOM.
BUT AS LONG AS WE'RE HERE, NO ONE'S GETTING IN OR OUT!!
빠샤
GO AMI! GET IN THERE!
THANKS!
How do you know those guys?
Oh, just seen 'em around.
Click
Click

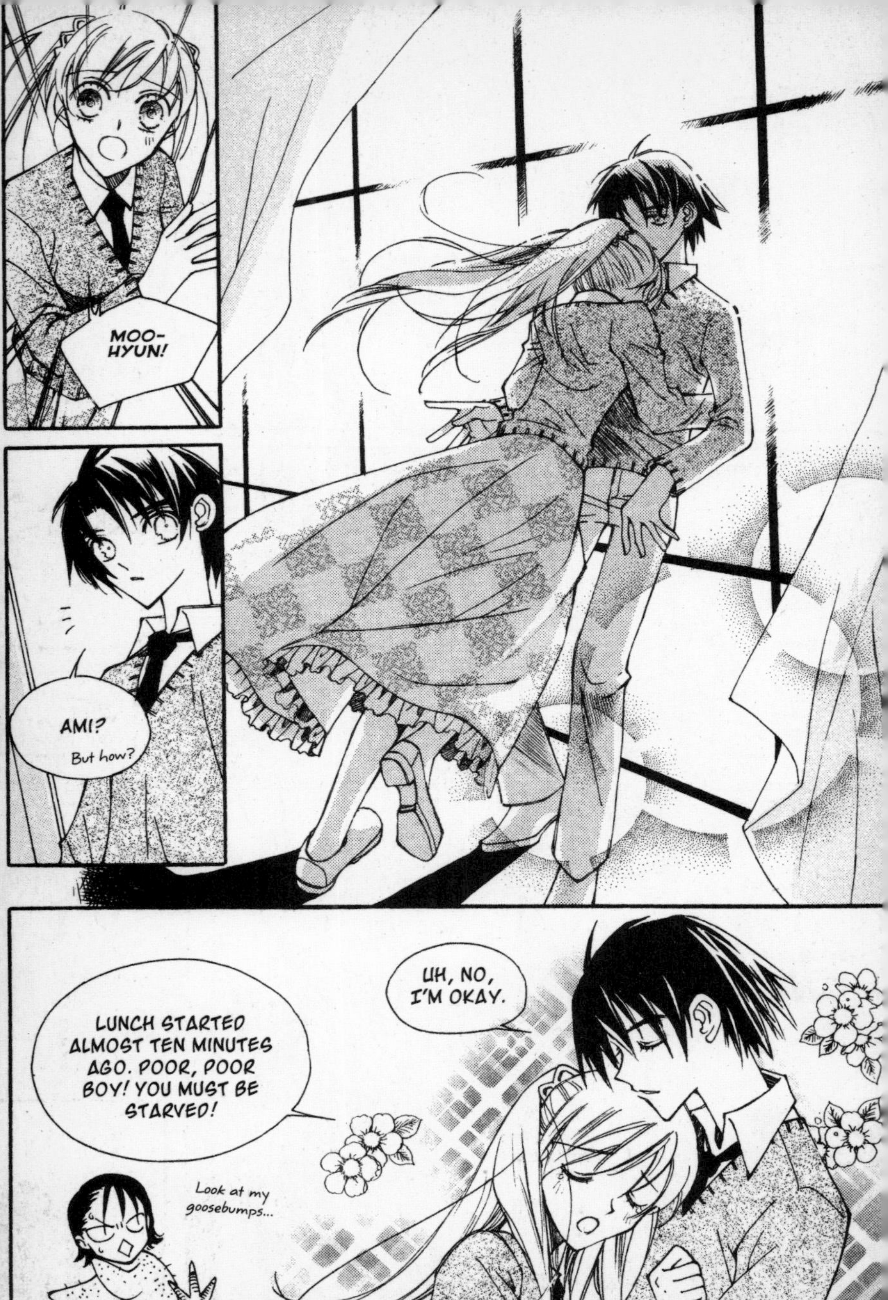

MOO-HYUN!
AMI?
But how?
LUNCH STARTED ALMOST TEN MINUTES AGO. POOR, POOR BOY! YOU MUST BE STARVED!
UH, NO, I'M OKAY.
Look at my goosebumps...

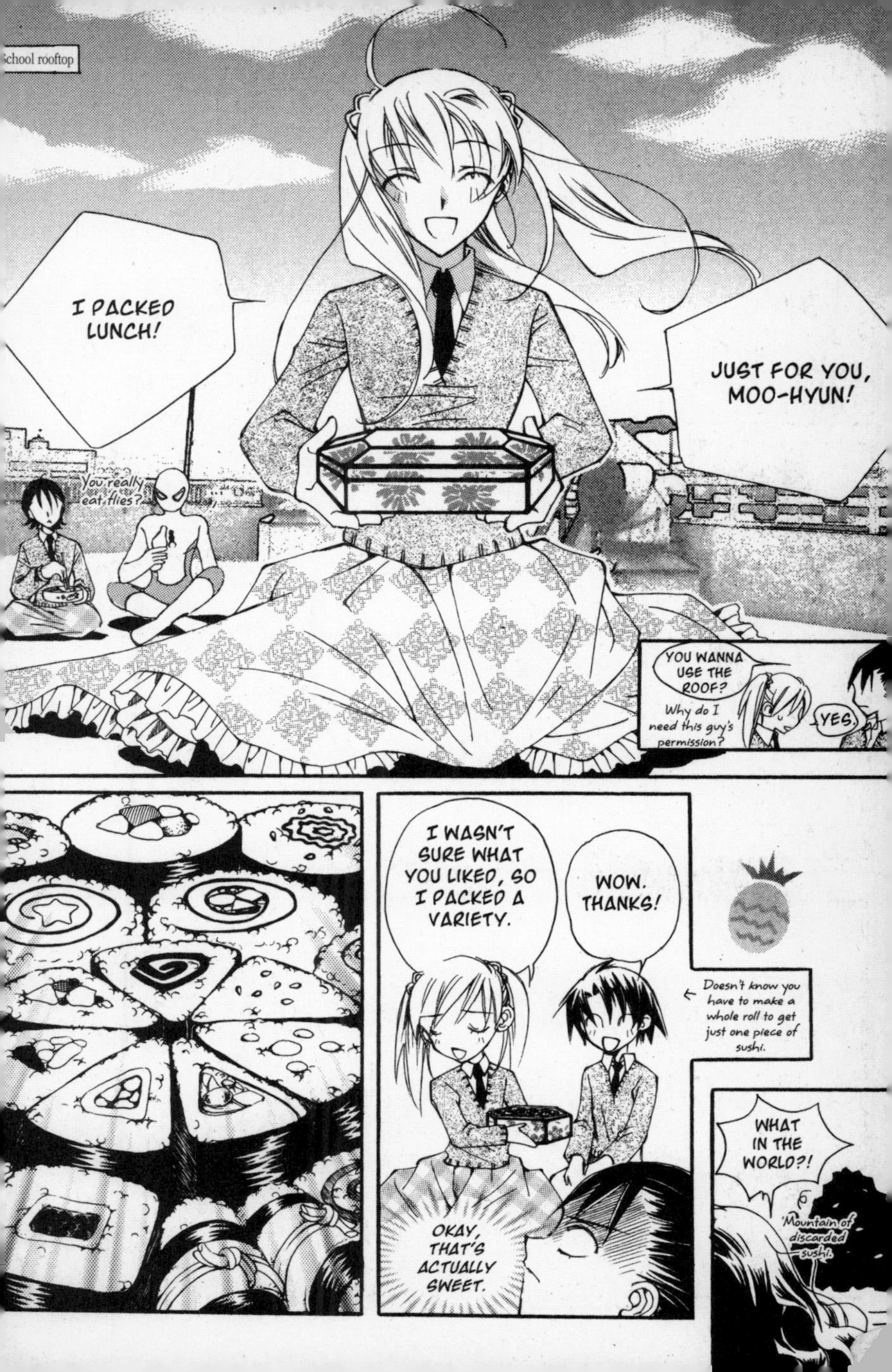
School rooftop
I PACKED LUNCH!
JUST FOR YOU, MOO-HYUN!
You really eat flies?
...
YOU WANNA USE THE ROOF?
Why do I need this guy's permission?
YES.
I WASN'T SURE WHAT YOU LIKED, SO I PACKED A VARIETY.
WOW. THANKS!
Doesn't know you have to make a whole roll to get just one piece of sushi.
OKAY, THAT'S ACTUALLY SWEET.
WHAT IN THE WORLD?!
Mountain of discarded sushi.

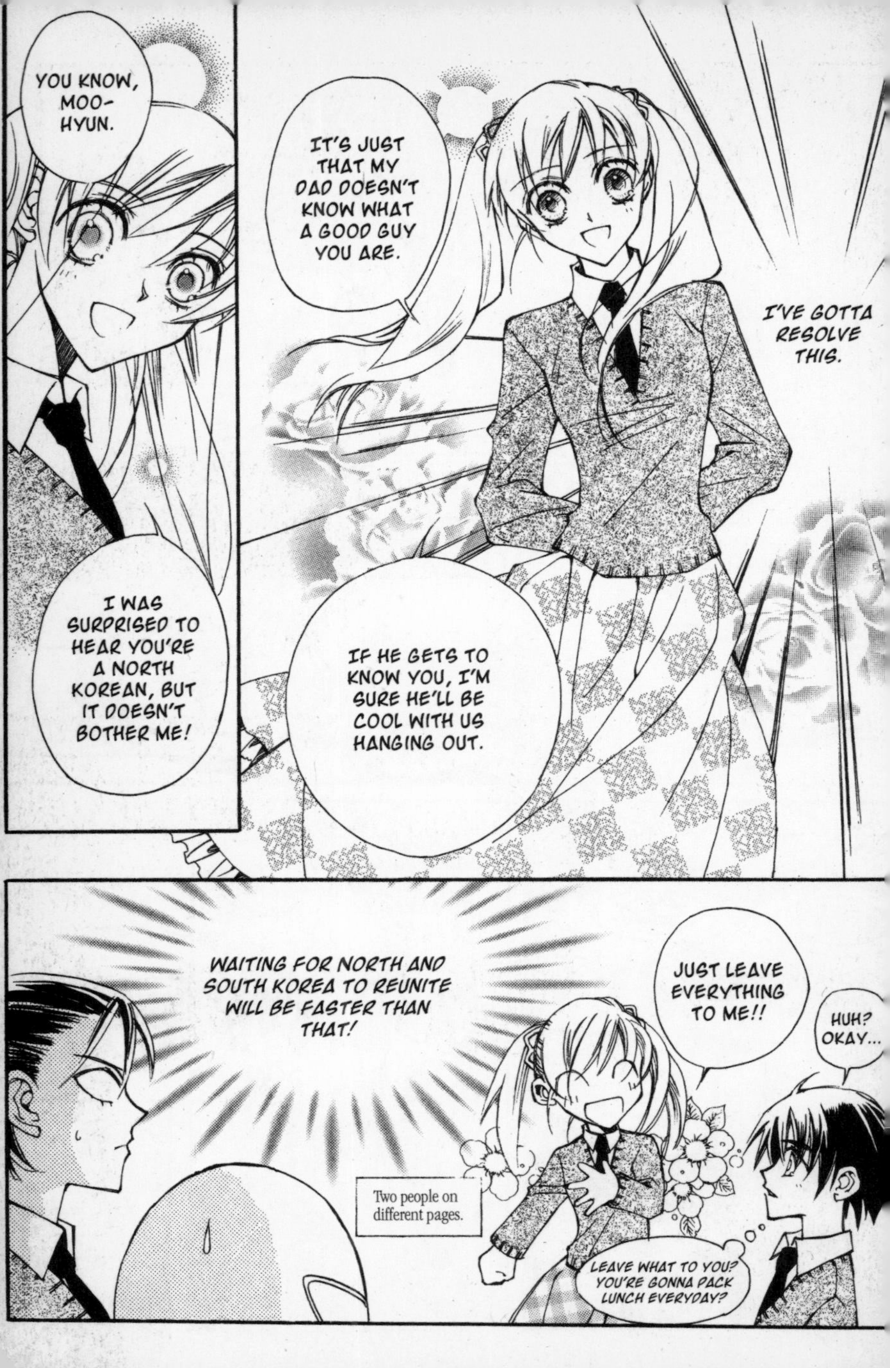
YOU KNOW, MOO-HYUN.
I WAS SURPRISED TO HEAR YOU'RE A NORTH KOREAN, BUT IT DOESN'T BOTHER ME!
IT'S JUST THAT MY DAD DOESN'T KNOW WHAT A GOOD GUY YOU ARE.
IF HE GETS TO KNOW YOU, I'M SURE HE'LL BE COOL WITH US HANGING OUT.
I'VE GOTTA RESOLVE THIS.
WAITING FOR NORTH AND SOUTH KOREA TO REUNITE WILL BE FASTER THAN THAT!
JUST LEAVE EVERYTHING TO ME!!
HUH? OKAY...
Two people on different pages.
LEAVE WHAT TO YOU? YOU'RE GONNA PACK LUNCH EVERYDAY?

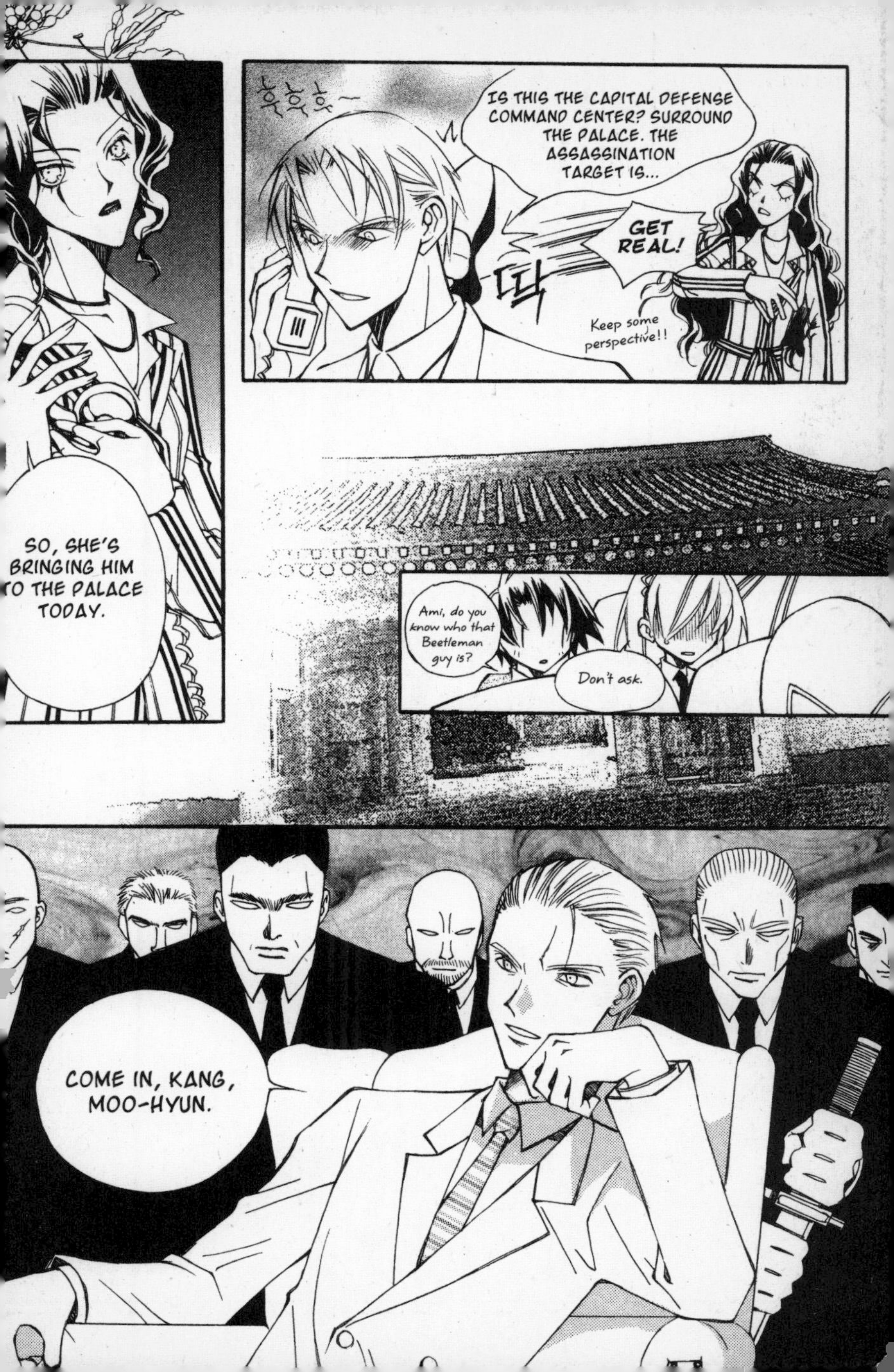
SO, SHE'S BRINGING HIM TO THE PALACE TODAY.
훗훗훗~
IS THIS THE CAPITAL DEFENSE COMMAND CENTER? SURROUND THE PALACE. THE ASSASSINATION TARGET IS...
GET REAL!
딱
Keep some perspective!!
Ami, do you know who that Beetleman guy is?
Don't ask.
COME IN, KANG, MOO-HYUN.

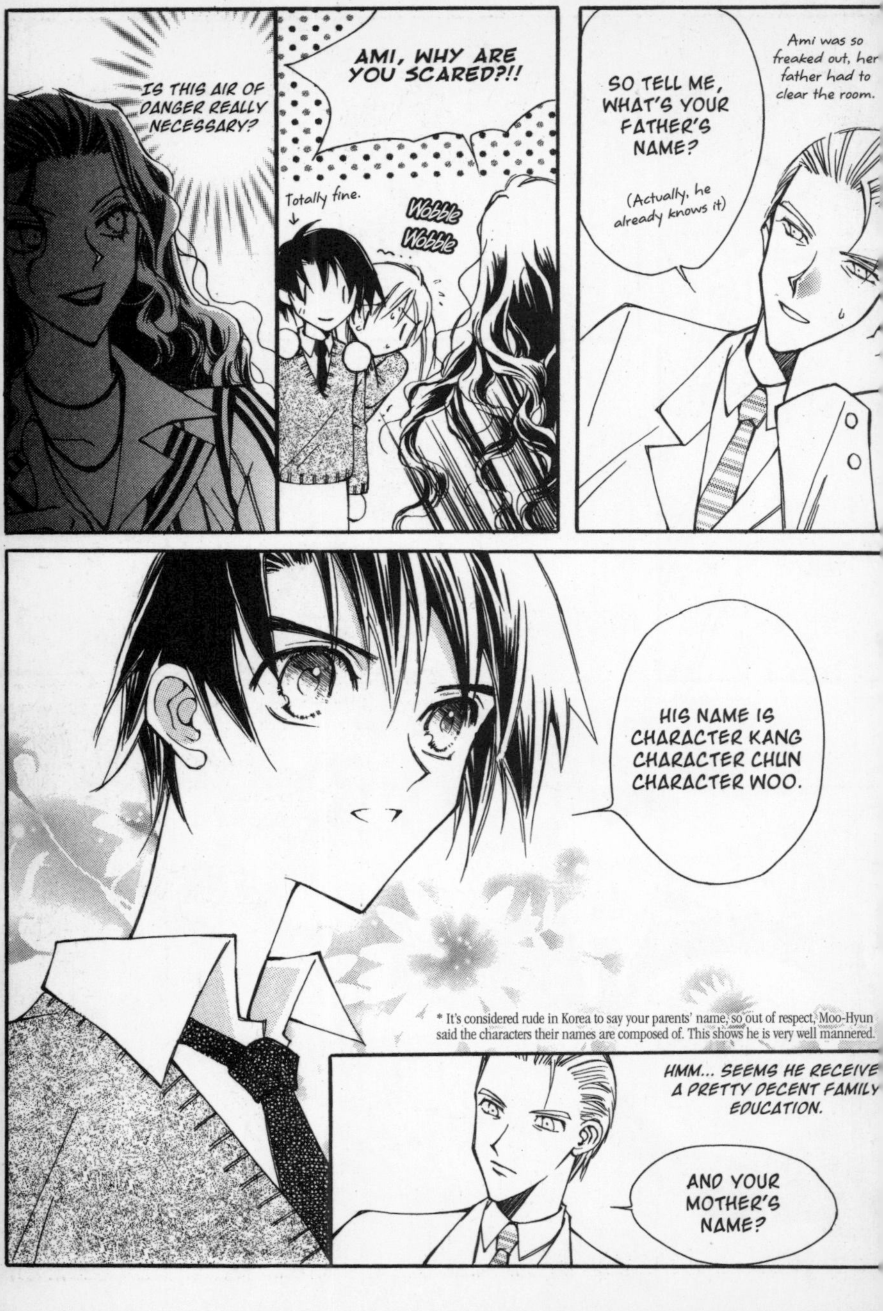
IS THIS AIR OF DANGER REALLY NECESSARY?
AMI, WHY ARE YOU SCARED?!!
Totally fine.
Wobble Wobble
SO TELL ME, WHAT'S YOUR FATHER'S NAME?
(Actually, he already knows it)
Ami was so freaked out, her father had to clear the room.
HIS NAME IS CHARACTER KANG CHARACTER CHUN CHARACTER WOO.
* It's considered rude in Korea to say your parents' name, so out of respect, Moo-Hyun said the characters their names are composed of. This shows he is very well mannered.
HMM... SEEMS HE RECEIVE A PRETTY DECENT FAMILY EDUCATION.
AND YOUR MOTHER'S NAME?

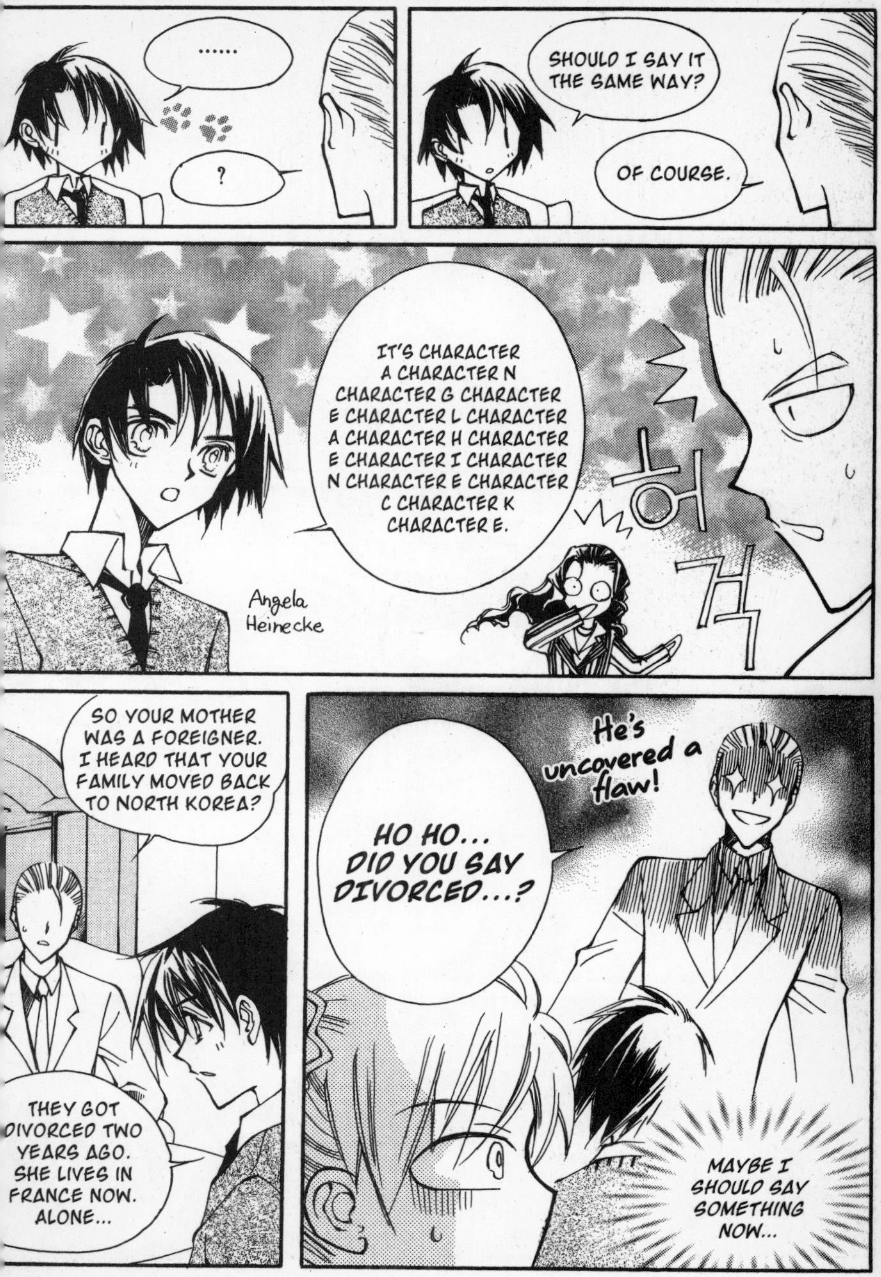
......
?
SHOULD I SAY IT THE SAME WAY?
OF COURSE.
IT'S CHARACTER A CHARACTER N CHARACTER G CHARACTER E CHARACTER L CHARACTER A CHARACTER H CHARACTER E CHARACTER I CHARACTER N CHARACTER E CHARACTER C CHARACTER K CHARACTER E.
허걱
Angela Heinecke
SO YOUR MOTHER WAS A FOREIGNER. I HEARD THAT YOUR FAMILY MOVED BACK TO NORTH KOREA?
THEY GOT DIVORCED TWO YEARS AGO. SHE LIVES IN FRANCE NOW. ALONE...
HO HO... DID YOU SAY DIVORCED...?
He's uncovered a flaw!
MAYBE I SHOULD SAY SOMETHING NOW...

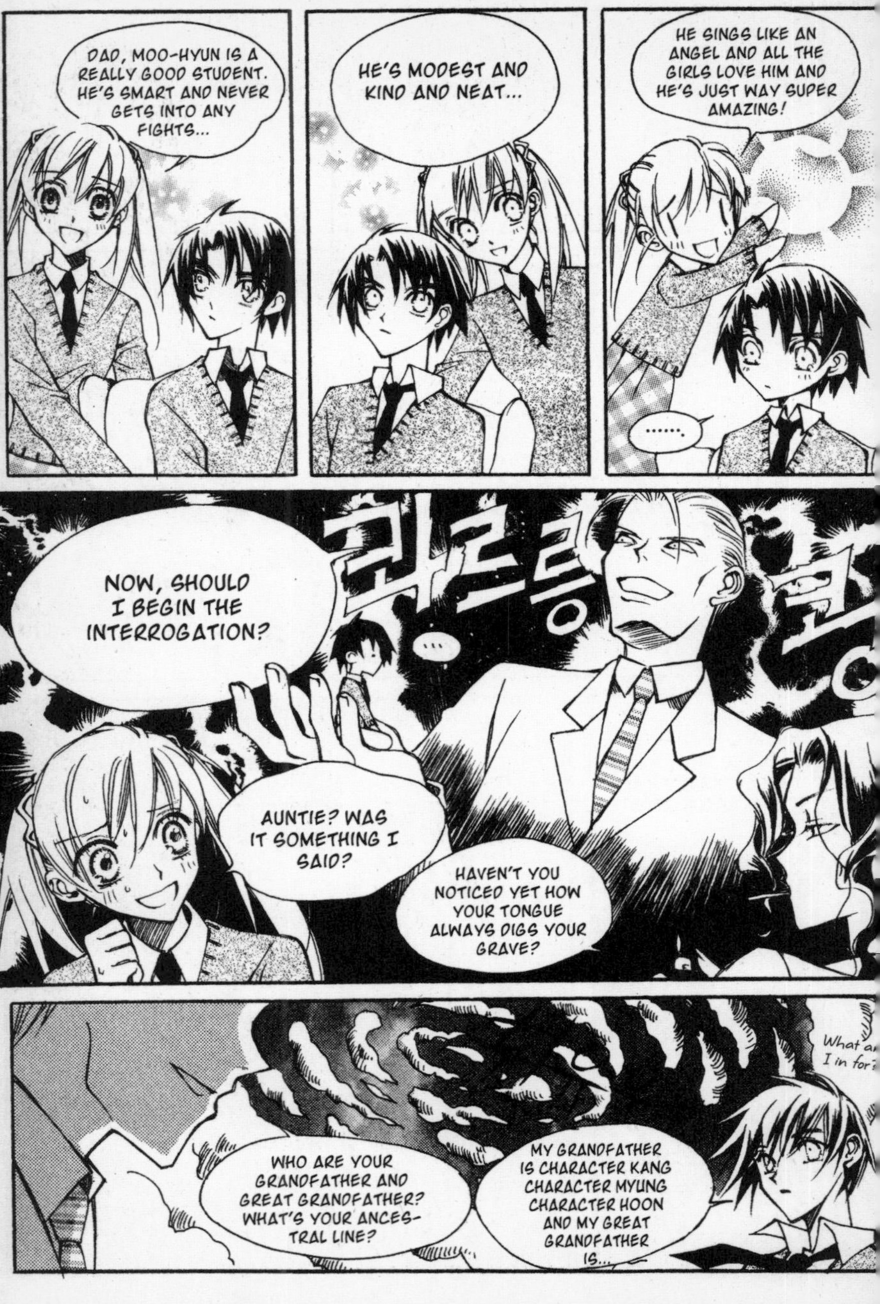
DAD, MOO-HYUN IS A REALLY GOOD STUDENT. HE'S SMART AND NEVER GETS INTO ANY FIGHTS...
HE'S MODEST AND KIND AND NEAT...
HE SINGS LIKE AN ANGEL AND ALL THE GIRLS LOVE HIM AND HE'S JUST WAY SUPER AMAZING!
....
콰르릉
NOW, SHOULD I BEGIN THE INTERROGATION?
...
AUNTIE? WAS IT SOMETHING I SAID?
HAVEN'T YOU NOTICED YET HOW YOUR TONGUE ALWAYS DIGS YOUR GRAVE?
What a
I in for?
WHO ARE YOUR GRANDFATHER AND GREAT GRANDFATHER? WHAT'S YOUR ANCES-TRAL LINE?
MY GRANDFATHER IS CHARACTER KANG CHARACTER MYUNG CHARACTER HOON AND MY GREAT GRANDFATHER IS...

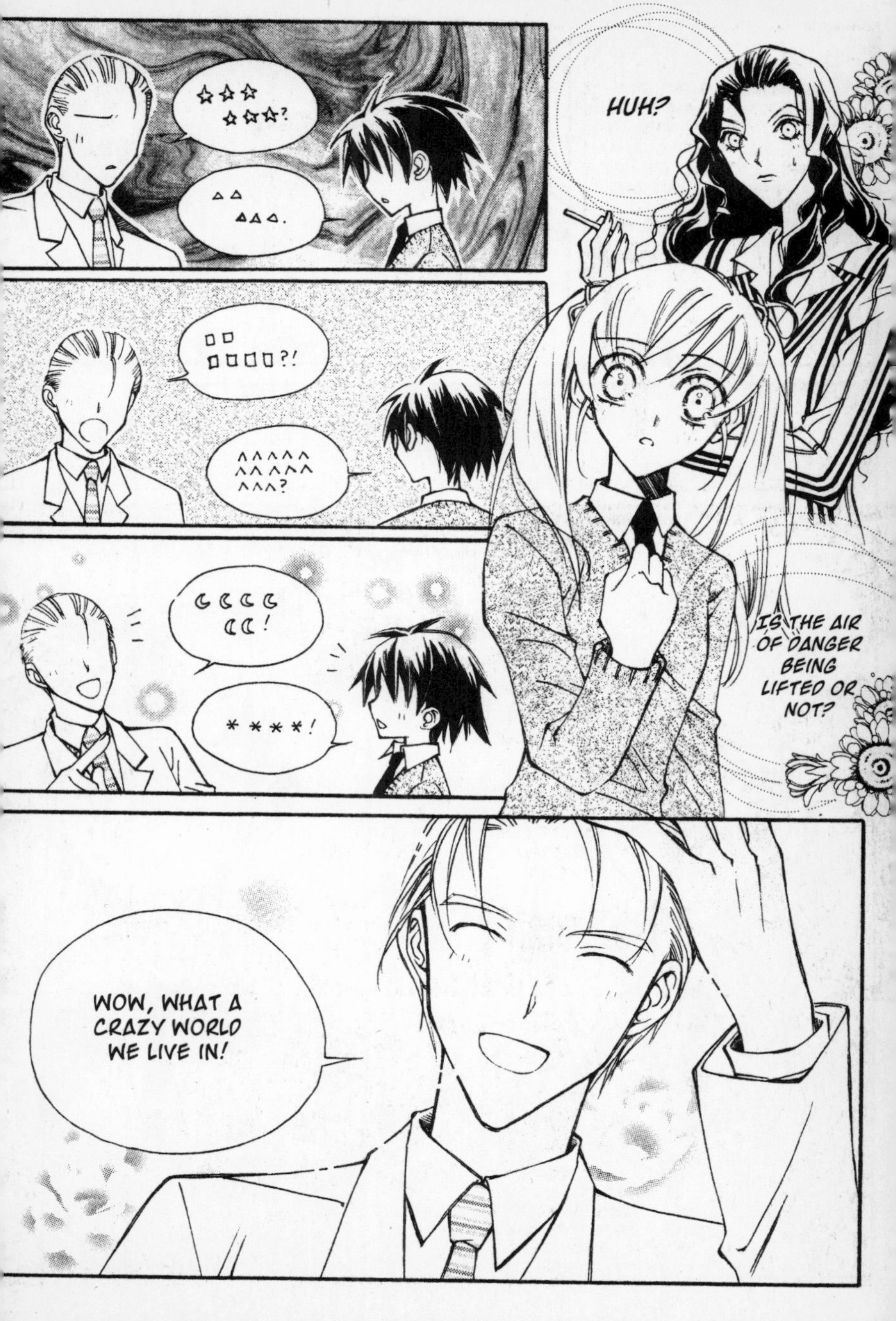

☆☆☆ ☆☆☆?
△△ △△△.
□□ □□□□?!
^^^^^ ^^^^^ ^^^?
☾☾☾☾ ☾☾!
****!
HUH?
IS THE AIR OF DANGER BEING LIFTED OR NOT?
WOW, WHAT A CRAZY WORLD WE LIVE IN!

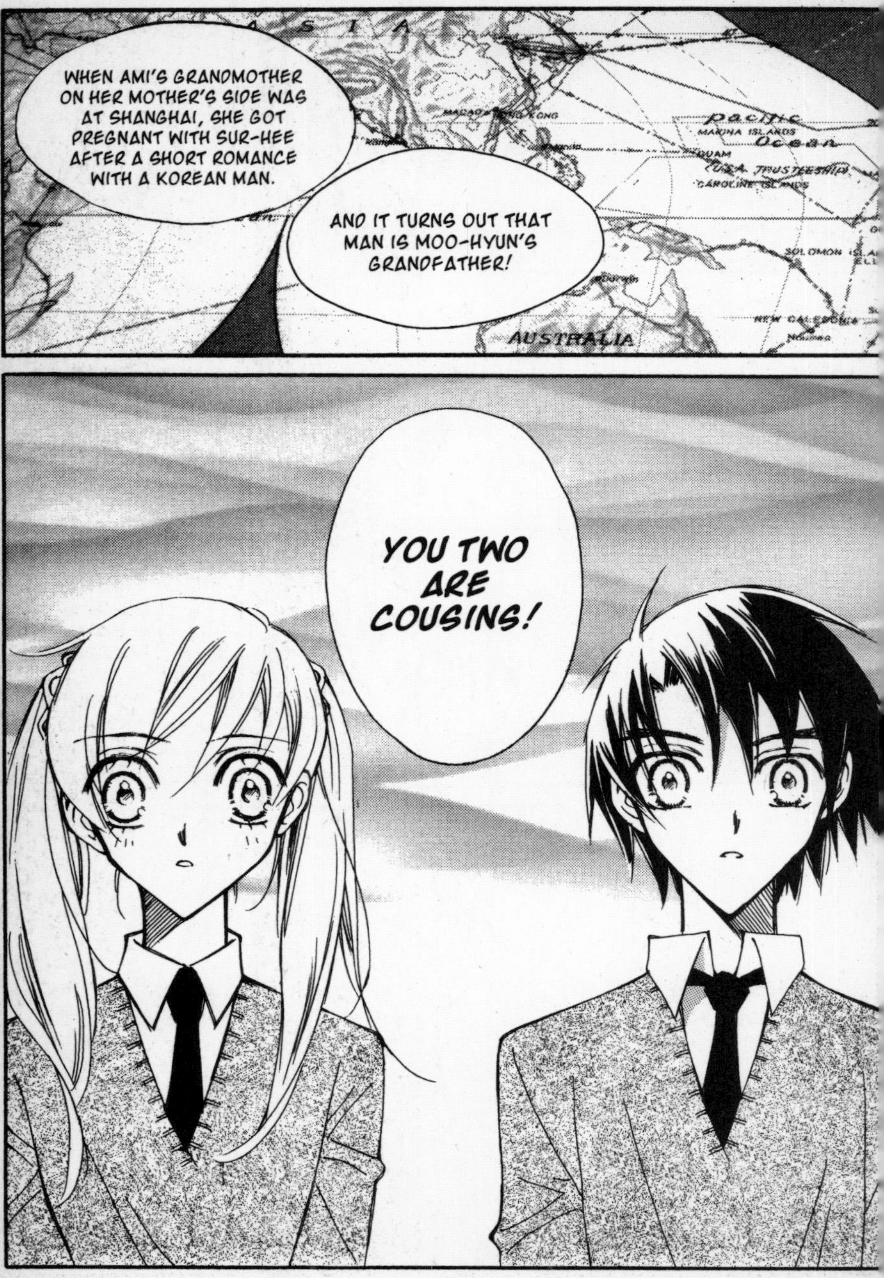
WHEN AMI'S GRANDMOTHER ON HER MOTHER'S SIDE WAS AT SHANGHAI, SHE GOT PREGNANT WITH SUR-HEE AFTER A SHORT ROMANCE WITH A KOREAN MAN.
AND IT TURNS OUT THAT MAN IS MOO-HYUN'S GRANDFATHER!
AUSTRALIA
YOU TWO ARE COUSINS!

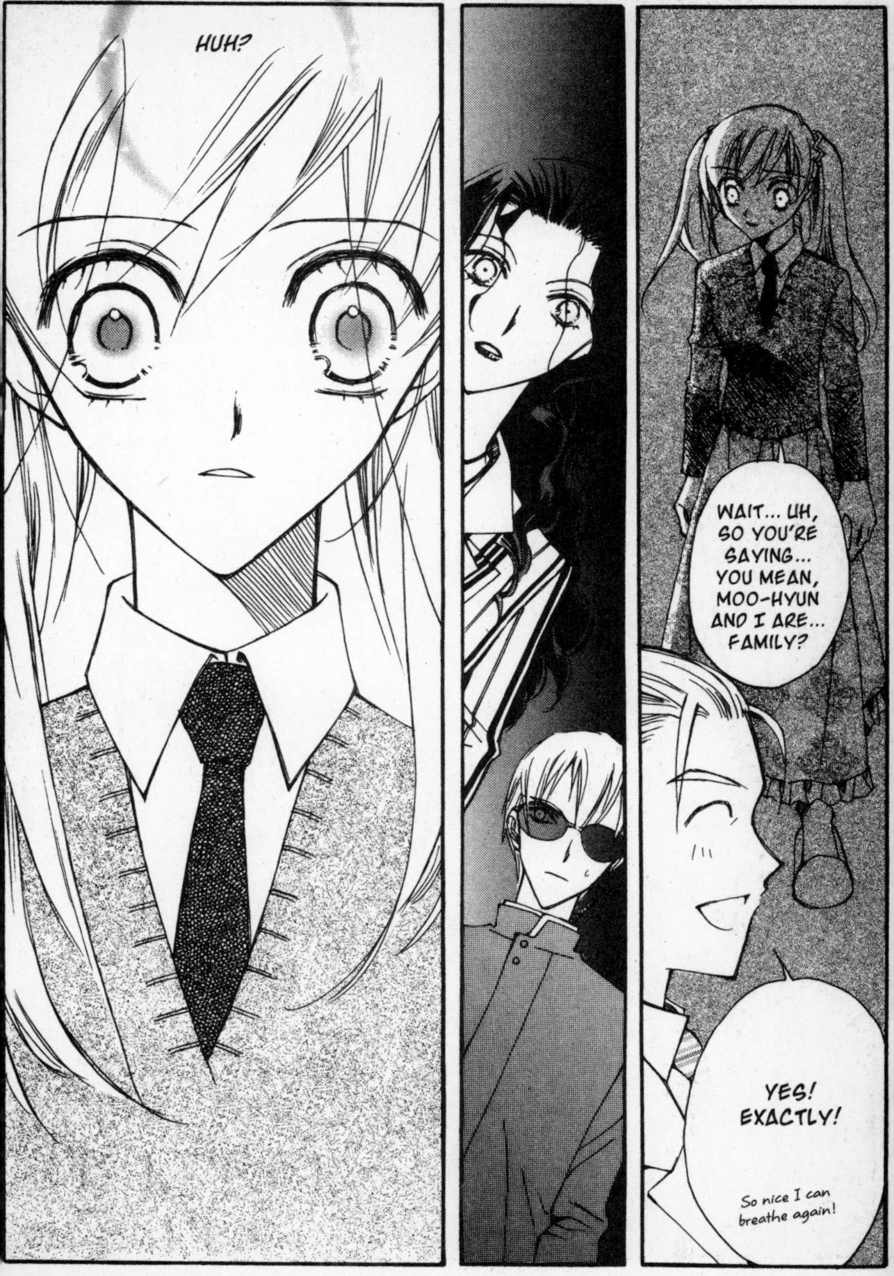
HUH?
WAIT... UH, SO YOU'RE SAYING... YOU MEAN, MOO-HYUN AND I ARE... FAMILY?
YES! EXACTLY!
So nice I can breathe again!

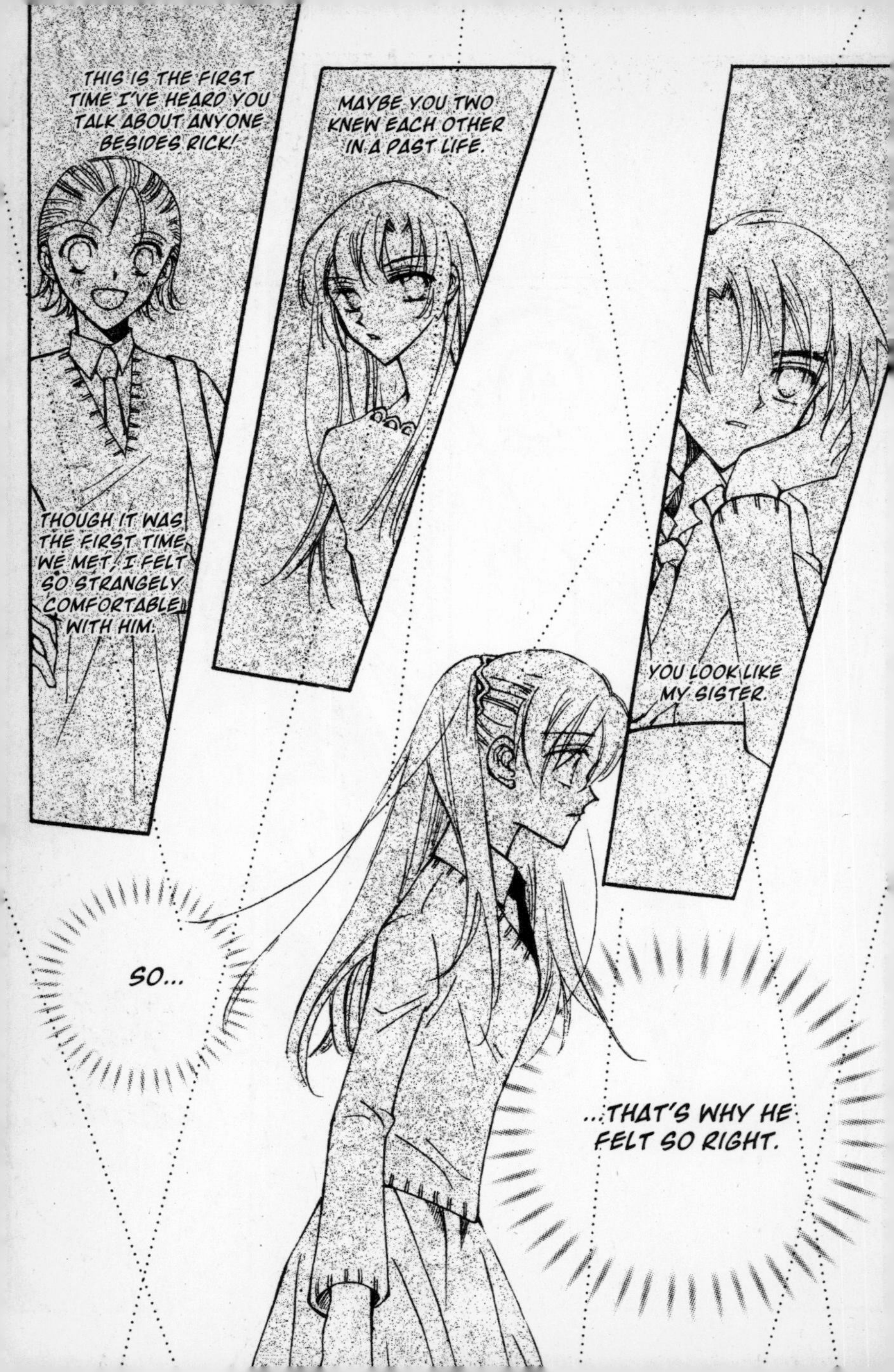
THIS IS THE FIRST TIME I'VE HEARD YOU TALK ABOUT ANYONE BESIDES RICK!
THOUGH IT WAS THE FIRST TIME WE MET, I FELT SO STRANGELY COMFORTABLE WITH HIM.
MAYBE YOU TWO KNEW EACH OTHER IN A PAST LIFE.
YOU LOOK LIKE MY SISTER.
SO...
...THAT'S WHY HE FELT SO RIGHT.

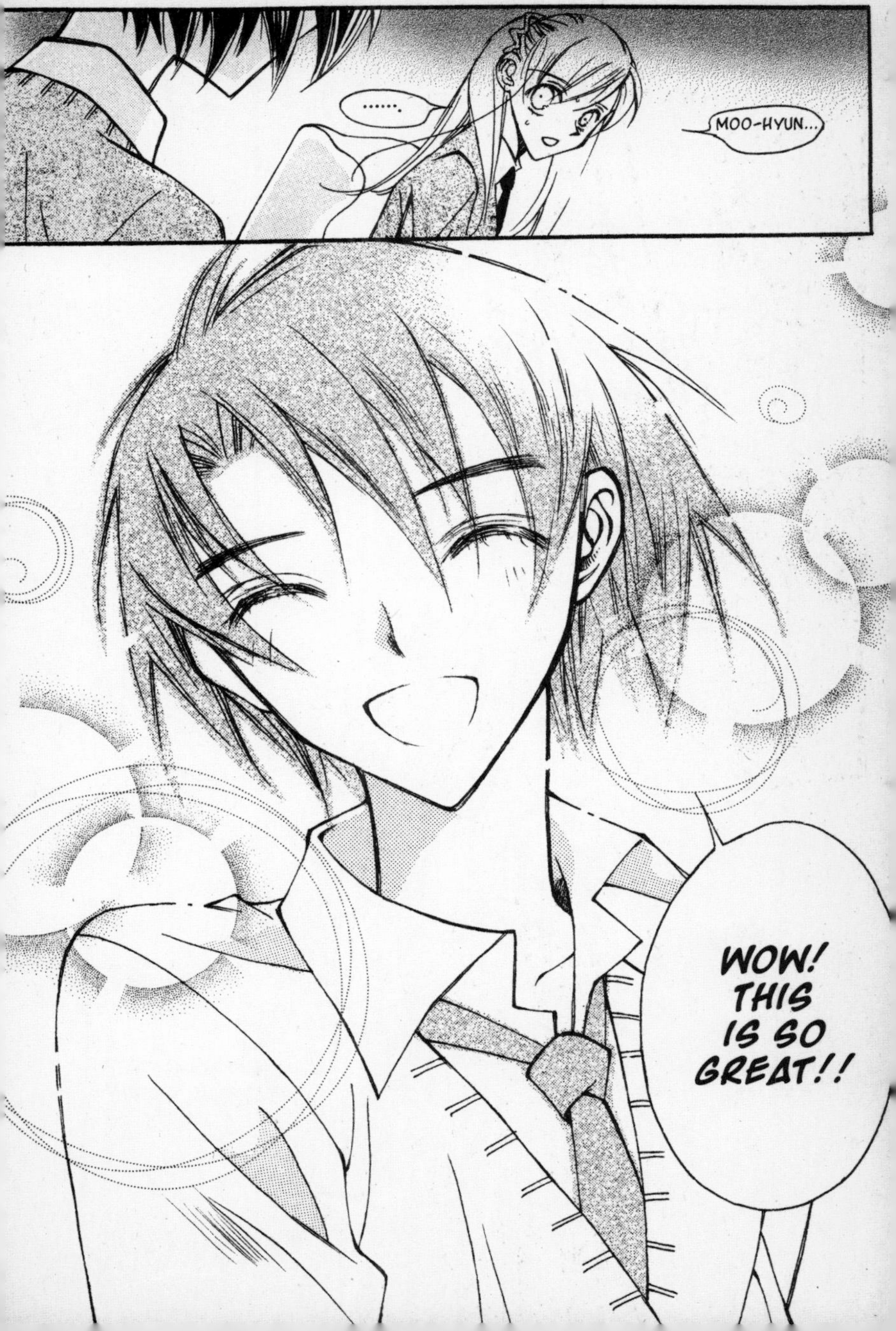
....
MOO-HYUN...
WOW! THIS IS SO GREAT!!

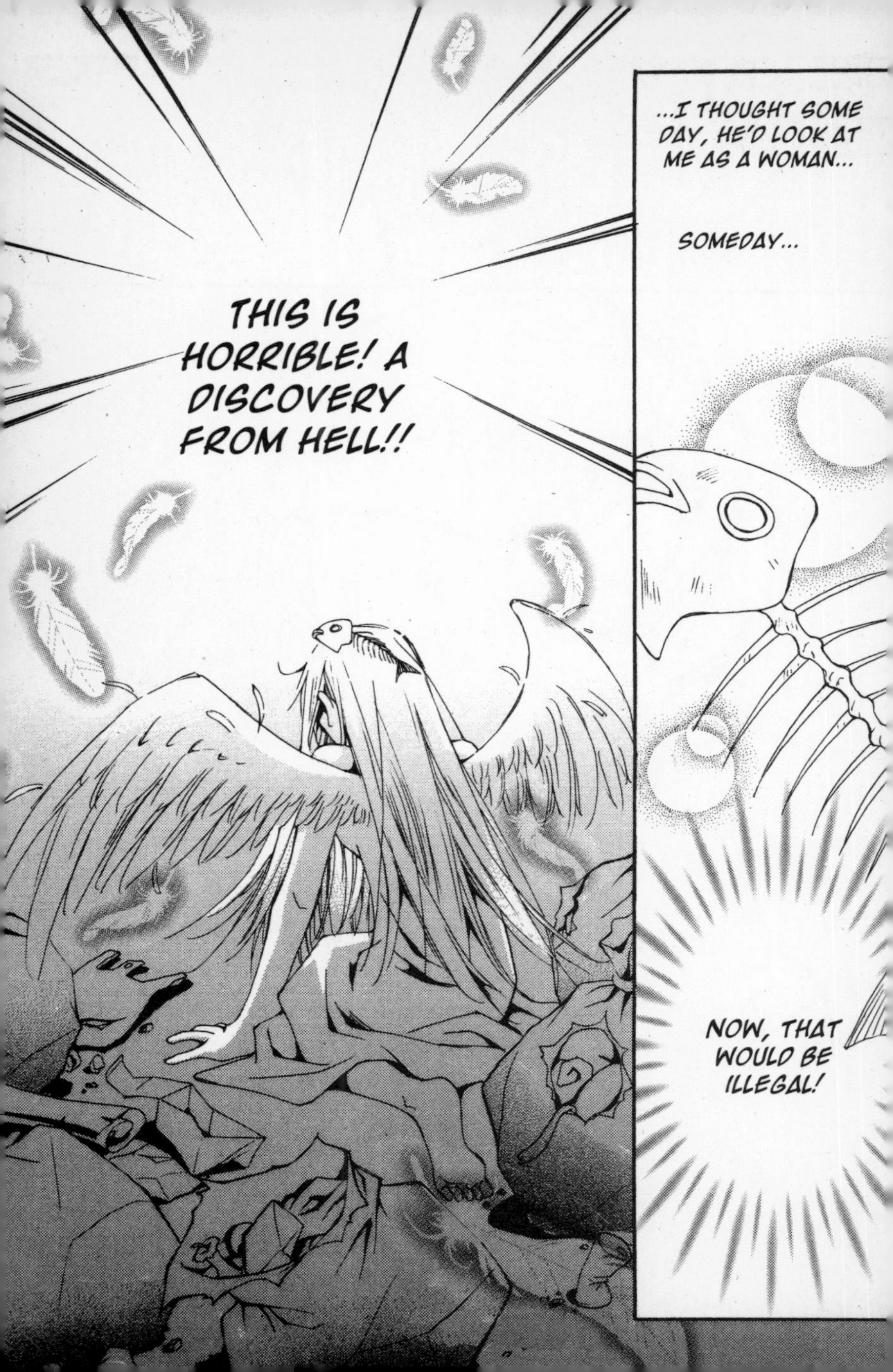
THIS IS HORRIBLE! A DISCOVERY FROM HELL!!
...I THOUGHT SOME DAY, HE'D LOOK AT ME AS A WOMAN...
SOMEDAY...
NOW, THAT WOULD BE ILLEGAL!

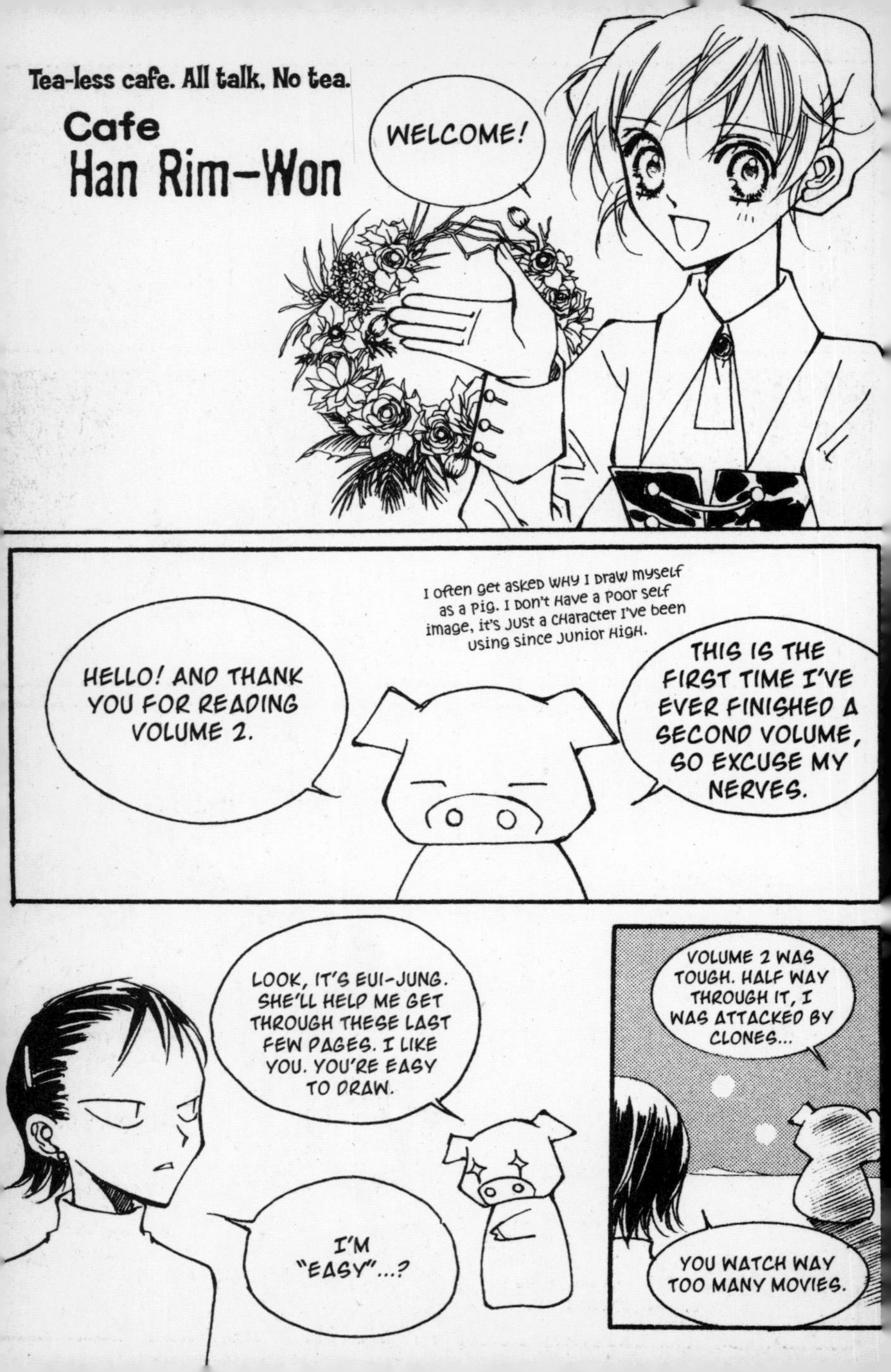
Tea-less cafe. All talk, No tea.
Cafe Han Rim-Won
WELCOME!
HELLO! AND THANK YOU FOR READING VOLUME 2.
I often get asked WHY I Draw myself as a Pig. I Don't Have a Poor self image, it's Just a cHaracter I've been using since Junior HiGH.
THIS IS THE FIRST TIME I'VE EVER FINISHED A SECOND VOLUME, SO EXCUSE MY NERVES.
LOOK, IT'S EUI-JUNG. SHE'LL HELP ME GET THROUGH THESE LAST FEW PAGES. I LIKE YOU. YOU'RE EASY TO DRAW.
I'M "EASY"...?
VOLUME 2 WAS TOUGH. HALF WAY THROUGH IT, I WAS ATTACKED BY CLONES...
YOU WATCH WAY TOO MANY MOVIES.

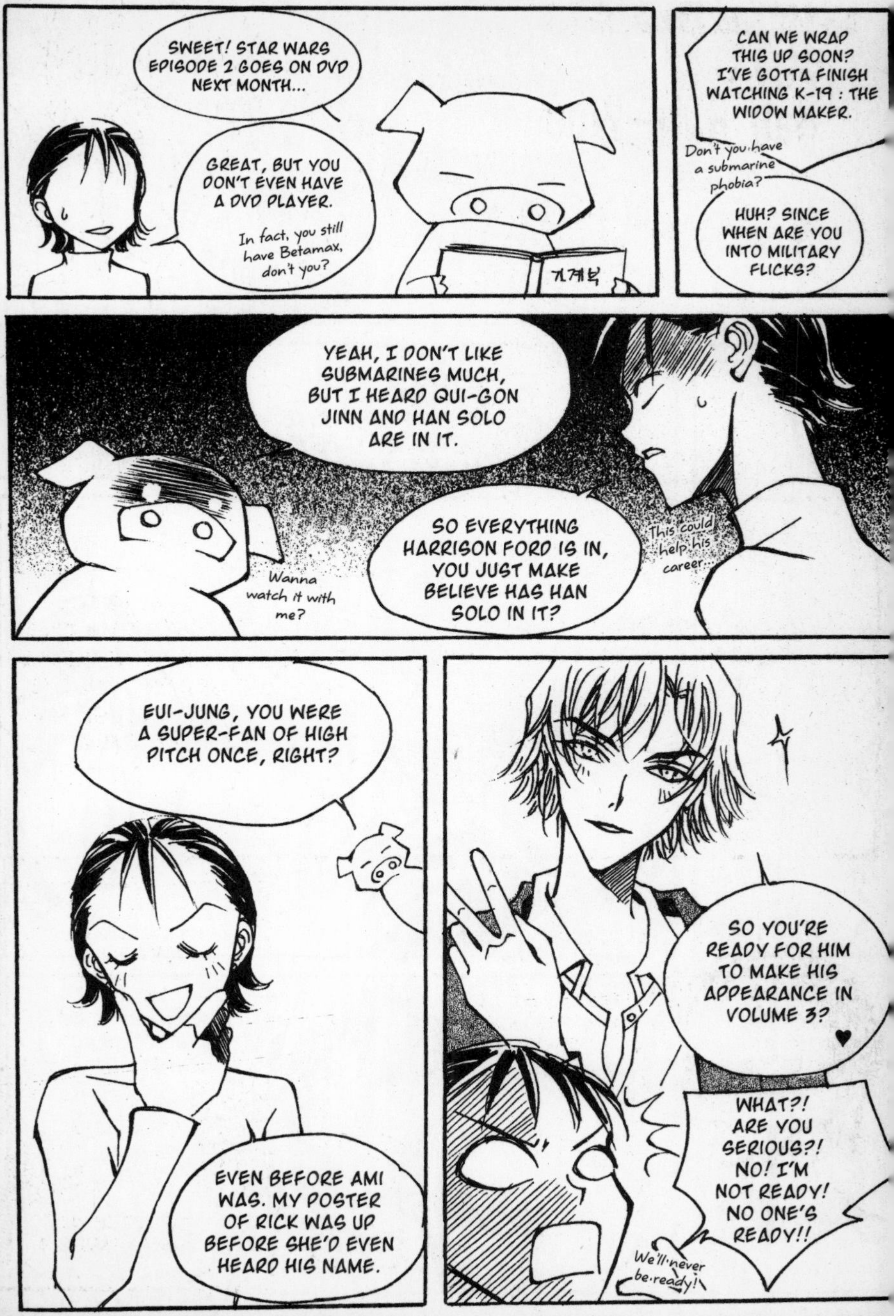
SWEET! STAR WARS EPISODE 2 GOES ON DVD NEXT MONTH...
GREAT, BUT YOU DON'T EVEN HAVE A DVD PLAYER.
In fact, you still have Betamax, don't you?
가계부
CAN WE WRAP THIS UP SOON? I'VE GOTTA FINISH WATCHING K-19 : THE WIDOW MAKER.
Don't you have a submarine phobia?
HUH? SINCE WHEN ARE YOU INTO MILITARY FLICKS?
YEAH, I DON'T LIKE SUBMARINES MUCH, BUT I HEARD QUI-GON JINN AND HAN SOLO ARE IN IT.
SO EVERYTHING HARRISON FORD IS IN, YOU JUST MAKE BELIEVE HAS HAN SOLO IN IT?
Wanna watch it with me?
This could help his career...
EUI-JUNG, YOU WERE A SUPER-FAN OF HIGH PITCH ONCE, RIGHT?
EVEN BEFORE AMI WAS. MY POSTER OF RICK WAS UP BEFORE SHE'D EVEN HEARD HIS NAME.
SO YOU'RE READY FOR HIM TO MAKE HIS APPEARANCE IN VOLUME 3? ♥
WHAT?! ARE YOU SERIOUS?! NO! I'M NOT READY! NO ONE'S READY!!
We'll never be ready!

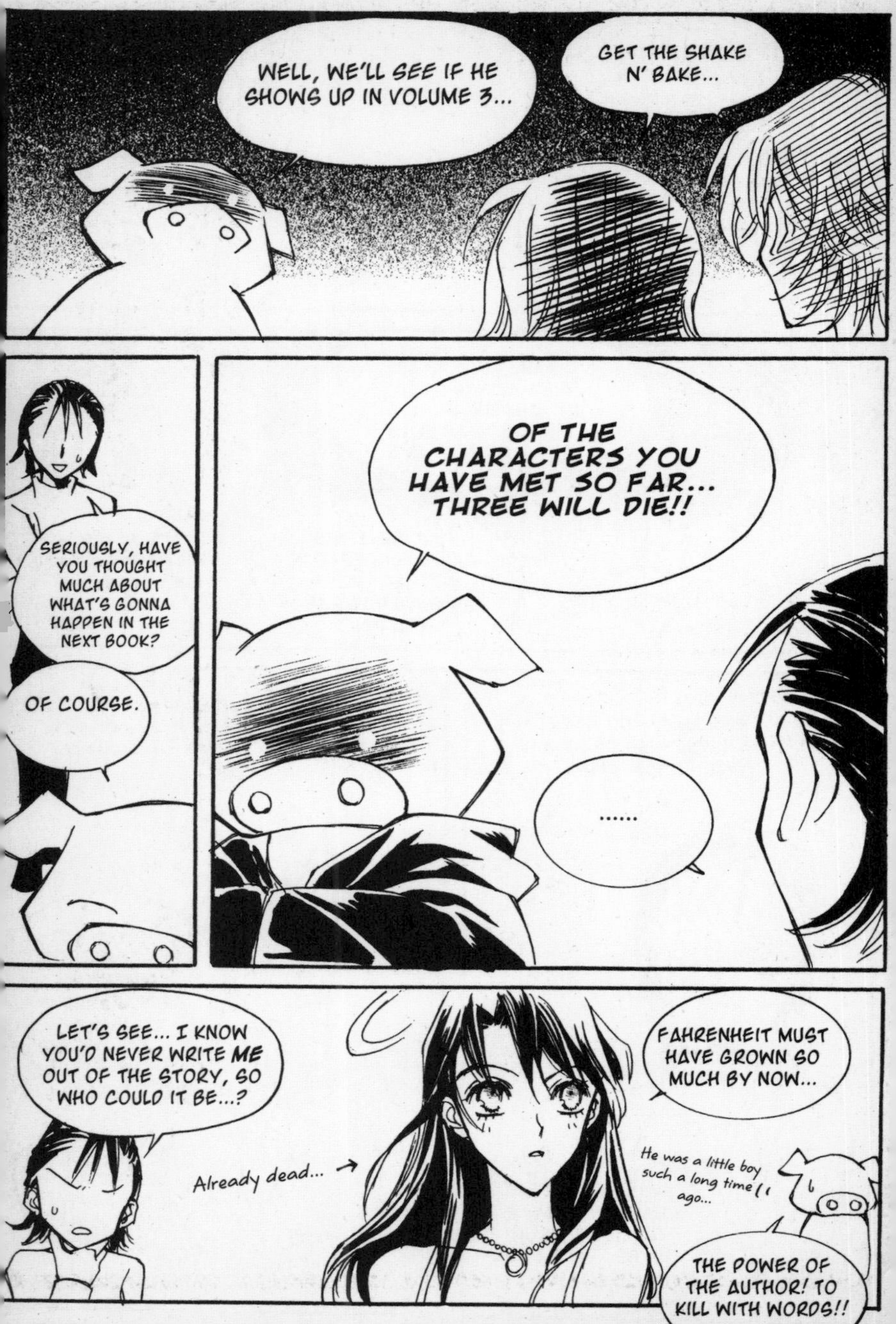
WELL, WE'LL SEE IF HE SHOWS UP IN VOLUME 3...
GET THE SHAKE N' BAKE...
SERIOUSLY, HAVE YOU THOUGHT MUCH ABOUT WHAT'S GONNA HAPPEN IN THE NEXT BOOK?
OF COURSE.
OF THE CHARACTERS YOU HAVE MET SO FAR... THREE WILL DIE!!
......
LET'S SEE... I KNOW YOU'D NEVER WRITE *ME* OUT OF THE STORY, SO WHO COULD IT BE...?
Already dead...
FAHRENHEIT MUST HAVE GROWN SO MUCH BY NOW...
He was a little boy such a long time ago...
THE POWER OF THE AUTHOR! TO KILL WITH WORDS!!

The Leading Characters' Early Designs

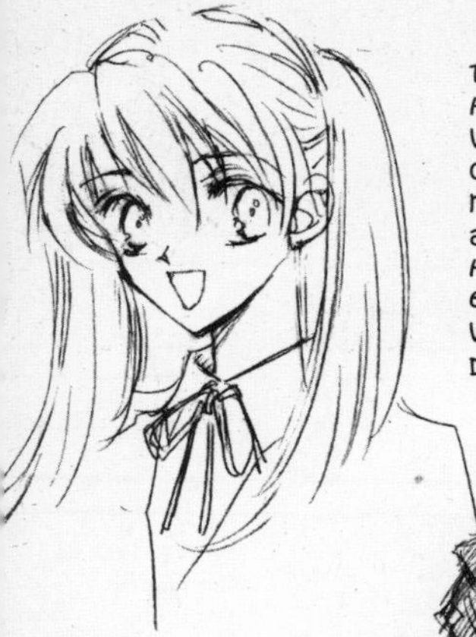

◄ Ami

The directions of her bangs have changed and her hair was a little shorter at first. Originally, I was thinking I'd make her a really lively (average) girl. But after changing her bangs, I rethought her entire character and ended up with someone who's a bit sadder than I first envisaged.

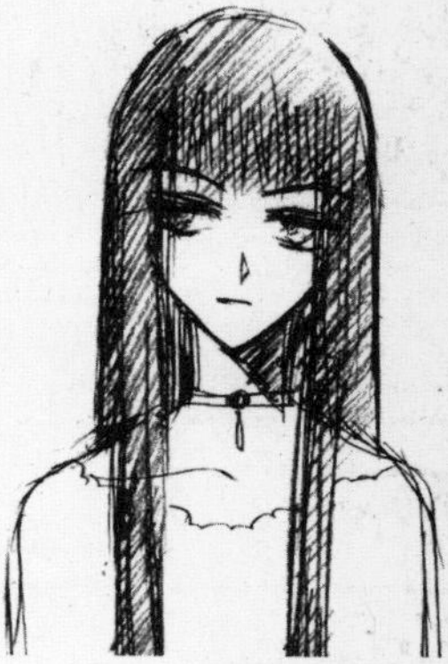

▲ Bi-Na

Bi-Na's concept was basically to create a "Dark Juliet".

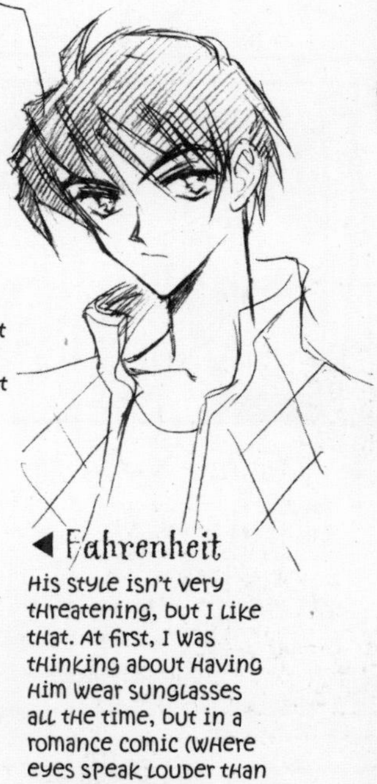

► Moo-Hyun

In Moo-Hyun's case, his personality changed a lot. At first, I was thinking about a cold, tough, vulgar boy... but that initial direction obviously took a turn.

Hwa-Ryun

▼ One of my old high school friends actually gave me this hairstyle once...

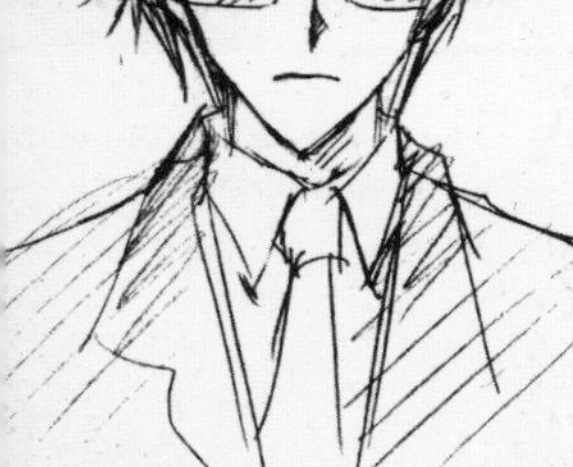

◄ Fahrenheit

His style isn't very threatening, but I like that. At first, I was thinking about having him wear sunglasses all the time, but in a romance comic (where eyes speak louder than words), it just wouldn't have worked.

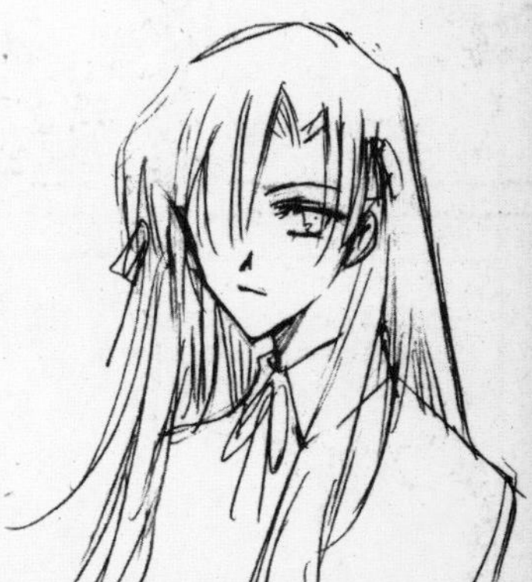

To be honest, it was the editor's idea to change Moo-Hyun's character, but I think it was a good move.

I remember a time when I couldn't afford to hire an assistant.

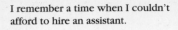

All the people who helped out for free back then...

...get special thanks from me.

Mr. Pa-sa
The one who turns a J Publisher's Fantasy novel's cover illustration into a work of art.

Main role: Masuri (from the Im Changrongjin)

He let me borrow that movie once.

DRAWING LOOKS LIKE FUN. LET ME TRY!

I'm sure you can do better than me...

No, no. Your perspectives are all wrong.

I... I know. Let's not talk about it.

Main role: East Shiba (In The Magician Ofen)

← Aste and Nas →

Not only the author's art teacher, but Daiwon NT novel's (Magician Ofen) translator.

She's one tough nut!

Circle's younger member. Be healthier Nas!! (I'm your number one fan!)

You didn't do your homework, did you?

And so I finally found an assistant. Miss Jung!

I look forward to many assignments.

Main role: Donkey Mother (In Dodgeball Donkey)

Main Role: Mirguardia (in Slayers)

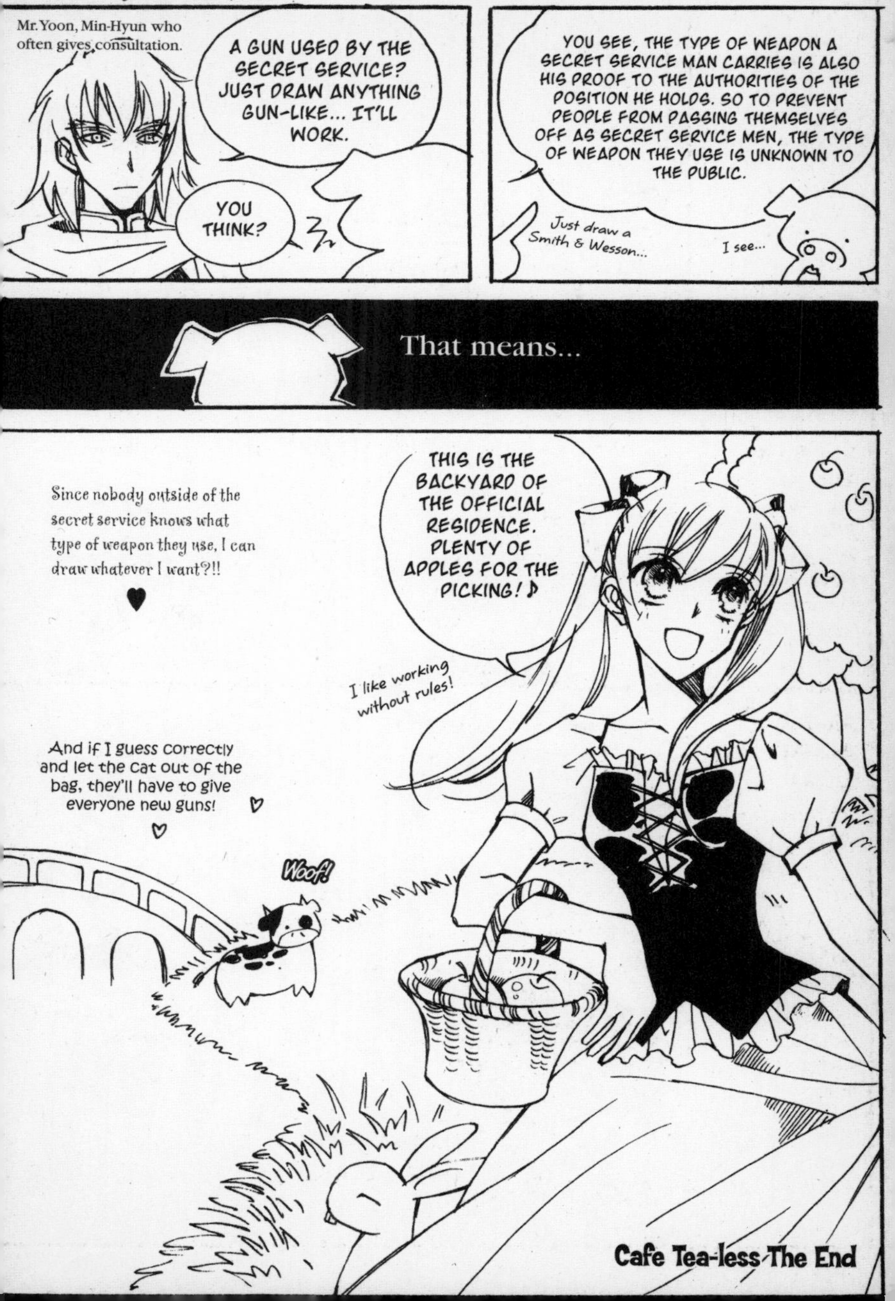
Mr. Yoon, Min-Hyun who often gives consultation.
A GUN USED BY THE SECRET SERVICE? JUST DRAW ANYTHING GUN-LIKE... IT'LL WORK.
YOU THINK?
YOU SEE, THE TYPE OF WEAPON A SECRET SERVICE MAN CARRIES IS ALSO HIS PROOF TO THE AUTHORITIES OF THE POSITION HE HOLDS. SO TO PREVENT PEOPLE FROM PASSING THEMSELVES OFF AS SECRET SERVICE MEN, THE TYPE OF WEAPON THEY USE IS UNKNOWN TO THE PUBLIC.
Just draw a Smith & Wesson...
I see...
That means...
Since nobody outside of the secret service knows what type of weapon they use, I can draw whatever I want?!! ♥
THIS IS THE BACKYARD OF THE OFFICIAL RESIDENCE. PLENTY OF APPLES FOR THE PICKING! ♪
I like working without rules!
And if I guess correctly and let the cat out of the bag, they'll have to give everyone new guns! ♡ ♡
Woof!
Cafe Tea-less The End

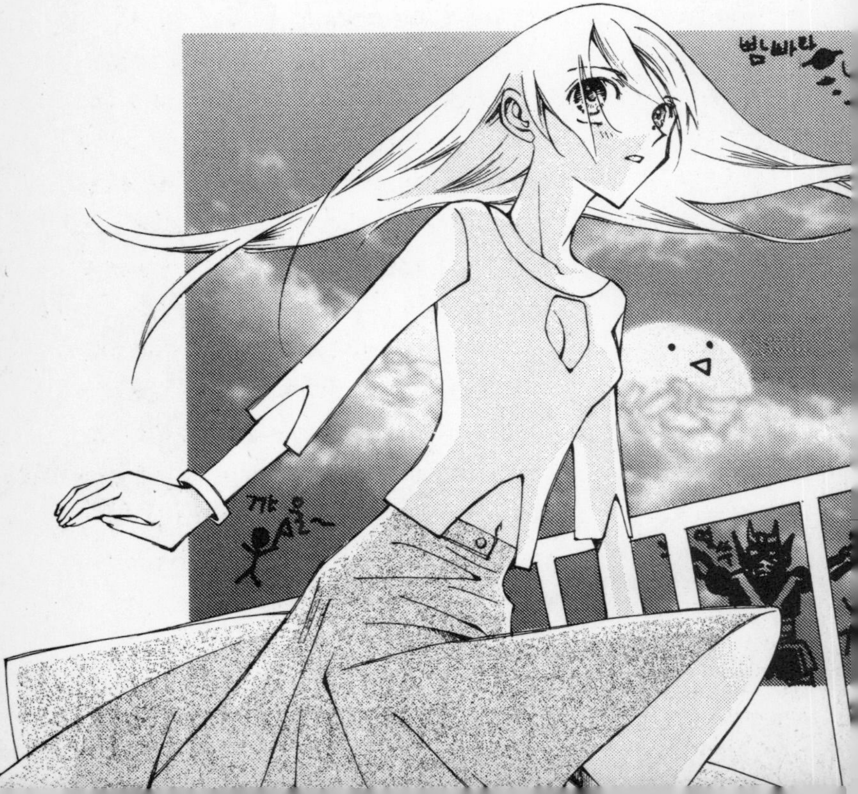

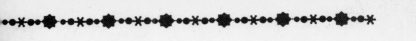

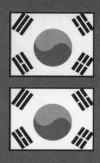

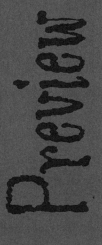

Preview

President Dad

Ho-Chan Won's inauguration day has arrived and Ami Won has come to terms with the fact that she's going to have to get used to cameras, reporters, fans, and the youth of Korea depending on her to show them the way. Not the most settling thought when just a week ago her biggest concern in the world was whether or not RICK got her letter. As if being hurled into the public eye wasn't bad enough, her aunt and her cousin are right around the corner ready to sabotage her ascension in the hopes that they will in turn rise to a position of prominence. And the new friend she made at school, Moo-Hyun, may also have ulterior motives.

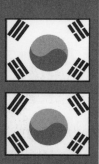

TOKYOPOP SHOP

WWW.TOKYOPOP.COM/SHOP

HOT NEWS!

Check out the
TOKYOPOP SHOP!
The world's best
collection of manga in
English is now available
online in one place!

WARCRAFT

SLAYERS MANGA NOVEL

THE TAROT CAFÉ

- LOOK FOR SPECIAL OFFERS
- PRE-ORDER UPCOMING RELEASES!
- COMPLETE YOUR COLLECTIONS

SOKORA REFUGEES

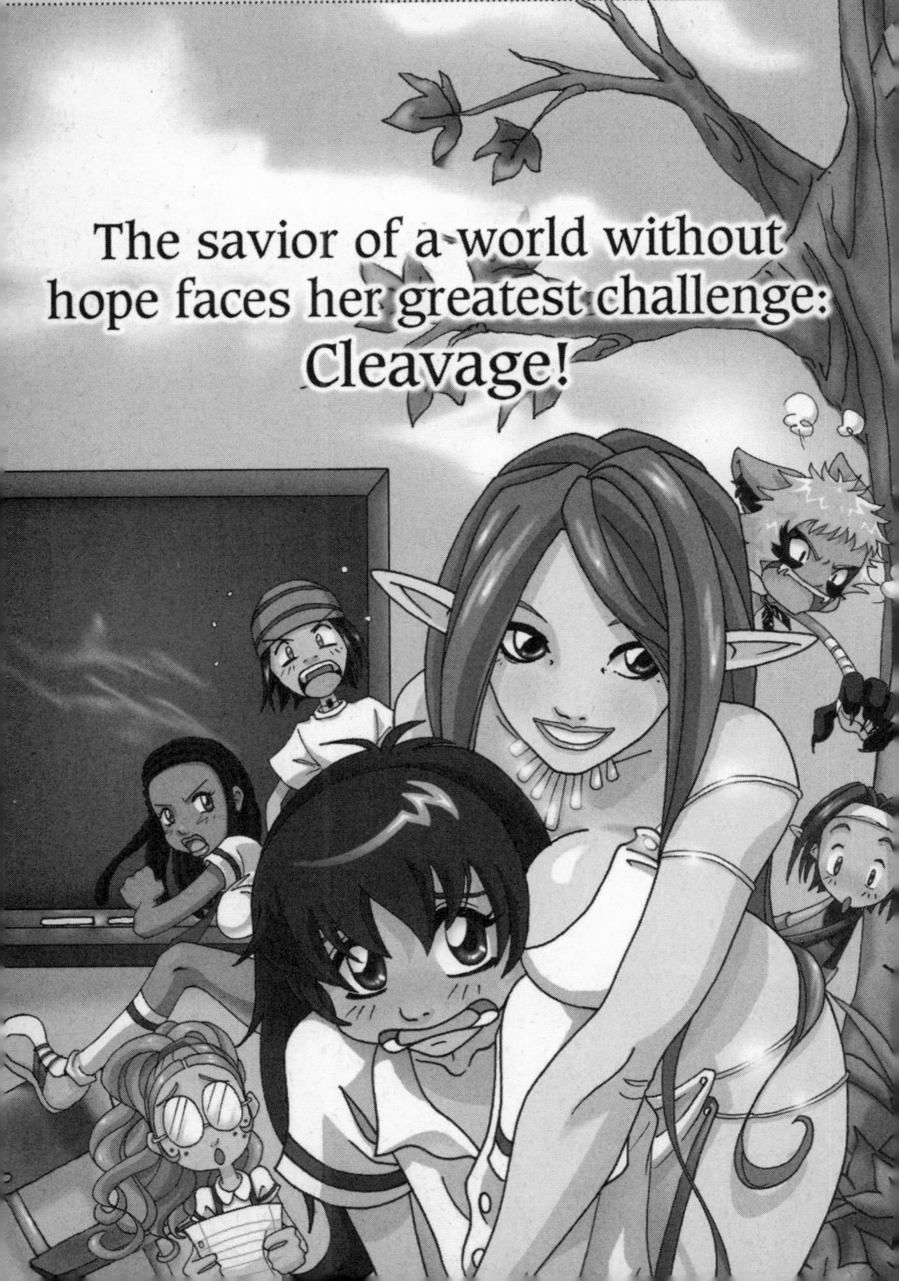
The savior of a world without hope faces her greatest challenge:
Cleavage!

SOKORA REFUGEES™

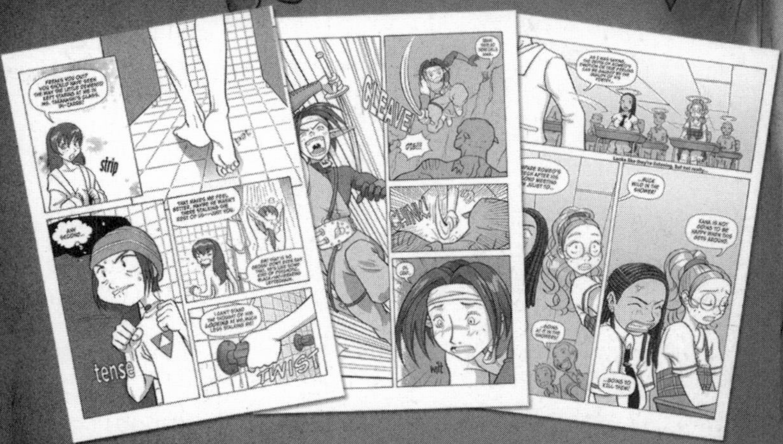
strip
tense
TWIST
CLEAVE!

Kana thought life couldn't get any worse—behind on her schoolwork and out of luck with boys, she is also the only one of her friends who hasn't "blossomed." When she falls through a magical portal in the girls' shower, she's transported to the enchanted world of Sokora—wearing nothing but a small robe! Now, on top of landing in this mysterious setting, she finds that her body is beginning to go through some tremendous changes.

Preview the manga at:
www.TOKYOPOP.com/sokora

T
TEEN
AGE 13+

TOKYO TRIBES

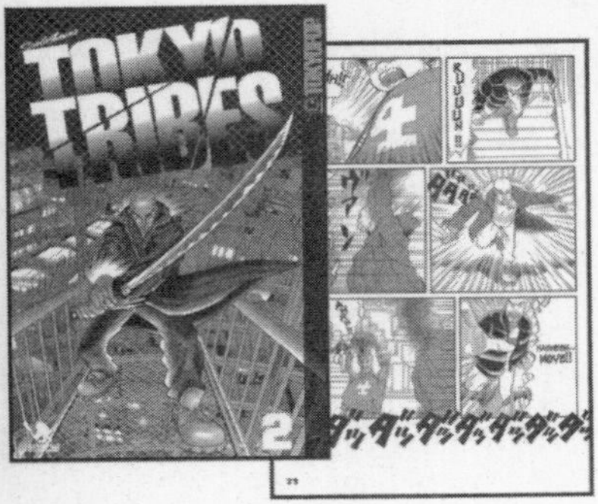
TOKYO TRIBES
2

BY SANTA INOUE

Tokyo Tribes first hit Japanese audiences in the sleek pages of the ultra-hip skater fashion magazine *Boon.* Santa Inoue's hard-hitting tale of Tokyo street gangs battling it out in the concrete sprawl of Japan's capital raises the manga storytelling bar. Ornate with hip-hop trappings and packed with gangland grit, *Tokyo Tribes* paints a vivid, somewhat surreal vision of urban youth: rival gangs from various Tokyo barrios clash over turf, and when the heat between two of the tribes gets personal, a bitter rivalry explodes into all-out warfare.

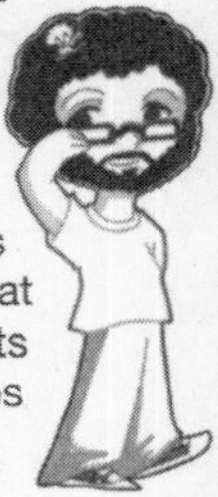

~Luis Reyes, Editor

LEGAL DRUG

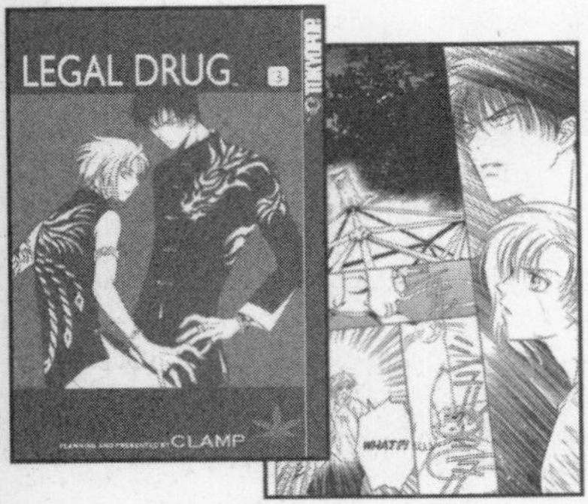
LEGAL DRUG
3
CLAMP
WHAT?!

BY CLAMP

CLAMP is the four-woman studio famous for creating much of the world's most popular manga. For the past 15 years they have produced such hits as the adorable *Cardcaptor Sakura,* the dark and brooding *Tokyo Babylon,* and the sci-fi romantic comedy *Chobits.* In *Legal Drug,* we meet Kazahaya and Rikuou, two ordinary pharmacists who moonlight as amateur sleuths for a mysterious boss. *Legal Drug* is a perfect dose of mystery, psychic powers and the kind of homoerotic tension for which CLAMP is renowned.

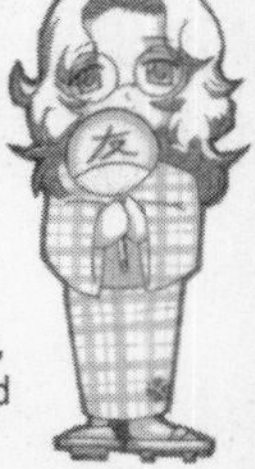

~Lillian Diaz-Przybyl, Jr. Editor

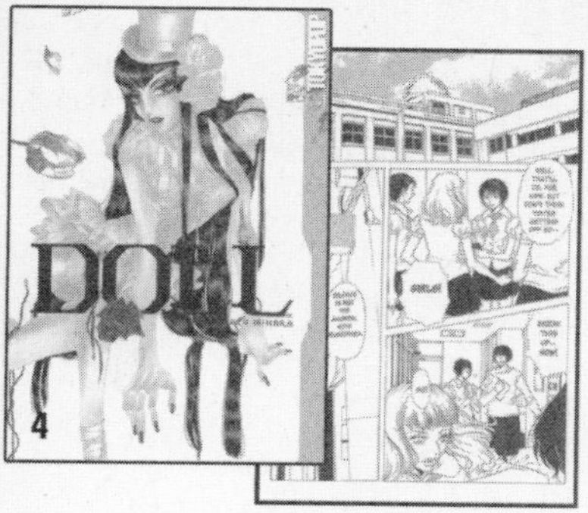
DOLL
4

BY MITSUKAZU MIHARA

DOLL

Mitsukazu Mihara's haunting *Doll* uses beautiful androids to examine what it means to be truly human. While the characters in *Doll* are draped in the chic Gothic-Lolita fashions that made Mihara-sensei famous, the themes explored are more universal—all emotions and walks of life have their day in *Doll*. *Doll* begins as a series of 'one-shot' stories and gradually dovetails into an epic of emotion and intrigue. It's like the *Twilight Zone* meets *Blade Runner!*

~Rob Tokar, Senior Editor

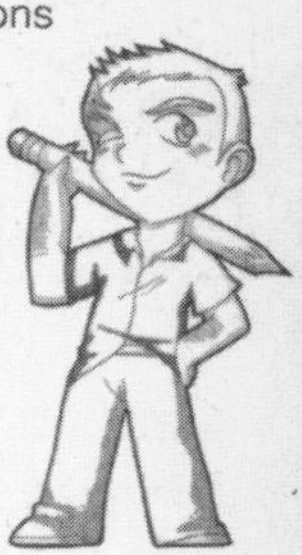

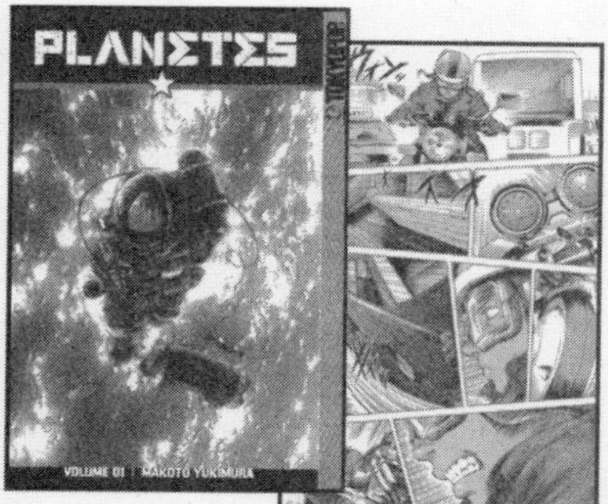
PLANETES
VOLUME 01 | MAKOTO YUKIMURA

BY MAKOTO YUKIMURA

PLANETES

Makoto Yukimura's profoundly moving and graphically arresting *Planetes* posits a near future where mankind's colonization of space has begun. Young Hachimaki yearns to join this exciting new frontier. Instead, he cleans the glut of orbital junk mankind's initial foray into space produced. He works with Fee, a nicotine-addict beauty with an abrasive edge, and Yuri, a veteran spaceman with a tragic past in search of inner peace. *Planetes* combines the scope of Jules Verne (*Around the World in Eighty Days*) and Robert Heinlein (*Starship Troopers*) with the philosophical wonder of *2001: A Space Odyssey.*

~Luis Reyes, Editor

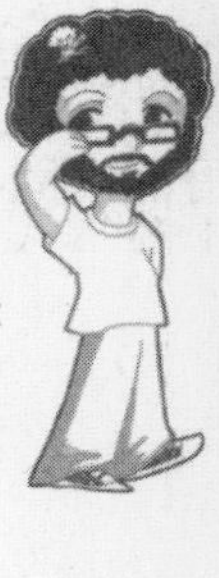

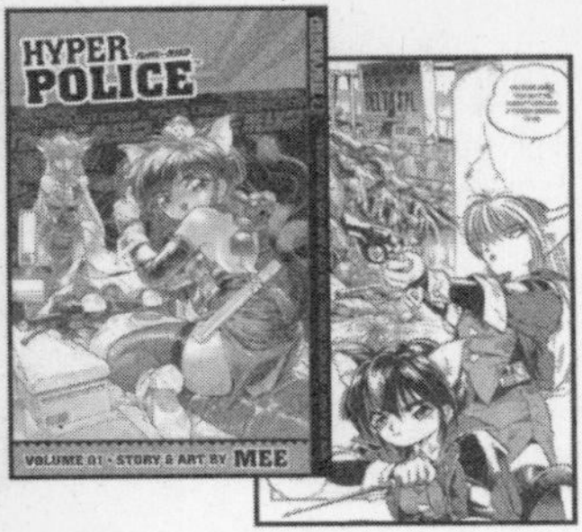
HYPER
POLICE
VOLUME 01 · STORY & ART BY MEE

HYPER POLICE

BY MEE

In a future rife with crime, humans are an endangered species—and monsters have taken over! Natsuki is a cat girl who uses magical powers to enforce the law. However, her greatest threat doesn't come from the criminals. Her partner Sakura, a "nine-tailed" fox, plots to eat Natsuki and gobble up her magic! In this dog-eat-dog world, Natsuki fights to stay on top!

OT
OLDER TEEN
AGE 16+

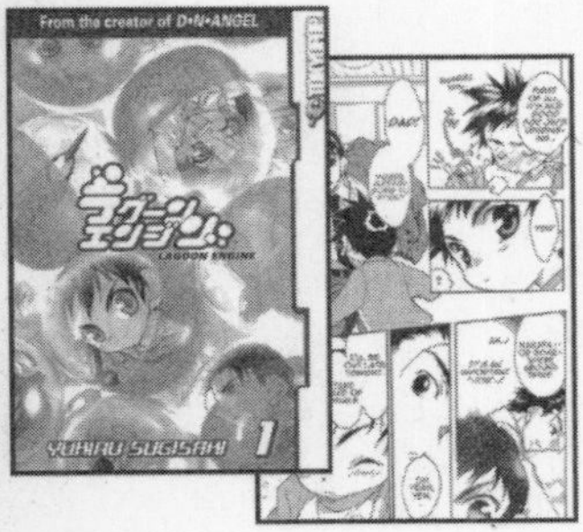
From the creator of D•N•ANGEL
LAGOON ENGINE
YUKIRU SUGISAKI 1

LAGOON ENGINE

BY YUKIRU SUGISAKI

From the best-selling creator of *D·N·Angel!*

Yen and Jin are brothers in elementary school—and successors in the Ragun family craft. They are Gakushi, those who battle ghosts and evil spirits known as "Maga" by guessing their true name. As Yen and Jin train to join the family business, the two boys must keep their identities a secret...or risk death!

T
TEEN
AGE 13+

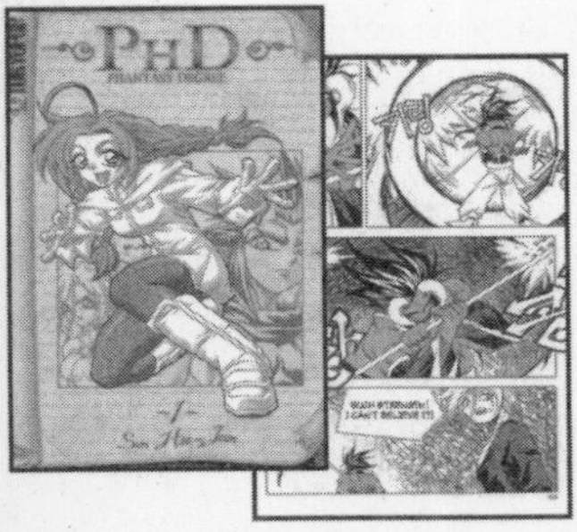
PHD
PHANTASY DEGREE

PHD: PHANTASY DEGREE

BY HEE-JOON SON

Sang is a fearlessly spunky young girl who is about to receive one hell of an education...at the Demon School Hades! She's on a mission to enroll into the monsters-only class. However, monster matriculation is not what is truly on her mind—she wants to acquire the fabled "King's Ring" from the fiancée of the chief commander of hell!

T
TEEN
AGE 13+